General George Wright

General George Wright

Guardian of the
Pacific Coast

By Carl P. Schlicke

University of Oklahoma Press
Norman and London

Library of Congress Cataloging-in-Publication Data

Schlicke, Carl Paul, 1910–
  General George Wright, 1803–1865 : guardian of the Pacific Coast /
by Carl P. Schlicke.—1st ed.
    p. cm.
  Bibliography: p.
  Includes index.
  ISBN 0-8061-2149-1 (alk. paper)
    1. Wright, George, 1803–1865.   2. Generals—United States—
Biography.   3. United States Army—Biography.   4. Indians of
North America—Wars, 1815–1875.   5. United States—History,
Military—To 1900.   I. Title.
E181.W94S35   1988
973'.092'4—dc19
[B]   88-10020
                                                                CIP

The paper in this book meets the guidelines for permanence and durability of the Committee on Production Guidelines for Book Longevity of the Council on Library Resources, Inc.

To Hilda

Contents

Preface   ix
Chapter   1 Origins   3
          2 Duty on the Frontier   14
          3 Wright's First Independent Command   24
          4 More Frontier Duty   37
          5 The Seminole War   50
          6 The Mexican War   67
          7 Return to the United States   85
          8 Off to California   94
          9 The Ninth Infantry Goes West   109
         10 The Indian War of 1858   141
         11 Under a New Commander   197
         12 Civil War Days: 1860–1861   213
         13 Civil War Days: 1862   238
         14 Civil War Days: 1863   264
         15 Civil War Days: 1864   291
         16 Civil War Days: 1865   315
         17 A Watery Grave   327
         18 Epilogue   349
Abbreviations Used in the Notes   357
Notes   359
Bibliography   385
Index   397

Illustrations

Fort Howard 16
Jefferson Barracks 21
Fort Niagara 43
Gen. William Jenkins Worth 48
Battle of Churubusco 76
Battle of Molino del Rey 78
Fort Ontario 87
Col. George Wright, 1855 110
Gov. Isaac I. Stevens 115
Walla Walla Council 117
Gen. John E. Wool 118
Kamiakin 126
Wright's quarters at Fort Dalles 130
Fort Walla Walla 134
Battle of Spokane Plains 171
Wright's Troops at the Spokane River 173
Gen. Newman S. Clarke 188
Gen. George Wright, 1863 289
S.S. *Brother Jonathan* 328
The Wrights' grave 346

Maps

Wright's Expedition to Council Bluffs, 1829 26
Florida at the time of the second
    Seminole War, 1840–44 52
Mexico during the Mexican War, 1846–48 70
Eastern Washington Territory during the
    Indian War of 1858 142
Department of the Pacific during the Civil War 216

Preface

GENERAL GEORGE WRIGHT was a career soldier who spent forty-three years in the United States Army. The history of the Republic was a troubled one during much of that time. Any attempt to document his life becomes a study of the problems which then beset the United States. He marched, he scouted, he fought, he planned, he administered, and for the most part he did these things competently. He loved his country, and he served it well. Finally he lost his life in the line of duty.

My interest in Wright was aroused shortly after I moved to Spokane following World War II. I heard about places and things named for Wright and saw granite markers at sites of events with which he had been connected. I found that Wright was mainly remembered for happenings which transpired during a few months of his life in the summer of 1858. At that time, in a carefully planned and well-executed military campaign, he quickly, effectively, and permanently quelled the Indian depredations and disturbances which had plagued the eastern portion of Washington Territory with increasing intensity during the early part of the nineteenth century. For that he earned the gratitude of the territorial authorities, the travelers to the mines who passed through the area, and the settlers who gradually moved in. To the conquered his terms were harsh, ruthless, and deadly. He hanged a number of Indian "criminals" and destroyed an Indian horse herd. For these acts he is currently in disrepute; yet the only criticism which came from his superiors was that he had been too lenient.

I was interested in attempting to determine what kind of man Wright really was and in finding out something about the rest of his life, concerning which little seemed to be known. What did his contemporaries think of him? Is

the opprobrium currently associated with his name justified? Is it fair to judge Wright's actions in the summer of
1858 out of the context of the times in which he lived?

Information concerning other periods of Wright's life
has not been easy to come by. A few of his letters, numerous military dispatches by him and others, and a few rare
reminiscences by contemporaries are available. Sometimes
it has been necessary to depict him solely against the background in which he was serving, after personal visits to
many of those sites.

Actually, Wright's most important contribution to his
country was his service during the Civil War, although he
was denied the opportunity to participate actively in the
battles for its defense. As commander of the immense Department of the Pacific he was responsible for all the land
and its occupants between the Rocky Mountains and the
Pacific Ocean, from the Canadian to the Mexican border. He is widely credited with having performed this
monumental task, at a difficult time, with wisdom, firmness, and tact. Yet in spite of the valuable service he rendered, Wright's actions were not publicly acknowledged by
his superiors or the government. His last years were spent
in bitterness and frustration at being passed over for
promotion.

As the state of Washington approaches its centennial
year, 1989, I hope that this account will draw attention to a
man who played such an important part in its territorial
days that it will lay the groundwork for future studies of
his life.

Many people were of inestimable help in collecting and
collating what information was available. It would be impossible to name them all, but I would like to express my
special appreciation to a few individuals and institutions:
the staff of the National Archives and of the Library of
Congress, Washington, D.C.; Mary Johnson, Elizabeth Gil-
bert, and Nadine Miller, of the reference department of
the Spokane Public Library; Betty W. Bender (now chief
librarian, Spokane Public Library), Eleanor Kelly, Douglas

Olsen, and Edward Nolan, in the library of the Cheney Cowles Museum, Spokane; Abbie Metcalf, former librarian in the Thayer School of Engineering at Dartmouth College, Hanover, New Hampshire, who lived next to the old Wright homestead in Norwich, Vermont; the individuals in the Norwich town hall who made old records available to me; Ann Turner, reference librarian in Norwich University, Northfield, Vermont; Marjorie Butler, of the Norwich Historical Society; Kenneth W. Rapp, archivist in the U.S. Military Academy, West Point; the Reverend William Schoenberg, the Reverend Clifford Carroll, and the Reverend Richard Sisk, of the Gonzaga University Archives, Spokane; Thomas E. Waggaman, former marshal of the U.S. Supreme Court; Mrs. Arthur Felt, of the Missouri Historical Society, Saint Louis; Priscilla Knuth, of the Oregon Historical Society, Portland; the Bancroft Library, Berkeley, California; Terry Davis, in the California State Library, Sacramento; the California State Archives, Sacramento; the Shasta County Library, Redding, California; Esther Marden, of the Redding Museum and Art Center; Mary Lou Miller, of the Del Norte County Historical Museum, Crescent City, California; the Reference Department, New York Public Library; James Abajian, of the California Historical Society, San Francisco; Richard Dillon, of the Sutro Library, San Francisco; the Historical Society of Pennsylvania, Philadelphia; the Erie County Historical Society, Erie, Pennsylvania; the Historical Society of Dauphin County, Harrisburg, Pennsylvania; the Kentucky Historical Society, Frankfort; the Filson Club, Louisville, Kentucky; John K. Mahon, Gainesville, Florida; Jonathan Club, Los Angeles; Ewing B. Hawkins (the grandson of John M. Wright), Wilmington, Delaware; Veronica Satorius, Redding, California; Mrs. Don M. Chase, Sebastopol, California; Judge Thomas I. Oakshott, Colville, Washington; Congressman Thomas Foley and the late Senator Henry Jackson, Washington, D.C.; H. Dean Guie, Yakima, Washington; and Roscoe Scheller, Sunnyside, Washington. My thanks also go to Jerome Peltier, Spokane, Washington, for sharing with me his knowledge of Northwest history; to William Lang and Chris McGonigle, for their help in editing this work; and to the late Reverend Lyle Davis, former chairman of the History Department, Gonzaga University, for his encouragement.

Spokane, Washington   CARL P. SCHLICKE

General George Wright

1.
Origins

FROM ITS ORIGIN in a chain of mountain lakes near the Canadian border, the Connecticut River winds southward in the broad glacial trench between the White Mountains of New Hampshire and the Green Mountains of Vermont. Leaving the northern wooded country, it passes through a land of rolling hills checkered with tilled fields and pastures. Here and there one sees a neat, quiet village, with green-shuttered white houses, sheltering maple trees, and a tall white church spire. Flowing ever southward, the river cuts across Massachusetts and Connecticut to empty, almost four hundred miles from its source, into the waters of Long Island Sound. Although hydroelectric dams now interrupt its flow, and large cities have sprung up along its banks, long stretches of the river still delight the eye of the traveler. With its hills and meadows, forests and fields, bluff and marshes, the Connecticut River valley remains a place of beauty, peace, and quiet industriousness.

As late as the middle of the eighteenth century much of the land in what are now New Hampshire and Vermont was wilderness, traversed only by Indians or an occasional white hunter. The first explorers and settlers of the lower Connecticut Valley were the Dutch, who arrived early in the seventeenth century and initiated a period of active trade with the Indians. By 1634, however, the Puritan exodus had brought more than ten thousand settlers to what was already being called New England, and the Dutch gradually were pushed out. Despite all this activity the land between the Merrimack Valley on the east and the military posts at Fort Ticonderoga and Crown Point on Lake Champlain on the west remained an entirely uninhabited and almost trackless forest. It was not until Quebec was captured by the British in 1759 and the French and Indian

War finally ended in 1760 that the development of this area became possible.

Once freed from the terrors of the massacres, burnings, and harassments that the war had brought to the border settlements, the restless New Englanders, who already regarded their communities as intolerably crowded, were on the move again. Town charters were obtained from the royal governor of the province of New Hampshire, under whose jurisdiction that territory was presumed to lie. The charters which he granted were unique for that day and age in that they conferred on the inhabitants of each township the right of self-government by means of town meetings. To them was given the privilege of selecting their own officers and the responsibility for the general direction of the town affairs.[1] Unfortunately, most of the lands sold to the colonists were also claimed as the property of New York, whose governor asserted title to them under the old grant from Charles II to the duke of York. That led to a decade of jurisdictional quarrels and partisan strife which ended only when the shots fired at Lexington in 1775 united all the disputants in a greater struggle against a common foe.[2]

Most of the immigrants to the land just beginning to be known as the New Hampshire Grants came from Connecticut. One such group, from the vicinity of Mansfield, was awarded a charter on July 4, 1761, for the development of a township to be known as Norwich, 150 miles to the north on the west bank of the Connecticut River. The charter required each grantee to plant and cultivate within five years five acres of land for every fifty acres contained in his share. Thereafter he was to continue to improve and settle his tract on penalty of forfeiture.[3]

The Wright Family of Norwich, Vermont

In 1763 three men became the first permanent residents of Norwich, "alone in the unbroken forest, where the echo of the woodsman's axe had never yet been heard." Two years later four more men arrived, bringing their families with them. One of them was George Wright's great-grand-father, Aaron Wright, from Preston, Connecticut, who took up a 100-acre hillside tract. Aaron Wright was born in Hebron, Connecticut, in 1700, the only son of Samuel and Elizabeth Wright. He brought with him his wife, Elizabeth, who was the daughter of the Reverend Samuel Bliss and his wife, Elizabeth, and their six sons and two daughters. Aaron Wright died in Norwich at age eighty-three.

Another settler, also from Preston, who arrived with his family the same year was Samuel Partridge, Sr. He took up land just south of the Wrights' tract. Accompanying him were his wife, neé Ruth Woodward, and seven children. His daughter Olive married Aaron Wright's twenty-four-year-old son, John, in 1768, and his son Samuel, Jr., married one of Aaron Wright's daughters, Elizabeth, in 1770.[4]

In 1768 the first town meeting was convened in Norwich. In 1770, John Wright became a member of the committee formed to lay out into lots all the undivided land in the township. He was also elected "collector," although the first tax was not levied until two years later. His father was named one of the three "overseers of the poor, . . . thus showing that the poor, even in the newest settlements, are ever with us." By 1771 forty heads of families were living in Norwich. In this group, later known as the "Fathers of the Town," were three Wrights: Aaron and his sons John and Samuel.[5]

The colonization of Norwich and its environs was extraordinarily homogeneous. Of the first 1,000 settlers in the area, almost all came from eastern Connecticut. Their lives were not easy. They lived in sparsely furnished log houses and dressed in homespun clothes. They spent many long hours felling trees to construct their habitations and clear the rocky, inhospitable land for farming. Yet, interestingly enough, education of the young was high among their priorities, for in 1769, just across the Connecticut River, Dartmouth college was founded, and the first classes were held a year later. To this pioneer enterprise in higher education the settlers of Norwich contributed 589 acres of land and thirty-five pounds, fifteen shillings, in cash. Aaron

Wright is listed as having donated one shilling, tenpence, and his son John, one shilling.[6]

It was not long before the luxury of self-government which the inhabitants of Norwich enjoyed was placed in jeopardy. One of the effects of the French and Indian War was a general tightening of control by Great Britain. Troops were quartered throughout the thirteen colonies, and taxes and duties were levied on the colonists to support them. By 1770, resentment was running high, and on the evening of March 5, British troops fired on a protesting crowd, a calamity that went down in history as the "Boston Massacre." After the "Boston Tea Party" in 1773, Parliament ordered the port of Boston closed, sent in troops, and suppressed town meetings. Pressure continued to mount; in 1775 the first real battles against British troops took place at Lexington and Concord.

The first mention of a Wright participating in the Revolutionary War occurred in 1777. In July of that year John Wright was called out because of an alarm at Stafford, Vermont, where a gathering of Tories had taken place. Here he served for five days until the Tories were captured. On August 3, John Wright was again summoned to join a company of militia.[7]

The British, meanwhile, had initiated a campaign that was designed to bring a speedy end to the war. On August 15 and 16, John Wright fought as a private in the Battle of Bennington, Vermont, in which a force of Tories and Hessians was defeated by the Hampshire Grants Militia. John was also present two months later when a British army of 5,500 men and 300 officers laid down their arms at Saratoga, a historic event that marked the turning point of the war.

John Wright returned to his farm in December and was not called out again until August, 1780. This time he served as a sergeant, guarding and scouting the frontiers of Vermont, although most of the military activity had shifted to the south. In October the British raided Royalton, in central Vermont, and John Wright was again called up. On that occasion he was promoted to lieutenant, and he did not obtain his release until April, 1781.[8] The independence of the colonies was finally recognized by Great Britain in 1782, and a peace treaty was signed in 1783 and ratified by the U.S. Congress in 1784.

After the close of the Revolutionary War, John Wright settled down to cut his trees, tend his fields, and raise his family. He and his wife, Olive Partridge, had four sons and seven daughters. Three of the children died in infancy. Five daughters, Anna, Ruby, Polly, Olive, and Betsy, reached maturity and married. Three sons grew to maturity: Roswell, born in 1781; Ebenezer, born in 1783; and John, Jr., born in 1792. Roswell would become the father of George Wright.

On the afternoon of September 10, 1799, when Ebenezer was sixteen years old, he was leading a team of oxen to remove some timber that John had cut down to prepare the ground for sowing grain. The family heard Ebenezer cry out and hurried to the spot. John's granddaughter Mercy related that they witnessed "a sad spectacle indeed. Grandfather [John] had attempted to roll a log down a descent, and by a sudden movement had got under the log (across his heart) and when his son arrived life was extinct."[9] Thus died that sturdy patriot at the age of fifty-six. The spot where the tragedy occurred is marked by a small granite monument later erected by his son John, Jr. The hillside clearing overlooking the Connecticut River where the marker stands seems hardly to have changed since the day the accident occurred. The marker bears the following inscription: "This monument is erected to commemorate the name of Lieut. John W. Wright who was killed instantly at this place by the pressure of a log on the 9th of Sept. 1799 Aet 56 years In the Midst of Life We Are in Death."[10]

Ebenezer Wright attended Dartmouth College and subsequently moved to Pennsylvania. There he became a distinguished lawyer, practicing first in Lebanon and then in Lancaster.

John Wright, Jr., attended the U.S. Military Academy at

West Point, graduating with a class of thirty in 1814. He was appointed second lieutenant in the Corps of Engineers and later that year became assistant professor of mathematics at West Point, where he also served as post adjutant. He resigned from the army on July 23, 1818. After leaving the army, he moved to Pennsylvania, where he read law with his brother Ebenezer and was examined for the bar by James Buchanan, who later became president of the United States. John then returned to his native town, where he established himself in his new profession and became a prominent citizen.[11]

The oldest son, Roswell Wright, married Jemina Rose, of Lisbon, Connecticut, on February 20, 1803. Roswell and his wife had three children, George, Mercy R., and Olive Partridge. Roswell bore arms in the War of 1812 but whether he served in any of its battles is not known. He spent the rest of his life in Norwich, where he died October 9, 1866. His two daughters also lived out their lives in Norwich.

Boyhood and West Point, 1803–22

George Wright, the oldest of Roswell Wright's three children, was born in Norwich on October 21, 1803.[12] Little is known of his boyhood, although it has been said that early in life he illustrated in himself the sterling virtues of the New England character. He was honest, industrious, and ambitious, a genial and faithful friend. He was devoted to his family and he loved his country. He knew the importance of an education and received a good one for the times. Later in life he also showed himself a firm adherent to democratic principles and to the obligations of civic responsibility. The development of such values is evidence of the influence of his family, his community, and his ancestry.

It has been written that George "received his early education at Partridge's Military School,"[13] but that Norwich institution did not open its doors until 1819. During the winter of 1816–17 he trudged across the bridge spanning the Connecticut River to Hanover to attend classes at Dartmouth College Academy.

As George grew up, he determined to follow in the footsteps of his uncle John Wright, Jr., and become a career officer in the U.S. Army. In 1817 he applied for admission to the U.S. Military Academy at West Point, from which his Uncle John had graduated three years earlier and where he was serving on the staff. One of those who recommended George's appointment was the Reverend James W. Woodward, pastor of the "Old Meeting House," as the original Congregational Church was called. His duties as pastor included the secular education of some of the children of the community, as well as their spiritual guidance.

On July 11, 1817, Mr. Woodward addressed a letter to the authorities at West Point:

> This certifies that I have been acquainted for several years with George Wright of Norwich, Vt. and know him to be a youth of excellent disposition and manners and who possesses a fair reputation among all his acquaintances. Having attended to his instruction in several branches of education I can recommend him as a youth of superior natural endowments and whose acquirements, especially in arithmetic and the English language are far beyond his age.

The second recommendation accompanying his application was from Samuel Merrill, his preceptor at Dartmouth Academy. Merrill wrote:

> This certifies that George Wright, of Norwich, Vermont, son of Roswell Wright of said town and state, attended the Academy in this place during the last winter, in which he made good proficiency in his studies and was regular in his conduct. His disposition and talents highly recommend him.

Bvt. Maj. Sylvanus Thayer, superintendent of the U.S. Military Academy, enclosed the foregoing recommendations in a letter to the secretary of war with the comment:

> I enclose herewith the recommendations in favor of George Wright, Norwich Vt., aged fifteen years who asks to be appointed cadet. No. 1 is the certificate of the Revd. James Wood-

ward and No. 2 a certificate of Preceptor Merrill of Dartmouth College Academy. Both gentlemen are well known and highly respected in that section of the country.

On May 20, 1818, John C. Calhoun, secretary of war to the newly elected president, James Monroe, notified young George of his appointment to the academy. Ten days later George wrote to Calhoun:

> Sir, I have the honor to acknowledge receipt of your letter of the 20th inst, appointing me a Cadet in the Service of the United States and to inform you of my acceptance of same.
>
> Very respectfully
I am, Sir
Your Obt. Srvt.
George Wright
Cadet U.S. Service[14]

On September 4, 1818, at the age of fourteen years, eleven months, George Wright entered the U.S. Military Academy at West Point.

George Wright's matriculation at the academy occurred at a time of tribulation and transition at that institution. The worst of the trouble was over when he arrived, but the atmosphere was still emotionally charged. Most difficult of all, for a boy barely into his teens, must have been that some of his own relatives had been deeply involved in the recent troubles.[15]

For several years until 1817, the year before George Wright appeared on the scene, Capt. Alden Partridge, a first cousin of George's father, Roswell, had been acting as superintendent of the academy. A bitter feud that broke out between Partridge and his faculty, together with complaints from other sources, had led to charges against Partridge of incompetence, mistreatment of cadets, nepotism, and peculation. Partridge had been exonerated by a court of inquiry, but the situation at West Point had continued to deteriorate, and after a visit to the academy President James Monroe ordered Partridge tried by court-martial and in July, 1817, replaced him as superintendent by Major Thayer.[16] George Wright's uncle John, Jr., also became caught up in the complicated series of events that followed. Thayer relieved John of his duties at the academy, and John resigned his commission.[17]

The court martial found Partridge guilty of disobedience of orders and assumption of command without authority but cleared him of charges of mutiny that had been added when he failed to acknowledge Thayer's position. The court ordered Partridge's dismissal from the army, but President Monroe permitted him to resign instead.[18]

Partridge returned to his native Norwich, where he founded the first private military academy in the United States, which subsequently was incorporated by the Vermont legislature as Norwich University and later moved to Northfield. Partridge went on to attain far-reaching influence as an educator.[19]

Meanwhile, Thayer, who ultimately came to be known as "the Father of the Military Academy," was proceeding with his task of reorganizing West Point and establishing a system of education, vestiges of which persist to the present. "In all his activities—study, recitation, drill and ceremony—the cadet lived under a rule of strict discipline."[20] Most important of all, a rigid code of honor was established for the corps of cadets. Lieutenant Ethan Allen Hitchcock, who owed his given names to his illustrious maternal grandfather, graduated in the class of 1817 and returned to West Point in 1824 as a member of the faculty. He regarded Thayer as "one of the most accomplished officers and one of the most finished gentlemen of the Army." Hitchcock wrote, "During many years the Military Academy owed to Major Thayer nearly all of its reputation."[21]

Nevertheless, the spartan austerity and discipline established by Thayer did not sit well with some of the older cadets, who had grown accustomed to the earlier, easygoing regime. Affairs at West Point reached another climax in the fall of George Wright's plebe year, 1818, when hot-tempered Capt. John Bliss, Thayer's commandant of cadets, publicly manhandled a disobedient member of the corps. Shortly thereafter a delegation of cadets appeared before Major Thayer bearing a petition for the removal of

Captain Bliss and threatening a revolt of the entire corps if he was allowed to remain. Thayer ordered the members of the delegation off the post until further notice. The national furor that followed ultimately led to yet another official investigation, but Thayer's conduct was upheld by the inquiry.[22]

Notwithstanding this crisis, a steady improvement in conditions was taking place at the academy. In March, 1820, Maj. William J. Worth replaced Captain Bliss as commandant of cadets and instructor in military tactics. Although "not of high intellectual capacity or attainments," Worth had considerable ability and undaunted courage and had risen rapidly through the ranks to become an officer. Badly wounded by grapeshot at the Battle of Lundy's Lane, he had become permanently lame. In spite of his disability he retained a fine military bearing and was an accomplished horseman.[23] Hitchcock described him as "the very ideal of a gallant soldier in the field." He was highly thought of by the cadets, helped shape the high standards of conduct and bearing that became traditional at the academy, and in later years played an important role in Wright's life.

Lieutenant Hitchcock had this to say about the atmosphere at West Point at the time of his return to the post in 1824:

> I can never forget the joy with which I mingled with the young assistant professors at the Academy, all of whom were graduates of high standing in their classes. The amount of culture among them was considerable; their conversation was enlightened—turning upon subjects of science and literature—in the greatest possible contrast to that with which I had been associated during the [previous] five years.[24]

George Wright was fortunate in being a beneficiary of the general upgrading that was taking place at West Point while he was there, although his position at times must have been somewhat difficult because of his family connections. In any event, he persevered and on July 1, 1822, graduated twenty-fourth in a class of forty. On the same

day the eighteen-year-old graduate received a commission
as second lieutenant in the U.S. Army. The next week he
penned the following letter:

> West Point, July 8th, 1822
>
> Sir:
>
> I have the honor to acknowledge the reception of my ap-
> pointment as second Lieut. in the 3ᵈ Regt. of Infantry and my
> acceptance of same.
>
> It is my request to obtain a furlough for a reasonable time
> for the purpose of visiting my friends at the town of Norwich
> in the state of Vermont.
>
> > I am, Sir, with respect
> > Your obedient Servt—
> > George Wright
> > 2nd Lt. 3ᵈ Regiment Infantry
>
> To the Honorable J. C. Calhoun
> Secretary of War
> Washington
> City[25]

If one is to judge by the experience of another Vermonter,
Ethan Allen Hitchcock, this may have been Wright's first,
or at least one of his few, opportunities to return home in
the four years he attended the academy.

Duty on the Frontier

AT THE TIME of Lt. George Wright's assignment to the Third Regiment of Infantry the fortunes of the army were at a low ebb. Congress had reduced its strength to seven regiments of infantry and four of artillery, a total of 5,211 men. The "Third" was an old regiment formed under the direction of President George Washington by the act of March 6, 1792, to afford more effective protection to the frontiers of the United States. When Wright joined the regiment in 1822 most of its activities were in the region of the Great Lakes. Wright's first post was Fort Howard, which guarded the eastern end of the Fox-Wisconsin waterway between Lake Michigan and the Mississippi River.[1] It was here that he was to spend the better part of the next four years and where he was to have his first taste of frontier duty, in which he would spend more than half his forty-three years in the army.

Fort Howard, 1822–26

Fort Howard was one of a series of forts established in 1816 to assert the authority of the United States over the Great Lakes and the upper Mississippi region. It was named after Gen. Benjamin Howard, who had distinguished himself in the War of 1812. H. R. Schoolcraft, who accompanied Lewis Cass, the governor of Michigan Territory, on a visit to the post in the 1820s, left this description: "The fort is situated on a handsome grassy plain on the north bank of the Fox River, near the point of entrance into Green Bay. It consists of a range of log barracks facing three sides of a square parade, and surrounded by a stockade of timber, thirty feet high, with block houses at the angles. The whole is white-washed and presents a neat military appearance."[2]

The post was first occupied by several companies of the Third Infantry and a detachment of artillery. Their chief duties were conciliating the settlers whose allegiance was questionable and controlling the hostile Winnebago Indians, who regarded themselves as the custodians of the Fox River Valley and sought to levy toll on anyone passing through the area.

For two years the post was vacated and fell into a dilapidated state, but in the fall of 1821 Col. Ninian Pinkney assumed command and fully restored Fort Howard. By now a sizable settlement had developed on the river embankment below the old stockade. Except for half a dozen Americans, its residents were for the most part retired voyageurs and half-breed French and Menominee Indians. Also adjacent to the fort was a huge campground for the Indians when they came to trade. Colonel Pinkney moved the headquarters of the Third Infantry from Detroit to Fort Howard, and it soon became a large, busy post and a meeting point for all the troops operating in the region.[3]

In spite of its isolated location Fort Howard offered an active social life. Otherwise, the long, cold winters would have been periods of desolation and despair. A number of the officers had their wives and children with them. Many French settlers became naturalized U.S. citizens and mingled freely with the young officers at the fort. The handsome French Creole women, "of graceful deportment," were in great demand as partners at the dances held on the post. There were games and amateur theatricals. Passes were readily obtainable for those who wished to fish or hunt the abundant fowl and game nearby. The young lieutenants whom Wright joined at Fort Howard found it an attractive assignment.[4]

Colonel Pinkney retired as post commander the year following Wright's arrival and was replaced by Col. John McNeil, a veteran of the battles of Chippewa and Niagara. He stood six feet, two inches tall and had a stiff knee from a wound sustained in battle. A strict disciplinarian, he promptly terminated the easygoing regime of his prede-

Fort Howard, Wisconsin, ca. 1830. From F. deCastelnau, *Vues et souvenirs de l'Amérique du Nord* (1842). Courtesy Library of Congress, Washington, D.C.

cessor. No longer were passes easily obtained; the "frolicsome lieutenants were obliged to lay aside their games and dissipation and rigid military duty became the rule."[5] Needless to say, initially this created dissatisfaction among the enlisted men and younger officers. But as old buildings were renovated and new ones erected, it soon became apparent that Colonel McNeil was genuinely concerned with the welfare of his command and with keeping the troops as comfortable as possible during the coming winter. A school was established on the post and all children were required to attend. Religious services were held regularly in the new mess building.

With the coming of spring the winter's social activity ended. Everyone was called out for extra duty—drilling, marching, cleaning, whitewashing. Again the complaints began to mount but when Insp. Gen. John Wool arrived in May he gave the post his unqualified commendation as one of the best ordered garrisons he had inspected in years.

Colonel McNeil appears to have made a strong impression on George Wright, who began to earn a reputation as a strict disciplinarian himself. However, this tendency was always tempered by a sense of fairness and a genuine concern and even affection for the men who served under him.

After two years at Fort Howard, Wright was detached and placed on recruiting duty at a time when the army's entire system of recruiting was undergoing reform. Prior to 1822, all recruiting had been carried on by individual regiments, often with meager results. In 1824, the General Recruiting Service was established. Depots were set up in New York, Philadelphia, and Baltimore to enlist men and train them before they were assigned to specific units. The new system was much more successful than the old. Eventually more depots were opened, but for a number of years some regimental recruiting continued.[6]

It was during this tour of duty, 1824–26, that Wright studied under the instruction of Captain Partridge at the academy in Norwich.[7] In spite of the opportunity to further his education, Wright grew tired of the humdrum existence of a recruiting officer. He was energetic and aggressive and yearned for active service. Consequently, in March, 1826, he applied to the adjutant general for permission to exchange regimental assignments with a lieutenant of the First Artillery. Two weeks later he withdrew his request, asking for orders to rejoin his old regiment.[8]

On May 6, 1826, Wright was ordered back to frontier duty at Fort Howard. Marked changes had taken place at the fort during his absence. Colonel Pinkney had died and Col. Henry Leavenworth was regimental commander. A busy frontier town was growing up around the post, stimulated by the needs of supplying a large garrison. The old fur-trading population was being replaced by American settlers.

The hostility of the Indians continued as settlers made increasing demands for their land. In an effort to cope with this problem, Secretary of War Calhoun had laid a plan before Congress in 1825 to move all the eastern Indian tribes west of the 85th meridian. This became the official policy of President James Monroe, although the Indian Removal Act was not passed until 1830, during the administration of Andrew Jackson. Meanwhile, to enforce treaties made with the Indians, prevent tribal warfare, and protect the frontier, a chain of forts was constructed extending from Fort Snelling, Minnesota, at the confluence of the Minnesota and Mississippi rivers, to Fort Jesup between the Red and Sabine rivers in Louisiana.[9]

Jefferson Barracks, 1826–28

In September, 1826, the Second Infantry took over at Fort Howard and the Third Infantry Regiment was transferred down the Mississippi to the vicinity of Saint Louis. Although surrounded by wilderness, Saint Louis had already become an important trading center and the starting point for numerous military and exploratory expeditions. In addition, a new era of commerce had opened when Mexico attained its independence from Spain in 1821; with the removal of the old Spanish trade restrictions, caravans began to move over the Santa Fe trail. Construction of a large new military post was started in July, 1826, among the heavily wooded, rolling hills on the west bank of the Mississippi River just below Saint Louis. General Henry Atkinson, commander of the Western Department, had placed Maj. Stephen W. Kearny in charge of the project, which was planned as a school of practice for infantry. It was named Jefferson Barracks in honor of Thomas Jefferson, who had just died.

On September 19, 1826, Bvt. Brig. Gen. Henry Leavenworth, Lt. George Wright and the remainder of the Third Infantry arrived and set up an adjoining camp, called Cantonment Miller after a former colonel of the regiment. The troops lived in tents and huts protected by fences, while the officers and their families occupied huts lower down on the hillside. By Christmas, log barracks were constructed. For the first few months, the sole recreation seems to have been listening to concerts by the regimental band, but in January, 1827, a grand military ball was held in the new central building. Another social event of that month was a banquet held at Gen. William Clark's home. Clark had achieved fame on the Lewis and Clark Expedition and served as Superintendent of Indian Affairs from 1822 to 1835.[10]

A commission in the army was an entree to the best society, and officers mingled freely with the hospitable social set of Saint Louis. Yet not all the officers were socially sophisticated. At numerous military installations, large numbers of high-spirited, hot-headed young men were crowded together, with time weighing heavily on their hands. Captain Hitchcock tells of an assignment in New Orleans with some thirty idle officers, a majority of them dissipated men without education: "They had no refinement of any sort and no taste for study. The general talk was of duels—of what this one said and that one threatened. Many a time I have taken a small volume in my pocket, started into the woods and remained a whole day, for no other reason than to be out of hearing of the profanity, ribaldry and blustering braggadocio." Many of these men were leftovers from the heterogeneous group of untrained officers brought into the army by the War of 1812. The result was confusion, disorder, and quarreling: "From ignorance and maladjustment came numberless duels, till an officer could scarcely consider himself entitled to respectability till he had been engaged in one." Hitchcock felt many of his fellow officers "were dissipated, in the worst sense of that word: profane, indecent and licentious and very many of them drunkards."[11]

Jefferson Barracks, with its numerous, diverse troops,

was especially plagued by the pernicious practice of dueling as a means of settling personal differences. Because of its frequent use for dueling, a nearby island on the river came to be known as "Bloody Island." Ultimately the War Department became sufficiently concerned to threaten severe disciplinary action if further dueling occurred within military circles.[12]

In 1827 the army began construction of permanent stone buildings and laid out a large parade ground. Four blocks of officers' quarters were built. Jefferson Barracks soon became one of the largest and most important military establishments in the United States. Promising young officers were sent to the infantry school there, troops were dispatched to the frontier garrisons, and Gen. Henry M. Atkinson established the headquarters of the Western Department at the post. But as more and more of the eastern Indian tribes were being forced west of the Mississippi and the Missouri rivers, the need for another post became apparent.

In their new homes the dispossessed tribes came into conflict with native tribes, such as the Sioux, Chippewas, Pawnees, Cheyennes, Arapahoes, Comanches, Kiowas, and Osages. Many of the eastern Indians wished to return to their homelands, but to others the horses, arms, ammunition, and articles of commerce moving down the Santa Fe Trail offered an irresistible lure.[13] Settlers and traders called on the government for protection.

In response, "Four companies of the 3d Regiment of the United States Infantry left Jefferson Barracks April 17, 1827 in keelboats under the immediate command of Captain W. G. Belknap for the Little Platte on the Missouri."[14] The troops were accompanied by some of the wives and children. They occupied what was thought to be an excellent site for a post near present-day Leavenworth, Kansas, on the west bank of the Missouri River. The troops disembarked and set up quarters in tents and huts made of logs and slabs of bark. The new post, named Cantonment Leavenworth in honor of their colonel, was situated in dry rolling country which it was hoped would prove conducive to

Jefferson Barracks, Missouri, ca. 1835. From J. C. Wild, *The Valley of the Mississippi* (1841). Courtesy Missouri Historical Society, Saint Louis.

the good health of the troops. The original garrison consisted of Companies B, D, E, and H with fourteen officers and 174 enlisted men. The site did not prove particularly healthful, however; during the first summer there was much sickness, and at one time between one-third and one-half of the men were stricken with malaria.[15]

Fort Leavenworth, 1828–29

Wright did not accompany the expedition to Cantonment Leavenworth but remained in garrison at Jefferson Barracks. As one of the more capable, industrious, and dependable young officers, he served intermittently as regimental adjutant. This elevated Wright, although only a second lieutenant, to the status of a staff officer and assistant to his commanding officer. His status demanded his presence at headquarters, with the specific duties of handling all official correspondence and the transmission of orders. This position of responsibility, at the center of activity, indicated the high regard in which he was held by his superior. On September 23, 1827, he received his first promotion, to first lieutenant. By the spring of 1828 there was very little improvement in the health of the garrison at Cantonment Leavenworth, but because of increasing Indian problems the remainder of the Third Infantry Regiment, including Wright, moved there. They continued the work of constructing the new post and built a road to connect it with Liberty, Missouri.

While large numbers of soldiers were being withdrawn from frontier posts to build and attend the Infantry School at Jefferson Barracks, a number of serious outbreaks occurred among the Indians. The Winnebagos, already aroused by the encroachment of settlers, were further provoked when lead mining began on their lands. Led by Chief Red Bird, they carried out numerous attacks in 1827 and destroyed several white families. They also attacked a keelboat loaded with provisions from Fort Snelling, with casualties among both the soldiers and the Indians. The following year Fort Winnebago was built on the right bank of the Fox River near the portage to the Wisconsin River. This afforded protection to the settlers, traders, and miners; it also prevented the Indians from attempting to levy tolls and helped to maintain an uneasy peace after the capture and imprisonment of Red Bird.[16]

Marriage

Sometime in the late 1820s, George Wright and Margaret Wallace Forster were married. Margaret was born to Thomas and Sarah Forster, an illustrious Pennsylvania family, on September 10, 1806, in Erie. Margaret's great-grandfather, John Forster, a native of County Antrim, Ireland, was of Scottish parentage. He emigrated to America before 1722, settling in Paxtang Township, Lancaster, now Dauphin County. Margaret's father, Thomas, was born there in 1762. He was educated at Princeton College and trained as a surveyor but owed his reputation to his civic and military activities.[17] In 1786 he married Sarah Pettit Montgomery, the daughter of the Reverend Joseph and Elizabeth Reed Montgomery.[18] In 1799 he moved his family to the newly developed frontier settlement of Erie, where he had purchased some large tracts of land.[19]

Thomas Forster and his wife, Sarah, had eleven children, of whom Margaret was the youngest. Interestingly enough, of six daughters who reached maturity, five married military men. One of these officers was Edwin Vose Sumner, who became a close friend and confidant of Wright. Margaret's mother died when the little girl was only a year old; her forty-six-year-old father never remarried. He died at his home in Erie in 1836.[20]

As Margaret grew up, there were some exciting times in Erie. In 1813, during the second war with Great Britain, the Americans gained full control of the waters of Lake Erie with the defeat and capture of the entire British naval squadron, and a great celebration was held in Erie. In 1825 her father was host to the aging Revolutionary War hero, the Marquis of LaFayette, when he visited Erie on his American tour.[21]

Unfortunately, I have not been able to determine where and how George Wright and Margaret met or the exact date or place of their wedding. Since George's Uncle Ebenezer practiced law in Lebanon and Lancaster, and his Aunt Polly married a man who was a lawyer and later a judge in York, George may have visited them in Pennsylvania during his periodic barnstorming tours as a recruiting officer.[22] The marriage was a happy one, and George appears to have been a loving husband and, after the birth of their three children, a devoted family man.

3.
Wright's First Independent Command

As THE WINTER of 1829 drew to a close, George Wright received his first independent command, an expedition to Council Bluffs. He had been in the army almost seven years and had received his first promotion a year and a half earlier. He had spent the previous year at Cantonment Leavenworth, where his duties were mainly administrative with periodic stints as regimental adjutant. However, his superiors must have recognized his soldierly qualities to entrust him with the important and potentially dangerous mission he was about to undertake.

Expedition to Council Bluffs, 1829

The expedition to Council Bluffs was an armed reconnaissance by a small detachment of soldiers from the Third Infantry sent out from Cantonment Leavenworth under the command of First Lieutenant Wright. His mission was to assess the strength, degree of hostility, and intentions of the powerful Pawnee nation by visiting their villages. Before undertaking this hazardous task, he spent almost two weeks at Council Bluffs, interviewing knowledgeable white traders and Indians for general information about the Pawnees' conduct and the risk he might be taking in visiting their villages. Wright had already earned a reputation for intelligence, dedication, dependability, and a capacity for maintaining strict discipline. These attributes could be important to the very survival of his men during such a mission. The Council Bluffs Expedition shows the careful planning Wright carried out before embarking on a campaign or dangerous undertaking. It was his first opportunity to display his qualities of leadership, courage, ability in the field, cool judgment, and common sense.

Cantonment Leavenworth, in the meantime, was fast becoming the guardian of the area, the watchdog of the Indian-trade traffic on the Missouri River, and the starting point for the fur-trading expeditions to the Rocky Mountains and the caravans bound for Santa Fe. The previous bastion in this region had been Fort Atkinson, further up the Missouri River above the mouth of the Platte. That post had been founded by Colonel Henry M. Atkinson in 1819.[1] It later became one of the largest and most advanced posts on the western frontier until it was abandoned and replaced by Cantonment Leavenworth. However, the district in which Fort Atkinson had been located was still an active trading area known as Council Bluffs after a council held there by Lewis and Clark with the Oto and Missouri Indians in 1804. Across the river and twenty-five miles upstream from the present city of the same name in Iowa, Council Bluffs had been the site of numerous trading posts. One of the most active of these was founded in the mid-1820s by John P. Cabanné for John Jacob Astor's American Fur Company.[2]

By the early nineteenth century, the whites regarded all the land acquired by the Louisiana Purchase as part of the United States. The Indian tribes of the area were understandably disturbed by the increasing influx of whites into their territories, and the Pawnees, in particular, were unhappy since the main highway of commerce to Santa Fe passed through their lands. One half of this road, which started at Independence, Missouri, lay within the United States, the other half in Mexico.

The result of these disputes with the Indians was almost continuous bloody conflict, although the Pawnees were never officially at war with the United States. In fact, in the Treaty of Fort Atkinson in 1825, the Pawnees acknowledged the supremacy of the United States and agreed to submit all grievances to the government.

The Pawnee confederacy was made up of four principal tribes: the Grand, the Republican, the Tappage, and the Loup.[3] These four tribes occupied the valleys of the Platte and Kansas rivers and their tributaries. The names were

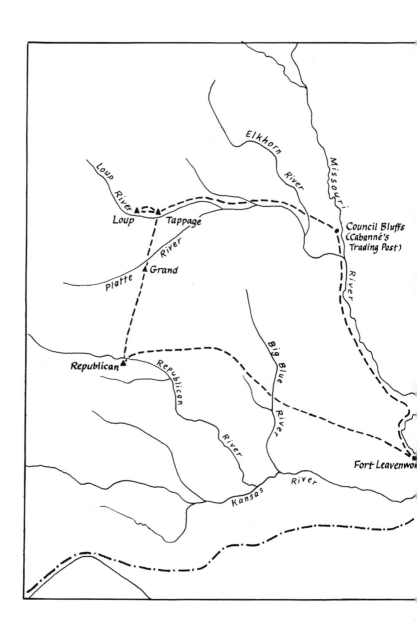

Map of Wright's expedition to Council Bluffs, on the Missouri River, in the spring of 1829, showing the approximate location of the Pawnee villages visited by Wright, his approximate route, and part of the Santa Fe Trail. The map is based on Wright's description in the National Archives and on maps in George E. Hyde, *The Pawnee Indians,* new ed., Foreword by Savoie Lottinville (Norman: University of Oklahoma Press, 1974).

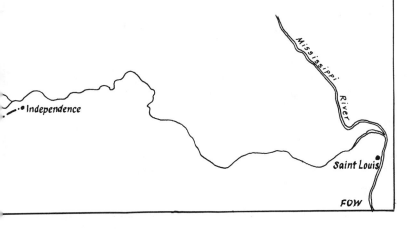

▲ Pawnee villages visited by Wright in spring of 1829 (approximate locations)

— — — — — Approximate route followed by Wright

—·—·—· Santa Fe Trail

0   25   50   75   100 MILES

given to the Indian groups by French traders who roamed the area in the eighteenth century. The same names were often applied to the rivers on which their villages of earthen lodges were situated.[4]

By early March, 1829, Wright and his men were at Cabanné's Trading House at Council Bluffs. Second Lt. Edwin B. Babbitt kept a meticulous record of the interviews carried out there by Wright.[5] Wright submitted this account and descriptions of his subsequent visits to the Pawnee villages to Maj. John Bliss, the commanding officer at Cantonment Leavenworth.[6]

The first person Wright interrogated was Louis L. Jennesson, an employee of Cabanné's. Jennesson had spent three years trading with the "republics" and one fall and winter with the Loups. Although ostensibly in search of buffalo and beaver, the Loups had sent out war parties against the Arapahoes, Crows, and Sioux. Only one of these parties had returned by the time Jennesson left the Loup villages. He had heard of no injury the Pawnees had done the whites. According to Jennesson, the tribe had been told by their "partizan"* not to hurt the whites upon whom they depended for supplies. They were also admonished to "listen to what they had promised in relation to the treaty with the United States." Some of the chiefs always sent a "reasonable man" with their war parties to keep their pugnacious young men from "beating and plundering" the whites. Of all the Pawnee tribes Jennesson regarded the Tappages as the most unfriendly to the whites.

Wright then questioned Martin Dorion, Cabanné's interpreter. Dorion had spent six years in the area and was particularly well acquainted with the principal men of the Otos, Omahas, and Ioways. Members of these tribes frequently visited the Pawnees and sometimes accompanied their hunting and war parties. Dorion thought Omaha vil-

---

*Partizan was the name of a Sioux chief who gave Lewis and Clark a good deal of trouble. Here it is used as a generic term for a chief or subchief. In the fur trade the *partizan* (or *partisan*) was the leader of a white field expedition, in contrast to the *bourgeois*, who was in charge of a trading post.

lages could be safely visited; only "some clerks who would trade high with them" would be ill-treated.

Dorion told Wright that the Omaha chief Big Eyes had demanded a large quantity of goods from Cabanné by presenting himself as worthy of pity, since his daughter had been accidentally killed in the house of one of Cabanné's clerks. Big Eyes was determined to satisfy himself for this loss, and Cabanné gave him what he requested at no cost. As a consequence, word spread among the Indians that others should emulate Big Eyes and get goods from the whites for nothing.

Wright asked Dorion whether he ever heard the Pawnees or other tribes say that the whites were afraid of them. His answer: "When I speak to the chiefs of the small tribes and ask them why they don't listen to the words of their [Great White] father, they reply, why don't you scold at the Pawnees, we are a small nation and you scold at us, but the Pawnees are a large nation and you are afraid of them." The only act of Pawnee "outrages or depredations" against the whites during the past winter that Dorion knew of was the theft of five horses by the Loups from a Cabanné employee. Dorion had been in the Republican village the preceding March when a party had returned with Spanish horses, mules, and scalps. A few months later, Big Nose, an influential man in the village, said to Dorion and several others that "he would in future make the Santa Fe road his home, that he would do all the injury to the whites that he could and he would see whether those [other Indians] who have received medals at the council last spring would dare to interfere."[7] Big Nose was angry because Maj. John Dougherty, U.S. Indian agent, had not given his brother a medal. While his father was one of the foremost chiefs of the nation, Big Nose "was looked upon by the whites as nothing."

Major Jonathan F. Bean, an Indian subagent, had told Dorion that the Sioux were well disposed toward the United States and that their long-standing hostility toward the Pawnees would make them of "great service to the U. States" in case of war with that nation. The Omaha band living on the Missouri was also said to be friendly, more so than the band living on the Elk Horn.

Big Elk, a chief of the Omahas whom Wright expected to accompany the detachment to the Pawnee villages, told Wright: "I believe that they [the Pawnees] don't like the whites at all. When they meet any of them with goods or anything they generally plunder, kill or flog them. And when they go on a visit to their father below [General William Clark] and return to their villages and get sick, they lay it on the whites." When last he had visited the Grand and Republican villages, no one was there but the old men, the others having all gone to war toward the "Spanish country." None of the war parties had returned. When asked whether the detachment could safely make a friendly visit to the Pawnee villages at this time, Big Elk diplomatically replied, "I cannot be certain whether a party could visit the different villages without any danger; as should I say they *could*, I might tell a lie; and should I say they could not, I might also tell a lie." The Omahas, he said, were not very friendly toward the Pawnees, although they had to trade with them, especially for horses. "They are very hard with us," he observed.

Perhaps the best-known person Wright interviewed was Lucien Fontenelle, "a gentleman of high respectability and veracity," who lived at Council Bluffs.[8] Fontenelle gave Wright an account of Pawnee misdeeds over a period of ten years, apologizing that it was not as extensive or as explicit as he could wish. "Had I taken notes of depredations . . . I could undoubtedly point out many more instances in which the Pawnees have been indulged." In spite of this disclaimer, Fontenelle recited a dismal tale of floggings, beatings, kidnappings, plunder, horse stealing, murders, scalpings, and desecration of the flag. Victims included individuals, large trading parties, and military detachments in search of deserters. There had even been attacks on remote military posts. One Indian was quoted as saying, "It was nothing to rob white men, they were such dogs and cowards." Some where robbed of all they owned and had been obliged to make their way homeward on foot, without food, weapons, or shelter, fortunate if they escaped with their lives.

Fontenelle told Wright of Abraham Ledoux, an interpreter residing with the Pawnees, who "was shot by one of them in three different places with arrows."[9] He was expected to die but amazingly, after several months, recovered from his wounds. After this event the Pawnees began to boast of their strength and courage and to express their contempt for American troops. The Pawnees said that they would be happy to fight Americans and demonstrate that they could be "used up like buffaloes in a chase." When Dougherty sought to have the responsible warrior surrendered to the authorities, the chiefs came to the council with concealed weapons in case the agent or anyone else attempted to take them hostage until the malefactor could be brought in.

The most gruesome event related by Fontenelle occurred in April, 1827. Word came to Major Dougherty at Council Bluffs that there was at one of the Pawnee villages a Cheyenne woman prisoner "who had been promised by one of their chiefs to their 'Holy Star' and that she was to be sacrificed according to ancient custom."* Dougherty and a few soldiers set out from Council Bluffs

to obtain, if they could, the poor wretch from her murderers. On their arrival at the village where she was, they demanded her, and after some long deliberations on the part of the Indians, and after some presents were made to them by the agent, they agreed that the prisoner should be sent into this place by some of their own people, and delivered to the whites; they immediately prepared and started to come in, in company with the party which had went [sic] from this place, and

---

*The practice of human sacrifice by the Loup Pawnees (Skidis) as a rite of Morning Star worship was well known. It was usually carried out on special occasions such as before the spring crop planting, at the summer solstice, or during harvest ceremonies.[10] Hyde refers to this particular incident as occurring in 1833, but in 1829 Fontenelle told Wright it happened in April, 1827.[11]

as they were getting out of the village, some eight or ten Pawnees, prepared for the act, rushed on them, killed the woman,
and cut her body into pieces in presence of the party. I never
have been apprised that any personal insults were offered to
any of the party, but the act itself taken in proper light, and so
the Indians themselves would take it, was in my opinion and
not less in theirs a great insult to the American Government.

The Americans threatened reprisal and punishment but
never took action.

Fontenelle remarked, "It has been a continual scene of
abuses since I have inhabited the country." Since the Pawnees held the firm belief that no American forces could in-
jure or molest them, the hostilities to travelers on the Santa
Fe road and on the upper Missouri would continue.

Wright sent the journal of these interviews down the
Missouri River with Major Bean to Cantonment Leavenworth. In his cover letter to the commanding officer,
Wright called attention to the "outrages and abuses committed by the Pawnees against our citizens during the last
ten years." In spite of the promises the Pawnees had made
in the Treaty of Fort Atkinson, "they have continued to kill
and plunder our citizens engaged in trade." This powerful
tribe felt itself capable of battling any nation on earth and
publicly proclaimed that the whites were afraid of them.
"As long as the Government forbear to chastise them for
these depredations, so long will they continue them," he
wrote. Neighboring tribes, Wright believed, might share
the views of the Pawnees but would probably side with the
United States in the event of hostilities. Although he judged
the Pawnees to be decidedly unfriendly, he did not think he
would incur any undue risk in visiting their villages.

Having gathered information at Council Bluffs, Wright
and his detachment marched westward on March 18, 1829.
They arrived at the Tappage village on Monday, March 22,
shortly after noon, but remained there only a few hours.
Although this band had been reported as particularly unfriendly, the Tappage chief, Wild Horse, rode out to meet

them, conducted them to his lodge, and, on their departure later in the day, led them to the nearby Loup village. The soldiers were surprised to detect no evidence of ill will or disrespect from any of the Tappages during their short stay.

At the Loup village they encountered a Mr. Sapine, Cabanné's resident trader. Sapine said the Loups were well disposed toward the whites but were concerned because Major Dougherty had not sent for them when he was at Cabanné's Trading House the preceding fall. They wondered if their theft of a large herd of horses from some traders the year before had been responsible for this "slight." Sapine knew of no recent depredations by the Loups.

The next day Wright met with the Loup chiefs, Antoine and Big Axe, who expressed to him and the assembled village braves their friendship for the whites. They admitted that some of their young men, against the wishes of their chiefs, had stolen sixty horses and mules from a party of whites. They begged forgiveness, although because of their poverty they were unable to return any animals. They promised good behavior and hoped to be invited to the next council.

On March 25, the detachment left the Loup village, but was unable to cross the Loup Fork because of moving ice on the river. In order to please Wild Horse they returned through his village on their way to the Grand Pawnees. As a result of his visits with the Loups and Tappages Wright formed the opinion that they were, "notwithstanding [their] constant protestations of friendship, a most confirmed race of thieves and rascals, and it was only by the constant exercise of all the vigilance in our power, that we could prevent their stealing from us every article which was portable under cover of a blanket or buffalo robe." One Tappage, under the guise of friendship, even followed them eight miles to their next encampment in order to carry out petty thefts.

The next day there was less ice flow in the river, and the

party crossed the Loup Fork by swimming their horses and transporting their baggage in an elk skin. Although two Tappage Indians accompanied him as guides, Wright was pleased to have the river as a barrier between him and the remainder of their band.

On Friday, March 27, they arrived on the Platte opposite the village of the Grand Pawnees. Here they encamped while constructing a means of conveyance for their baggage. Numerous visitors from the village "began already to annoy us by becoming quite too familiar with ourselves, but much more so with our property."

On Saturday, in the midst of a violent storm of snow and rain, the soldiers crossed the Platte with the assistance of some Indians from the village. The troops suffered considerably from the cold weather and their wet clothing, and were particularly glad to be kindly received by Bad Chief, Sun Chief, and a number of braves. Both chiefs professed friendship toward the whites but admitted that some of their young men "were not all of the same disposition."

Mr. La Marche, Cabanné's resident trader in the Grand village, told Wright he had accompanied a hunting party during the last winter. They saw no whites but encountered a Tappage band who stated they had killed three Kickapoos. La Marche was sure the "Kickapoos" had been whites, an opinion confirmed by Big Elk, the Omaha chief, who heard it from a Pawnee.

The Grands had sent out several war parties, one of which encountered sixty or eighty shod horses and mules running unaccompanied on the "Arkansaw," but they only brought back seven or eight, the chiefs said. However, a friendly Oto Indian, Satan, whom Wright had sent for, said that the Pawnees had stolen the animals and left them at a convenient spot from which they could be brought in a few at a time.

Wright relied on La Marche's opinion that

> if a war party should meet a party of traders on the Santa Fe road or elsewhere, if the whites were superior they would probably pass on without saying anything to them, but if the

Pawnees were the superior, they would rob them and if resistance was made, they would kill them. The chiefs . . . speak very friendly to the whites but they do not say what they think.

Starting out at daylight on April 1, Wright and his men reached the Republican village at noon, having marched twenty-four miles. They moved on another eight or ten miles and then encamped. The Pawnee Republicans were found to be "nearly in a state of starvation," having to leave their village daily to obtain food from their neighbors.

At this village Wright encountered another of Cabanné's traders, Francis Dorion, who confirmed the threats Big Nose had made. Although the Republics would not attack whites at or near the Indian village, should they meet whites on the road or elsewhere, they would rob and kill them, Dorion said.

As for three whites known to have been killed while eastbound on the Santa Fe road, Dorion did not believe the Republics had been responsible. These murders were subsequently attributed to the Comanches.

Wright returned to Cantonment Leavenworth on April 9, only a day or two later than he had anticipated. In his final report to Major Bliss, Wright reemphasized the opinion expressed in his previous letter that the Pawnees regarded themselves as invincible. The large number of horses and mules found "accidentally" by the Grand and Republican Pawnees in the Arkansas River valley had probably been stolen by these bands from a Santa Fe caravan the previous season. He concluded his report by expressing his "entire conviction that the Pawnees never entertained the most distant intention of prosecuting an open war with the United States, but until decisive measures are taken by the government, they will continue to rob and murder the whites as heretofore."

Malaria had begun to take such a toll at Cantonment Leavenworth that in May the post was temporarily abandoned, and the depleted garrison moved back to Jefferson Barracks by steamboat. The following month a battalion of the Sixth Infantry served as the first military escort to a Santa Fe caravan. In November these troops returned and took over possession of the miserable huts and shacks left by the Third Infantry at Cantonment Leavenworth. In 1832 the post was designated as Fort Leavenworth by an order of the War Department which directed that henceforth all cantonments should be called forts.[12]

4.
More Frontier Duty

IN JULY, 1829, two months after Lt. George Wright returned to Jefferson Barracks from Cantonment Leavenworth, fighting broke out in Randolph County, Missouri, between the Sauk and Iowa tribes and the settlers. Although Colonel Leavenworth dispatched detachments of the Third Infantry to the trouble spots, by the next year general warfare among the Indian tribes seemed imminent. Wright did not accompany any of these expeditions because of his increasing duties at headquarters.[1]

During 1830, Wright's wife, Margaret, then twenty-four years of age, gave birth to the couple's first child, at Jefferson Barracks. The boy, named Thomas Forster Wright,[2] caused his parents a great deal of anxiety in the years to come.

Fort Jesup, 1831–36

As the year 1830 drew to a close, Maj. S. W. Kearny and the First Battalion of the Third Infantry were sent to Natchitoches, on the Red River in Louisiana, in Choctaw country. On March 11, 1831, General Leavenworth reported to the adjutant general that two months earlier Wright had been officially appointed the regiment's adjutant, a position that he filled with distinction for the next five years.[3] Since troops were dispatched to various assignments from Jefferson Barracks, Wright served as post commander on several occasions.

In September the remaining troops of the Third Regiment of Infantry were transferred to the Red River valley; they were transported down the Mississippi by steamboat. Leavenworth established his headquarters at Fort Jesup and assigned Wright to that post. Wright spent part of 1832 as judge advocate of a general court-martial. He appar-

37

ently devoted considerable time to reading. Later observers referred to him as a man of refinement and culture, with high intellectual and moral qualities.[4] His speeches and proclamations, and his surviving letters, suggest a well-educated, sensitive man with a high degree of patriotism.

Fort Jesup, named after Thomas S. Jesup, quartermaster general of the army, was situated in Sabine Parish, Louisiana, on a ridge between the Red and Sabine rivers, twenty-five miles southwest of Natchitoches.

By the Treaty of Washington signed with Spain in 1819, Florida had been ceded to the United States and the Sabine River designated as the western boundary of this portion of Louisiana. Bvt. Maj. General Edmund P. Gaines, commander of the Western Department (one of two U.S. military departments), ordered construction of a group of forts in this area. Cantonment Jesup was erected in 1822, but it was not officially designated a fort until ten years later. The farthest southwest of the U.S. posts, Fort Jesup had comfortable quarters, but because of the lack of a surrounding stockade, it was said to look "more like a little hamlet in the midst of the forest" than a crucial bastion of defense.[5] When relations between the United States and Mexico became more strained as a result of the independence movement in Texas, the post became increasingly important. It was progressively strengthened and new buildings constructed.

Companies B, D, F, and H of the Third Infantry made up the garrison at Fort Jesup. Other companies of the regiment were stationed farther up the Red River at Fort Towson, Oklahoma. With the arrival of its remaining companies in Louisiana, the Third Infantry came back under the immediate command of Leavenworth, now a brevet brigadier general. A brevet was an honorary commission by which the United States could promote an officer in recognition of bravery and distinction without providing him with the additional pay or full authority of the new rank. His troops spent much of their time building roads to connect the various posts. He faced the vexing problem of his soldiers drinking liquor they bought from squatters.[6]

In 1834, Leavenworth was placed in command of the left wing of the Western Department. During this year he led an expedition against the Pawnee and Comanche Indians in what was subsequently referred to as Indian Territory. While in the field he contracted a violent fever and died within a few hours. On August 10, Wright informed the adjutant general of Leavenworth's death.[7] After his death, news reached Leavenworth's command that he had been promoted from brevet brigadier general to brigadier general.

Colonel James B. Many now assumed command of the Third Infantry. His first field operation, in 1835, was chiefly a reconnoitering and fact-finding expedition among the Caddo Indians. It resulted in the Caddo Treaty, the only Indian treaty ever executed in Louisiana. Wright's duties as adjutant kept him at regimental headquarters and he was disappointed at being unable to participate in any of these operations.[8]

About this time occurred the first indication that Wright was having some trouble with other officers, particularly those who outranked him. This problem, not unique in the army of those days, was to plague Wright periodically in later years. In 1835 he sent a letter to the adjutant general requesting clarification of his duties as adjutant, specifically regarding his relationships with field-grade officers. Were they authorized to interfere with his duties as adjutant or, in the absence of the commanding officer, to make him, as regimental adjutant, perform the duties of post adjutant?[9] No reply to his query has been found, but it is known that Wright was punctilious in conforming to military rules. He was dedicated to firm discipline and obedience to orders, although if he felt that orders were not in strict conformity with army regulations, he would resist. This behavior could easily annoy a superior and suggests a stubborn, contentious streak that may explain Wright's occasional problems with personal relationships.

The year 1835 was an important one in the history of Fort Jesup. The raging revolt of Texas against Mexico was watched with great interest, particularly by the southern states. Reinforcements poured in, and the post was enlarged. On January 23, Lewis Cass, secretary of war in the cabinet of President Andrew Jackson, ordered General Gaines to assume command of all troops near the boundary.

After the Mexican slaughter of Americans at the Alamo and at nearby Goliad in 1836, Gaines requested volunteers and additional federal troops and established Camp Sabine on the west bank of the Sabine River, just three miles from the Gulf of Mexico. On April 18, 1836, the Texans, under Gen. Sam Houston, defeated the Mexicans at San Jacinto, and captured the Mexican president and commander, Antonio López de Santa Anna. This victory deprived Gaines of any immediate prospect of a personal military success; however, in June the murder of several settlers in northeastern Texas by Indians provided him with another opportunity. Gaines sent out troops from Fort Jesup and Camp Sabine and occupied Nacogdoches in Texas with several companies of infantry and some dragoons.

Texas, meanwhile, had sent an envoy to Washington, D.C., demanding annexation by the United States or recognition as an independent republic. President Jackson had decided on a plan of watchful waiting regarding Mexico and Texas. Gaines was ordered to withdraw his troops to Fort Jesup and Camp Sabine. In October, Gaines left the frontier, never to return.[10]

Wright appears to have remained at his post at regimental headquarters during all of this activity. It was difficult for a patriot like Wright to sit by while events of great importance to his country were taking place. As a prudent individual, Wright would be unlikely to seek identification with a rash, temperamental man like Gaines, but he could hardly have watched with complacence what was happening to some of his fellow citizens. Moreover, Wright was an ambitious man with an intense desire for accomplishment and he was becoming impatient at not achieving higher rank. Promotion was a slow process, and it was not unusual for officers to call attention of Army Headquarters to their current status.

In April and May, 1836, Wright wrote letters to the adjutant general soliciting a captaincy for himself, pointing out that he had spent fourteen years in the army, the last nine as a first lieutenant.[11] His promotion to captain finally came through on October 30, and he was granted leave until February of the following year.[12] While he was on leave, he requested reassignment to the recruiting service.[13] His request was granted, and he remained on this duty until October, 1838. During this time he took his wife to Harrisburg, Pennsylvania, where in May, 1837, their second child, a daughter, Eliza H. Wright, was born.[14]

As for Fort Jesup, after the departure of General Gaines, it relapsed into a dreary little garrison, and remained so until a decade later when it became an important post during the war with Mexico.

The Patriot War, 1837–39

Captain Wright's duty in the recruiting service assumed increased importance as tension along the border with Canada created a turmoil that nearly led to a third war with Great Britain. It was not long before Wright was recruiting along the northern border of New York State.

In Canada the Patriots, an insurrectionary party headed by William Lyon MacKenzie, sought to establish a democratic government responsible to the people, a concept totally unacceptable to the royal governors. A network of secret societies known as Hunters' Lodges, made up of Patriots and their American sympathizers, fomented discontent with conditions in Canada, armed themselves, drilled, and prepared for action. They planned a revolution with the goal of establishing a republic of Canada or possible annexation to the United States. The movement initially had little popular support, but in the latter part of 1837 a few rebels were killed in skirmishes with the Canadian armed forces. MacKenzie fled to the United States, while some of his lieutenants were executed for treason. This was the start of the Patriot War, a poorly planned and supported "comic-opera rebellion"; while it failed completely

as a military coup, it initiated a successful political movement which led to an independent Canada.[15]

MacKenzie found considerable support for his beliefs in
some of the American border states, and he soon gathered
a large band of Canadian refugees and adventurous Americans. They established a base for the planned invasion of
Canada on Navy Island, on the Niagara River. Arms and
supplies were accumulated and taken to the island aboard
the American steamer *Caroline.*

Wright, on recruiting service in Buffalo, informed the
adjutant general, Col. Roger Jones, in a letter of December 30, 1837, that Navy Island was in the possession of the
Patriots and that U.S. soil had been violated by Canadian
loyalists attempting to dislodge them. The *Caroline* had descended the Niagara River the preceding day and tied up
on the U.S. side. During the night 150 Canadian troops
crossed the river, set fire to the *Caroline,* and sent her over
Niagara Falls in flames. The body of an American was
found on the wharf, and others from the crew were said to
be missing. The U.S. militia was organizing to prevent any
repetition of this act, which had been perpetrated by the
authority of the Canadian government. Wright reported
the rumor that the British intended to occupy Grand Island, which belonged to the United States, and that the
British commander was prepared to ignore "the law of nations" and occupy Navy Island as well. Only a strong U.S.
force, he said, could preserve the peace.[16]

Wright's apprehensions were not unfounded, for the
border states regarded this episode as an overt act of war.
However, President Martin Van Buren and Congress were
reluctant to become involved in a border quarrel; their
main concerns were domestic, for the United States was
fighting an economic depression in 1837. Far from supporting MacKenzie, American authorities had him slapped
into jail in Rochester, New York.

Early in 1838, Wright was ordered to reestablish Fort
Niagara with a garrison of sixteen recruits, which he reported accomplished on January 14.[17] A few months later
tensions on the border escalated after an American named

Fort Niagara, New York, ca. 1850. From *Ballou's Pictorial Drawing Room Companion* (1856). Courtesy Library of Congress.

Bill Johnson led a party of desperadoes dressed as Indians to burn the Canadian steamer *Sir Robert Peel* at Ogdensburg, New York.

In May, Wright wrote from Buffalo to one of his subordinates to warn him that many disaffected Canadians were "coming to our shores." Wright ordered him to keep his commanding officer informed, notify the civil authorities if any violations of law were likely to occur, and offer authorities the help of troops if needed. Wright reported to the adjutant general that these disaffected Canadians would probably return to Canada if there was any prospect of success for their cause. He pointed out how difficult it was to prevent insurgents from crossing the long frontier between the United States and Canada, particularly with the small number of troops available.[18] Wright had the satisfaction of being at least peripherally involved in international affairs and doing something for his country.

Madison Barracks, 1838–40

By summer Congress had become sufficiently alarmed about the Canadian rebels to pass the act of July 5, 1838, which ordered the formation of the Eighth Regiment of Infantry. Colonel William J. Worth, who had been commandant of cadets when Wright was at West Point, was placed in command. On July 7, Captain Wright was transferred to the new regiment. Headquarters were originally in Troy, New York, but by October the entire regiment had been raised and was assembled at Madison Barracks at Sacket's Harbor, New York, at the eastern end of Lake Ontario. Wright was given command of Company F.[19]

Construction of Madison Barracks had begun in 1815. Handsome buildings of hand-chiseled limestone were erected in the dense forest surrounding the post, where as recently as 1834 wolves and panthers had been hunted for a ten-dollar bounty. Little thought was given to the comfort of the soldiers, who slept either on the floor or on wooden platforms, often without even a straw mattress. It was a scene of hard work and harsh discipline. Corporal punishment was common and led to many desertions. Deserters, if apprehended, were either hanged or shot. Boredom, quarrels, and dissipation marked the long winters. Originally regarded as a healthful spot, Madison Barracks later was plagued with much sickness. The arrival of many recruits and the overcrowded barracks led to a good deal of disability from dysentery and intermittent fever.

Hopeful of preventing active hostilities with England, the government gave Colonel Worth unusual authority to complete the post, repair its defenses, and fit it for the large number of troops being enlisted. By October, he had ten companies of one hundred men each. Worth was an inspiring commander and soon had his command trained and in shape.

The Eighth Infantry was to act as an international peacemaker. Constant patrols of the border between Detroit and Swanton, Vermont, were maintained to preserve neutrality and prevent aggression by the Patriots and their adherents in the United States against the established government of Canada. In the summer of 1838, the steamer *Telegraph* was fitted out at Sacket's Harbor; manned by a company of the Eighth Infantry, it patrolled among the Thousand Islands to protect navigation on the Saint Lawrence River. In the early fall the steamer *Oneida*, with another company of the Eighth Infantry aboard, joined the river patrol. Additional details were placed on all Saint Lawrence River passenger steamers. In spite of close cooperation with British officials, raids across the border continued, and in September, 1838, the Patriots met in Cleveland to plan the invasion of Canada. Both governments protested and a serious rupture seemed imminent. General Winfield Scott was sent north to dissuade the governors of the border states who openly condoned such activity.

By October, a thousand Patriots and sympathizers were in Ogdensburg, poised for a coup which they hoped would unite all of North America. Two hundred crossed into Canada on the steamer *United States,* where they engaged in a futile battle with Canadian troops at Windmill Point near Prescott, Ontario. A number of "enthusiastic young men" were killed by the Canadian soldiers and aroused loyalists who resented this armed invasion of their country. After a five-day siege the survivors surrendered. They were tried, imprisoned, and two of their leaders hanged; the others were exiled to Van Diemen's Land. During this encounter the two American patrol boats lay nearby, but Colonel Worth and his men could not intervene as allies of the Canadians since the battle was waged on foreign soil.[20]

This disastrous defeat dampened the ardor of the Patriots. Colonel Worth captured the steamer *United States* and a number of other boats, schooners, and barges, many of which were laden with munitions of war. All were taken to Sacket's Harbor and sold, with their cargoes, by the U.S. marshal.

In May, 1839, another international incident occurred when the American schooner *G. I. Weeks* was seized by loyalist militia off Brockville, Ontario. Worth averted serious consequences by promptly sending Captain Wright to the scene to demand the release of the schooner. Wright was threatened by a mob, and his ultimatum was rejected by the Canadian authorities. Worth then ordered the steamer *Oneida* to run into the harbor and level her guns on the town of Brockville. The Canadians thereupon backed down and released the schooner. The U.S. secretary of state demanded an explanation of the affair from the British government. Following this episode the Eighth Regiment of Infantry spent the remainder of 1839 on routine patrols.[21]

On February 21, 1839, at Madison Barracks, Margaret Wright gave birth to her third and last child, a boy, whom they named John Montgomery Wright.[22]

At various times during the absence of Colonel Worth, Wright was in command of the post. An incident in January, 1839, offers a glimpse of Wright's soldierly qualities and the high esteem in which he was held by Worth. Company G, under 1st Lt. N. D. Reeve, was moved from Madison Barracks to duty in Ogdensburg. While they were there, the men were guilty of some unidentified disorderly conduct. The next month the company, now commanded by Lt. Thomas Johns, was returned to Madison Barracks with orders to report to Captain Wright. Colonel Worth wrote to Wright: "I send you Company 'G' almost ruined; the company has discredited the Regiment. I desire to subject it to rigid discipline, and withhold all indulgences, except what the law allows, until reputation is retrieved."[23] A year later Wright was able to report marked improvement; the officers of the regiment, including those fresh from civilian life, were making good progress in the school of instruction that he had organized.[24]

Because of its strategic location during the border troubles and the danger of war with England, Madison Barracks attracted many distinguished visitors. Colonel Worth was proud of the appearance of his men on parade and usually honored his guests with a special drill: "The men of the Eighth were a fine sight as they marched to the music of their band, with their long tailed coats drawn together by frogs across their chests, spotless white canvas trousers covering their black, square toed boots, buttons gleaming like silver. . . . Their caps were high and brilliant with decoration. When bayonets were affixed to their long unwieldy muskets, they were a foot higher than the soldiers' heads."[25]

A near disaster occurred during a review held in honor of President Van Buren. The president had arrived the day before on the government steamship *Oneida* and had been welcomed with a booming cannon salute. The subsequent formal review was held on the parade ground between the barracks:

> After the men had completed the customary evolutions, Colonel Worth ordered them to load and fire toward the lake as a finish to the exercise. The reviewing party was standing near the sally port on a line with the flank of the troops; and when the pieces were discharged, the iron ramrod from one of the muskets flew like an arrow and lodged in the ground between the President and Colonel Worth, who were standing close together, talking. The President was calm and did nothing more than move backward slightly from where he was standing, but both he and Colonel Worth were thankful to see the erratic piece of metal where it was.[26]

Throughout his career, Wright usually enjoyed good relations with the nonmilitary population in the communities where he was assigned. His dealings with civilian officials were conducted with tact, understanding, and cooperation. Disagreements occurred when the health, welfare, or effectiveness of his men were threatened, or the interests or property of the government jeopardized. In January, 1840, Wright had some difficulty with a hostile civilian judge. A private from Company D, after six months

Gen. William Jenkins Worth, ca. 1848. Wright's commander during the Seminole and Mexican wars. Courtesy Fort
Worth (Texas) Museum of Science and History.

of service, wished to be discharged. The judge ordered the man released from the army, arguing that he had enlisted as a minor without parental approval. At the hearing no parent had appeared and no proof of age was offered. Wright believed that this decision might encourage other soldiers to follow the same route and felt frustrated at his inability to do anything about it.[27]

Forts Winnebago and Crawford, 1840

On April 14, 1840, the Eighth Infantry was ordered to report to General Atkinson at Fort Winnebago, Wisconsin. Here they were scheduled to take part in an operation against the Winnebago Indians who had left their reservation and were "committing depredations." The regiment left Sacket's Harbor on May 2; traveled by steamer on Lakes Ontario, Erie, and Huron; and reached Fort Howard at the head of Green Bay on Lake Michigan on May 18. Worth and six companies marched from there to Camp McKeown near Fort Winnebago. Wright and the remainder of the regiment reached Camp McKeown on May 29, after bringing the equipment and stores up the Fox River in shallow draft boats. After Wright's arrival, an inspection and review were held for General Atkinson, who was favorably impressed with the soldierly appearance and health of the regiment. This show of strength led to satisfactory negotiations with the Indians and the avoidance of warfare. In a treaty, the Winnebagos agreed to move west of the Mississippi, and they dutifully headed in canoes toward their future home.[28]

During the month of June, the troops bivouacked near Fort Crawford at Prairie du Chien, Wisconsin, and the following month the regiment was transferred to Jefferson Barracks, traveling down the Mississippi in transports. Wright visited his family briefly at Madison Barracks before going to Missouri and spent the remainder of the summer in garrison at Jefferson Barracks.[29]

The Seminole War

As TENSIONS EASED along the northern frontier, an ugly war was being fought in the southernmost part of the country. The Seminole Indians were one of the five "civilized" tribes of colonial days. Under the pressure of American expansion, during the eighteenth century, they had migrated to Florida from the lower Creek towns on the Chattahoochee River. While Florida was still under Spanish domination the Seminoles became involved in hostilities with the United States.[1] During the War of 1812, frequent border clashes occurred between the Seminoles and U.S. militia, and in 1816, renewed fighting broke out. Referred to as the First Seminole War, it was an outgrowth of the violence which resulted when settlers in Georgia and Alabama attempted to recover runaway slaves who had found sanctuary with the Seminoles. In an effort to bring the Seminoles under control, Gen. Andrew Jackson invaded Florida with 3,500 men, killed a few Indians, burned their towns, seized their cattle and supplies, executed two British subjects accused of abetting the Indians, and drove the Spaniards out in "self-defense." A militarily weak Spanish government could do nothing more than utter a feeble protest. In 1819, Spain ceded Florida to the United States.[2]

Jackson urged that the Indians be moved west to Louisiana Territory. Instead, the government induced a few chiefs near Saint Augustine to sign the Treaty of Moultrie Creek, whereby the Seminoles ceded 28 million acres of their land for a miserable 4-million-acre reservation in central Florida.[3] The government's failure to live up to its treaty promises led to discontent and periodic raids and murders by the Seminoles. Nevertheless, settlers and adventurers continued to pour into Florida and the pressure for complete removal of the Indians increased.

In 1832 a new treaty was negotiated at Payne's Landing, on the Oklawaha River. The Seminoles were to give up all of their land in Florida and emigrate west of the Mississippi River within three years. A large segment of the Seminole Nation denied the authority of the emissaries to make such a commitment and, under the guidance of War Chief Osceola, prepared for resistance.

Troop reinforcements began to come into Fort Brooke, at the head of Tampa Bay, in 1835. Frequent clashes with the Seminoles occurred; Charley Emathla, a chief favoring emigration, was slain by Osceola; plantations were attacked; wagon trains were captured; and the Second Seminole War was under way. On December 27 a large party of Indians ambushed Maj. Francis L. Dade and two companies of artillery serving as infantry. Of eight officers and one hundred enlisted men, only one man survived to tell the tale. On the same day Osceola bushwhacked and killed Indian Agent Gen. Wiley Thompson and four other men.[4]

During the next seven years the army waged a series of small but bloody battles against the Indians. Although Captain Wright did not personally enter the theater of operations until 1840, every existing regiment of infantry, in addition to dragoon and artillery units, served at one time or another in the effort to expatriate the Seminoles; 10,169 regulars and 30,000 citizen soldiers were involved. The regular army suffered 1,460 deaths, 328 of which were due to enemy action, the remainder to disease. The navy lost 69 men, and 55 militiamen were killed in action. As the war dragged on, many commanders' reputations were severely damaged. The cost of the war was estimated to be between $30 and $40 million, and the destruction of property was appalling. The total number of Indian warriors probably never exceeded 1,400.[5] Osceola marveled that "the whites would use all that gold to kill Seminoles and only a handful . . . to buy their land or give them help."[6]

It would be difficult to overemphasize the harsh conditions the combatants had to cope with: disease was rampant; the summers were hot and humid, the winters cold

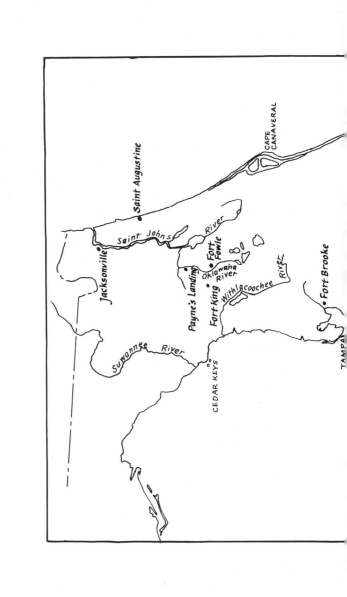

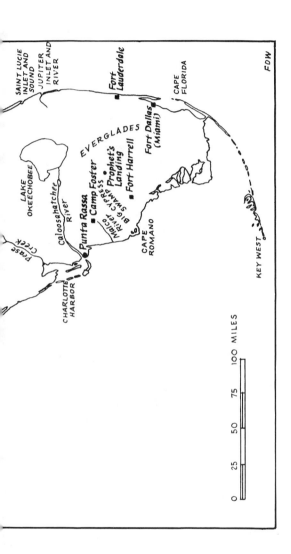

Florida at the time of the second Seminole War. The map shows a number of sites where Wright served between 1840 and 1844. Based on a map compiled in 1843 by Captain McClellan and Lieutenant Humphries, U.S. Topographical Engineers. Courtesy National Archives, Washington, D.C.

and damp. The troops spent long hours wading through mud in dense cypress and mangrove swamps; struggling from one pine- and palmetto-covered hummock to another; groping through grass sometimes five feet tall which could cut like a blade; coping with chiggers, mosquitoes, snakes, and alligators; following narrow trails through dense forests; seeing their wagons and cannons bog down in the mud. The stillness of the day was broken by Indian war cries, the night by the howls of wolves and the shrieks of wild birds. The soldiers were seeking an elusive foe who was familiar with the terrain, who watched every move the soldiers made, and who was seemingly able to disappear at will. The men were in constant danger of ambush or running attack, and faced the problem of maintaining communication or supply lines. The Indians, for their part, saw their families scattered and terrorized, and their camps, crops, and cattle destroyed. They were often on the verge of starvation, and occasionally ran out of guns and ammunition, leading to their increasing reliance on bows and arrows in the later days of the war. Many officers, including Maj. Ethan Allen Hitchcock, who acted as inspector general, felt that "To carry on such a war seems an idle, if not wicked waste of life and treasure."[7]

Maj. William S. Harney of the Second Dragoons, who later played a prominent role in the Pacific Northwest, first earned his reputation for hanging Indians after a disastrous night raid which had cost him eighteen of his twenty-six men.[8] Hitchcock later observed, "I never did believe in Harney's method of dealing with Indians—to hang them wherever they were found—but in friendly overtures."[9]

Congress by now was becoming increasingly concerned about the cost of the war. The antipathy between the army regulars and militia, and the conflicting interests of the pro- and anti-slavery elements were becoming increasingly apparent. The seemingly fruitless and extravagant management of the war was one of the issues that led to the defeat of President Van Buren in his bid for reelection. William H. Harrison, who defeated Van Buren, died after only a month in office, and Vice President John Tyler succeeded to the presidency. Tyler believed that the steadily increasing white population in Florida would soon accomplish what the army could not. Hitchcock maintained that "the government is in the wrong; and this is the chief cause of the persevering opposition of the Indians who have nobly defended their country against our attempt to enforce a fraudulent treaty." [10]

Operations Against the Florida Indians, 1840–41

In the fall of 1840, Col. William J. Worth was ordered to carry out a campaign of Indian extermination in Florida in an attempt to end the tedious and expensive war, with Capt. George Wright as his adjutant. On September 24, Wright accompanied eight companies of the Eighth Infantry under Lt. Col. Newman S. Clarke down the Mississippi River by steamer and then by sailing vessel to Tampa Bay. From there they marched to Fort King, which they reached November 5, and found Colonel Worth and two reorganized companies awaiting them. [11] In mid-November Wright commanded two companies of the Eighth Infantry and one of the Second on a scouting mission to the Oklawaha River from Fort King. One night he camped on a hummock near Fort Fowle. At daybreak he was surprised to find that a bridge that was supposed to be nearby had disappeared. No sign of Indians or recent passage by troops was to be found. [12]

In December the Eighth Infantry was back at Fort Brooke, and Gen. Walker K. Armistead, then in command of Florida, turned over all field operations to Worth, although the latter did not officially assume command until May, 1841.

On March 20, Wright reported from Camp East Toajaka that he was awaiting the arrival of Chief Halleck Tustenuggee. He had in his camp fifty-four destitute Indians who had surrendered to him. Wright had given them some supplies as they were even without blankets. [13] A few weeks later he was stricken by illness and obliged to take sick leave.[14]

The mood of the Florida war changed sharply after Worth took charge. He planned to use his troops as small bands of guerrillas and keep them on the move all year around. He discharged many civilian employees and discontinued the use of citizen soldiers. About five thousand regulars, from the First, Second, Third, Sixth, Seventh, and Eighth Regiments of Infantry, the Second Dragoons, and most of the Third Artillery, were at his disposal.[15]

During the summer of 1841 the army undertook a concerted drive to round up the Indians remaining in the Withlacoochee cove. Villages, crops, and supplies were burned. Worth's effort was aided by implementation of the policy of white resettlement. Wright was on sick leave during this drive. In July he was in Carlisle, Pennsylvania, planning to spend the summer in Norwich. Major Samuel Cooper had taken over Wright's duties as regimental adjutant.[16]

On June 25, Maj. General Alexander Macomb had died and Gen. Winfield Scott had been appointed to take his place as commander-in-chief of the U.S. Army. For many years Scott had been a friend and mentor of Worth. In August, Wright, though still in poor health, asked to join a detachment going south so that he could return to his regiment. In September, however, he was back at Carlisle, requesting a few weeks' delay before departing for the port of embarkation on Governor's Island, New York. When he finally set out to sea on a troop transport vessel, the voyage was marred by a bad storm and the loss of one of the 210 soldiers overboard. By the end of October, Wright was back at Fort Brooke.[17]

In spite of Worth's best efforts, Indian depredations continued. Between November, 1841, and February, 1842, the army traversed the entire theater of operations in every direction. In one part of the campaign, which came to be known as the Big Cypress Expedition, the Indians were hunted like animals, their crops and homes burned, their canoes and provisions destroyed. Although this phase of the war was marked by increasing cooperation between the army and the navy, the results often seemed disappointingly small.

After his return to Florida, Wright did his share of scouting in search of Seminoles as part of the Big Cypress Expedition. On November 30, Companies F and G of the Eighth Infantry were dispatched under his command to the mouth of the Malco River, eighteen miles south of Punta Rassa, traveling on the U.S. steamer *Adams*. They started their ascent of the river in canoes on December 5 and moved eastward into the Everglades, encircling the southern extremity of the swamp to Chief Billy Bowlegs' Landing. Wright hoped to round up resisting Indians on the way and then establish communications with Maj. Thomas Childs and Navy Lt. John T. McLaughlin, who were also in the area.[18]

Capt. Richard B. Screven and his company returned to one of the rendezvous points in the swamp on December 16 and left a communication for Wright from Maj. William G. Belknap, who was in command of the whole southern operation while Worth was in the north. At Prophet's Landing, Screven had found a letter to Colonel Worth from Lieutenant McLaughlin, dated December 2, saying that he had taken a detachment of soldiers on board his ship.[19]

On December 16, near Prophet's Landing, Wright had found letters from Major Childs, Major Belknap, and Captain Thomas Lawson. From these he learned that the Prophet (Otulke Thlocco) and his people were thought to have moved southward so he headed out "with all dispatch" in an attempt to join Belknap at Fort Harrell. He reached Fort Harrell on December 22 but saw no sign of Belknap or the enemy. On the twenty-eighth, having run out of provisions, he was back at Fort Dallas. He had paddled twenty-four successive days to get there. The men slept in the canoes most nights, usually feeling it unwise to have fires or lights after dark. Wright apologized that his muster rolls for Companies F and G were late; he explained that while he was in the Everglades he had run out of paper for reports. Surprisingly, his 6 officers and 102 men remained well during this arduous effort.

Wright had with him an Indian and a Spaniard as interpreters. The Indian could talk to the Spaniard, and one of his soldiers translated the Spanish to English.

On December 29, Wright reported from Fort Dallas, at the site of the present-day Miami. He told more about his scouts and about his futile efforts to obey the orders to coordinate and communicate with the other columns. Wright found old fields cultivated by the Indians, but no Indians. At Biddle's Harbor he found the U.S. schooner *Otsego* awaiting McLaughlin. Wright searched along numerous rivers, but the only Indian sites he discovered were unoccupied. He believed that the Indians were unlikely to return to the area, since they knew that with the aid of competent guides the army could easily find them.

Two weeks later Wright left Fort Dallas with two companies in sixteen canoes. He reported reentering the Everglades on January 17, 1842, and then carefully searching Biddle's Harbor. To add to their discomfort, a severe gale struck on the twenty-first. His soldiers remained healthy but were gradually being worn down by the strenuous canoe service. Although this scout lasted less than two weeks, in the last five or six days Wright was so sick he was unable to sit up in his canoe. His Spanish interpreter also became ill, and his Indian guide collapsed from exhaustion. Again, Wright and his men did not see Major Belknap or the enemy. Wright's difficulties in the swamp convinced him that 1,000 men would be unable to rout a small band of Indians without efficient guides.

On February 1, 1842, he was again encamped on the Malco River in the Everglades. Lieutenant A. B. Lincoln had reported finding the trail of another column, so Wright ordered Lincoln to leave some men to guard his canoes and march overland to Camp Foster to deliver and pick up messages regarding troop movements. Wright thought the enemy had been driven out of Big Cypress Swamp and had probably moved southwest toward the Gulf of Mexico. In a report to Assistant Adjutant Cooper, Wright said he was unable to march at that time because of rheumatism in his knees. Two days later Lincoln returned, having found

Camp Foster deserted; Wright was at a loss about how to communicate with the other forces, in spite of his orders to do so. He began to wonder whether the enemy had moved north, since he had so carefully examined the south without finding a trace of the Indians. On February 4, Companies F and G reboarded the *Adams,* which transported them to Punta Rassa. Three days later they were picked up by the *Harney,* which took them to Fort Pierce, on the shore of Saint Lucie Sound on the Atlantic seaboard. There Wright assumed command of the post.[20]

By the end of February, Worth believed that Big Cypress Swamp had been cleared of hostiles. Only a few chiefs, such as Sam Jones and Billy Bowlegs, and a handful of warriors remained at large. A total of 230 Seminoles had been shipped out. Lieutenant John T. Sprague remarked: "Thus ended the Big Cypress Campaign, like all the others: drove the Indians out, broke them up, taught them we could go where they could; men and officers worn down; two months in water; plunder on our backs; hard times; trust they are soon to end."[21]

Fort Pierce was the only remaining post on the Atlantic coast of Florida. Before Wright's arrival it had been occupied by eight companies of the Third Artillery commanded by Major Childs. Earlier in February these troops had been ordered north to the Saint John's River to examine the retreats of Halleck Tustenuggee, thence to Cedar Key, and finally to stations on the Gulf Coast.[22] Worth believed that only 300 Indians now remained in all of Florida but that the army could not bring them in by force. This view aroused such an outcry from the Floridians that the government ordered Worth to carry out a relentless pursuit. Soldiers were offered one hundred dollars for every warrior captured or slain.[23]

Scouts from Fort Pierce at the end of March found signs of Indians, whom they pursued futilely. A few days later the soldiers destroyed an encampment believed to have been Chief Sam Jones's along with the nearby fields of corn and pumpkins but encountered no Indians. On April

14, Wright went out with his command in skiffs and canoes
to explore Saint Lucie Sound. Seeing smoke at the mouth
of the Jupiter River, the troops disembarked and marched
rapidly in its direction. Several Indians were seen on a
hummock, but they promptly took to their heels, leaving
their packs, arms, cooking utensils, and a raft. The soldiers
hacked their way through the palmettos in pursuit. From
the packs, bows, arrows, spears, a rifle, hatchets, and a
quantity of flour found on the spot, Wright concluded that
it had been a large camp. He decided that to destroy their
crops or dig up their sweet potatoes was futile, since these
Indians seemed too well supplied to be starved out. The
men found bales of cotton and cases and barrels of supplies. Whether the Indians had plundered these objects or
had been supplied from a ship the troops saw offshore was
not determined.[24]

On April 19, 1842, Halleck Tustenuggee and 40 of his
fighting men were brought to bay in central Florida. Worth
directed 400 regulars against the barricaded hummock
but the Indians seemed to vanish into thin air. One soldier
was killed, 3 wounded. This was the last action of the Second Seminole War that could be called a battle. Ten days
later Halleck Tustenuggee came to Worth's camp for a
conference. The commander took Halleck and 112 of his
followers to Fort King, where they were plied with food
and liquor and then summarily seized. The new secretary
of war, John C. Spencer, had informed General Scott that
the administration wished to end hostilities as soon as possible but gave Worth authority to end the war by any means
and at a date he thought proper. Through Halleck, Worth
informed the Seminoles that those remaining would not
be molested if they stayed south of Pease Creek, which
flowed into the Gulf at Charlotte Harbor. However, those
already in custody like Halleck and his band were shipped
west in July.[25]

While some of Wright's troops were on a scouting expedition on the Jupiter River in June, they had a near disaster. A severe gale struck as they were on their way back to

Fort Pierce, and their boats became separated because of the poor visibility. One of the boats overturned. The men clambered onto the bottom of the boat and managed to reach shore, although they lost all their clothing, accouterments, and blankets. Fortunately, all the men ultimately made their way back to Fort Pierce safely. Wright submitted a plea that the men be issued new gear without charge. Colonel Worth approved the request.[26]

Throughout his career in the army Wright consistently exhibited a sincere concern for the men under his command, individually and collectively. Sometimes he chose to try to rehabilitate a young recruit who was in trouble, to spare him from disgrace rather than mete out severe punishment. Or he would intercede with an unsympathetic quartermaster to keep his men properly clothed and equipped. Many of his disciplinary orders and measures were for the protection of his men and in their best interest. He also showed concern for his foes, as when he had issued supplies to weak and shivering, captured Indians. On numerous occasions Wright remarked that it was often better to feed Indians than to fight them, from both humanitarian and economic standpoints, a view usually frowned upon by the commissary department.

A Brevet for Wright

On August 14, 1842, from his headquarters at Cedar Key, Colonel Worth announced the official termination of the war. He was granted ninety days' leave and breveted as a brigadier general by a grateful President Tyler for his distinguished service. Hitchcock, who earlier had served with the Eighth Infantry in Florida and was now a lieutenant colonel in the Third, wryly remarked:

> At last General Worth reports a thorough pacification of Florida! How? By doing precisely that which was so urgently recommended nearly two years ago by myself, first to Mr. Poinsett, Secretary of War, and then to Mr. Bell, his successor. Worth was chosen to supercede Armistead by my urgent ar-

gument, that he might carry out this very policy. He has 'pacified' the Indians, probably in the precise manner I suggested after nearly two years of additional and expensive war costing twenty million dollars and now he is made Brigadier General for it! This almost makes me exclaim against the humbug of the world![27]

An officer of the Fourth Infantry derisively exclaimed: "We killed the Indians and they killed us. We sucked water through our handkerchiefs in the Everglades swamps, lived on calomel and alligator tails; then came a fine band with the National air, fresh from old Madison [Barracks], and on high bugle, the war ended."[28]

Actually, in spite of the proclamation, the war did not end immediately. Sporadic Indian attacks on stagecoaches and settlements, murder, and rapine continued. The Floridians felt that all Indians should have been deported or exterminated. Tiger Tail and Octiarche dallied too long before moving to the new reservation in southern Florida, and an order was issued to capture them and their followers. A $300 bounty was offered for each remaining chief, and $100 for each warrior. Soon 250 more Seminoles were captured and sent to Indian territory in the West. The war gradually petered out. Three years later, because of the swelling tide of white immigration, Florida became a state.

On October 4 and 5 a destructive hurricane devastated Cedar Key, and the army headquarters there had to be abandoned. The base of operations was moved to Saint Augustine, where it remained until September 1845.[29]

The Seminole War, in its length, its cost in lives and money, the harsh conditions under which it was fought against an able and elusive foe, and its effect on the morale of the soldiers and of the country at large, bears a resemblance to the Vietnam War of the following century. About 1,500 men lost their lives in battle or to disease so that 3,200 half-starved Indians could be expatriated. In both wars the vast power of a great nation was checkmated by a lesser force. The Second Seminole War was the costliest war ever fought against Indians. It was also the only Indian war in which the U.S. Navy played a significant role. When the war finally limped to an end, it had failed in its purpose of removing all the Seminoles from Florida. No peace treaty was ever signed, and even today descendants of these Indians truthfully and proudly say that they never surrendered to the United States.[30]

Concerning Captain Wright's performance in Florida, Gen. G. W. Cullum, the biographer of West Point graduates, wrote, "[In] this tedious and expensive war, amid the pestilential swamps of Florida . . . the success of our arms was in no small degree due to Wright, whose efficiency won for him the esteem and confidence of the Army."[31] On April 25, 1842, Colonel Worth sent a letter to Army Headquarters in Washington in which he said:

> In compliance with repeated instructions, I have the honor to submit the following list of officers for the distinction of promotion by brevet.
>
> The peculiar nature of this service, offering constant occasion for the display of zeal, energy and talent, patient endurance of hardship and privation, but few opportunities for the more brilliant exhibitions of those qualities which attract and fix attention in the presence of an enemy "worthy a soldier's blade" renders this a difficult and delicate duty.

Twenty-four names were submitted. Worth praised Wright's meritorious conduct throughout the war, although his efforts had not brought him in contact with the enemy. Worth added that Wright was "qualified to command a regiment under any circumstances" and that he was "recommended for major by brevet."[32]

Garrison Duty, Fort Brooke and Key West, 1843–44

After the end of hostilities the troops remaining in Florida were moved to more healthful stations. Wright spent the early part of 1843 in garrison at Fort Brooke. On March 19 he received word that President Tyler had appointed him brevet major. In June he was serving as commanding officer at Fort Brooke. Six months later, along with Company F, he was assigned to Key West, where he was again commander of the post; he remained there until April, 1844.[33]

While in command at Fort Brooke, Wright once again became involved in legal problems. On February 4, 1844, he sent Worth a report of the matter. In its December, 1843, term, a grand jury representing three counties of Florida had made a presentment accusing army officers of perpetrating outrages on citizens of Florida, including sending off the sheriff of Hillsborough County on a military transport and threatening to do the same to the local magistrate if he attempted to hold court. Because of lack of evidence the jurors withheld suggesting prosecution or punishment, but the very fact that they made the presentment indicated, said Wright, that they were either unintelligent or eager to publicize their slander of the army and show their support of civilians. There is no doubt that many Floridians hated the army. They felt that it kept them from land they wanted, had not prosecuted the war with sufficient vigor, and had shown little enthusiasm for helping capture runaway slaves. Another sore point was the low esteem in which the army held the state militia.

Wright explained to Worth that the army had surveyed Fort Brooke to determine the boundaries of the land reserved for the garrison and that the deputy marshal had been instructed to remove intruders. A few citizens had been allowed to remain, but their proximity proved an obstacle to troop discipline. The most obnoxious ones were asked to leave, although no force was used to evict them. The sheriff was given permission to travel to New Orleans on a government ship. The "magistrate," a former soldier, now justice of the peace, held court on the post, which he considered a "suitable arena for civil litigation." He was finally ordered to depart when it was discovered that he had been selling liquor to the soldiers and running a disorderly house. These events had been widely publicized and exaggerated by the *Saint Augustine News.* Nothing finally came of this tempest. Wright pointed out that the current justice of the peace in the area had told him that he was having no problem with the army.[34]

Recruiting Service, 1844–46

It is not known where Mrs. Wright and the three children lived during the Seminole War. In 1845, however, Wright's oldest son, Thomas Forster Wright, returned to Norwich to live with his grandparents and for the next three years attended the Partridge Academy.[35]

Wright spent the period from May, 1844, to September, 1846, in Philadelphia at his old job of recruiting. During this time the aggregate strength of the army dropped from a wartime peak of 11,189 to 8,349. Wright preferred recruiting to the boredom of peacetime garrison duty. After almost four years in Florida, often on arduous duty, recruiting was a welcome change. He made numerous suggestions for changes in the regulations regarding the inspection of recruits and for improvement of the recruiting service. At times he complained that "business" was dull and wondered about putting advertisements for recruits in the newspapers. As time went on, however, this assignment must have seemed increasingly important, for war clouds were gathering again. In September, 1846, Wright reminded the adjutant general that he had promised General Worth to return to his regiment if there should be any signs of activity, and he was ordered to do so.[36]

Another conflict with Great Britain had been narrowly avoided. President James K. Polk had been elected in 1844 on a platform that asserted the claims of the United States to sole possession of the Oregon Country with the campaign slogan "Fifty-four Forty or Fight." This advanced the American claim up to the border of the Russian possessions in Alaska. The agreement made with Great Britain in 1818 and formalized by treaty in 1827 had called for joint occupancy of Oregon. This arrangement became increasingly impractical with the steady influx of American settlers. Great Britain again began to make warlike sounds. In April, 1846, Congress abrogated the Treaty of 1827. Great Britain decided that Oregon was not worth fighting over as long as she maintained possession of British Columbia. In 1846 a new treaty established the forty-ninth parallel as the boundary between the United States and Canada.

6.
The Mexican War

BY THE TIME Bvt. Maj. George Wright set out to rejoin his regiment, the United States was involved in a full-scale war with Mexico, with the Eighth Infantry in the thick of it. President John Tyler interpreted the election of the Democratic candidate, James K. Polk, to succeed him as a mandate for the annexation of Texas. The Senate failed to pass the treaty that Tyler submitted, but in the closing hours of his administration Congress passed a joint resolution to admit Texas to the Union. Accordingly, in 1845, nine years after the Alamo and the Texas declaration of independence, Texas became the twenty-eighth state. Mexico had served notice that such an event would be considered an act of war and immediately broke off diplomatic relations. Polk believed that a show of force might induce the Mexican government to make some sort of settlement leading to a satisfactory negotiated peace, and in June, 1845, he ordered Gen. Zachary Taylor to lead an army to the disputed area.[1]

After numerous border clashes near Fort Brown, Texas, it became apparent that hostilities were inevitable. The Eighth Infantry Regiment was ordered to join General Taylor's Army of Occupation at Corpus Christi, where they spent the fall and winter, 1845–46. As the enlarging army was reorganized, the regiment was placed in the First Brigade. A bitter controversy broke out between the Eighth's commanding officer, Colonel Worth, and Col. David E. Twiggs of the Second Dragoons over who was to serve as Taylor's second in command. Twiggs was Worth's senior as colonel, but Worth believed that his brevet as brigadier general gave him precedence.[2] General Winfield Scott supported Worth's claim, but Hitchcock, who was serving at Corpus Christi and later became inspector general of the Army of Occupation, forwarded to the president of the

Senate a memorial signed by half the officers in the encampment favoring seniority in staff rank over brevet rank as a claim to command.[3] Although there was no question about where Wright's loyalty lay, he escaped having to take sides because he was still away on recruiting duty. Most of the officers at Corpus Christi aligned in cliques, with a resulting disruption of discipline and morale. Finally President Polk, to whom Taylor had appealed, overruled Scott and sustained Twiggs's claim to command. Worth submitted his resignation[4] and departed for Washington, D.C., to appeal to the president. Polk refused to accept his resignation. Five weeks after his departure Worth returned to Texas and resumed command of the First Brigade.[5]

On April 23, 1846, Mexico declared war on the United States. In the meantime U.S. troops had advanced southward toward Matamoros, near the mouth of the Rio Grande. In May, at nearby Palo Alto and Resaca de Palma, the Eighth Infantry participated in its first battles as a regiment.[6] Matamoros was occupied on May 18, and by midsummer Taylor had almost 14,000 soldiers at this point.

The United States offered to purchase disputed borderlands, but the Mexican government refused to negotiate. Accordingly, in August, Taylor started moving about half his army inland toward the strongly fortified city of Monterrey. Worth's troops assaulted and captured the fortifications surrounding Monterrey and then joined the rest of Taylor's forces in the attack on the city itself.[7] On September 23, the Mexican Army of the North had been destroyed as an effective fighting force, and Monterrey fell. On November 12, the city of Saltillo, fifty miles southwest, was occupied without opposition.

Although other successful offensives had been set in motion, control of the occupied lands was difficult to maintain. It appeared that the capital of the Mexican Republic would have to be taken. Major General Winfield Scott was placed in command of this operation. Scott chose Lobos Island, south of Tampico, as the staging point and gathered 9,000 men there. Soon after the capture of Saltillo Worth's

division moved out to join Scott, traveling down the Rio
Grande from Camargo to Matamoros on transports and
then on to Lobos.[8]

The Battle of Cerro Gordo, 1847

Meanwhile, Wright had been attempting to rejoin his regiment. On October 13, 1846, he wrote from New York City
to Col. R. B. Mason, superintendent of the recruiting service, protesting an order to accompany a detachment of
recruits to join four different infantry regiments in Mexico, with Bvt. Maj. E. L. Hawkins in charge. Wright insisted
that it was his own right to be in command and suggested
that Mason consult Major General Scott if he disagreed.
The orders were not changed.

Wright arrived safely at Saltillo with eighty-four men for
the Eighth Infantry. On December 30 he reported to Adj.
Gen. Roger Jones on how the Hawkins controversy had
turned out. Ironically, while he was still at sea on the *Massachusetts,* which later was Scott's command ship, Hawkins
had assigned Wright as major of the recruit battalion until the men in the detachment reached their respective
regiments. After the recruits arrived in Mexico, another
ship took them up the Rio Grande to Camargo. There the
men landed and, after proceeding only ten miles on foot,
Hawkins's deteriorating health forced him to drop out.
Wright wistfully expressed the hope that the War Department would recognize that he had been on field duty and
in command during this fiasco and was thus entitled to pay
commensurate with his responsibilities. Finally, on February 6, 1847, Wright, with six companies of the Eighth Infantry under his command, sailed from Brazos Santiago at
the mouth of the Rio Grande to join Scott.[9]

Scott had two divisions of regulars, the First under Worth
and the Second under Twiggs, and a division of volunteers
under Gen. Robert Patterson. By March 6 the army was at
sea off Veracruz. Three days later Worth, with Wright and
the remainder of the First Division, made a surprisingly

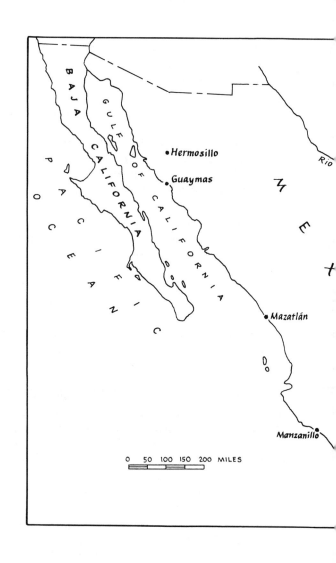

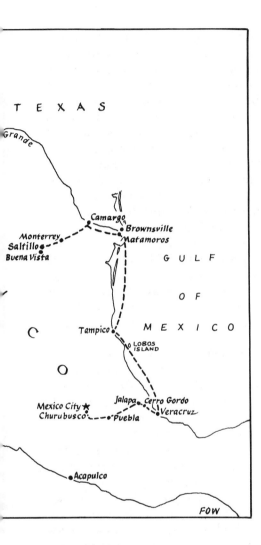

Mexico during the Mexican War.
The map shows the routes
followed by Wright, 1846–48.

unopposed landing three miles south of the Castle of San Juan de Ulúa, which protected Veracruz, and by nightfall 11,000 men had gone ashore safely. The troops rapidly encircled the land side of the city and began a siege and bombardment, rather than a frontal assault. The bombardment became more effective after some heavy guns were borrowed from the navy, dragged into position, and then served by their own navy crews. On March 28, Gen. Juan Morales surrendered the city, its castle, and his troops. Worth was appointed temporary governor of Veracruz, and his own brigade was designated as its garrison.[10]

In the meantime Generals Taylor and John E. Wool had won a precarious victory at Buena Vista, a few miles south of Saltillo, against Gen. Antonio de López Santa Anna. Santa Anna, now president of Mexico as well as commander-in-chief of its armies, had brought a large force north in the hope of wiping out Taylor's troops and then hurrying back to intercept Scott. Taylor and Wool's victory at Buena Vista effectively ended the campaign in northern Mexico.[11]

On April 8, General Scott's army started up the National Highway on the long climb to Mexico City, 240 miles to the west. Twiggs and his division led off, and Worth was miffed, believing that he had earned the honor of leading the advance. Wright and the Eighth Infantry did not leave the encampment near Veracruz until April 13.[12]

Santa Anna, anxious to keep Scott and his army in the lowlands, had prepared a strong position in the hills near the village of Cerro Gordo, fifty miles west of Veracruz, and occupied it with 12,000 troops. The Mexican hilltop positions were attacked on April 17 by Twigg's division, supported by Gen. James Shields's brigade and Gen. Gideon J. Pillow's Third Division. General Worth's troops remained in reserve. After his heroics at Monterrey, Worth was not happy in that role.

The Mexicans were routed, with 1,200 killed or wounded, compared to 67 U.S. casualties. Three thousand Mexican soldiers were taken prisoner, with one general killed and five captured. In addition, 4,000 weapons and

43 cannon were taken.[13] Santa Anna escaped, leaving behind his carriage, his money, and his wooden leg. Worth's division was left to guard the prisoners until they were paroled the next day, after which he escorted Scott to Jalapa, thirteen miles farther west, where the remainder of the army was awaiting him. There Scott established his temporary headquarters.[14]

Wright, with the remainder of Worth's division, then moved along the National Highway to Perote with its strongly fortified castle, destroying defensive works along the way. On April 22, Worth seized the castle and the arms left by the fleeing Mexicans. Worth wanted to pursue the enemy and move on toward Mexico City, but he was held in check by Scott. The general had presidential aspirations and did not want Worth gaining too much glory.

Finally, on May 6, Worth was ordered to move ninety miles to Puebla, Mexico's second-largest city, high in the Cordilleras. He took the city on May 15 after a brief skirmish with Santa Anna's cavalry. Wright and Companies D, E, and H of the Eighth Infantry were delayed at Perote in a mopping-up operation but caught up with the First Division when it entered Puebla.[15]

Scott and the rest of his army arrived at the end of May. In Puebla they halted for more than two months, albeit in a healthier location than the lowland; many enlistments had expired, and Scott believed that he could not proceed farther until replacements arrived. During this trying period Scott was disappointed by what he regarded as lack of support by the War Department, and he asked to be relieved from command in the fall.[16] During the halt at Puebla, Scott was extremely critical of Worth. Worth demanded a court of inquiry, which recommended that Worth be rebuked in orders. By this time Worth's long-standing friendship with Scott was beginning to turn to hatred.

Puebla was only seventy miles from the capital. There were no further physical barriers or concentrations of enemy troops to impede the army's progress. Mexico City had a population of 200,000 and was defended by 30,000 troops. The U.S. Army's delay had given the beaten and disorganized Mexican army time to regroup and strengthen the defenses of the capital. Worth was particularly impatient at the delay; he believed that the capital could have been taken with little loss of men in May.

Finally, on August 7, Twiggs's Second Division led the descent into the Valley of Mexico. Scott had 11,000 effectives for his attack. Wright accompanied Worth and his First Division as they moved south of Lake Chalco and on August 17 encountered the first resistance at San Agustín, ten miles south of Mexico City, on the highway to Acapulco. San Agustín was easily captured, but three miles to the north Santa Anna had fortified the hacienda of San Antonio. Two miles north of San Antonio, on the outskirts of the village of Churubusco, stood the large, stone Convent of San Mateo and the Church of San Pablo. All these structures were strongly fortified and surrounded by a wall and moat. The key to the defense of the area was an almost impregnable bridge which spanned the Churubusco River.[17]

On August 18, Scott arrived and ordered Worth to move on San Antonio the next morning. This advance was delayed by Worth's reinforcement of an attack by Twiggs's division on nearby Contreras. By the time Worth entered San Antonio on August 20, it had been evacuated, and the Mexican forces had retreated to Churubusco, the strongest position in the environs of the capital.[18]

The Battles of Churubusco and Molino del Rey

On August 20, Wright was with the American columns in pursuit of the fleeing enemy. The Fifth, Sixth, and Eighth Infantry, commanded by Col. Newman S. Clarke, moved to one side to cut off the enemy's retreat to the capital, and the First Brigade went to the other side to cut the enemy's force in two. There was no time for reconnaissance of Churubusco, on which all the U.S. forces advanced against the enemy's main battle array.

At this juncture Scott arrived on the field and assumed command of the assault on Churubusco. At first all commands were repulsed by the enemy's heavy artillery and musket fire. Wright and the men of the Eighth Infantry then advanced through some corn fields, crossing deep, water-filled irrigation ditches on the way, and at 3 P.M. they carried the crucial position, the *tête-de-pont*, with a bayonet charge.[19]

The final assault on the stronghold was led by the troops of the Eighth Infantry. Major Carlos D. Waite was now in command, for Colonel Clarke had received a chest wound. Brevet Major Wright, who had been serving as a battalion leader, acted as second in command. Captain James S. Bomford and Company H moved out ahead of the line bearing the regimental colors. The color-bearer fell near the moat, and Bomford picked up the colors. At the moat he handed them to Lt. James Longstreet while he crossed over. Longstreet then threw the colors over to Bomford and crossed the ditch, closely followed by Lts. George E. Pickett and G. S. Snelling, Company H, the rest of the regiment, and then by the men of the Fifth. After several attempts to enter the fortification, Captain Bomford stood on the shoulders of some of his men and climbed into the work through an embrasure, dragging the colors with him. Among the first to follow were Captain Larkin Smith and his company, who captured a Mexican cannon and turned it on the enemy. Wright appears to have been everywhere, rallying, forming, and keeping the troops moving, while his beloved Eighth Infantry was moving into the fray. Its regimental colors were the first American flag to fly over the fortress. The routed Mexicans fled into Mexico City with Shields and Worth in pursuit.[20]

In his official report of the battle Worth commended the officers and "conspicuously named" Major Waite and Brevet Major Wright for recognition of their performance. Colonel Clarke also commended them in his report of the activities of the Second Brigade. "The gallantry of these officers," he wrote, "entitles them to favorable notice." Major Waite wrote: "To Brevet Major Wright I am greatly indebted for the assistance he rendered on all occasions and particularly in forming the troops, and moving them on to the assault. To his activity, coolness and good judg-

The Battle of Churubusco, August 20, 1847. Lithograph by Carl Nebel in the possession of the author (originally appeared in a folio by Nebel accompanying G. W. Kendall, *The War Between the United States and Mexico, Illustrated* (New York, 1851). The illustration shows troops advancing through a cornfield and attacking an outlying fortification. A convent and church are in the background.

ment the success of the attack is in considerable degree to be attributed."[21] For his "gallant and meritorious conduct" in the Battles of Contreras and Churubusco, Wright was breveted lieutenant colonel.[22]

The Battle of Churubusco was widely regarded as one of the most brilliant exploits of the war. About 2,600 Americans engaged in two and one-half hours of hand-to-hand battle against 7,000 Mexicans around the Church of San Pablo, where many of the latter had taken refuge. The victory was a costly one, the Americans suffering more than 1,000 casualties—133 killed, 865 wounded, and 40 missing. Santa Anna lost one-third of his army—4,297 men killed or wounded and 2,637 taken prisoner.[23]

Among the latter were at least 65 members of the San Patricio Brigade. All these "Irish deserters" from the U.S. Army, who wore Mexican uniforms and fought for the Mexicans, were tried by court-martial and condemned to death. General Scott commuted the death sentences of more than half to fifty lashes.[24] To Colonel Harney was given the responsibility of executing the remaining 30, because of the proficiency he had acquired hanging Seminoles in Florida.[25]

On the day after the Battle of Churubusco, notwithstanding the hard service performed and the depleted condition of the Eighth Infantry, the regiment pushed on at the head of the First Division to Tacubaya, two and one-half miles from the capital. Scott moved his headquarters to Tacubaya, attempted to negotiate a peace, but settled for a two-week armistice.

Before moving against the city, Scott ordered Worth to attack the nearby Molino del Rey. He was under the mistaken impression that the long, low stone buildings of this "mill of the king" contained a cannon foundry, that a large quantity of powder was stored there, and, moreover, that they were lightly defended. Here, near the gates of their capital, the Mexicans made a stalwart defense.

Worth's division was under arms at 3:00 A.M. on September 8, and by 4:00 A.M. it was in position and ready for the assault as soon as it became light enough to distinguish the enemy's position. The First Division was reinforced by three squadrons of dragoons and one company of mounted riflemen, all commanded by Major Sumner; three pieces of field artillery under Capt. Simon Drum; two 24-pound battering guns under Capt. Benjamin Huger; Gen. George Cadwalader's brigade; a volunteer regiment; and the Eleventh and Fourteenth Regiments of Infantry. The operation was to be a limited one, the division withdrawing to Tacubaya as soon as the Molino and the

The Battle of Molino del Rey, September 8, 1847. Lithograph by Carl Nebel in the possession of the author (originally from the folio accompanying Kendall, *The War Between the United States and Mexico, Illustrated*). The illustration shows an attack on the Molino. Chapultepec Castle is
in the left background.

adjacent sturdy stone citadel called Casa Mata were captured and the guns, ammunition, and machinery thought
to be in them destroyed.

A reconnaissance by Captain Mason of the Engineers revealed the enemy's position within the Molino to be strong
and to extend left to a grove under the guns of Chapultepec Castle. The enemy's right rested on the Casa Mata. A
field battery of seven guns was out front between these
points.

With the center seemingly the weakest spot, an assault
party of five hundred carefully selected officers and men
was designated to open the attack and capture the artillery

in the center of the enemy's line. As a mark of esteem for his soldierly qualities, Worth chose Brevet Major Wright to lead this party.

Colonel John Garland's brigade was on the right with two pieces of Drum's artillery to sustain the assault party and protect the battering guns, which were placed on a ridge 500 yards from the Molino. The Second Brigade under Col. James S. McIntosh was posted on the ridge with Col. James Duncan's battery of flying artillery. Cadwalader's brigade was in reserve between McIntosh and the battering guns. The cavalry under Lieutenant Colonel Sumner was on the extreme left.

Huger's heavy guns opened a bombardment that shook the center of the enemy's line. The Molino seemed quiet and possibly deserted, so the bombardment was cut short, and Wright and his assault party were directed to move forward. What happened next is best described by Wright:

> The Assaulting Column consisted of twelve officers and five hundred men taken in proportion from the Regiments comprising the 1st Division, the whole divided into five comps. of one hundred men each. . . .
> At 3 O'Clock on the morning of the 8th the Column was paraded, and at 4 O'Clock, I reached the field and remained in compact order in front of the enemy's Batteries and lines until it was light enough to distinguish his position, when I deployed to the left of our Siege Battery. After a few rounds from our Battery, I ordered the Battalion to advance in line, the point of direction being the enemy's Battery; The line moved forward in good order, and at the distance of two hundred yards the enemy opened on us with round and grape shot with considerable effect, the ground being perfectly level; I instantly ordered the double quick step; the line advanced rapidly, and immediately came within close musket range; I found the enemy securely and strongly posted within his Fort and his lines on either flank, extending beyond view; He had abandoned his Artillery, which was placed a little in advance, and with his immense superiority in numbers, and comparatively secure, was enabled to concentrate all his fire upon our ranks, already very much reduced in numbers; Myself struck down with a musket ball, I was unable to see the state of the

contest for a few moments, and was soon after obliged to leave the field, not however before witnessing the movement of the gallant Light Battalion to support the advance.

The Assaulting Column continued the combat in conjunction with the other corps of the Division, until the enemy's positions were all carried and we remained in possession of the field; after which there being but 3 officers left, and the rank and file very much reduced, they joined their respective Regiments.

The conduct of all the Officers and men on this occasion is worthy of the highest commendation.[26]

The enemy's infantry and artillery had been driven back at bayonet point, their cannons seized and turned on them. Suddenly, before Wright's men could fire the cannons, the Mexicans realized they had been driven out by a comparative handful of men. Aided by infantry firing from housetops, they made a desperate rally. Eleven of 14 officers (two Engineer Corps officers had joined the column) in the assault party, including Wright, were struck down (2 of them killed), and 111 enlisted men fell, 27 of whom were killed. Lieutenant Isaac I. Stevens, of the Corps of Engineers (who would be associated with Wright in the Pacific Northwest), helped carry Wright from the battlefield after he was wounded.[27]

When the assault party broke and fell back, the Mexicans recaptured their guns and murdered many of the wounded. Captain Kirby Smith and the light battalion, and the right wing of Cadwalader's brigade, were ordered forward, and the enemy was again driven back, this part of the line being carried and fully possessed by the U.S. troops. Garland attacked the enemy's left and drove him from his seemingly impregnable position. Duncan's battery pounded the enemy's right and the Second Brigade was ordered to move on the Casa Mata.

Garland and his men entered the west end of the Molino and fought from room to room. Smith fell mortally wounded during this operation. In the assault on the Casa Mata, McIntosh and his second in command were mortally wounded. Approaching enemy cavalry was driven back by artillery fire, and Sumner and his dragoons joined in the attack on the Casa. The U.S. troops briefly drew back, and heavy artillery fire forced the Mexicans to abandon the Casa Mata.

When the enemy was driven from every point in the field, the American troops blew up the Casa Mata along with a few worthless cannon molds and some useless ammunition found in the Molino. They captured or spiked most of the enemy's cannons and seized a large quantity of small arms and ammunition. They took 800 prisoners, including 52 commissioned officers. Worth estimated the enemy force at more than 14,000 men under the personal command of Santa Anna. His second and third in command were killed, and his total loss in killed, wounded, and prisoners numbered 3,000. In the two-hour contest Worth's command of 3,100 had 9 officers killed outright and 49 wounded (3 mortally) and 107 noncommissioned officers and privates killed, 604 wounded, and 18 missing. These casualties represented one-fourth of those engaged. Wright was breveted colonel that day for gallant and meritorious conduct.[28]

The action, however heroic, had its critics. Justin Smith referred to the assault party as "glued fragments of steel, not a forged blade," since a large number of the men were separated from their comrades and officers. As a result, when they were subjected to the terrible fusillade of fire that poured forth from the Molino del Rey, the column broke, and one-third of the men bolted, leaving their wounded behind to be butchered by the enemy.[29] Hitchcock referred to the operation as a "sad mistake" and added, "A few more such victories and this army would be destroyed."[30] Worth had often accused Scott of needlessly dragging his feet during the campaign. Now it was Scott's turn to complain. He blamed Worth for the tragic losses at the Molino, saying that the bombardment had been ended prematurely and that the operation was poorly planned and executed. Scott's accusations did little to ease the growing animosity between the two officers. In fairness to Worth, it must be noted that Scott had approved his battle

plan in advance, and neither Scott nor Inspector General
Hitchcock had said that the position was anything but
lightly held and easy to carry. At least some of the blame for
this costly battle must be borne by Scott and Hitchcock.[31]

In the battles of Churubusco and Molino del Rey, Wright
proved himself a courageous and capable soldier. Although
in Florida he had begun to show that he was a good leader,
able and willing to endure the same hardships and priva-
tions as those of his men, he did not have to do any actual
fighting. Nonetheless, in recommending him for major by
brevet, Worth alluded to his zeal, energy, talent, and intelligence and expressed confidence in his ability to perform
the duties of a colonel and command an entire regiment.

In the bloody battles in Mexico his performance was favorably mentioned in the reports of his divisional, brigade,
and regimental commanders. He was described as con-
spicuous for his ability to organize his men, adapt to chang-
ing conditions, and maintain the momentum of assaults.
Waite attributed a considerable degree of the success of
the attack at Churubusco to Wright's activity, coolness, and
good judgment. For his performance at Churubusco,
Wright was rewarded by being breveted lieutenant colonel.

When Worth needed someone to lead the storming
party against the formidable Molino del Rey, he selected
Wright as a mark of special favor. Wright did his best, advancing in the face of withering fire and superior numbers
until he was wounded and unable to continue. For his gallant and meritorious conduct he earned his second brevet,
as colonel, in less than three weeks.

Most of what was left of the Mexican army was now in
the capital. The defenses of Mexico City were formidable.
The city could be approached only over eight causeways,
which crossed the surrounding marshes and led to the
heavily fortified gates. Scott decided to attack over two
western causeways that were under the protection of the
castle on the heights of Chapultepec. The castle fell to the
Americans on September 13, and the next day U.S. troops
entered the city. By this time Santa Anna and his army had

fled. The American flag was raised over the National Palace, and later in the day General Scott made a triumphal entry and reviewed his troops in the Grand Plaza. The battered Eighth Infantry took part in these activities, but Wright was unable to participate because of his wound. A formal peace treaty was not signed until February 2, 1848, at Guadalupe Hidalgo. By this document Mexico ceded to the United States more than half of its land. The United States agreed to pay $15 million in cash and assume the claims of American citizens against the Mexican government. The Eighth Infantry remained in Mexico City until peace negotiations were completed. Of 90,000 men who served in the U.S. Army during the Mexican war, 11,300 died from disease or accidents and 1,930 were killed in action.[32]

Discord in the Army

Wright's wound was not serious, and for most of the time between September 20, 1847, and February 20, 1848, he was able to command his regiment and for part of this time the Second Brigade as well. After his recovery he was on detached service in Mexico City for a month and then was granted three months' leave of absence for "the benefit of his health" by Gen. William O. Butler.[33]

Although the United States celebrated successive victories during the Mexican War, in its wake the increasing disharmony, jealousies, resentments, and frayed tempers grew among the officers of General Scott's command. In November, 1847, the last straw was provided by the publication of some letters that General Pillow had sent to U.S. newspapers extolling his own prowess and disparaging his peers and superiors. Other officers also engaged in altercations and recriminations until finally Scott laid charges of insubordination against General Pillow, a friend and former law partner of President Polk, and against General Worth and Lt. Col. James Duncan and arrested them. Pillow had aggravated the dispute by writing to the War Department castigating Scott. Worth appealed directly to the president, accusing Scott of conduct unbecoming an officer and a gentleman.

Dismayed by this scandalous quarrel, after consultation with his Cabinet, Polk relieved Scott of his command, released the officers from arrest, and appointed a court of inquiry to investigate the charges and countercharges. Major General William O. Butler took command of the army in Mexico, and the court finally convened March 17, 1848, in Puebla. Worth requested permission to withdraw his charges against Scott in the interest of harmony in the service. Scott did the same in regard to Pillow and Duncan, but Pillow insisted that the court review his case, and Worth testified in his favor. In April the court adjourned to Frederick, Maryland. When Worth returned to Washington in June, he was still insisting on an investigation of Scott's charges against him, claiming that he had been unjustly censured, but the whole matter was finally shelved by higher authorities.[34] Perhaps the saddest feature of the affair was that the once close friendship between Scott and Worth degenerated into implacable enmity. Worth even changed the name of his son, whom he had named after Scott, to William.

Wright had served for almost ten years under Worth, who regarded him as a valued and capable officer. Wright loyally supported Worth and closely identified with him. As the bitter animosity developed between Worth and Scott, one senses that Wright was beginning to fall into disfavor as well. To a man of Scott's temperament Wright's leadership of the costly assault on the Molino could also make him a likely scapegoat, when one was needed.

7.

Return to the United States

IN JANUARY, 1848, George Wright was promoted to the rank of major and transferred to the Fourth Infantry. Wright acknowledged receipt of the orders from Washington three months later in Carlisle, Pennsylvania.[1] On April 16 he received the following note from R. Jones, adjutant general:

> Your report of the 20- rec'd. Before returning to your regiment on the expiration of your leave of absence please report by letter as your services may be required at that time. If any light duty should arise which you might perform, I will take pleasure in receiving your tender of services.[2]

On June 1, Wright reported his health satisfactory for light duty but did not immediately join his new regiment.[3] The Fourth Infantry returned from Mexico to Camp Jefferson Davis, Mississippi, a month later.

As it turned out, Wright was fortunate to have been separated from his old regiment. After its return to the United States, the Eighth Infantry stayed briefly at Jefferson Barracks and was then stationed at Fort Lavaca, Texas. There, in December, one-third of the men fell victim to a cholera epidemic in six days, and one-half of them died within a few hours. On May 7, 1849, Bvt. Maj. Gen. William J. Worth succumbed to the same disease at Camp Worth, near San Antonio, Texas.[4]

In July, 1848, Major Wright was back on duty after his sick leave, mustering out volunteer troops in Philadelphia. Later in the month he was ordered to Pittsburgh to muster and discharge two regiments of Pennsylvania volunteers and other companies from Maryland, the District of Columbia, and some independent companies. In August, having completed his duties in Pittsburgh, he was ordered to New York to help muster troops out of service.[5]

In Command of Fort Ontario, 1848–52

In October, 1848, the Fourth Infantry was ordered to what was then called the Northwest Frontier; Wright joined the regiment in November.[6] It was dispersed to garrison various forts in the area. Headquarters were established in Detroit, and companies were assigned to Forts Mackinac and Gratiot, in Michigan, and Fort Niagara, Madison Barracks, and Plattsburgh Barracks, in New York. On November 16, Wright reported the occupation of Fort Ontario, Oswego, New York, by Company F.[7] The fort was on the right bank of the Oswego River where it flows into Lake Ontario. Wright retained command of the post until July 15, 1852.[8] There was still considerable unrest in Canada at this time, with riots and burning of the assembly hall in Montreal. Embittered loyalists even suggested annexation to the United States, but there was no longer any interest in this south of the Canadian border. With the arrival in 1849 of one of Canada's greatest governors, James Bruce, earl of Elgin and Kinardine, an era of goodwill began. Responsible government was established, and sanity was introduced into U.S.–Canadian affairs.[9]

Wright spent much of his time at Fort Ontario capturing and processing deserters from various posts, whom he regarded as "miserable specimens." He complained of the difficulty he had keeping the recruits who had been sent to Fort Ontario. Some deserted a few days after enlisting, and others secured discharges as minors. Wright regarded most of them as a worthless lot and urged that recruits be sent to him from outside New York State, as they were less likely to desert the farther they were away from home. Catching deserters was a popular pastime, since a reward of thirty dollars was paid for each one captured.[10]

Wright bemoaned the quality of postwar recruits compared to those obtained before the war. As a patriotic and idealistic soldier, he believed that the guarding of his country was a citizen's privilege and that the men chosen for this task should be of high caliber. The illiterate and often dis-

Fort Ontario, New York, ca. 1852. From *Ballou's Pictorial Drawing Room Companion.* Courtesy Library of Congress.

abled specimens he was getting, many of them new immigrants, disgusted him, and he had little sympathy for the deserters. He requested that a report be submitted by the recruiting service to explain how such men could have been passed. In response, one officer wrote to the chief of the recruiting service that he had been directed to send deserters to the nearest post. With asperity he added, "I regret that Colonel Wright's repugnance to receiving them, should make the performance of my duty the subject of his unwarranted criticism."[11]

Many of Wright's problems at Fort Ontario were disciplinary. Numerous courts-martial were held, and some of the miscreants were drummed out of the service. However, one does not read of the floggings, shootings, and hangings of earlier days. Only by enforcing strict discipline was Wright able to maintain the military effectiveness of the heterogeneous group of soldiers serving under his command. The chief activities of the troops at Fort Ontario were general garrison duty, frequent drilling, and occasional artillery practice.

Thomas Forster Wright, in and out of West Point

In July, 1848, the Wrights' older son, Thomas Forster Wright, received a presidential appointment to West Point and matriculated at the U.S. Military Academy at the age of seventeen years and seven months.[12] Given George Wright's strong feelings about a citizen's duty to serve his country, it must have been a great source of satisfaction when Thomas decided to follow his father's footsteps in a military career. However, his pleasure was to be short-lived, for Thomas did not do well in his studies at West Point. A year after his admission Colonel Wright received a disheartening letter from the superintendent:

> U.S. Military Academy
> West Point, N.Y. Nov. 17, 1849

My Dear Colonel:

I regret to inform you of the dismissal of your son from the service. He was arraigned before a General Court Martial of which Colonel Waite was President and which convened at West Point on the 29th of last month. The charge against your son was a violation of the 124 par: of the Academic regulations, in absenting himself from his tent at night between tattoo & reveille for a longer period than half an hour on the 25th of August last. He plead not guilty to the charge, but guilty to the specification— The court found him guilty of both & sentenced him to be dismissed the service; but recommended a remission of the sentence in the following words, viz: 'In consequence of the previous good and exemplary conduct of the accused, as shown in evidence by the chief Officers of the Institution, the members of the General Court Martial do earnestly & unanimously recommend him to the mercy of the Executive.' The recommendation was not approved and the sentence of the Court was directed to be carried into effect. . . .

Although your son was doing much better in his studies, still I am led to believe from a conversation I had with his Professor, that he could not probably have been able to pass his examination in the higher branches of Mathematics studied by the 3rd Class.— This being the case it is to be regretted, now that this unfortunate affair has happened, that he did not resign upon his failure last June. His good conduct then permitted him to be turned back.

As your son had not money to take him home, I have advanced him twelve dollars for that purpose—he is also indebted in the settlement of his acct. at the Academy the sum of $3 92/100, which you can remit at your convenience.

With the renewed expression of my sincere regret at this unpleasant occurence

I remain, with much esteem
Very truly yours,
Henry Brewerton
Capt. Corps of Engs. Supt. M.A.

In a second letter to Tom's father, after his debt had been paid, Captain Brewerton said:

I assure you it was a matter of great regret to me that the blow should have fallen on your son, but suppose the execution of the sentence in his case grew out of the reprehensible course of the previous administration, in allowing flagrant violations of the regulations of the Academy to go unpunished, by which the discipline of the Institution was greatly endangered.[13]

Considering the high standards that Major Wright set for those who served under him and his aspirations for his son, the boy's dismissal must have been a bitter blow and a source of embarrassment. Tom immediately sought reinstatement, but Captain Brewerton wrote back that the Academic Board was unlikely to recommend his "restoration," since it would be in violation of usual practice.

In March, 1850, Major Wright requested a copy of the proceedings of his son's court-martial.[14] Powerful influences apparently were brought to bear, for on May 25, 1850, Secretary of War George M. Crawford, by direction of President Zachary Taylor, ordered that Thomas Forster Wright be restored to the U.S. Military Academy and rejoin his former class.[15] Upon Tom's return to West Point,

Captain Brewerton reported to the chief of engineers, Gen. Joseph C. Totten, that young Wright had "not been pursuing his studies since he left the Academy & is of course not prepared to be examined with his former class, the present 4th." He suggested that Wright be placed in the class just entering instead, and this was done. He also inquired whether Wright was to receive pay for the time he was separated from the Academy.[16] There is no record that he did so.

Controversy with Civil Authorities

Bvt. Col. George Wright and Capt. Henry W. Judah constituted a board of officers assembled at Fort Niagara in May, 1850, to investigate the destruction of a number of buildings by fire. They determined that the blaze had originated from a barrel of ashes on a windy day and not from arson.

In June, for the first time, Wright was pleased with the quality of recruits he was receiving. He described this group as "fine young men," far better than any previous ones. He hoped soon to bring the strength of his company to approximately fifty men.[17]

In February, 1851, he recommended Lt. A. B. Lincoln for brevet as captain. Lincoln had served with Wright in Florida and then with zeal and gallantry from Veracruz to Molino del Rey, where he was severely wounded and suffered a crippled hand and wrist. He had been promoted to first lieutenant about the time he had been recommended for a brevet to that rank, so Wright urged that he be awarded the higher brevet.

The next month Wright interceded on behalf of Ed Lanagan, a fifer who was in some sort of trouble. Wright said that Lanagan was "a smart, active boy who served faithfully during the War with Mexico. His youth and former service induce me to recommend that he be restored to duty without trial and attached to this company. I think I can make something of him."[18]

These examples illustrate Wright's concern for the men serving under him: seeking promotion for a deserving officer and suggesting rehabilitation rather than punishment and disgrace for a young veteran. On another occasion he requested the transfer of a recruit from Syracuse because the man's brother was in Wright's command at Fort Ontario.[19] This fatherly gesture was characteristic of Wright's interest in the well-being of his men. As a result of his consideration for them, he usually enjoyed their confidence and esteem.

In 1850, Congress passed the Fugitive Slave Law to govern the return of runaway slaves. Its main effect was to increase antislavery sentiment in the North. On October 9, 1851, Wright requested guidance from Adjutant General Roger Jones about his obligations under this law:

> I am likely to be called upon any moment by the Commissioner appointed under the Act of Congress relative to fugitive slaves— my object in addressing you is to procure the decision of the Commanding General of the Dept, as to the course I am to pursue in such cases, and whether it is expected that I will furnish the Commissioner with my disposable force, without express orders from the War Dept.— I have thus far been under the impression, that before furnishing a military force to carry into effect this law, I should be furnished with special orders.[20]

As Wright's stay at Fort Ontario drew near its close in the spring of 1852, he became involved in a legal controversy with the civilian authorities in Oswego. At this post, as at others, Wright had usually gotten along well with the citizens of the community and earned their respect. However, when a local politician attempted to carry out some harbor "improvements" which Wright felt would interfere with the defensibility of his fort, he vigorously protested.

On February 9 he informed the acting adjutant general that the New York State Legislature had passed a bill granting the city title to underwater land in front of the fort. This entitlement was illegal since it did not have the sanction of the government, which should have at least the same shore rights as a private owner, Wright said. General John Wool, the division commander, in endorsing Wright's report, agreed that the act of the legislature was illegal and that any construction by the city in front of the fort would interfere with its rights as well as its defenses. Wright, on instruction from Adjutant General Jones, wrote to Mayor John Thurman of Oswego that the government would obtain an enjoinder against the city.

The city attorney wrote to Secretary of War C. M. Conrad, saying that the city merely wanted to excavate and improve the harbor and erect a few wharves. He was careful to avoid mentioning any legal aspects.

Brevet Brigadier General Totten, commander of the Corps of Engineers, received a letter from Congressman Leander Babcock saying that Wright had objected to a similar bill the previous year because the construction of wharves, warehouses, and piers would be injurious to the fort's defenses. Because of the government's objections, when the bill was passed, it stipulated that the erection of buildings was forbidden without War Department approval. Babcock thought the question of legal title to the land should be waived and that the commander of the post should have a legal instrument prepared which would permit wharves only and no buildings. Unconvinced, Wright insisted on the detrimental effects of any such bill.[21] Wright believed that, as a loyal citizen, he had an obligation to protect his country and that, as a soldier, he had the added responsibility to ensure the effectiveness of his military establishment.

Wright was spared further involvement in this controversy when in May orders arrived for his regiment to move to California. With this change of station, the first phase of Wright's career came to an end. A new era began for him as a guardian of the Far West, where he increasingly exercised his qualities of leadership.

Wright's life to date had prepared him well for the broadening responsibilities he was to assume. At West Point he learned about the "code of honor." At various frontier posts in the Old Northwest and the Mississippi Valley he learned the necessity of strict discipline. When he set out on the expedition to Council Bluffs, he discovered the importance of prudence and careful preparation. As he advanced in rank, he demonstrated his concern for his men. The Seminole War prepared him to endure hardships. In the Mexican War he displayed courage under fire. And during these thirty years of military service he discovered that getting along with civilian authorities might present problems.

Off to California

WITH THE ADVENT of the year 1852 there was an increasing need for regular army troops on the Pacific Coast. In 1851 there were only 350 regulars between Mexico and Puget Sound, a shortage that was especially critical in light of recent events. A great deal had transpired since July, 1846, when Commodore John D. Sloat had raised the American flag at Monterey and declared California free from Mexican rule. Two years later, by the Treaty of Guadalupe Hidalgo, California officially became a territory of the United States. In the meanwhile, on January 24, 1848, James Marshall discovered gold in the tailrace of a sawmill he was building on the American River for John Sutter. The following year hordes of prospectors arrived to pursue the great mineral wealth of California, creating problems in maintaining law and order. What the authorities were unable to accomplish vigilante committees attempted to do, even after California became a state in 1850.[1]

The entrance of gold seekers into Indian lands caused other problems. The history of white relations with the Indians in California was for the most part one of debauchery, enslavement, and extermination. However, the Indians of the Sacramento Valley and the northern mountains were less docile than the Diggers of the south. They raided settlements, attacked travelers and supply trains, stole cattle, and perpetrated murders and atrocities. Peace commissioners were sent out by President Millard Fillmore in 1852, and E. F. Beale was appointed superintendent of Indian affairs, with instructions to move the Indians onto reservations.[2]

The continuing flow of settlers into Oregon Territory was creating problems in the Pacific Northwest as well. In May, Major Wright received orders to move out of Fort Ontario, and the Fourth Infantry was gradually assembled at

Fort Columbus on Governor's Island in New York Harbor
in preparation for its move to the West Coast. Wright was
unhappy when he found himself assigned to sail around
Cape Horn with two of his companies. He was able to persuade the regimental commander, Lt. Col. B. L. E. Bonneville, to allow him to accompany the main body of the regiment across the Isthmus of Panama rather than taking the
lower route. He alleged that such a long sea voyage would
be injurious to his health, and most of his junior officers
had been offered a choice of routes.[3]

On July 5, Wright and the designated troops sailed to
Aspinwall, Panama, arriving there on the twentieth. They
crossed the Isthmus of Panama, boarded another ship,
and commenced north on August 5. Three weeks later the
regiment arrived at Benicia, California, which the previous commander of the Pacific Division, Gen. Persifor F.
Smith, had selected as his headquarters. Of 500 recruits
who had preceded them earlier in the year, more than 100
had already succumbed to the lure of the gold fields and
deserted. The Fourth Infantry, however, was of little use
on arrival—the command was almost completely incapaci-
tated by disease contracted in crossing the isthmus.[4]

In Command of Fort Reading, 1852–55

California at the time of Wright's arrival was divided into
four military districts. He was placed in command of the
Northern District, with headquarters at Fort Reading. On
September 24 he reached that post, which was then occupied by Company E, Second Infantry, whose men had
erected it a few months earlier. He was joined by Company
D of his own regiment the following month. Regimental
headquarters and five companies under Lieutenant Colonel Bonneville went on to Columbia Barracks at Fort Vancouver, in what was shortly to become Washington Territory. Two companies remained at Benicia, and two others
were still en route to California in December. Some of the
companies were later distributed to The Dalles, Oregon,
under Maj. Gabriel J. Rains; Fort Steilacoom, Washington

Territory, under Maj. C. H. Larned; Fort Humboldt under Lt. Col. R. L. Buchanan; and Fort Jones in California under Capt. B. R. Alden.[5] Breaking up the regiment into widely separated small detachments was hard on organization and morale.

Colonel Ethan Allen Hitchcock was serving as commander of the Division of the Pacific at this time. In the spring of 1852 he had ordered the establishment of Fort Reading to protect the mining district and the wagon trains moving between Oregon Territory and northern California and to guard the upper Sacramento Valley against Indian depredations. Hitchcock believed that many of the outbreaks were the fault of the whites. The slightest Indian incident often led to massive retaliation by the settlers, many of whom had developed a hatred of Indians while crossing the plains. Wholesale murders were sometimes committed in reprisal for petty or suspected Indian thefts. The settlers complained that the military could not protect them and that their only defense lay in concerted civilian action or the formation of militia units.

Some of the Indian conflicts were of sufficient magnitude to be designated wars: the Shasta War of 1851, the Klamath War of 1852, the Rogue River War of 1853, the spring campaign against the lower Klamaths in 1854 and 1855, and the Kern River War of 1856. Hubert Howe Bancroft later wrote that California could not claim a single Indian war that bordered on respectability: "It can boast, however, of a hundred or two of as brutal butcherings on the part of our honest miners and brave pioneers as any area of equal extent in our republic."[6]

The most troublesome Indians in California were those of the extreme northern area that extended from the headwaters of the Sacramento River to Oregon. They had been hostile to early trappers and emigrants, and became more relentless after every contact with the whites. The growing white population fought through to their future homes with little scruple, exacting terrible vengeance for every outrage. Indians were kidnapped, enslaved, and debauched, and the women molested.

Fort Reading, the first army post in northern California, was situated on the west side of Cow Creek, a tributary of the Sacramento River, two and a half miles above their confluence, near the present city of Redding.[7] The post occupied a ten-acre tract in a grove of oak trees and was composed of more than twenty buildings of wood or whitewashed adobe.[8] It was named after Pierson B. Reading, a former trapper and hunter for John Sutter who became a prominent citizen with extensive landholdings.[9] The city is named after B. B. Redding, a pioneer and later a Central Pacific Railroad agent.[10]

Shasta County had a population of about 4,000 whites, and about 400 Indian warriors within seventy-five miles of the fort and possibly 1,000 in the entire Northern District, most of them armed with bows and arrows.[11] The troops spent almost as much time protecting the Indians as they did the settlers.

The fort soon had a good garden with fresh vegetables, and Cow Creek supplied an abundance of clear water. Other than fresh meat, supplies had to be brought thirty-one miles by oxcart or pack train from the steamer landing at Red Bluff or farther south when the water was low. When the water was high, much of the post was flooded, and bridges had to be built to connect some of the buildings.[12] During Wright's first winter at the post, floodwaters isolated many miners and ranchers. As food shortages became acute, settlers complained that the soldiers were "living in clover" and would not let outsiders have supplies.[13] Worst of all, the site was plagued with "fever and ague," which kept many members of the garrison on the sick list and unfit for field duty, although quinine was administered daily.[14] For armament the fort had two mountain howitzers in addition to the soldiers' sidearms.

Early in 1853 the comparative inaction of the settlers owing to the severe winter encouraged the natives to supply their own wants by thefts of cattle. A few whites were murdered. These acts provoked avenging campaigns. Ruffians took advantage of the lawlessness and mistreated the natives. They hoped that provoking the natives into retaliation would force the government to mount a formal expedition against the Indian marauders. Indian agent Beale had little success in persuading the natives to leave their homes and hunting grounds for a reservation. Further, he was unable to convince many of the white citizens of the wisdom of placing the Indians on reservations or caring for them at all.[15]

During the time Wright was at Fort Reading, the peak aggregate strength of his command was 212, with a maximum of 10 officers, including one or two assistant surgeons. Units and detachments came and went, and most of the time there were no more than four to 6 officers and 40 to 70 enlisted men on the post. During his first year, 21 men deserted, a few of whom were captured and placed in confinement to await trial. After September, 1853, only 5 additional desertions were recorded during Wright's tenure. Officers were occasionally listed as absent without leave, but this usually occurred when they were reassigned while on leave, before word reached the post, or when they were late returning from leave because of illness or travel difficulties. The command was constantly plagued with illness. In July, 1853, 18 of a total of 66 men were reported sick. There were numerous discharges for disability, and during a seven-month period in Wright's first year there were twelve "ordinary deaths," but only one after that.

Maintaining morale was a challenge. Often the soldiers' pay was four or five months late in arriving, and spectacular views of the snow-capped Cascade Range provided scant compensation. Yet disciplinary problems were not common. In most months there was only one enlisted man in confinement, sometimes three or four; one month there were seven. Many of them were returned deserters. Disciplinary problems were not confined to enlisted men. When Company D of the Third Artillery arrived in June, 1854, it was accompanied by Capt. Bvt. Maj., Francis O. Wyse, who had been placed under arrest in April at Fort Columbia for some infraction of regulations. In July the findings of his general court-martial were received at Fort Reading, and Wyse was suspended from duty for six months. When his sentence expired in January, 1855, he resumed command of his company, and after Wright's departure Wyse assumed command of the post and the Northern District.[16]

Another disciplinary problem concerned one of Wright's surgeons. Wright believed that his civilian employees were entitled to the benefits of the post doctors. Under his interpretation of army regulations it was the duty of his surgeons to treat such civilian patients without fee. When Assistant Surgeon John Campbell refused Wright's order to see a civilian patient in the hospital, Wright had Campbell placed under arrest. Said Wright, "Obedience to orders, the *first* duty of a soldier, has been my pole star for more than thirty years." Wright's actions were approved by Hitchcock. Assistant Surgeon William F. Edgar assumed the duties of the medical department and by Wright's decision, which was upheld by Hitchcock and later by Gen. John E. Wool, was required to attend employees without additional remuneration.[17]

With Campbell under arrest it became necessary to hire a civilian physician, a Dr. Stark. Campbell, meanwhile, appealed directly to Secretary of War Jefferson Davis. In his appeal he reduced the matter to a personal vendetta, held Wright responsible for the fees he had been forbidden to charge, and accused him of misuse of government funds, property, and personnel.[18] Although Wright received the support of his departmental commanders, Davis settled the conflict with a mild rebuke to Wright and transferred Campbell to Fort Miller, on the San Joaquin River. As with Wright's other personal difficulties with fellow officers, the problem was precipitated by differing interpretations of army regulations, undoubtedly augmented by clashing personalities.

Wright also seems to have had frequent trouble with the army auditors. While he was in Florida, he was disgruntled at the return of a voucher for twenty-five dollars he had submitted, as acting assistant quartermaster, for use of a steamer for troop movement during the Patriot War; the expenditure had been authorized by Colonel Worth.[19]

During his tenure at Fort Reading there was a good deal of correspondence over whether he should receive the pay of his brevet rank, since as commander of the Northern District he was performing the duties of a lieutenant colonel.[20] Later his right to engage a civilian physician was questioned. There is no reason to believe that Wright was anything but a man of integrity and that this financial quibbling galled him. Whether he ever received the money he thought the army owed him is not known.

A few days after Wright's arrival at Fort Reading, Companies A and E of the First Dragoons arrived. About ten days later they headed north to establish Fort Jones, in the Scott River valley near the town of Yreka. In spite of the arrival of Company D of the Fourth Infantry in October, the attrition produced by men leaving as their terms of enlistment expired, and to a lesser degree by desertions, led Wright to submit an urgent appeal for recruits to fill out his command.[21]

That fall, for the first time, California participated in a presidential election. To Hitchcock's dismay, his old friend and commander Gen. Winfield Scott was defeated by a former subordinate, Franklin Pierce.

Lieutenant Russell Killed by Indians

Although many Indian skirmishes occurred farther north, Wright's command had few problems with the Indians in the immediate vicinity. The only death of a soldier in enemy action during Wright's command of Fort Reading occurred on March 24, 1853. First Lieutenant Edmund Russell, Fourth Infantry, chief commissary for the Northern District, was killed by the Indians about twenty miles from Tehama at the headwaters of Thomes Creek. Wright had dispatched Russell with a small detachment southward to punish the Indians who had been committing numerous depredations on the ranch owners in a portion of the Coast Range that formed the western boundary of Tehama County. The command was accompanied by one other officer, Bvt. 2nd Lt. J. A. Moore; an old mountain man, who served as guide; and an Indian boy, who acted as interpreter. Moore had arrived at Fort Reading a few weeks earlier to join Company A of the First Dragoons, which had just returned from Fort Jones.

On his way to a rancheria in the mountains Russell encountered a band of hostile Indians, eight or ten of whom he captured and disarmed, placing their bows and arrows in the charge of his young interpreter. Continuing toward his destination with his prisoners, his guide, and the interpreter, Russell became separated from the rest of his men as the two parties passed around opposite sides of a small hill. As soon as the other party was out of sight, the Indians speedily regained possession of their arms, "either by force or through the treachery of the interpreter" and fell on Russell. By the time the guide, who was lagging behind, reached the spot, the Indians had unhorsed Russell, shot seven arrows into his body, and beaten his brains out with a club. The lieutenant was able to kill one of his assailants and wound another before he died, and the guide killed two or three more; the rest escaped.[22]

Lieutenant Russell's body was returned to Fort Reading for burial. Public reaction to the event was expressed by an editorial in the *Shasta Courier:*

> The news of this unfortunate affair excited the utmost indignation among the acquaintances of Lt. Russell and the citizens generally. When such instances of the fate of white men at the hands of the savages are occurring in this section of the State every day, is it at all strange that our people are exasperated to an extraordinary degree? and that they are determined, unless this great evil be speedily removed, to wage a war of extermination against the Indians? . . . What are the lives of a hundred or a thousand of these savages to the life of a single American citizen?— to the life of Lt. Russell? Our citizens below should not censure us and call us inhuman, if we fight the Indians in their own mode of warfare. The man—away from all danger, living securely in a comfortable home, surrounded by all the safeguards of a well organized city, is but illy capable of telling the miner, the packer and the traveller— who are nightly exposed to the attacks of these brutal devils— what course they should pursue in defending themselves.

Our people, like all right thinking men, desire the esteem
and approbation of their fellow citizens throughout the State;
but if they have to buy it with their lives, then, they prefer
doing without it. If the Indians cannot be made to live on
terms of amity with them, they are determined they shall not
live at all. We say shoot them down wherever you find them.
Slay them as you would so many panthers or bears. Show
them no mercy until they give satisfactory evidence of a sincere wish for peace–and thereby protect the lives of your own
and your fellow citizens.[23]

It is difficult to grasp the intensity of feeling that followed Russell's death. Hitchcock was shocked when a Methodist minister upon whom he called in San Francisco observed that Providence had designed the extermination of
the Indians and suggested that it would be good to intro-
duce smallpox among them.[24]

Several times in 1853, Wright visited posts throughout
the Northern District, which included southern Oregon.
No serious engagements resulted, to the dismay of the
white settlers, for the newspapers carried frequent accounts of Indian attacks on homes and pack trains and periodically expressed fears of a general war. In June, Wright
reported on a tour to Fort Jones, Yreka, and the northern
section of his district. He found the country quiet. He neither saw nor heard of Indian aggression in the area but
was aware that the Indians to the west on Cottonwood and
Thomes Creek had been making forays and driving off
stock. Only a mounted force could prevent such activity,
and he had none to spare. He also knew that even the Indians in the immediate vicinity of Fort Reading were likely
to be hostile, although there had been no recent overt acts.

The dragoon squadron at Fort Jones was ordered to be
ready for field duty early in July, to escort a survey crew
for a new pack-train trail to Crescent City on the coast, and
to patrol the emigrant road for 100 miles to the east and
protect new arrivals. Better routes to the coast would
greatly reduce the cost of supplying Fort Jones and enable
Wright to use the dragoons at Fort Orford for duty in the

Sacramento Valley, replacing them with infantry. Wright was pleased to find the garrison at Fort Jones in excellent health and good order.[25]

In spite of the infusion of troops on the West Coast and the raising of volunteer companies by the California legislature, Indian hostilities in some areas seemed to increase rather than diminish and there was much loss of emigrant life and property. Settlers still had to defend themselves and much of southwestern Oregon was virtually unprotected. Fort Orford had been established on the Oregon coast in 1851 but did little good, since it was separated by the Coast Range from the inner country, where the principal problems were. Finally, on September 28, 1853, Fort Lane was established by Maj. G. W. Patten in the Rogue River valley, about eight miles north of present Jacksonville, Oregon.[26] Fort Reading then became the supply depot for all of northern California and Fort Lane, and the added work made it necessary to engage thirty-three civilian employees. Administratively, both Fort Lane and Fort Jones, as well as Fort Reading, were under Major Wright's command.[27]

General Hitchcock Replaced by General Wool

It was not long before changes on the national political scene affected military affairs on the West Coast. After assuming office, President Pierce appointed as his secretary of war Jefferson Davis, who shared Pierce's antipathy for Scott and his supporters, such as Hitchcock. In September, 1853, Hitchcock uncovered a plot by an adventurer named William Walker to overthrow Mexican authority and set up a revolutionary government in the state of Sonora, adjoining California. President Fillmore had previously instructed Hitchcock to thwart any such enterprise. Hitchcock dispatched Capt. E. D. Keyes with a party of soldiers to seize the freebooter's vessel and turn it over to the U.S. marshal. This action led to litigation against Hitchcock. A month later Walker took off with a fragment of his force on another vessel and attempted to seize Baja California, but he was abandoned by most of his men and forced to return to San Francisco.[28]

Hitchcock's actions received official government approval but made him enemies among influential local politicians. He was replaced on February 16, 1854, by Gen. John E. Wool so as to "allow freer play to the champions of free enterprise."[29] Wool had a fairly distinguished military record, but he turned out to be a highly controversial character during his stay on the West Coast. In Bancroft's opinion, before Wool's arrival military affairs in California had been conducted with reasonable ability—perhaps without vigor, but with few collisions between the army and the militia or the army and civilians. Wood had continuous and acrimonious quarrels with the civil authorities. His intentions were honest, but many of his measures were arbitrary and ill-advised.[30]

General Wool's assumption of command of what was now called the Department of the Pacific was soon to have a profound effect on Wright's life. Wool's views and policies toward the Indians, white immigration, and the militia determined much of Wright's early conduct in the Pacific Northwest and inevitably embroiled him in Wool's controversy with the governor of Washington Territory, Isaac I. Stevens.

A Visit by the Inspector General

In June, 1854, Company D, Third Artillery, arrived at Fort Reading from Benicia. On July 18 the inspector general of the army, Col. Joseph K. Mansfield, visited the post. In his report he described an abundance of wood, grazing, and water but pointed out that all other supplies except pork and beef had to come from San Francisco:

> It appears to me . . . that this post is not at this time properly located, however suitable it might have been when established in 1852. I would therefore recommend this post should be removed further eastward towards the Emigrant Trail at the

mountains, after a suitable reconnaissance as a post in that quarter seems necessary. Another objection to this post is its decidedly sickly locality (the Sacramento Valley) where the ague and fever prevails & the officers and men are kept constantly sick and unfit for duty in the field.—Further it is exposed to overflows in the rainy season.

In his cover letter to General Wool, Mansfield wrote: "I found that post well commanded by Col. Wright, and the troops in excellent condition. . . . The quarters are good & there is an excellent stable & the store houses &c. ample. . . . Its locality is not in my opinion of importance to supress Indian depredations. . . ." He recommended a location between the junction of the Pitt River and McLeod's Fork, "thus placing the troops between the wild Indians & the population."[31]

In the summer of 1853, Wright requested an increase in rank if the army should be expanded. He pointed out that he had served in the army for thirty-one years, spending much of that time in arduous duty on the frontier. During those years he had had only a few months' leave, a good portion of it for the recovery of his health after his illness in Florida. He had not seen his family during the two years he had been in California. On September 3, 1854, he requested six months' leave. Wool's endorsement of the application says that Wright was entitled to leave but that Wool could not approve it since he had no officer of equal merit and standing to take Wright's place. Secretary of War Davis approved Wright's request, provided a suitable replacement became available.[32] It appears that by this time Wright had firmly established his reputation as a capable and dependable commander. He was strict with his men and would tolerate no hint of insubordination, but they knew of his interest in their well-being.

In October, Major General Wool paid a visit to Fort Reading. He was received with full military honors by the little garrison. The next day he inspected the troops and the post.

Although intermittent fighting with the Indians in Shasta County continued throughout 1854, it mainly involved volunteers rather than the army. The most decisive battle took place after Wright's departure in the spring of 1855, when Capt. Henry Judah and 100 regulars defeated the warriors of several Indian tribes at Castle Rock.[33]

On February 3, 1855, Wright was promoted to lieutenant colonel in the Fourth Infantry. Indian troubles were brewing in newly created Washington Territory, and General Wool persistently emphasized to the War Department the need to expand the army to defend the extensive frontier. On March 9, Congress authorized the organization of two new regiments and the reorganization of the Ninth and Tenth Regiments of Infantry, which had been disbanded at the end of the Mexican War.[34] Wright was promoted to full colonel just a month after his previous promotion and placed in command of the Ninth Infantry.[35] Word of Congress's action was reported in the *Shasta Courier* on April 14, 1855. The esteem in which Wright was held by the civilian community is indicated by an excerpt:

> The following is a list of the field officers of the four new regiments—nearly all of them being promotions. Among the number, we have observed with feelings of peculiar pleasure the name of Brevet Colonel George Wright, promoted to be Colonel of the 9th Infantry. Col. Wright has been commanding officer at Fort Reading for the past two years or more. During this time, many of our citizens have sought occasion to make his acquaintance and enjoy those hospitalities at his quarters, which he dispenses with that liberality and delicacy so characteristic of the service of which he is an ornament. No one, we venture to say, has ever left his presence without feeling sentiments of the warmest admiration and friendship for the officer and gentleman. His promotion will not fail to be received with satisfaction by all who have the pleasure of his acquaintance.[36]

Wright gave up his northern California command on May 9, turning it over to Wyse, and sailed back to the East Coast, where in July he established the headquarters of his new regiment at Fort Monroe, Virginia, and proceeded with its organization.

Thomas Wright Joins William Walker

While George Wright was still at Fort Reading, he received word that his older son, Thomas Forster Wright, had been finally and permanently separated from West Point in the summer of 1853 because of a deficiency in a philosophy examination.[37] Major Wright was a man with strong family ties, a dedicated soldier, and a proud patriot. His older son's debacle at West Point was a sad disappointment to him.

When he was next heard from, Tom had joined the company of the notorious William Walker.[38] Walker was a quixotic adventurer with a burning ambition and a natural flare for leadership. He had been a physician, a lawyer, and a newspaper editor before embarking on his career as a filibuster, or freebooting warrior.

At this time the embryo Confederacy had its eyes directed southward, and there was nothing Secretary of War Davis would have liked better than a revolution in the Mexican border states. Many other American citizens, both northern and southern, shared a yearning for more Spanish soil and mineral wealth. Now that the doctrine of manifest destiny had carried the nation to the shores of the Pacific, perhaps the United States should start moving south toward the Isthmus of Panama and even to Tierra del Fuego! The need for a shorter route from the eastern United States to California had already given rise to thoughts of a canal, and entrepreneurs like Cornelius Vanderbilt and Charles Morgan were maneuvering for control of possible routes. Great Britain was strongly opposed to such a project because of the trade advantages it would give to the United States.

Although several filibustering attempts, including his own, to invade parts of Mexico had failed, Walker continued his Latin-American intrigue. In 1855 he was invited by a losing political faction in Nicaragua to join their cause. Walker, with George Wright's son and a band of fifty-eight men, sailed to Nicaragua and managed to turn the scales in favor of his new allies, who awarded him the title "gen-

eralissimo." One year and many battles later he was elected
president of Nicaragua. Walker regarded himself as the
liberator of the oppressed Nicaraguans and the standard-
bearer of the United States, but the support he had hoped
for from his own country never materialized. Ultimately
the combined efforts of his Nicaraguan enemies led to his
surrender in May, 1857, and he and the remnants of his
force departed on American warships.[39]

In 1860, Walker set out once more, this time to Honduras, because Britain was patrolling Nicaraguan waters as
a protection against filibusters. He had with him 100 men,
including Tom Wright. Walker now sought the expansion
of U.S. interests into the Caribbean and the creation of a
Central American federation. He captured the fortress
that guarded the Honduran port of Truxillo and then
seized the customs house. Soon, however, the British warship *Icarus* arrived, and its commander, Capt. Norvell
Salmon, demanded Walker's surrender. Walker and his
surviving men fled south down a coast trail, hoping to join
forces with a rebel leader. However, they were soon surrounded by Honduran troops, and after nine days of futile
resistance Walker surrendered to Captain Salmon. He was
promptly turned over to Honduran authorities, was court-
martialed by them, and was executed by a firing squad.[40]

Tom Wright, who had been wounded in this brief campaign, was allowed to return to the United States with the
rest of the command.[41] He made his way to Washington
Territory, where his father was serving. The 1860 census
lists him as a clerk in the Quartermaster Department at
Fort Walla Walla.

George Wright must have been concerned about the
risks his son had taken in these dubious and unlawful enterprises. Wright may also have wondered whether Tom's
failures at the U.S. Military Academy and his filibustering
escapade would reflect unfavorably on Wright's own reputation or adversely affect his career.

9.

The Ninth Infantry Goes West

WHEN COL. GEORGE WRIGHT arrived in the East to begin
the organization and training of his new regiment, his first
stop was in New York City. He apologized to army headquarters for a delay while he bought a wardrobe suitable
for his new position, after three years on the frontier. He
then traveled to Oswego for a visit with his family.

Organizing the Regiment, Fort Monroe, 1855

On July 3, 1855, he assumed command of the Ninth In-
fantry at Fort Monroe, which had been designated as the
regiment's headquarters and assembly point.[1] Founded in
1819 as Fortress Monroe, the post was located at Point
Comfort, Virginia, on the west side of the entrance to
Chesapeake Bay, directly across the mouth of the James
River from Norfolk. Recruiting rendezvous for the new
regiment had been established in Maine, Connecticut,
New York, New Jersey, Pennsylvania, Virginia, Ohio, and
Tennessee.[2]

By the end of July, Wright hoped to have 600 men mustered in. His newly promoted field-grade officers were experienced regular army men. Lt. Col. Silas Casey came to
Wright from the Second Infantry, Maj. Edward J. Steptoe
from the Third Artillery, and Maj. Robert S. Garnett from
the First Dragoons. About half his other officers came directly from civilian life, and the rank and file were almost
entirely new recruits. A rigorous training program was in-
stituted: drill in Hardie's tactics, target practice, and physical toughening to prepare the men for marching twenty or
thirty miles a day.[3]

Wright reported to army headquarters that he hoped to
be able to have his regiment completely organized and

Col. George Wright on taking command of the Ninth Regiment of Infantry, U.S. Army, 1855. Courtesy United States Military Academy Archives, West Point, N.Y.

trained before it was broken into small detachments for frontier duty. If the regiment's ultimate destination was to be the West, he hoped it would be California or Oregon, since he felt familiar with the area and believed he could best do justice to both whites and Indians.[4]

Early in August an unexpected problem arose. A virulent epidemic of yellow fever had broken out at Norfolk and several nearby towns. Hoping to maintain the good health of his men, Wright suspended all interaction with these communities as a precautionary measure. Each day brought news of fresh cases of yellow fever, so Wright placed guards on the roads leading into the post and on the wharves. His prompt action in quarantining his post drew the wrath of the Norfolk and Hampton Steamship Company which, with others, filed suit against him for $10,000, alleging trespass. Wright told the War Department that yellow fever was still raging but so far "we have escaped." He was assured that it was within his discretionary power as post commander to isolate his post to protect it from disease without additional orders from higher authority.

Then, because no ships from the stricken communities were allowed to dock at the fort, a smear campaign was mounted against Wright. The *Norfolk Evening Star* decried "the inhumanity of the commander of Fort Monroe in refusing assistance to the starving men of the ship *Plymouth Rock*." Wright told the War Department he had never heard of the ship or its captain before seeing the article in the newspaper, which he described as "a tissue of falsehoods." Had the captain requested aid he would have received it, Wright said. Only ships from the locations where yellow fever was rampant were forbidden to land; his actions in trying to protect his men were not based on panic or lack of sympathy but on his surgeon's advice.

Secretary of War Jefferson Davis informed the U.S. attorney general that Wright had been summoned by the local sheriff to appear in court and requested an appropriate defense for him. As in the Oswego controversy, by the time the suit came to trial Wright was far away, this time at Fort Vancouver in Washington Territory, and the defense was carried on by the U.S. attorney for the eastern district of Virginia. An interesting postscript came in a letter Wright received from one of his officers, Capt. Frederick T. Dent, who had heard the *Norfolk Evening Star* story repeated by supper companions while traveling on the steamer *Louisiana*. The *Plymouth Rock*'s Captain Patterson, who happened to be seated at the same table, did not in any way object when Dent asserted that the accusation that Wright had driven off the starving captain, was a falsehood.[5]

In any event, Wright's men stayed well. His main complaint to army headquarters was that he had to reject one or more men from every batch of recruits sent to him because many had never been examined by a surgeon before. Some of the officers who came directly from civilian life, in contrast to those who had previously served, were not sturdy enough to endure the rigors of a campaign. He respectfully suggested to the secretary of war that "the gentlemen appointed from civil life" be examined for physical disabilities before being commissioned. By November he was able to report that his regiment was now complete, with more than 700 men. A month later he received orders from the general-in-chief to prepare for movement to the Pacific and to take as little baggage as possible.[6]

Yakima War, 1855–56

On December 15, the Ninth Regiment of Infantry embarked on the U.S. steamship *St. Louis,* arriving at Aspinwall, Panama, on December 24. After crossing the isthmus by rail, Wright, his staff, the regimental band, and seven companies boarded the S.S. *Oregon* the same afternoon. Crowding was so severe that one company was removed and placed on board the *Golden Age* with Lieutenant Colonel Casey, who had with him the remaining three companies and most of the regimental baggage. Though still crowded, the men were in good health and spirits, and the *Oregon* was soon under way, the *Golden Age* following later. On January 3, Wright reported from Acapulco harbor, complaining that the *Oregon* was slow and he was concerned that the *Golden Age* might arrive in San Francisco before him. Later, off the Oregon coast, Wright encountered a ship carrying General Wool back to San Francisco from a visit to Fort Vancouver. Wool ordered Wright to take over the command of the Columbia River District from Maj. Gabriel J. Rains and to move headquarters from Fort Vancouver to Fort Dalles, farther up the Columbia River. Casey, with two companies, was to go to Fort Steilacoom on Puget Sound.

Wright and his troops reached Fort Vancouver on January 20, 1856. Here Wright was reunited with part of his former regiment, the Fourth Infantry. Casey and his command, which had transferred to the *Republic* in San Francisco, arrived three days later.[7]

An account of the regiment's arrival at Fort Vancouver was given by then 2nd Lt. Philip H. Sheridan, who was assigned there with a detachment of the First Dragoons. Upon its arrival, the Ninth Infantry encamped in front of the officers' quarters "on the beautiful parade ground of that post" and set about preparing for the coming campaign.

> The commander, Colonel George Wright, who had been promoted to the colonelcy of the regiment upon its organization the previous year, had seen much active duty since his graduation over thirty years before, serving with credit in the Florida and Mexican Wars. For three years prior to his assignment to the Ninth Infantry, he had been stationed on the Pacific Coast, and the experience he had there acquired, added to his excellent soldierly qualities, was of benefit in the active campaigns, in which, during the following years, he was to participate.[8]

There were five military posts in the district at that time: Fort Vancouver, Fort Steilacoom, Fort Dalles, Fort Lane, and Fort Orford. With the arrival of the Ninth's twenty-seven officers, two surgeons, and 736 enlisted men, the number of regular army troops in Washington and Oregon was increased to 2,000. Of the thirty-three companies in the Pacific Department, twenty-seven were located in these two territories; nine of them, in the early months of 1856, were trying to wind up the Rogue River War in southern Oregon.[9]

Events of great significance had been happening in the Oregon country while Wright had been stationed at Fort Reading. Many of these contributed to the Indian unrest and uprisings in which Wright was to play such an important role. In 1853, by an act of Congress, a portion of Oregon Territory, including what is now Washington, northern Idaho, and western Montana, was established as a separate entity and designated as Washington Territory. President Franklin Pierce appointed Isaac I. Stevens, a native of Massachusetts and a graduate of West Point, as governor. On the way to his new assignment, Stevens carried out an extensive survey of the northern plains and mountains and demonstrated the feasibility of a northern railroad route to the Pacific coast. In addition to his duties as governor, he was also appointed Superintendent of Indian Affairs.[10]

That fall, about 7,000 emigrants passed over the Oregon Trail into the Pacific Northwest. The ever-swelling tide of new settlers was causing apprehension among the Indians, so Stevens traveled about making treaties with the native inhabitants of his huge territory, which extended from the Pacific Ocean to the Continental Divide. He planned to compensate the Indians for their lands, offer them certain amenities, and place them on reservations.[11]

In 1850, Congress had passed the Donation Land Law to encourage settlement in the Pacific Northwest. Three hundred and twenty acres was granted to every man, and a like amount to his wife, upon actual residence for four consecutive years, prior to December 1, 1850. Those who came later got 160 acres each for man and wife. The law made no provision for any possible Indian title, or for rights granted by treaty to the Hudson's Bay Company. The settlers were led to believe that the land was theirs for

Isaac I. Stevens, 1861, the first governor of Washington
Territory, 1853–57. Courtesy Washington State Historical
Society, Tacoma.

the taking; their growing numbers and the activities of Governor Stevens made it all too apparent to the Indians that the whites intended to take over their lands, and threatened their whole way of life. As a result, the frequency of clashes between Indians and whites increased.

Rains Expedition

In May, 1855, Governor Stevens, having concluded some treaties with Indians in the Puget Sound area, held a great council in the Walla Walla valley. Approximately 5,000 Indians, mainly from the Walla Walla, Cayuse, Umatilla, Yakima, and Nez Perce tribes, attended. The Indians were "far from unanimous" in their acceptance of the treaty terms, and some of the chiefs who signed were actually planning a war of extermination against the whites under the leadership of Leschi on the Coast and Kamiakin in the interior. As early as 1853, the Oblate missionary Father Pandosy and Capt. Benjamin Alvord, who was in command at Fort Dalles, had warned their superiors that the tribes were banding together to oust the whites. Rains forwarded the information to the headquarters of the Pacific Department, but he and Father Pandosy were regarded as alarmists.[12] Stevens, undismayed, continued on to the northern Rocky Mountain region to make treaties with the Flatheads, Pend d'Oreilles, Kootenais, and Blackfeet.

In 1855, gold was discovered near the Hudson's Bay Company's Fort Colvile in what is now northeast Washington, and an influx of miners began, which added to the white population. Later in the summer a number of prospectors on their way to the mines were murdered by the Indians in the Yakima country.[13] In September Indian Agent Andrew J. Bolon, who went to investigate, was treacherously murdered by a party of Yakimas after being advised by a friendly chief to turn back because of the agitated state of the tribe.[14]

Maj. Granville O. Haller was ordered to take 105 officers and men to find the killers of Bolon and the miners. About

Governor Stevens's Walla Walla Council, 1855. Sketch by Gustavus Sohon. Courtesy Eastern Washington State Historical Society, Spokane.

sixty miles north of Fort Dalles he ran into a throng of over 1,000 warriors who mauled his command badly. After three days of fighting he finally was able to make a nocturnal retreat to safety. Five of his men were killed, seventeen wounded, and he was obliged to leave behind his howitzer and most of his mules and provisions.[15] The Yakima War was now under way. Colonel Wright, whose regiment had been raised because of Wool's concern that such a conflict would arise, was still in Virginia training his men.

As fall passed into winter the coastal Indians committed numerous raids on the Puget Sound settlements. Block houses were built, and volunteer companies raised in Oregon and Washington. A company intended as an escort for Governor Stevens on his return from the Blackfoot council was disbanded by General Wool while he was visiting at Fort Vancouver. He suggested that the governor could return by way of Saint Louis and New York if he was concerned about hostile Indians. The Indians, said Wool, would cause no trouble if they were left alone.[16]

Maj. Gen. John E. Wool, ca. 1860, the controversial commander of the Department of the Pacific during the early days of Washington Territory. Photograph by Mathew B. Brady, engraving by J. C. Buttre. Courtesy California State Library, Sacramento.

Meanwhile Major Rains marched into the Yakima country with a force of 700 regulars and volunteers.[17] Instead of carrying on a vigorous campaign, Rains went into camp at St. Joseph Oblate Mission on Ahtanum Creek. The outnumbered Indians had fled and taken Fathers Pandosy and Durieu with them.[18] The volunteers proceeded to butcher the mission pigs and dig up the potatoes in its garden. In doing so they unearthed a keg of powder, buried by the priests to keep it from falling into the hands of the Indians. The volunteers assumed that the priests had been supplying the Indians with gunpowder and burned the mission to the ground.[19] Sheridan, who had accompanied the Rains expedition, commented, "The failure of the Haller expedition from lack of a sufficient force, and of the Rains expedition from the incompetency of its commander, was a great mortification to the officers and men connected with them."[20] When snow began to fall, Rains returned to Fort Dalles. He lost only two men, who drowned while attempting to cross the Yakima River.

Wool upbraided Rains for seeking the assistance of volunteers and accepting a commission as brigadier general from them. While Wool was impatient with civilian government and despised volunteer troops, another military observer commented that the hardy frontiersmen who made up the volunteers were more effective in fighting the Indians than the regular soldiers who had recently enlisted and were serving under officers fresh from West Point. He did concede that the volunteers' lack of discipline often impaired their usefulness.[21]

Cascades Massacre

The regulars spent the bitter winter of 1855–56, during which the Columbia River froze over, in garrison. Meanwhile, Col. James W. Nesmith kept the Oregon volunteers in the field. Lt. Col. James K. Kelley moved into the Walla Walla country, because there was considerable concern for the safety of Governor Stevens. In early December the Walla Walla chief, Peupeumoxmox, came into the Oregon volunteer camp under a flag of truce. He and six of his men were retained as hostages to assure the safe passage of the column as it moved on to the old Marcus Whitman Mission site at Waiilatpu. On the way the column encountered a large band of Walla Wallas and a fierce fight ensued. The chief shouted orders and encouragement to his warriors, and the troops attempted to silence him. In the ensuing scuffle, Peupeumoxmox and four of his fellow hostages were killed. The volunteers scalped him and cut off his ears as souvenirs.[22] After three days of fighting, the Indians were driven off.

Governor Stevens finally returned to the Coast in January, 1856, after a stormy council with the Spokanes on the way. He missed General Wool by one day when Wool returned to his headquarters in San Francisco. Stevens wrote to Secretary of War Davis charging Wool with incapacity and criminal neglect of duty, and requested his removal. Before long the Oregon legislature petitioned Congress and brought about Wool's recall. Wool regarded Stevens as "crazy," guilty of harassing friendly Indians and stirring up the hostiles.[23] J. Ross Browne, a special agent who later was sent to investigate the causes of the war, termed the quarrel between Stevens and Wool "undignified and unstatesmanlike."[24]

On January 26, 1856, an Indian attack on the village of Seattle was repulsed with the aid of the firepower and crew of the sloop of war *Decatur* under Capt. Guert Gansvoort.[25] This attack was simply another manifestation of the general uprising fomented by Kamiakin and Leschi. More blockhouses were built throughout the coastal settlements, and in February Lieutenant Colonel Casey marched into the White River valley from Fort Steilacoom. Numerous engagements occurred, involving regulars and volunteers. Most were won by the whites, but there were losses on both sides. By mid-March the war west of the Cascade Range was over.

In February, Governor Stevens had visited with Wright at Fort Vancouver and Casey at Fort Steilacoom in an attempt to coordinate the efforts of the army with those of the volunteers. Both officers had received specific instructions from Wool to have nothing to do with volunteers other than to disarm and eject them whenever possible. Initially, relations between Wright and Stevens were good.

Stevens remarked, "In Colonel Wright I have entire confidence, and if he were allowed to act according to his own judgement, there would be nothing to apprehend."[26] In his biography of his father, Hazard Stevens wrote:

> In truth, between the governor and his volunteers, who were so efficiently protecting the settlements and attacking the common foe, on the one hand, and his irate commanding general, who had positively ordered him to ignore the territorial authorities and forces, on the other, Colonel Wright was in something of a quandary, and it must be confessed that he conducted himself with no little diplomatic skill.[27]

Wool felt that the war was unnecessary, attributable to mistakes of civil policy. He said that the posts Wright had been ordered to establish were not needed for the defense of the inhabitants of Washington and Oregon territories, but to prevent Oregon Governor George Curry's militia from waging war against the Indians and taking possession of their land. The citizen soldiers, he said, were animated by eagerness to acquire Indian horses, cattle, and land; the territorial authorities, to promote their own ambitious schemes and advance the fortunes of pecuniary speculators at the expense of the federal treasury.[28]

Initially, Wright's sympathies also were with the Indians. Early in 1856, he protested to Governor Curry that he was "much embarassed by the wanton attacks of the Oregon Volunteers on the friendly Indians" who had been fired upon by the volunteers while fishing at The Dalles on the Columbia River. Governor Curry replied with some asperity to Wright's accusation and his request for withdrawal of the volunteers.

Wright's response to Curry indicated that his feelings regarding militia and relationships with civilian authorities were far different from those of his commander, General Wool:

> In conclusion, I beg leave to remark, that it has always been my aim to cultivate a good understanding with the authorities and people in the country where I am stationed. . . . [The

opinion that soldiers] have no feelings or sympathies in unison with civilians, and particularly that the regular army is hostile to volunteer troops . . . . is entirely a mistake.[29]

During a second brief visit to Fort Vancouver in March, Wool ordered Wright to establish posts in the Walla Walla and Yakima regions of eastern Washington, mainly to protect the Indians and exclude the settlers. Early in March, after "weeks of prudent preparation," Wright left Fort Vancouver and headed up the Columbia River, with all but three companies of his command, having been preceded by five companies of Oregon volunteers.[30] His orders were to maintain peace and to fight only as a last resort.[31] Wool also sent two of the remaining three companies at Fort Vancouver to Steilacoom and ordered away all but nine men of the company that had been guarding the blockhouse at the Cascades.[32]

The Cascades was a narrow gateway in the Cascade Range through which the Columbia River rushed, about forty miles west of The Dalles. Here, at the upper limit of navigation on the lower Columbia, troops and other travelers had to disembark and move to the upper landing on foot. It was a bottleneck through which supplies for the interior were moved on a five-mile, mule-powered wooden tramway on the north bank of the river. The accumulation of valuable material at this key point made it a tempting prize for the Indians. Wright was aware of the importance of protecting the area, yet it was left defenseless by Wool's order.[33] There were small settlements at the upper and lower landings of the portage and at its mid-portion stood the blockhouse.

When Wright and his troops reached a point five miles above The Dalles on March 26, a combined force of Yakimas, Klickitats, and Cascade Indians attacked the blockhouse and settlements. Fortunately the river steamers *Mary* and *Wasco*, which were at the upper landings, were able to get under way before the Indians could burn them and steamed up the river to overtake Wright. A friendly Indian made his way to Fort Vancouver carrying news of the skirmish there. A number of whites at the lower settlement escaped down the river by boat. At the upper landing about forty settlers took refuge in Bradford's two-story log store. The next day Lieutenant Sheridan arrived from Fort Vancouver on the steamboat *Belle* with a detachment of forty dragoons and a few Oregon volunteers. On March 28, Wright and his command returned on the *Mary* and *Wasco,* bringing 270 men and towing dragoon horses in barges. Sheridan had by this time crossed the Columbia to the Oregon side and was able to get back over the river to the blockhouse behind the shelter of an intervening island. The Yakimas and Klickitats dispersed as Sheridan was about to attack them, on hearing a bugle from Wright's troops who were moving down from the upper landing. Only the Cascade Indians remained and they were captured and placed on the island.

In the Indian attack fourteen civilians and three soldiers of the blockhouse detail were killed and twelve persons wounded. Two soldiers in the relief force were killed. The Cascades protested their innocence, but Sheridan demonstrated that their guns had been recently fired. Thirteen were arrested and taken to Wright at the upper landing, where they were tried by a hastily organized military tribunal. Nine of them were hanged and the others sent as prisoners to Fort Vancouver.[34] The hangings were thought to be justifiable punishment for the killing of nineteen whites in an "unprovoked" attack.

After the so-called Cascades Massacre, Wright ordered two more blockhouses erected at the Cascades. Capt. Charles S. Winder and his company were left to protect the portage.

Meanwhile, Governor Stevens sought to make political capital of the Cascades tragedy "by citing it as proof of army incompetence."[35] He also declared martial law on the Coast in his effort to control the activities of the white "squaw men" who were suspected of collaborating with the Indians. If it became necessary to detain these men, Stevens was prepared to ignore writs of habeas corpus

seeking their release. This act led to a conflict with the ju-
diciary, and Stevens was censured by the territorial legislature at its next meeting and reprimanded by President
Pierce and Secretary of State William L. Marcy.

Wright Campaign in Yakima Country

After the action at the Cascades, Wright returned to Fort
Dalles to establish his headquarters. Wool ordered him to
postpone going to Walla Walla and to move into the Yakima country first. Wright left Fort Dalles on April 28 and
followed Haller's route of the previous year. The Naches
River was impassable for infantry because of the spring
run-off so Wright halted nine miles from its point of entry
into the Yakima River. Here he threw up a field work to
contain his stores, protected by wicker containers filled
with dirt. He named it Fort Naches but it was later referred to as "Basket Fort." While here, he sent for Maj.
Bvt. Lt. Col., Edward J. Steptoe to join him with three
companies of the Ninth Infantry and one of the Fourth
from Fort Dalles and two companies of the Ninth from the
Coast under Maj. Robert S. Garnett. Wright now had 500
regulars with him to face a large body of Indians who had
recently forced the departure of five companies of Oregon
volunteers.

Wright seemed more interested in impressing the Indians with the strength of the army and patiently parley-
ing with them than in waging what he regarded as an unnecessary war. For this attitude he was roundly criticized
by the governor and the settlers. Stevens wanted unconditional surrender and peace by conquest while Wright was
content with a promise of peace. He felt that his peace-
keeping efforts were hampered by barbarous acts of the
volunteers, such as the strangling of a family of six friendly
Indians after the Cascades fight. Stevens blamed the army
for interfering with his efforts to bring the Indians under
control. In his commitment to the growth and development of his territory, Stevens favored encouraging settle-

ment, while the army wished to keep the whites out of the interior.

Stevens felt that as governor and Indian Superintendent he had the highest authority. He resented any interference with his views and his command of the Washington volunteers. The army, on the other hand, felt Stevens kept the Indians agitated and that an army officer should have authority when fighting occurred. Moreover, the volunteers were consuming supplies and using transport that the army needed. The volunteers were indignant that the army would no longer give them arms and ammunition.[36] Wright was caught in the midst of this controversy, and found himself in a no-win situation.

Within the Indian tribes there were sharp divisions between those who favored war and those who were opposed to it. The Indians were further confused by the conflict between the civil and military authorities.

Recent writers have taken Wright to task for resorting to full-scale war when police action alone was indicated.[37] Such a policy, they claim, created the intertribal unity he wished to avoid.[38] Yet limited activity had characterized Wright's actions for two and a half years. Initially, he shared Wool's belief that the Indians were basically peaceful and were only forced into aggression by the whites. Stevens wrote to the secretary of war deploring Wright's dilatory course of action in the Yakima country, which he said inflamed the Indians and incited them to prepare for war.[39] He was also disturbed by Wright's reluctance to hand over to him a group of chiefs he called "murderers" who had come into Wright's camp. Wright felt it would be unwise to prosecute them in the "present unsettled state"[40] and planned to turn them over to Casey for safekeeping nearer their homes. To Stevens's disgust, they managed to escape.

Chief Owhi and his brother Chief Teias, the father-in-law of Kamiakin, told Wright that Stevens's Walla Walla Treaty was the cause of all the trouble. Wright warned the chiefs against further depredations and they agreed to return stolen goods and comply with his demands, but once

Kamiakin, head chief of the Yakimas, 1855. Sketch by
Gustavus Sohon. Courtesy Washington State Historical
Society.

out of his camp they never returned. Kamiakin had been
across the Naches River but had declined to come in to
Wright's Basket Fort for a parley and soon left the area
with several hundred warriors.

By June 17, the Naches was bridged and Wright's command crossed over and marched north and west, leaving
Steptoe and three companies at Fort Naches. When they
reached the upper Yakima, they crossed the mountains

into the Wenatchee valley. About this time Wright wrote to
Assistant Adjutant General William W. Mackall requesting
250 recruits to fill out his regiment and expressed his regret at the delay in submitting his report while he had
been in the field for four months. He also said that two
companies of volunteers had moved into the interior and
gave his opinion that the Spokanes would not join Kamiakin but were guilty of harboring hostile Cayuses.[41]

In the Wenatchee valley, Wright encountered Father
Pandosy and a large number of Indians who were busily
catching their winter supply of salmon. Pandosy trusted
Wright and urged the Indians to cooperate by remaining
peaceful.[42] Teias and his family were picked up as hostages; Kamiakin and Owhi had already fled. By July 19,
Wright had descended the Wenatchee River to the right
bank of the Columbia and then entered the Kittitas valley.
Five hundred Indian men, women, and children accompanied him, thanks to the influence of Father Pandosy,
whose help he acknowledged in dispatches. The Indians
returned a few stolen horses and mules and Wright believed he had convinced the Yakima nation of the futility
of continuing the war.[43]

To the War Department Wright suggested that the country between the Cascade Mountains and the Columbia
River should be "given to the Indians; it is not necessary to
the white people." Wright was convinced throughout his
life that the only way to prevent total extinction of the Indians and secure their rights and property was to separate
them completely from the whites under protection of the
War Department. When the two races were in close contact
the Indians adopted the vices of the whites, fell victim to
their diseases, or were killed by them, he said. Stevens believed Wright's plan simply kept the Indians in a savage
state and delayed "civilizing" them and, most important, it
denied the settlers access to the Indians' land. Commenting on Stevens's plan to put the Indians on small reservations, Wright explained to headquarters that the Indians
could not live at one spot for the whole year unless the
government supplied them with subsistence.[44]

At the Ahtanum Mission, Chiefs Leschi, Nelson, and Kitsap and a small party of Nisquallies visited him. These were some of the "murderers" Stevens wanted delivered to him.[45] They told Wright they wished to return to their homes on the Coast but feared their reception by the civil authorities. Wright gave them notes assuring their safety from the military. Stevens, on the other hand, wanted them turned over for trial and urged Wright to make no arrangement which would "save their necks from the executioner."[46] Leschi returned to the Coast of his own free will, was betrayed into capture by his own nephew, tried, and hanged. While Leschi was on trial Wright asked that he be pardoned since the U.S. volunteers went unpunished for their savage deeds.[47] Another of the accused chiefs, Quiemuth, turned himself in and was brutally murdered in the governor's office.[48]

During July, Stevens concluded that Wright had little to show for his activities and ordered Lt. Col. Benjamin F. Shaw to lead a battalion of Washington volunteers into the Grande Ronde valley of northeastern Oregon. Wright told Shaw that he would get no help from the army and that the army needed none from him. On July 17, the Indians suffered a crushing defeat. Forty warriors were reported slain, and all of their provisions, ammunition, and more than 200 horses were captured. Three of Shaw's men were killed and four wounded. Wright reported that a number of the Indian casualties were old men, women, and children.[49] Richards also maintains that most of those killed were noncombatants and compares the action to subsequent, better-known massacres at Sand Creek (Colorado) and Washita (Indian Territory) and "deserving of an equal share of infamy."[50]

Capt. F. P. M. Goff and another detachment of Washington volunteers joined some Oregon volunteers in July and won the battle of Burnt River near present-day Baker, Oregon. Wright again complained that his peace-keeping efforts were thwarted by the actions of the volunteers.

Wright, following his orders to establish a post in the Yakima country, settled on a site between Simcoe and Toppenish creeks about forty miles southwest of the present city of Yakima. Major Garnett was placed in command, and Companies F and G of the Ninth Infantry were assigned the jobs of constructing the buildings and garrisoning them, while Capt. Frederick T. Dent with Company B was ordered to construct a wagon road to Fort Dalles, sixty-seven miles south. Wright reported that he had the situation in the Yakima country under control, and was commended by Wool. Kamiakin was far away and the Bolon murderers had fled.[51] Stevens scoffed that Wright had been duped by the wily Yakimas and that he had attained a quasi-peace without striking a blow or apprehending a murderer.

On August 2, General Wool announced that no whites except Hudson's Bay Company employees and missionaries were to be allowed to settle or remain in the Indian country east of the Cascades. Men on their way to the Colville mines could proceed but they were to be evicted and punished if they bothered the Indians or their squaws. On August 4, Steptoe was sent farther into the interior to establish Fort Walla Walla. Wright expressed the strongest faith in the friendship of the Klickitat chiefs and their people with whom he had met at the Ahtanum Mission site and said he could see no indication for any punitive measures.[52]

Captain Winder and his detail were moved to the lower blockhouse at the Cascades; Maj. Pinkney Lugenbeel was to send a detachment to the upper blockhouse; the middle blockhouse was abandoned as no longer necessary and because the people there "keep the soldiers drunk all the time."[53]

During August Wright returned to Fort Dalles and then went on to Fort Vancouver. Capt. Rodney Glisan, a medical officer, wrote of visiting Fort Vancouver where he saw Colonel Wright, "the chief in command of the United States troops now in Oregon and Washington." Wright informed Glisan that the hostile Indians of the eastern part of those territories had agreed to make peace and had asked for the protection of the troops. Old Kamiakin and other influential chiefs, however, had left their people and

Colonel Wright's quarters at Fort Dalles. The building was designed by Louis Scholl. Courtesy Oregon Historical Society, Salem, negative No. ORHI5350.

declined to come to terms. "The Colonel is busily engaged in erecting blockhouses and forts in the Indian country east of the Cascades," Glisan wrote.[54]

While Wright had been in the field, expansion of the post at The Dalles proceeded. The installation was expected to become the Fort Leavenworth of the Pacific Northwest and the supply depot for all the other posts in the area. Under Capt. Thomas Jordan, assistant quartermaster, a unique and attractive fort was built, replacing the previous decrepit log structures. The quartermaster department complained of the cost, and some visiting officers regarded the buildings as too elegant for a frontier post and castigated Jordan. Wright, as commanding officer, came in for most of the blame.[55]

Second Walla Walla Council

Governor Stevens was now planning a second Walla Walla council. Since many of the volunteer companies had been disbanded Stevens asked Wright for a company of regulars to guard his supply train. The request was referred to Wool, with foreseeable results: request denied. The governor and Wright traveled together from Fort Vancouver to Fort Dalles. Wright declined to accompany the governor to the council but assured him that Steptoe, who would be there with four companies to establish the new post, would cooperate with him as needed. Since Steptoe presumably would provide protection, Stevens countermanded the order for two more companies of volunteers and disbanded all those in the field except Goff's company. One company of the Fourth Infantry and two of the Ninth were left in the Kittitas valley under Haller and two of the Ninth with Garnett at Fort Simcoe.

On August 24, back at Fort Vancouver, Wright reported all was quiet in the Walla Walla country. At The Dalles, 1,500 Indians had surrendered their arms and horses and were being turned over to the Indian agent. Wright was also able to report the recovery, "unimpaired," of a howitzer Haller had abandoned on his retreat the previous year.

On September 1, Wool ordered Wright to meet with all the Indian tribes in the Walla Walla region. In view of Stevens's council and Steptoe's presence there Wright chose to delegate the responsibility to Steptoe. Wool had told commander-in-chief Scott he could foresee no further trouble with the Indians if the volunteers and settlers were kept out. About this time Wright informed Wool that as a result of "bad management" Stevens's packtrain had been captured by the Indians. Wright added, "In spite of all these little contretemps, I doubt not of the ultimate success of our arrangement for the pacification of all the Indian tribes." [56]

Stevens opened his council on September 11 and adjourned it on the seventeenth. Steptoe was encamped eight miles away. The Indians, always ready to exploit any discord among the white intruders, were quick to notice the antipathy between the military and the governor's forces, just as they had been able to see hostility among the missionaries during the previous decade. Many Indians boycotted the council and none of the main chiefs attended. As the council progressed, hostility increased and many of the Indians professed a readiness to fight rather than yield. On the third day of the council, Steptoe, appreciating the dangerous situation, invited Stevens and his party to move into his camp, an offer which they promptly accepted. Except for a few Nez Perces, the Indians at the council were intractable and nothing was accomplished. Steptoe had attempted to dissuade Stevens from holding the council as the Indians were still seething from the Grand Ronde slaughter.[57] When Stevens left for The Dalles with a few volunteers and Nez Perce auxiliaries, the Indians set fire to the grass around Steptoe's camp and attacked the governor's party before it had moved three miles.

Steptoe, now eager to join forces with the governor, sent a company of dragoons with a howitzer to escort him back. When this party returned, they found Steptoe under attack. The Indians were driven off and a blockhouse and stockade erected.[58] A company of regulars was left to guard the supplies and the two parties moved back to The Dalles together, arriving on October 2. Wool believed that the governor had called the council in order to force war on the Indians. At Wool's order Steptoe issued a proclamation similar to Wool's previous directive, closing off the interior.[59]

Wright reported nearly 4,000 Indians had attended the council: Nez Perces, Cayuses, Walla Wallas, and some Yakimas. The army was attempting to restore the Indians' confidence, which had been shaken by the volunteers, he said. As soon as regular troops were established in the country there would be a good understanding and a firm peace with the Indians. This important duty could not be more safely entrusted to anyone than the present commander at Walla Walla, Lieutenant Colonel Steptoe. When Wright received Steptoe's report of the recent fighting, he remarked that the governor should have waited until Fort Walla Walla was established before holding his council. Stevens blamed its failure on the lack of army cooperation, but the army claimed that his presence had embarrassed Steptoe and jeopardized his mission.

Because he sincerely believed there would be no cause for war if there were no treaties, Wright, like Wool, hoped that the Stevens treaties would not be confirmed. The management of the Indians should be assigned to the War Department, since the Indian Department could not control them without the aid of the military. Wright thought this would eliminate the confusion among the Indians caused by conflicting councils.[60]

Frances Fuller Victor, who in 1891 was directed by the Oregon legislature to record the history of the local Indian wars, wrote that in 1856 there was widespread discontent, jealousy, and hatred of the

> superior and encroaching civilization. That there was reason for much of the discontent in treaties compulsarily [sic] made, tardily ratified, and fraudulently executed, cannot be denied; nor that the fault was with the government rather than with the people. Every interest of the people . . . was in favor of peace; but the peace . . . many times, broken, the preservation of their lives and property forced upon them the alternative of war, even to extermination, the end of which was, . . . first conquest, and finally banishment for the inferior race. And all this, no matter where the responsibility rested, was in consonance with that law of nature which decrees the survival of the fittest.[61]

In 1857, however, J. Ross Browne, a special agent of the Treasury Department who was sent out to investigate the causes of the war, made a less arrogant and racist appraisal. In his report to the Commissioner of Indian Affairs, which the commissioner passed on to the Secretary of Interior and then to the Senate, Browne said that he did not think that the treaties were the cause of the war. Stevens had no more control over events than the Secretary

Fort Walla Walla, 1857. Sketch by Edward Del Gerardin.
Courtesy National Archives, Washington, D.C.

of War, in Browne's view. Leschi and Kamiakin had been
traveling the Oregon country rousing the Indians. The
chiefs had tried as early as 1853 to unite the tribes in a war
with the Americans. "The cause of this war is that the Americans are going to seize their lands," Browne wrote. Neither the commanding officer of the military nor the citizens could have prevented war, since its primary cause was
the "progress of civilization." There was no basis for the
charge that the wars were started in order to raid the federal treasury. The Donation Land Law, described earlier,
was a source of difficulty. It was unwise and impolitic, he
said, to encourage settlers to take land away from the
Indians.[62]

While Steptoe had been in the Walla Walla valley he had
selected a site for his new fort on Mill Creek, six miles from
its junction with the Walla Walla River, five miles from the

old Whitman Mission mill, and about thirty miles east of the abandoned Hudson's Bay Company's Fort Walla Walla on the east bank of the Columbia River. Wool took Wright to task for not having gone to the Walla Walla country earlier himself to talk with the Indians, rather than letting Stevens meet with them.[63]

When Steptoe, with one company each of the First Dragoons, Third Artillery, Fourth and Ninth Infantry, returned in October to erect the fort, Wright went with him with an additional company. The new post was completed by November 20, and Steptoe remained there in command. At Walla Walla Wright belatedly summoned a council of local chiefs with whom he reached an agreement to forget past differences, to "wash the bloody cloth," and to bury the hatchet.[64] Few chiefs attended, but Wright felt satisfied that peace would prevail and that the Indians had no objections to having a military post in their midst.[65] Wright at least helped placate the Indians who were so agitated by the Grande Ronde massacre and Stevens's council. He continued to urge nonconfirmation of Stevens's treaties. Although Wool had ordered Wright's meeting with the Indians, Stevens felt that Wright was usurping the governor's prerogatives.[66]

Family Developments

The Ninth Infantry's regimental adjutant at this time was a twenty-three-year-old Southerner named Philip Albert Owen. Born in Tennessee in 1833, Owen was appointed to the army from Alabama and commissioned a second lieutenant to serve in the Ninth Infantry when the regiment was organized in 1855.[67] He held the position of adjutant from July 1, 1856, to June 25, 1861. Of the many energetic and attractive young officers who served with Wright, many rose to high rank and fame during the Civil War.[68] However, it was to the blandishments of the dashing young Southerner that Wright's nineteen-year-old daughter Eliza succumbed. The *Weekly Oregonian* on September 20, 1856, contained a notice that "Lieutenant Owen, U.S.A., on

18 September, 1856, was married to Miss E. H. Wright, daughter of Colonel Wright, at Vancouver by Rev'd. J. L. Daly."[69] Years later, Col. Edwin J. Harvie reminisced, "Lt. Philip A. Owen, just above me on the list of second lieutenants, was married to the daughter of Colonel Wright . . . and I was complimented by an invitation to act as best man."[70] Capt. James J. Archer, who was serving at Fort Simcoe, went to Fort Vancouver to obtain some winter clothing for his company. He arrived there "Just two days late for Miss Lizzie Wright's wedding" but had the pleasure of dining with the bride and groom at the colonel's quarters.[71]

In August, 1857, Owen was promoted to first lieutenant, and toward the end of that year Eliza gave birth to their first child, a daughter whom they named Margaret F. Owen.[72] Later, two sons, Montgomery M. and Frank, were born to them.[73] Owen was promoted to captain in June, 1861. In September he relieved Capt. Philip Sheridan from command at Fort Yamhill, Oregon.[74] At the end of the Civil War he was in command at Fort Vancouver, but still a captain.[75]

Three days after his daughter's wedding, Wright presented the name of his younger son, John Montgomery Wright, to the War Department for consideration as a candidate for admission to the U.S. Military Academy.[76] Wright was anxious for at least one of his sons to follow in his footsteps in the military service. The following autumn he again applied on the boy's behalf for an appointment at West Point. Finally, in 1859, President Buchanan received an enthusiastic letter of support on behalf of John M. Wright's application, which accomplished what Colonel Wright's missives had been unable to do. This letter made some surprisingly complimentary remarks about Colonel Wright and his services to his country. It suggested "that such conduct should receive recognition. . . . We therefore urge the appointment of the son of this distinguished officer as a favor to each of us." The letter was signed by Isaac I. Stevens (former Washington governor and now delegate to Congress from Washington), Joseph Lane (delegate to Congress from Oregon), and two others.[77] One can only surmise that these former antagonists changed their views of George Wright once he was out from under Wool's thumb and especially after his successful campaign against the Indians in the Spokane country.

Little has been written about George Wright's personal appearance or characteristics. A photograph taken when he was in command of the Ninth Infantry shows a clean-shaven, well-nourished, not unpleasant-looking, middle-aged man. Gen. G. F. B. Dandy, who served under him as a second lieutenant in 1858, remembered him as a person

> of medium size, manly appearance and of rather handsome features. He was a fine looking soldier and a thorough gentleman. . . . [He] had a fine social side. When not engaged in the strict performance of duty, he was genial, whole-souled, kind and hospitable; full of wit and possessed a keen sense of humor. One could not be in his presence long without feeling charmed by his personality, his refinement, as well as a just and impartial commander.[78]

Another veteran of 1858, identified only as I. G. T., had this to say:

> In personal appearance Colonel Wright was not of lofty figure or martial form, but his face showed dignity and his presence was commanding. In his handsome countenance was written justice, a sign the soldier is quick to detect, and to which he will respond with obedience and valor. No worry, confusion or doubt was ever discernible in our commander, and everything went forward with alacrity and confidence. Promptness and strict attention to orders was exacted, but no ostentation enforced these requirements.[79]

General Clarke Replaces Wool

On the Coast, residents still feared the fierce Haidas and other tribes from Alaska and British Columbia, who periodically made raids down the Coast in their huge, fifty-man war canoes. During the summer of 1856, a large marauding band of these northern Indians was removed from the vicinity of Port Gamble, near the mouth of Hood

Canal, by the crew of the U.S.S. *Massachusetts* under Capt.
Samuel Swartwout. The Indians resisted this effort and in
the resulting fray a number were killed or wounded and
their canoes destroyed. In August, Fort Bellingham was
established for protection against these warriors and Capt.
George E. Pickett placed in command. Two months later
Major Haller and a company of the Fourth Infantry erected
a second fort for this purpose at Port Townsend on the
Olympic Peninsula. In spite of these precautions, the following year the Indians staged a gruesome reprisal for
the shooting of one of the northern Indian chiefs at Port
Gamble. "Colonel" Isaac N. Ebey, who had been U.S. Collector of Customs at Port Townsend, was decapitated at his
home on Whidbey Island by a party of vengeful Haidas.[80]

On the whole, however, 1857 was a comparatively quiet
year. James Buchanan was inaugurated as president and
John B. Floyd appointed Secretary of War. In the Northwest, upgrading of forts, blockhouses, and roads continued. In spite of the official censure by the legislature of
Washington Territory for his martial law actions, Stevens
was elected the territory's third delegate to Congress. James
Nesmith was appointed to replace Stevens as superintendent of Indian affairs for Washington, and Oregon as well.

While territorial governor, in his frustration with what
he regarded as the army's inactivity and lack of cooperation, Stevens sent frequent complaints about Wright to the
Secretary of War. When Stevens went to Congress, he was
regarded as the voice of authority on the Pacific Northwest. There can be no doubt that Stevens's criticism damaged Wright's reputation. Although Wright was simply
carrying out Wool's orders, he made some enemies in influential places at a time when he was already in disfavor
for the "lavish and pretentious" construction at Fort Dalles.

In March, partly at his own request, Maj. Gen. John
Wool was withdrawn and replaced by Brig. Gen. Newman S. Clarke as commander of the Pacific Department.
Initially Clarke continued the policies of his predecessor
and excluded whites from the interior. The 1,500 to 2,000
troops in the Columbia District were kept in garrison.

Their commander, Colonel Wright, maintained his head-quarters at Fort Dalles with a view to policing the interior and protecting the Indians. There was no war, only an un-stable peace, and the continuation of the "exclusion pol-icy" was attacked as a high-handed outrage at the next ses-sion of the Washington territorial legislature.[81]

Clarke did not visit the Columbia River District until June. However, it had gradually become apparent to him that in spite of the army's conciliatory policy, the Indians of the interior remained as hostile and menacing as ever.

Clarke said nothing at the time of his visit to Fort Dalles, but in subsequent reports he found fault with what he re-garded as the extravagant style of its buildings and issued an order that in the future any construction at nonperma-nent posts should be of the plainest character, serving only to protect the troops from undue exposure. He regarded the commandant's quarters as far too large and elaborate, even though Wright and his wife shared their home with the Owens and used part of it for office space. Clarke ordered that there be no further construction of any kind at Fort Dalles, which meant no replacement of the old log cabin serving as a hospital and no adequate water system for fire control, which later proved a serious problem. Clarke's order was subsequently reinforced by a War De-partment directive, although expenditures during the three previous years at Fort Dalles had been less than those at Forts Vancouver, Benicia, or San Francisco.[82]

In the spring of 1857, Kamiakin's brother, Skloom, un-expectedly returned what remained of some horses and cattle stolen by his warriors from Fort Simcoe a few months earlier. Along with the livestock, a herder named White had been seized by the Yakimas. He was released after two weeks in captivity, and had learned the details of the Bolon murder.[83] The whites had suspected Owhi's son, Qualchin, but in spite of his involvement in many attacks on whites and many killings, he had no connection with this one. The information White gave the army ultimately led to the apprehension of the guilty. The instigator of the crime was Mosheel, a son of Bolon's friend Ice and a nephew of Kamiakin. One of the Indians involved later shot himself, and at the end of the 1858 campaign, the other three were captured. Mosheel was shot and killed attempting to escape and the remaining two were hanged from an oak tree near the Fort Simcoe parade ground.[84]

During the winter and early spring of 1857, Capt. Dickinson Woodruff commanded Fort Simcoe while Garnett was granted leave to go East to be married. In January Chiefs Owhi and Qualchin and a son of Teias came in to parley. Woodruff was not convinced of their sincerity and was particularly upset by the "sauciness" of Qualchin.[85] Still, as the year went on the signs seemed propitious for peace. Kamiakin had not been heard from and none of the Indians seemed disposed to renew the war. In May Garnett returned to Fort Simcoe with his new bride. Later in the month Woodruff and Company F left Simcoe to serve as an escort to the American Northwest Boundary Commission surveying the boundary line between the United States and the British possessions to the north.[86]

10.

The Indian War of 1858

With the advent of the year 1858 the peace Colonel Wright thought he had established with the Indians east of the Cascade Range was becoming ever more precarious. After his visit to the area the preceding summer, General Clarke had taken over the command of the Northern District of the Department of the Pacific, leaving Wright in charge of Fort Dalles. Ultimately, however, it was Wright who was destined to play the leading role in one of the most tense periods of Indian-white conflict in Washington Territory. The activity is sometimes considered an extension of the Yakima War, but it was chiefly a campaign against the formerly friendly Spokane and Coeur d'Alene Indians and the Palouse Indians. The struggle had its immediate origin in a disastrous and poorly planned reconnaissance mission from Fort Walla Walla, under the command of Wright's subordinate in the Ninth Infantry, Maj. Edward J. Steptoe.

As the easternmost post in the interior, Fort Walla Walla did not have a prepossessing appearance. It consisted of a huddle of log barracks and other structures around a central parade ground with its symbolic flagpole, scattered tents, and ramshackle outbuildings. Lacking a stockade or bastions, it hardly seemed defensible. But then, of the neighboring tribes, only the Palouse Indians were considered hostile. The Nez Percés and the Walla Wallas were thought to be friendly. The garrison consisted of a few companies of the Ninth Infantry, the Fourth Infantry, and the Third Artillery. Most of the dragoons had been sent for the winter to Fort Vancouver, where better forage was available for their horses. In command was Maj. Bvt. Lt. Col., Edward J. Steptoe—a proud Virginian, graduate of West Point, and veteran of the Seminole and Mexican

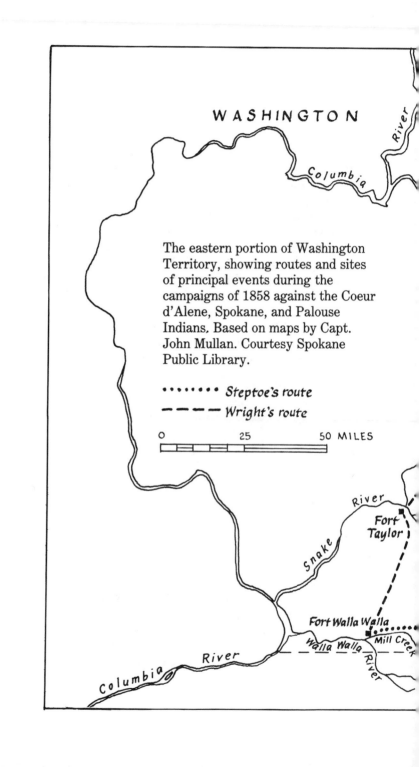

WASHINGTON

Columbia River

The eastern portion of Washington Territory, showing routes and sites of principal events during the campaigns of 1858 against the Coeur d'Alene, Spokane, and Palouse Indians. Based on maps by Capt. John Mullan. Courtesy Spokane Public Library.

•••••••• *Steptoe's route*

– – – – *Wright's route*

O   25   50 MILES

River

Fort Taylor

Snake

Fort Walla Walla

Mill Creek

Walla Walla River

Columbia River

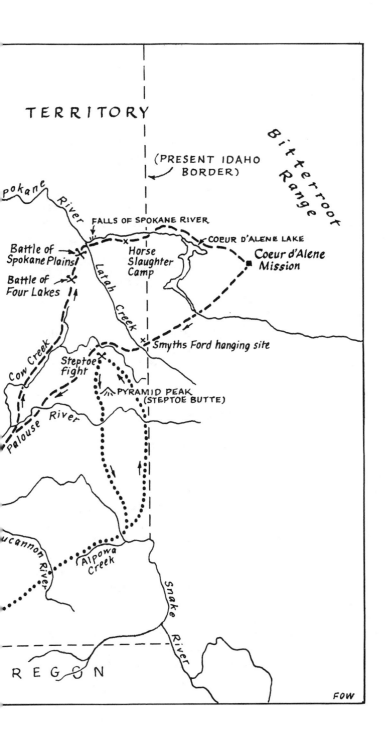

TERRITORY

(PRESENT IDAHO
BORDER)

Bitterroot Range

Pokane River

FALLS OF SPOKANE RIVER

COEUR D'ALENE LAKE

Battle of
Spokane Plains

Horse
Slaughter
Camp

Coeur d'Alene
Mission

Battle of
Four Lakes

Latah Creek

Cow Creek

Smyths Ford hanging site

Steptoe
Fight

PYRAMID PEAK
(STEPTOE BUTTE)

Palouse River

ucannon River

Alpowa Creek

Snake River

REGON

FOW

wars. During the Mexican War he had received two brevets for gallantry.

Late in 1854, Steptoe had been sent west from Fort
Leavenworth with two companies of the Third Artillery
and eighty-five dragoon recruits. They had wintered at
Salt Lake, where Brigham Young was serving as governor
of Utah Territory, and trouble with the Mormons was
brewing. While he was there, Steptoe was offered the gov-
ernorship of Utah Territory by his friend President Pierce.
Although the appointment received the consent of the
Senate, Steptoe declined and continued his military career. He was subsequently appointed major in the Ninth
Infantry, reported to his new commander, Colonel Wright,
and proceeded to Fort Vancouver at the end of 1855.

The following year, while traveling between Vancouver
and Fort Walla Walla, Steptoe, although only forty-one
years old, developed signs of transient right-sided palsy.
This ailment temporarily disabled him to the extent that
he needed help to mount his horse or get into a carriage.[1]
Although he seemed to make a complete recovery, evidence of a mild stroke was an ominous event in the life of a
man who was soon to assume great responsibilities.

The Steptoe Disaster

The "peace" in the interior became increasingly uneasy.
General Clarke had reported the Indians' concern about
whether the Bolon murderers would be punished or
whether there would be retaliation against their tribes if
they were not apprehended. The matter was still under
consideration in Washington, D.C. The Indians asked
Clarke about the stipulations and promises of the Stevens
treaties, which were still unconfirmed. Clarke and Nesmith opposed the treaties, saying that they could be enforced only by war. On the other hand Special Agent J.
Ross Browne was telling the Indians that confirmation was
definitely forthcoming.[2] Meanwhile, Kamiakin, Tilcoax,
Qualchin, and some of the other chiefs were doing everything they could to arouse the tribes.

The Indians, who had seen some surveying parties in the field, were certain that the government planned to seize their lands. In fact, Congress had authorized the construction of a military road to connect the upper limit of navigation on the Missouri River at Fort Benton with old Fort Walla Walla, the Hudson's Bay Company post on the Columbia. First Lieutenant John Mullan of the Second Artillery, who had gone west as a member of Governor Stevens's party in 1853, directed the surveys.[3] Work on a road between The Dalles and Fort Walla Walla had already been started.[4]

The whites were unhappy as well. In March the Washington territorial legislature sent a resolution to the secretary of war protesting the military's exclusion and removal of settlers from the Walla Walla Valley. Referring to this action as "the worst form of military law, proclaimed by tyrants," the members requested the governor and territorial delegate to make available to the proper officials in Washington, D.C., information pertaining to the conflict between the army and the civil authorities.[5] Furthermore, rumors circulated that the Mormons were supplying the Indians with arms and ammunition and inciting them to hostility.[6] The residents of Washington Territory feared that the troubles in Utah, where the Mormons were resisting the federal government and turning away its designated territorial appointees, might spill over onto the northwest frontier.[7]

Early in January, 1858, Steptoe was ordered to put his command in a state of field efficiency. The dragoons and their horses were to be recalled as soon as the condition of the roads and the availability of forage permitted.[8] Steptoe had planned to send three companies of dragoons toward the Hudson's Bay Company's Fort Boise to investigate Mormon activity among the Snake Indians,[9] but in April he informed departmental headquarters that, since there was much "excitement" among the Spokane and Palouse Indians, he would send an expedition to their country first. He intended to investigate reports of a murder by the Palouse Indians of two whites on their way to the mines in the vicinity of Fort Colvile and to visit the nearby settlement, Colville, where forty of the residents had drawn up a petition requesting the presence of troops. The Palouse Indians also had raided the Walla Walla Valley and stolen horses and cattle, including thirteen government head.[10]

On May 2, Steptoe reported that he planned to depart later in the week. "It is proper for me to say," said Steptoe, "that there appears to be some probability of considerable disturbance among the neighboring tribes, but I hope to check it."[11] Meanwhile, Wright was modernizing, enlarging, and strengthening Fort Dalles and asking the War Department for 150 more recruits to fill out his regiment.[12]

On May 6, Steptoe set out on his expedition. His command consisted of Companies C, E, and H of the First Dragoons under Bvt. Capt. Oliver H. P. Taylor, Lt. William Gaston, and Lt. David M. Gregg, respectively, and twenty-five men from Company E of the Ninth Infantry, mounted, commanded by Capt. Charles S. Winder. Lieutenant James Wheeler, Jr., was attached to Taylor's company, Lt. H. B. Fleming was the acting quartermaster, and John Randolph was assistant surgeon.[13] Packmaster Thomas J. Beall led a packtrain of assorted civilian packers and herders, eighty-five mules, and some cattle. A half-blood Indian accompanied the troops as a scout. The total number of soldiers including officers was 158.[14]

Three of the combat officers were in impaired physical condition. Steptoe had experienced a mild stroke, Winder had just returned from a two-year leave because of illness, and Gaston was hoping that he would fall in battle rather than succumb to a cancerous growth in his neck.[15] Remaining to guard Fort Walla Walla were half of Company E, all of Company B of the Ninth Infantry, a few artillerymen, and one company of the First Dragoons under Capt. Frederick T. Dent. Major William Grier was left in overall command.

The men of the expedition were poorly armed. Most of the dragoons carried musketoons which, according to one authority, "couldn't kill a rooster across the barnyard."[16] A few of the dragoons had Sharps breechloading carbines, and some had pistols, but their sabers had been left behind. The mounted infantry and the remaining dragoons carried Mississippi Jaeger rifles, which were too long for loading on horseback. Worst of all, there were only three muleloads of ammunition in the packtrain, amounting to about forty rounds per man. Officers and sergeants carried swords. Two small mountain howitzers completed the armament. Nobody really expected a fight—a few arrests and perhaps a light skirmish or two—but mainly, they believed, this was to be a training exercise for Steptoe's new recruits, a fact-finding expedition, and a pleasant spring excursion to impress the Indians and allay the fears of the whites.

When the column reached the Snake River at the mouth of Alpowa Creek near what is now the Idaho-Washington border, their guide refused to go farther, fearing a battle. Nez Percé Chief Timothy and some of his warriors ferried the troops across the Snake and then took over as guides. By this time the command was far east of the usual road to Fort Colvile and on its way north from the river it passed east of Pyramid Peak, now known as Steptoe Butte. After an uneventful advance northward, on Sunday morning, May 16, the command crossed Pine Creek just southeast of the present town of Rosalia. Suddenly Steptoe found himself confronted by 800 to 1,000 "armed, painted and defiant" Spokanes, Palouses, Coeur d'Alenes, Yakimas, and others. Most of them carried Hudson's Bay trade guns, which had a longer range than most of the arms of Steptoe's men; others had bows and arrows and lances. Even the arrows carried farther than many of the army's guns and could inflict wounds more deadly than bullets.

Steptoe narrowly avoided a trap that had been set for him in a nearby ravine and encamped a little farther away. "The whole, wild, frenzied mass [was] moving parallel to us, and by yells, taunts, and menaces, apparently trying to drive us into some initiatory act of violence,"[17] he recounted. At nightfall some of the chiefs rode up and asked the reason for this intrusion by the soldiers. Steptoe said that he was simply on his way to Colville, where he hoped to restore good feeling between the whites and Indians. When he expressed surprise at the hostile attitude of Indians he had thought were friends, the Indians pointed out that he was in Spokane and Coeur d'Alene country, far east of the Colville road, and that the howitzers did not look friendly.

Steptoe certainly knew the importance of not antagonizing these tribes and thereby forcing them into joining up with the Yakimas. Both Father Anthony Ravalli and Angus McDonald, then chief trader at the Hudson's Bay Company's post Fort Colvile, had advised two years earlier against sending troops into Spokane country.[18] There is some reason to believe that his guides brought him this way for reasons of their own.[19] When the hostile chiefs told him that they would not let him have canoes for crossing the Spokane River, he decided to return to Fort Walla Walla.

Earlier, near the Palouse River, Steptoe had been able to send a message to Major Grier requesting a detachment to protect the Snake River crossing. Now he sent a second message describing his dilemma, but it was never delivered. The bearer, an Indian named Wie-cat, assumed that Steptoe's command would be wiped out and tried to rouse the local Indians at Walla Walla to assault the now pitifully defended post.[20] Meanwhile, a few of the chiefs, eager to avoid a battle, had sent word to Father Joseph Joset, S.J., who hurried down from the Coeur d'Alene Mission.[21] Arriving on Sunday evening, he was unable to quiet the Indians who were skeptical of Steptoe's protestations of peaceful intent. The soldiers slept little that night, with fires burning and Indians drumming, dancing, and shouting in the surrounding camps.

Before dawn the next morning the troops began their "retrograde movement" toward Fort Walla Walla. Father Joset attempted to arrange a conference with Steptoe; though he felt it would be dangerous to halt, he agreed to meet with the chiefs while he was on the move. Only a few appeared, and, except for some pushing and slapping between the prowar and antiwar Indians, nothing was accomplished. About 8:00 A.M., before the column had moved three miles, the Indians began their attack. Taylor and Gaston, with their companies, were assigned the difficult and dangerous task of protecting the flanks, "to both of whom it proved fatal."

First Sergeant William C. Williams tried to fill Gaston's place but fell mortally wounded. Casualties mounted, ammunition ran low, and the soldiers began using their guns as clubs. The ferocity of the Indian attacks increased after some of their chiefs were killed, and more Indians joined the fray. About noon part of the packtrain and some of the cattle were run off. After six hours of steady fighting, further retreat seemed too hazardous, and Steptoe occupied a hilltop just south of Rosalia. He arranged his men in a circle around the supplies and remaining animals. His dragoons were not performing well as skirmishers, and the howitzers were ineffectively handled.

After several vigorous attacks on the new position the Indians resorted to crawling toward the hilltop through the tall grass. The soldiers were hot, thirsty, and scared. They were soon down to four rounds of ammunition per man, and the bangs of musketry, whistling of arrows, groans of the wounded, and yells of the enemy were demoralizing to them. As the day wore on, two of their officers and three enlisted men were killed, and fifteen wounded, two of them mortally. Interpreter Connor was the only civilian fatality, but two Nez Percé scouts were killed in the action, and a Nez Percé youth, the son of one of the expressmen, who had gone after some loose horses, was run through by a sergeant's sword when he was mistaken for a hostile Indian.[22] The Indians are known to have had nine killed and forty or fifty wounded, although Gregg later said that he counted fifteen dead.[23]

At sundown the Indians, as was their custom, broke off fighting for the night, in spite of Kamiakin's efforts to organize a charge to annihilate the soldiers. Among the soldiers there was not a man who did not expect death in the morning. The end of Steptoe's command would also mean the end of Fort Walla Walla with its minuscule remaining garrison, for there was no help anywhere near. Steptoe was prepared for a last-ditch stand, but his officers persuaded him that an attempt to escape was preferable to certain death.

Exactly how the escape was accomplished is uncertain. The credit is usually given to Timothy, a Spalding Mission convert, for finding a gap in the ranks of the surrounding Indians. Brown says that Steptoe's Nez Percés made a deal with the Coeur d'Alenes, offering them first access to the booty if they allowed the soldiers to escape.[24] Bond suggests that Father Joset arranged matters.[25] Or it may simply be that a reconnaissance party discovered the gap.

In any event the howitzers and any bodies that could be retrieved were buried. Everything that might impede progress was abandoned. Fires were kept burning, and wounded and unneeded animals were picketed; packs, supplies, and provisions were left behind to deceive the enemy. Light horses were blanketed, their hoofs muffled, the severely wounded lashed to their saddles. About 10:00 P.M. the column began a cautious descent from the hilltop, forded Pine Creek, and took off southward at a full gallop. Miraculously, they got away. When the Indians rushed the camp sometime after midnight, they found the soldiers gone but then became too preoccupied dividing the fabulous spoils to mount an effective pursuit.

On the trail the pace of the column was too much for the two mortally wounded men, Sergeant Williams, who had commanded the rear guard during the fighting march, and Pvt. Victor DeMoy, a former captain in the French army. During the hand-to-hand conflict while using his gun as a club, DeMoy had cried, "My God for a saber!" The two had to be left along the way. DeMoy is said to have used his revolver to shoot and wound two Indians who found him and then to shoot himself, while Williams is said to have been cared for by an aged Indian woman during his last hours.[26]

By dawn the fleeing soldiers had reached the Palouse River, and at ten o'clock that night they reached the Snake, a distance of seventy miles in twenty-four hours. There they rested and were fed by friendly Nez Percés, who ferried them across the river the next morning. On their way south they had passed west of Steptoe Butte, a site often mistakenly referred to as the scene of "Steptoe's Last Stand." When they crossed the Snake River, they were met by Captain Dent and sixty-six men, who brought food for the weary troops and their steeds. There could be no thought of returning for further combat, although Chief Lawyer urged them to do so when they encountered him and a large band of Nez Percés on the evening of May 20.

Two days later the beaten and disheartened little army arrived at Fort Walla Walla. Their escape was a disappointment to the hostiles, but the defeat represented a terrible setback for the U.S. Army. In his subsequent report Steptoe paid tribute to his officers, his men, and his surgeon. Listed as missing was one man, 1st Sgt. Edward Ball, Company H, First Dragoons.[27] Ball was a member of a small party that had been left behind when the rest left the hilltop. These men were to help round up the skirmishers, keep the fires going, and maintain signs of activity until everyone else was under way. Among his duties Sergeant Ball was responsible for disposing of the surgeon's medicinal alcohol, and it is supposed that his faithful performance of this task is what led to his awakening in a clump of bushes the next morning and finding everyone gone. Making his way alone on foot, he reached Fort Walla Walla six days later.[28] As far as is known, he was never reprimanded, probably in view of his heroic conduct during the fighting and his subsequent hardships.

The army appreciated Father Joset's peace-keeping efforts. In a complete account of the Steptoe affair to his superior, Father Congiato, Joset wrote: "What breaks my heart is to see Colonel Steptoe, the zealous protector of Indians, exposed to the blame which ordinarily attaches itself to bad success; however, in the eyes of reflecting men, who know his situation, his retreat will do him infinite honor."[29] General-in-Chief Winfield Scott, in his endorsement of Steptoe's report, was less charitable: "This is a candid report of a disastrous affair. The small supply of ammunition is surprising and unaccounted for."[30] Packmaster Beall later admitted to leaving two cases of ammunition behind for lack of transport, but the responsibility was still Steptoe's.

On his return to Fort Walla Walla, Steptoe found an order directing him to furnish Lieutenant Mullan with an escort of one officer and sixty-five soldiers. He responded that Mullan's survey would be impossible at this time and that Father Joset had told him that if Mullan had started his project before Steptoe's expedition he and his party would have been massacred by the Indians.[31] On May 30, Mullan returned to Fort Dalles and disbanded his party.

Word of the disaster reached Walla Walla on May 20, The Dalles on the twenty-second, and Vancouver on the twenty-fourth. No details were available until Steptoe's report of the twenty-third went through channels. Army headquarters in New York did not receive the news until July.[32]

When Wright received the news, he informed headquarters of the Department of the Pacific that "all the Indians in that section of the country have combined for a general war." A large body of troops, about 1,000 men, would be necessary to bring them under subjugation and to punish them for this attack on Steptoe. He hoped that the troops could be gathered without reducing the small posts east of the Cascades.

As if transport and communication were not sufficiently serious problems, the only steamboat on the upper Columbia had recently been lost in the Cascade Rapids, "a serious detriment to us as well as the owners." Wright predicted a protracted war which should be prosecuted "systematically, with an ample supply of the *personnel* and *material,* to guard against a possibility of failure." He regarded the proposed opening of a road through Indian country as the primary cause of the attack on Steptoe and stated that there was no chance of any construction this year.[33]

There was little question that stronger measures would be required. The "Steptoe Disaster," as it came to be called, was the second defeat of regulars in two and a half years. The army represented the power of the United States. Its misfortune was not like the defeat of a party of volunteers; aside from its duty to protect citizens, the army's prestige was at stake. Moreover, quick action was needed to prevent a general northwest Indian war, and the Indians would have to be beaten before the road survey could proceed. Steptoe thought 300 or 400 men and three companies of dragoons could defeat the confederated tribes, consisting of "about half of the Spokanes, Coeur d'Alenes, and probably of the Flatheads, nearly all of the Palouses, a portion of the Yakimas and I think a small number of Nez Perces."[34]

Steptoe believed that the tribes were getting their ammunition from the British traders at Fort Colvile or from the Mormons, not from the priests, as some were suggesting, although any suspicions that might have attached to Father Joset were dispelled when the contents of his letter to Father Congiato were made generally known. Steptoe thought it unfortunate that a force could not move immediately while the Indians were still out gathering roots in preparation for the winter. As a first step in any campaign he suggested a temporary post on the Snake River to secure a crossing near the mouth of the Palouse. "Our defeat encourages the wavering to active hostilities," he said. All the tribes were watching to see what they might gain by joining the hostiles.[35]

After word of the Steptoe Disaster reached Stevens in Washington, D.C., he reported that the event had created a great sensation there. "The sentiment of condemnation of the temporizing measures of the military is universal and overwhelming," he said. "The officers whose councils here lead [sic] to it, have pretty much lost all reputation they ever had." Surely the delegate meant to include Wool and Wright in this appraisal.[36]

The Campaigns of Wright and Garnett

On June 2, General Clarke informed army headquarters that he was leaving for Washington Territory to assume personal charge of matters in that troubled area.[37] He urged that a delegation of chiefs be invited to the nation's capital to impress them with the number and power of the whites. All the troops that could be spared from California and Oregon were ordered to follow him north, and supplies and equipment were rushed to the region.

Following General Scott's instructions, General Albert S. Johnston at Salt Lake City dispatched the Sixth Infantry overland to San Francisco. From there they were to proceed by ocean and river to Walla Walla, but by the time they reached the coast, the campaign was over.

General William S. Harney was stopped on his march to the Mormon War in Utah and ordered to return to New York, from which he would embark for Fort Vancouver by way of Panama to take full command of the Northwest Indian War. He had set out from Fort Leavenworth in May and planned to reinforce General Johnston with 3,000 men. It is usually said that he was given the Northwest assignment because of his prowess as an Indian fighter, but his biographer suggests that he was recalled because the authorities regarded some of the measures he had in mind for permanently settling the Mormon problem as too vigorous. Indeed, he had planned to capture Brigham Young and the twelve Mormon apostles, hang them, and then spend the winter in the temple of the Latter-Day Saints.[38]

Clarke arrived at Fort Vancouver on June 23 and summoned Wright, Steptoe, and Garnett for consultation. Interested in getting any help he could from the missionaries, Clarke asked Father Joset to inform the Indians of the conditions under which they could have peace. These were: (1) recognizing the right of troops to move about their country; (2) acknowledging the right of the United States to construct a road to the Missouri River on which troops and travelers could move unmolested; and (3) admitting their crimes, restoring plundered government property, driving hostile Indians from their lands, and giving up the warriors who had fired on Steptoe against the orders of the chiefs. "They must suffer for their disobedience, and atone for their guilt," the general said. Troops sent into their country would do them no harm if they did as he demanded; if not, they would be punished severely.[39]

On July 4, Clarke placed Wright in command of the troops north and east of Fort Walla Walla. He was to move to the fort and assume command there of four companies of the First Dragoons, two companies of the Ninth Infantry, and six companies of the Third Artillery. In addition he was ordered to move out with no fewer than 600 men early in August, leaving Steptoe and an adequate garrison behind. His objectives would be to punish and obtain the submission of the Indians engaged in the attack on Steptoe; further, he was to obtain the surrender of the Palouses who had murdered the two miners in April. The conditions that Clarke had laid down in his letter to Joset were to be his guide in fixing the terms for receiving the submission of the Coeur d'Alene and Spokane Indians. The delivery of the Indians who fired on the troops and the recovery of the two howitzers "must be conditions precedent to any accommodation; these conditions complied with, you are authorized to make such reduction in the lesser demands, as may seem to you proper, on the spot."

Clarke also enclosed the terms of a treaty that he wanted Steptoe to make with the friendly Nez Percés and, if possible, with the Coeur d'Alenes and the Spokanes after their submission. In any event, hostages were to be taken from the Coeur d'Alenes and the Spokanes to ensure future good conduct. If the offenders from these two tribes were given up, they were to be guarded securely until further orders from Clarke, or Wright could turn them over to the commander at Fort Walla Walla on his return. If the terms were not accepted, Wright was to make vigorous war on the Coeur d'Alenes, the Spokanes, the Palouses, and any hostile Nez Percés. Clarke said, "You will attack all the hostile Indians you may meet, with vigor; make their punishment severe, and persevere until the submission of all is complete." If possible he was to visit the Colville settlement. Wright was authorized to employ friendly Nez Percés if he wished, supplying them with arms, ammunition, and old army uniforms. He was denied permission to declare martial law and instructed not to interfere with Hudson's Bay Company employees or U.S. citizens who presented no danger.[40]

Two weeks later Garnett was ordered to take the field with two companies of the Fourth Infantry and any of his own troops he could spare. He was to punish the Indians who attacked the party of miners in the Yakima country in June and secure the lives and property of the whites in that region. If individual offenders did not surrender, the whole tribe was to be driven to submission by severe punishment, and hostages were to be taken: "The interest of the government and the safety of the Indians equally require that the Indians be established and maintained in a state of pupilage." There was to be no more temporary neutrality. Kamiakin and Qualchin were to be surrendered or driven away; any tribe giving them asylum was to be considered hostile. Garnett was given a copy of the same model treaty as Wright. It stipulated that the tribes agreed to perpetual peace with the United States, that they would aid the United States against all enemies, that they would receive help from the United States against their own enemies, and that the two parties agreed to treat at all times for their mutual benefit.[41]

At Steptoe's suggestion, Wright made the treaty with the Nez Percés lest the Indians think that the two officers entertained different sentiments. Clarke approved the treaty, although he thought it "more amplified and especial" than he wanted. Wright had specified that when the Nez Percés helped the United States the government would furnish them "arms, ammunition, provisions, &c.," as was to be done in the present campaign, but when the United States helped the Indians, they would not be required to furnish anything to the troops unless they were repaid for it. Any misunderstanding between the troops and the Nez Percés was to be settled by their respective chiefs in council.[42]

A number of the officers felt that Clarke's treatment of Steptoe did not give him "opportunity to retrieve his fortunes" with some sort of active role in the campaign.[43] Sadly, Steptoe was not only a ruined man but a sick one. Early in 1859, he departed for the East on sick leave. He was well enough in 1860 to marry at his home in Virginia, but the following year he was paralyzed by a severe stroke. In the fall of 1861 he received a promotion to lieutenant colonel in the Tenth Infantry but two months later he resigned from the army because of failing health. In 1865, at the age of forty-nine, Steptoe died.

In August, 1858, word reached General Clarke that George Blenkinsop, the Hudson's Bay Company trader at Fort Colvile, was buying captured or stolen army horses and mules from the Indians and supplying arms and ammunition to tribes with whom the United States was at war. Clarke sent a vigorous letter of protest to James A. Grahame, chief trader at Fort Vancouver, demanding that these practices be stopped.[44] Grahame promptly issued cease-and-desist instructions to Blenkinsop and told him to return any unlawfully obtained animals or property. Realizing that this policy might jeopardize the lives of his employees and endanger the company's property, Grahame said that he would hold the United States responsible for any damages sustained. He also protested the demolition of one of the company's buildings at Fort Vancouver by order of the army quartermaster.[45] This incident marked the beginning of a serious deterioration in relations between the army and the Hudson's Bay Company.

Father Congiato wrote to Clarke from the Coeur d'Alene Mission telling him that Kamiakin had stirred the Indians into a great state of excitement and eagerness for another encounter with the troops. Chief Vincent was in disrepute for having made peace proposals to Steptoe without consulting the relatives of those killed in the battle, with whom, by tradition, the decision for war or peace belonged. The Indians objected to Clarke's conditions for peace, especially to surrendering the attackers of Steptoe and returning the booty. Father Congiato enclosed letters from Chiefs Polatkin, Melkapsi, and Garry, all saying that they would not surrender their "neighbors" or their land. Indians, they said, made peace by forgiving each other and giving presents.

Garry's letter was the most conciliatory. He said, "Withdraw this one word [surrendering the attackers] and sure you will make peace." The Indians knew only too well the fate in store for any "attackers." To them, death in battle was far preferable to death by hanging.

Congiato assured Clarke that the missionaries would do everything in their power "in order to open the eyes of those poor savages and prevent them from going to war." [46] The Jesuits traveled far and wide, working unceasingly for peace. Numerous military dispatches of the time express appreciation for their efforts.

Wright spent most of July assembling, organizing, and training his enlarging command and accumulating supplies at Fort Walla Walla. Clarke ultimately brought 2,200 soldiers to the Pacific Northwest, one-sixth of the active field force of the U.S. Army. Although Governor Stevens had said that only cavalry could cope with mounted Indians, most of the troops were foot soldiers. Arms, ammunition, horses, mules, and flour came by boat from San Francisco. Pork came from as far away as New York.

At Fort Walla Walla the troops engaged in parades and guard mounts, but mostly they were drilled in light infantry and skirmishing tactics, learning the use of their new weapons. One of Wright's young officers, Lt. Lawrence Kip, mentioned that the drilling was unlike the pro forma peacetime drilling. "Now it is invested with a reality, since all are conscious that our success in the field depends perhaps upon the state of discipline." [47]

Wright's second in command, Capt. Erasmus D. Keyes of the Third Artillery, later an aide to General Scott and a major general, had this to say about his commander:

> I had never before served under the orders of Colonel Wright, but from a slight personal acquaintance with him and many favorable reports I had conceived great respect for his military capacity. I was glad, therefore, to be his lieutenant, and to

receive from him the command of a battalion of six companies of artillery serving as infantry.

Later he wrote:

> My position of second in command was one the difficulties of which have always been recognized by military men. The chief sometimes dislikes or envies his junior, and the latter fancies or discovers faults that he, if in command, would have avoided. From the commencement to the end of the campaign my relations with Colonel Wright were confidential and cordial, and if I were to give expression to my admiration and respect for that gallant soldier and gentleman, I fear my style would appear more flowery than the rules of rhetoric prescribe for a narration of facts. The discipline he enforced was extremely rigid and severe. . . . Nothing in his conduct indicated that an acknowledgement of my deserts would dwarf his fame, and his order after the battle of Spokan [sic] plains was profuse in the praise of the conduct of others, while it was silent in regard to his own.[48]

Lieutenant, later General, George B. Dandy, four times breveted for gallantry in the Civil War, considered Wright the best commanding officer under whom he had ever served.[49]

On August 4 a large delegation of Nez Percés under Chief Lawyer met with Wright at Fort Walla Walla. After the prescribed treaty was signed, thirty Nez Percé volunteers were selected as guides and scouts under the command of Lieutenant Mullan, who had been given permission to join the expedition after his road survey was deferred.

"A Fine Body of Troops, Well-Trained, Well-Armed"

On August 7, Captain Keyes moved out with the first detachment of the command to select and fortify a point for the crossing of the Snake River.[50] He had with him the artillery battalion serving as infantry, one company of dragoons, and two twelve-pound howitzers and two six-pounders. The supply train moved with him to the Snake

and then returned to Fort Walla Walla for reloading, escorted by the dragoon company. The supply train brought
30,000 rations in wagons and on mules. The march north
over the rolling prairie was hot and dusty. As the troops
came closer to the river, they found that much of the coun-
tryside had been burned over by the enemy. Clarke had
anticipated that Wright's greatest difficulty might be the
evasive tactics of the hostiles and their grass burning,
which might "seriously embarrass the operations of the
troops."[51]

On the eighth it was found that the Indians had driven
off thirty-six oxen from Fort Walla Walla, and a party of
dragoons under Lt. H. B. Davidson was sent in pursuit.
The next day small parties of Indians were seen hovering
about the column, and one Walla Walla was taken prisoner
but later released. After another day's march over the des-
olated country, the column encamped where the Tucannon River empties into the Snake. The troops constructed
a road from the bluffs adjoining the Snake River to the
river's edge. Keyes and Mullan set out to select a site for
the temporary fort to guard the crossing.

Meanwhile, the sentries exchanged shots with some Indians across the Snake. Two who had crossed over were
captured but immediately broke free and leaped into the
Snake River. Lieutenant Mullan, who was not a large man,
jumped into the water and tried to recapture one far big-
ger than he. When the Indian began to hurl rocks at him,
Mullan attempted to fire his pistol, but it was too wet to discharge. The ensuing hand-to-hand struggle ended when
the combatants stepped into a hole in the river bottom.
Mullan lost his grip and the Indian swam away.[52]

The command remained until August 27 building a post,
which they named Fort Taylor in honor of one of the officers killed in the Steptoe battle. Meanwhile, they awaited
supplies and reinforcements. The fort, in which the two
six-pounders were mounted, was built of basalt rock with
bastions of alder at the diagonal corners. Construction was
directed by Bvt. Maj. F. O. Wyse, who, with Company D of
the Third Artillery, was to garrison the post and protect

the crossing as well as the boats and supplies left there. The high basalt cliffs bounding the mouth of the Tucannon were named after Taylor and Gaston.

At the site of Fort Taylor the Snake River was 275 yards wide with a deep, swift current. Captain R. W. Kirkham, the expedition quartermaster, had a large flatboat built and, with some boats brought from Walla Walla, established a ferry. Wright reached the Snake River camp with the rest of the command on August 18, and the next day the packtrain returned with the remaining supplies. Although much of the land had been burned, the army was fortunate in having good grass for forage around Fort Taylor.

Reports came in that the Indians were present in force five days' march away on the Palouse River and were ready to fight. Day and night extensive fires burned in the north, and Wright worried that the Indians might content themselves with laying waste the land in his advance. After viewing the desolate landscape, he wrote Clarke: "It will be mortifying, after all our preparation, to fail in the objects of the expedition. . . . We have a lake of fire before us, but no human effort will be spared to overcome all obstacles."[53] A few days earlier he had begun to report his misgivings:

> I have a body of troops, both officers and men, in the highest order, and on whom I feel that I can rely with perfect confidence; yet, with all these circumstances in my favor, I am greatly apprehensive that the results of the campaign may fall short of what is expected by the general and the country. From all that I can learn, we must not expect the enemy to meet us in pitched battle; although haughty, insolent, and boastful now, when I approach he will resort to guerilla warfare, he will lay waste the country with fire, and endeavor by every means in his power to embarrass and cripple our operations.

People familiar with the country had told Wright that the Indians would probably let him advance to the Spokane River and then fire any unburned country behind him. Still, he said, he would try to chastise them severely: "Should they burn the grass in my rear, we can live on our animals, and if they die, we can take our provisions on our backs and march. I have no doubt we shall have some hardships to undergo; but I shall advance cautiously and prudently, and try to do all that can be done."[54]

Superintendent Nesmith also feared that the Indians would elude Wright. Others felt the campaign promised nothing more than another futile, "titanic game of hide and seek . . . , a repetition of his 1855 [sic] fiasco."[55] Without a supply line Wright had to be totally self-sufficient and could not stay anywhere very long without starving.

After the Steptoe disaster the Indians had reportedly said that "the white soldiers were women and could not fight and the more that should be sent into that country the better they would like it, for they would kill them all."[56] They were confident that U.S. troops could not stand up to them; being well supplied with arms, ammunition, and provisions, they expected another easy victory. So far, however, action had been limited to occasional exchanges of gunfire across the Snake River.

As Fort Taylor neared completion, the troops prepared to cross the river, taking only one light wagon to carry the instruments of Lieutenant Mullan, who was also serving as topographical engineer for the expedition. The crossing of the Snake River was planned for August 23, but had to be postponed for two days because of a violent storm. On the twenty-fifth the Third Artillery began crossing at 5:00 A.M., followed by the Ninth Infantry companies and part of the quartermaster's train. The dragoons and the rest of the train crossed the next day. Men and packs were taken over on the raft and in boats, and animals were swum across, with Indian allies swimming after and driving them. Both crossings were made "without loss or incident" under the direction of Captain Kirkham.

After he crossed the river, Wright had with him four companies of the First Dragoons under Bvt. Maj. William N. Grier, five companies of the Third Artillery under Capt. E. D. Keyes, and two companies of the Ninth Infantry under Capt. F. T. Dent—a total of 570 regulars. Wright's staff officers included his son-in-law, Lt. P. A. Owen, acting assistant adjutant; Captain Kirkham, quartermaster and commissary; and Assistant Surgeons James E. Hammond and John Randolph. Other officers with the First Dragoons were Lts. Henry B. Davidson, William D. Pender, and David M. Gregg; with the Third Artillery, Capts. E. O. C. Ord and James A. Hardie, Lts. Horatio G. Gibson, Robert O. Tyler, James L. White, Michael R. Morgan, Dunbar R. Ransom, George P. Ihre, H. B. Lyon, George F. B. Dandy, James T. Howard, and Lawrence Kip; and with the Ninth Infantry, Capt. Charles S. Winder and Lt. H. B. Fleming. Thirty friendly Nez Percé Indians were serving under Lieutenant Mullan. Assistant Surgeon J. B. Browne had been left with Major Wyse at Fort Taylor.[57] Of the combat officers only Winder, Gregg, and Fleming were veterans of the Steptoe campaign. Seventeen of these officers later became generals during the Civil War, 12 serving in the Union army and 5 in the Confederate army. Also accompanying the column were 100 civilian employees, herders, packers and the like; 800 "animals of all kinds," including the dragoon horses; and subsistence for thirty-eight days.

On the morning of August 27 the entire column marched a short distance down the right bank of the Snake River and then moved north fifteen miles across the tableland to the Palouse River. It was another hot, dusty day, and the foot soldiers were miserable. As a rule the order of march called for the dragoons in the lead, followed by the mountain howitzer company under Lieutenant White, then the battalion of Third Artillery serving as infantry, the rifle battalion of the Ninth Infantry, the packtrain of the corps, headquarters, one company of infantry, and the general train of the quartermaster and commissary, with one troop of dragoons as rear guard. Whether on the march or in camp, formalities were observed: the companies paraded at reveille and retreat, roll call was taken, and all arms and ammunition were inspected.

The discharge of firearms was forbidden except in the line of duty or when authorized by the commanding officer. Each evening at sunset one company mounted guard

for the night. The men habitually kept their arms at hand
and wore their ammunition belts at all times, even when
sleeping. The arms they carried were quite different from
those of Steptoe's men.[58] The artillery acting as infantry
carried the new Springfield 58-caliber rifle musket, 1855
model; the infantry carried the improved Mississippi Jaeger rifle, which, like the newer guns, could fire the highly
effective minié ball; each dragoon was armed with a breechloading Sharps carbine and a Colt revolver or an old cavalry
pistol. This time the dragoons also carried their sabers.[59]
The two howitzers were manned by well-drilled crews.

On the twenty-eighth the troops traveled only eight
miles. When they saw tracks of Indian horses, Wright
wisely decided to head toward the falls of the Spokane
River rather than continuing toward Fort Colvile. The
next day they made twenty miles through rocky and hilly
country. As they advanced, the country became more level,
with scattered timber; in the distance they could see the
Coeur d'Alene Mountains.

The troops spent the night of the twenty-ninth at a place
they called Aspen Camp. On the thirtieth they passed
through fairly level but rocky country, marching eighteen
miles. Water was scarce and of poor quality. During that
day they passed a small lake around which wild parsnips
grew; two of the men died from eating the poisonous
roots. The night's camp, amid basaltic outcroppings, was
called Camp Pedrigal. Wright had hoped to rest at this
spot for a day but decided to keep moving since the terrain
would be difficult for maneuvers or defense.

They had no sooner encamped than the Nez Percé scouts
announced the approach of a large body of Spokanes. The
dragoons saddled their horses and made ready to mount.
Shots were heard from the advance pickets as well as from
the enemy. Wright and some troops set off in pursuit for
three miles. They drove off what was probably a scouting
party but accomplished little else. On August 31 the command moved into the scattered pines marking the border
of the Great Spokane Plain. Small parties of hostile Indians were seen on the hills at their right, and their num-

bers gradually increased. The command marched eighteen miles, the scouts occasionally exchanging shots with
the Indians. They halted frequently to close up the baggage and supply trains, a timely measure, for the Indians
made a strong demonstration on the trains in the afternoon. They were repulsed by a rectangle of troops formed
around the crucial supplies.

At 4:00 P.M., having found a suitable site with wood,
grass, and water southeast of the present-day town of
Medical Lake, the soldiers went into camp. Because of a
nearby cluster of four small lakes, Wright referred to the
area as Four Lakes. As they set up camp, the Nez Percé
auxiliaries, who were out scouting, were charged by the
enemy. Wright saw what was happening and sent a squadron of dragoons under Grier and Davidson, who drove the
Indians off. The Indians fired the grass at many points,
but the flames did not reach the camp. A large number of
Indians assembled on a hill northwest of the camp but dispersed at nightfall. Wright saw that his men and horses
were exhausted and decided to remain at the camp through
the next day to give them some rest. But that was not to be.

Battle of Four Lakes

The Indians had planned their strategy carefully and chosen the field for battle. Their objectives were to draw off
the cavalry and then wipe out the infantry. Their main
goal was to capture the supply train, which would have
spelled disaster for Wright and his men, who had no supply line and only enough rations for a little over thirty
days. The Indians had had the army under close observation since the start of the campaign, and after their experience with Steptoe they felt that they had nothing to fear
from white soldiers. Indeed, they were excited by the prospect of the booty soon to be theirs.

Colonel Wright's report of the events of the next few
days presents the military viewpoint.[60] A more romantic
account was given by Lieutenant Kip,[61] and the action was
later described by Keyes[62] and by Dandy[63] in their reminis-

cences. Recent writers have considered Wright's reports "pompous; fatuous; self-serving." Burns, for example, speaks of a "euphoric Wright composing lyrical effusions" rather than reports.[64] Yet Captain Keyes, who as second-in-command was invited by Wright to read all the letters, reports, and orders, had this to say:

> I made a careful examination of every document written by the colonel during the campaign, and found in them continual proofs of justice, impartiality, and the absence of prejudice. It seemed to afford him especial satisfaction to set forth the merits of his subordinates, and he omitted no subject worthy of praise, saving his own activity and fitness for command.[65]

Wright's report of the Battle of Four Lakes follows:

HEADQUARTERS EXPEDITION AGAINST NORTHERN INDIANS
Camp at the "Four Lakes," W.T., lat. 47° 32′ N
Long. 117° 39′, September 2, 1858

SIR: I have the honor to submit the following report of the battle of the "Four Lakes," fought and won by the troops under my command on the 1st instant. Our enemies were the Spokane, Coeur d'Alenes and Pelouse Indians.

Early on the morning of the 1st I observed the Indians collecting on the summit of a high hill, about two miles distant, and I immediately ordered the troops under arms, with a view of driving the enemy from his position, and making a reconnaissance of the country in advance. At half past 9 A.M. I marched from my camp with two squadrons of the 1st dragoons, commanded by Brevet Major W. N. Grier; four companies of the 3d artillery; armed with rifle muskets, commanded by Captain E. D. Keyes; and the rifle battalion of two companies of the 9th infantry, commanded by Captain F. T. Dent; also one mountain howitzer, under command of Lieutenant J. L. White, 3d artillery and thirty friendly Nez Perce Indian allies, under command of Lieutenant John Mullan, 2d artillery. I left in camp all the equipage and supplies, strongly guarded by company "M," 3d artillery, commanded by Lieutenants H. G. Gibson and G. B. Dandy; one mountain howitzer, manned; and in addition a guard of fifty-four men, under Lieutenant H. B. Lyon; the whole comanded by Captain J. A. Hardie, the field officer of the day.

I ordered Brevet Major Grier to advance to the north and
east around the base of the hill occupied by the Indians, with a
view to intercept their retreat when driven from the summit
by the foot troops. I marched with the artillery and rifle battalion and Nez Perces to the right of the hill, in order to gain a
position where the ascent was more easy, and also to push the
Indians in the direction of the dragoons. Arriving within six
hundred yards of the Indians, I ordered Captain Keyes to advance a company of his battalion, deployed, and drive the Indians from the hill. This service was gallantly accomplished by
Captain Ord and Lieutenant Morgan with company "K," 3d
artillery, in cooperation with the 2d squadron of dragoons
under Lieutenant Davidson; the Indians were driven to the
foot of the hill, and there rallied under cover of ravines, trees
and bushes.

On reaching the crest of the hill I saw at once that the Indians were determined to measure their strength with us,
showing no disposition to avoid a combat, and firmly maintaining their position at the base of the hill, keeping up a constant fire upon the two squadrons of dragoons, who were
awaiting the arrival of the foot troops. In front of us lay a vast
plain, with some four or five hundred mounted warriors,
rushing to and fro, wild with excitement, and apparently
eager for the fray; to the right, at the foot of the hill, in the
pine forest, the Indians were also seen in large numbers.

With all I have described, in plain view, a tyro in the art of
war could not have hesitated a moment as to his plan of battle.

Captain Keyes, with two companies of his battalion, commanded by Lieutenants Ransom and Ihrie, with Lieutenant
Howard, was ordered to deploy along the crest of the hills, in
rear of the dragoons, and facing the plain. The rifle battalion,
under Captain Dent, composed of two companies of the 9th
Infantry, under Captain Winder and Lieutenant Fleming, was
ordered to move to the right, and deploy in front of the pine
forest; and the howitzer, under Lieutenant White, supported
by a company of artillery, under Lieutenant Tyler, was advanced to a lower plateau, in order to gain a position where it
could be fired with effect.

In five minutes the troops were deployed; I ordered the advance; Captain Keyes moved steadily down the long slope,
passed the dragoons, and opened a sharp, well directed fire,

which drove the Indians to the plains and pine forest; at the same time Captain Dent, with the rifle battalion, Lieutenant White, with the howitzer, and Lieutenant Tyler, with his company, were hotly engaged with the Indians in the pine forest, constantly increasing by fugitives from the left.

Captain Keyes continued to advance, the Indians retiring slowly; Major Grier, with both squadrons quietly leading his horses in rear. At a signal, they mount, they rush with lightning speed through the intervals of skirmishers, and charge the Indians on the plains, overwhelm them entirely, kill many, defeat and disperse them all; and in a few minutes not a hostile Indian was to be seen on the plain. While this scene was enacting, Dent, Winder, and Fleming, with the rifle battalion, and Tyler and White, with company "A" and the howitzer, had pushed rapidly forward and driven the Indians out of the forest beyond view.

After the charge of the dragoons, and pursuit for over a mile on the hills, they were halted, their horses being completely exhausted; and the foot troops again passed them about a thousand yards, but finding only a few Indians in front of us, on remote hill-tops, I would not pursue them with my tired soldiers. A couple of shots from the howitzer sent them out of sight. The battle was won; I sounded the recall, assembled the troops, and returned to our camp at 2 P.M.

It affords me the highest gratification to report that we did not lose a man, either killed or wounded, during the action— attributable, I doubt not, in great measure, to the fact that our long-range rifles can reach the enemy where he cannot reach us.

The enemy lost some eighteen or twenty men killed, and many wounded.

I take great pleasure in commending to the department the coolness and gallantry displayed by every officer and soldier engaged in this battle.

The report concludes with several pages of praise for the performance of individual officers and men and Wright's signature.[66]

Lieutenant Kip gave a colorful description of the Indians as they appeared in this battle:

Every spot seemed alive with the wild warriors we had come so far to meet. They were in the pines on the edge of the lakes, in the ravines and gullies, on the opposite hillsides, and swarming over the plain. They seemed to cover the country for some two miles. Mounted on their fleet, hardy horses, the crowd swayed back and forth, brandishing their weapons, shouting their war cries, and keeping up a song of defiance. Most of them were armed with Hudson Bay muskets, while others had bows and arrows and long lances. They were in all the bravery of their war array, gaudily painted and decorated with their wild trappings. Their plumes fluttered above them, while below skins and trinkets and all kinds of fancy embellishments flaunted in the sunshine. Their horses, too, were arrayed in the most glaring finery. Some were even painted, and with colors to form the greatest contrast . . . [and] fantastic figures. . . . Beads and fringes of gaudy colors were hanging from their bridles, while the plumes of eagles' feathers, interwoven with mane and tail, fluttered as the breeze swept over them, and completed their wild and fantastic appearance.[67]

Wright and his men were overjoyed by what they regarded as a triumph, with no casualties on their side except one dragoon horse. The exact enemy loss was difficult to determine because the Indians promptly removed their dead and wounded from the field as they fell. The number of their casualties was, however, substantial, and might have been greater but for the worn condition of the dragoon horses. Among the wounded were a brother and a brother-in-law of Chief Garry.

The range and accuracy of the army's new firearms took the Indians completely by surprise. Lieutenant Kip said that the soldiers began firing at 600 yards, and as they advanced, the minié balls began to bring the enemy down. The cavalry used their sabers to good advantage, and the howitzers were skillfully manned.

One can hardly blame Wright for exulting at his success. He had feared an ineffectual campaign against guerrilla tactics, but instead he engaged a great confederation of Indians in a pitched battle and drove them from the field. His success, moreover, was not entirely due to his new and accurate long-range weapons. His battle plan was sound, his men well disciplined and superbly trained. Their morale was high in spite of their long, tedious march, and they deployed with precision and enthusiasm. Their tactics were effective and because of intensive practice they were expert in the use of their arms. The Indians' plan of attack was upset by Wright's protection of the supply train.[68] Wright's report bestowed generous praise for the way his officers and enlisted men had performed. The long hours of drilling and the discipline he had established had paid off.

After the battle the soldiers returned to their camp by the "four beautiful lakes in the Spokane plains, skirted by beautiful open pine forests."[69] There the weary men and their worn-out horses rested for three days. Dispatches were written, and the Nez Percés reconnoitered, but no hostile Indians were seen. In spite of their defeat the Indians were regrouping and preparing for a full-scale battle in which they expected to annihilate the command.

While Wright was resting at the Four Lakes camp, the number of Indians in the area continued to increase. Detachments of numerous tribes arrived to join in the defeat of the whites and sharing of the booty. If the Indians had been more successful in the first battle, even more would have been attracted to join the fray.

Battle of Spokane Plains

Early on the morning of September 5, Wright and his command left the camp at Four Lakes. They marched northward along the eastern shore of Silver Lake, the westernmost of the four. After moving about five miles through "broken country," they emerged onto the great Spokane Plain. In the distance ahead of them they saw Indians moving along the edge of woods to their right. The Indians, their numbers rapidly increasing, formed a semicircle ahead of the troops. Wright halted, closed up his long packtrain, and assigned two companies of infantry and one company of dragoons to guard it. In front, four companies were deployed into a line of skirmishers almost a mile long, and the other companies were held in readiness.

The Battle of Spokane Plains, 1858. Sketch by Gustavus
Sohon. Courtesy Smithsonian Institution, negative No.
45744.

The Indians now began to set fire to the tall grass in
front and to the right of the soliders. Behind the flames,
preparing to attack the packtrain, were between 500 and
1,000 Indians. The tribes of the confederacy had been
joined by some Pend d'Oreilles, Yakimas, and disaffected
Nez Percés. Brisk firing began on both sides. As the flames,
fanned by a strong wind, threatened to envelop the soldiers, Wright ordered an advance. Led by a squadron of
dragoons, the skirmishers and the howitzer battery "dashed
gallantly through the roaring flames, and the Indians were
driven to seek shelter in the forest and rocks." The howitzers then sent shells among the Indians and routed them
from their cover with the dragoons in pursuit.[70]
Several attacks on the packtrain were repulsed as the
command moved forward. Dandy later commented:

If the enemy had succeeded in stampeding and capturing this
train, we would have been left in a desperate condition. . . .

But the packers and troops were quick to obey their officers and saved the train. . . . It was only by the very great coolness and courage of the officers and men that the calamity of a stampede was averted in this case.[71]

Firing was now general along the entire front. The Indians dashed about wildly, performing incredible feats of horsemanship in an effort to gain the upper hand. The troops continued their advance, now bearing to the right toward the Spokane River. As they reached terrain that was more rugged and less suitable for dragoon operations, most of the fighting was carried on by foot soldiers. The Indians repeatedly charged, but the troops continued to push them back to new positions. Wherever Indians congregated, shells from the howitzers scattered them.

The battle had started just north of the present Fairchild Air Force Base, twelve miles west of Spokane. Fighting continued for seven hours over a distance of fourteen miles. As the troops approached the Spokane River, they were able to regroup with flankers out and make better progress, but skirmishing and firing continued most of the way. When they finally reached the river, the Indians had dispersed and the soldiers went into camp on the south bank at the present site of the Fort George Wright campus in Spokane. The entire command, men and animals, was utterly exhausted. They had marched twenty-five miles that day without water; for two-thirds of that distance they had been under fire. Although the balls flew thick and fast through their ranks, only one man was wounded, and he only slightly.

The Indians lost two chiefs, one of whom was found with the pistol of Lieutenant Gaston, who had been killed in the Steptoe fight. Many other Indians are reported to have been killed or wounded, but there is no estimate of the number. Kamiakin was seriously injured by a branch torn from a tree by a howitzer shell.

Wright reported another victory to his superiors. As before, he ascribed it to superior weaponry and discipline. In closing the report, he said, "Again it affords me the high-

Wright's troops camped at the Spokane River following
the Battle of Spokane Plains. Sketch by Gustavus Sohon.
Courtesy Library of Congress.

est pleasure to bear witness to the zeal, energy, perseverance and gallantry displayed by the officers and men during this protracted battle." He again cited individuals whose
performances had been outstanding. With both of his reports Wright enclosed topographical sketches of the battle-
fields drawn by Lieutenant Mullan.[72]

In the Indian wars no war correspondents accompanied
troops into battle, so we are largely dependent on the reports of the commanders and their superiors. Secondary
opinions from contemporary sources which followed these

reports were generally favorable to Wright's conduct of the battles and accomplishments. Reminiscences by army participants, both officers and enlisted men, written in later years also spoke favorably of Wright. When Clarke received Wright's dispatches, he expressed his gratification to Col. Samuel Cooper, the adjutant general, and added, "I presume that the success narrated in these dispatches is a surety of peace henceforth with these Indians."[73] On the other hand, a twentieth-century historian asks:

> What, then, had Wright accomplished? He had been presented with the confederated tribes in one large body and had allowed them to disperse again. . . . It had been all flags and sabers, foam-flecked horses and a confusion of musketry: the game of war with an illusion of danger, an illusion of dedication. The Colonel was at the end of his tether, on short supplies and with winter in the offing. Unlike Garnett, he had enjoyed a great stroke of luck. But Kamiakin and his war leaders would hardly repeat the mistake of presenting him with a united force in the open field. Wright had used up his resources in a grand, futile gesture. He was back where he had started in 1855—to marches on the empty plains. In short, he had lost the war. . . . A new element was needed to bring meaning to Wright's situation and to precipitate a just and lasting peace. This element, in the upper country in 1858, happened to be the Jesuits.[74]

It is interesting to compare this opinion with that of a Jesuit who played an important part in 1858, Father Joset:

> From the first the colonel knew how to disable them, and it was practically no fight, but a complete rout. Before this the Indians smiled with pity when anyone suggested that they could not make head against the whites; but the brave Colonel Wright so well persuaded them that, by their own admission, they cannot even think of war any more. They are like men tied hand and foot, who cannot move.
> The effect produced by Colonel Wright's expedition is such that one must be on the spot to gain any idea of it. A general war was on the eve of breaking out. The volunteer expeditions had exasperated the Indians, without inspiring them with any dread; but by the able manner in which the colonel

made the most of his resources, he completely rid the savages of any desire to measure themselves with the American troops. Furthermore, he has terrified the bad Indians by his severity as much as he has won the hearts of the good ones by his clemency. In short, he has deserved well of the Republic, above all that can be said for him. And finally, the fine discipline that he enforced whenever he passed, has been an eloquent reply to the slanders by which it has been sought to render the military odious to these poor people, insomuch that the chief, Vincent, was able to say to the officers, and it is the expression of feeling of the whole nation [Coeur d'Alene]: "Before, we knew you only by hearsay, and we hated you; now we have seen you, we love you." [75]

Not only had Wright succeeded in dispersing the Indians; he had rendered them dismayed and despondent. They knew they had been beaten badly, and their will to fight was dissipated. The confederation was destroyed; a great many Indians realized that in the long run they were no match for the whites with their greater numbers, more efficient organization, and superior weapons. Immediately after the first battle, Mullan wrote a long letter from the camp at Four Lakes to Charles E. Mix, acting commissioner of Indian affairs, in Washington, D.C. Mullan said:

It is not my province to give you the details of a battle of which this point has been the scene. . . . Suffice it for me to say he [Wright] has fought a memorable, never to be forgotten fight; since he killed, discomfitted, and drove in dismay the enemy from the field without sustaining a single loss to his command. [76]

Years later, Keyes wrote:

I doubt if in the history of our country there has ever been an Indian campaign in which as much was accomplished at an equal cost. The good result was due to three causes: The proper instruction of the soldiers at the commencement, the excellence of the quartermaster's department, and the admirable fitness of our commander, Colonel George Wright. [77]

Wright rested his troops for a day at the riverside camp and then moved slowly east along the south bank of the

Spokane River. He was eager to gather the Indians for a
council and obtain their unconditional surrender before
they scattered to the four winds. He halted at a ford two
miles above the great falls of the river.

On September 7, Chief Garry arrived and told Wright
that he had always opposed fighting but that his young
men and some chiefs had defied him. Wright upbraided
him and demanded that he collect all his people and that
they surrender their arms and trust to Wright's mercy;
then Garry would learn the terms on which he could have
peace. The alternative, Wright said coldly, was extermination of the Spokane Nation.

War chief Polatkin and some of his braves then came
into camp. Polatkin had been a leader in the Steptoe fight
as well as in both the recent battles with Wright. He had,
moreover, written an offensive letter to Clarke. Polatkin
was detained in Wright's camp, along with a visiting Palouse who was suspected of being one of the murderers of
the miners in April.[78]

The March to the Coeur D'Alene Mission

The next day the command resumed its march along the
river with its two prisoners. Along the way two of Polatkin's
sons appeared on the other side of the river and demanded
their father's release. The troops shouted refusal, and
some shooting occurred in which both sons were wounded.
As the command neared the vicinity of Liberty Lake, they
saw a cloud of dust in the distance. Three companies of
dragoons were sent to investigate, followed by a few foot
soldiers. They discovered that the dust had been raised by
a large herd of horses that a few Indians were driving into
the mountains. Lieutenant Davidson with his troop and
Lieutenant Mullan with his scouts captured the whole herd
of 800 or 900 horses, which were thought to belong to a
Palouse troublemaker named Tilcoax. The herd was driven
back to the area where the column had made camp, sixteen miles above the falls. A subsequent attempt to capture

a herd of wild cattle was unsuccessful. Some lodges filled
with wheat were discovered and burned.

In the evening Wright "investigated the case" of his Palouse prisoner and, satisfied that the man had been involved in the death of the miners, had him hanged.[79] Clarke
had previously told Wright that Steptoe knew who·the
culprits were, and this information had been passed on to
Wright.[80]

The next morning at daybreak more storehouses of
wheat were discovered and burned. Wright was uncertain
what to do with the captured horses, for most of them
were unbroken. Horses were the most prized possessions
of the Indians, who would most certainly make an effort to
stampede or recapture them.[81] If a stampede occurred,
the command's horses could be lost as well. But keeping
the herd seemed out of the question; a herd of this size
could not be taken into the Coeur d'Alene country in the
mountains. Wright, hesitant to kill the valuable animals,
convened a board of officers to determine what should
be done.

The consensus was to let the officers, quartermaster department, and Indian auxiliaries select a certain number
that were not too wild and to kill the rest to prevent them
from falling back into the hands of the Indians. At first the
horses were shot one by one, but this proved too slow, so
the men were ordered to fire volleys into the makeshift
corral. This disagreeable task required the better part of
two days and earned for the site the name Horse Slaughter
Camp.[82] Watching the destruction of the herd from the
nearby hills, the Indians could hardly believe what they
saw—that anyone could be so indifferent to such a great
source of wealth. The capture of the herd did not completely deprive the Indians of transport, but it had a devastating effect on their morale.

On the evening of September 10, Wright received a dispatch from Father Joset, who was back at the Coeur d'Alene
Mission. He announced that the hostiles were "down and
suing for peace." Wright replied that the Indians who had

taken part in the war must come in with their guns, their families, and all that they had but that no lives would be taken for acts committed during the war.[83] The next day the column resumed its advance, forded the Spokane River at what is now the Idaho border, and then marched fourteen miles along the north bank to the northwest corner of Lake Coeur d'Alene, where Fort Sherman was later erected. Along the way they destroyed more Indian lodges filled with wheat and oats and some caches of dried cakes, wild berries, camas, and vegetables. Some captured cattle that could not be used were also killed.

Only a narrow Indian trail existed through the thickly timbered Coeur d'Alene Mountains, so Mullan's wagon and the limbers carrying the howitzers were abandoned. They were promptly burned by Indians who had been lurking in the rear.

On the twelfth the men moved along the trail on the north shore of the lake. The trail became progressively worse owing to dense undergrowth and fallen trees. By the next day the men had to move in single file, struggling uphill with their arms and equipment. They formed a column six miles long, without communication from head to rear and with no protection for the flanks except the dense forest. If the Indians had not been subdued, they could have created havoc from an ambush.

In spite of the difficulties, the column advanced nineteen miles to the Coeur d'Alene mission on the thirteenth, but the packtrain and the rear guard did not arrive until ten o'clock that night. Wright reported to Clarke: "The chastisement which these Indians have received has been severe but well merited, and undoubtedly necessary to impress them with our power. For the last eighty miles our route has been marked by slaughter and destruction."[84]

Father Joset was indefatigable in trying to bring in the hostiles with their women and children and inducing them to surrender the horses and mules belonging to the United States. Wright felt that he had struck the Indians a blow they would never forget. His troops were in good health and spirits, and he still had provisions, which, with economy and reduced rations, would last him until October 5. In the mountains the days were still warm, but ice a quarter-inch thick formed each night. Fathers Joset and Joseph Menetrey and three lay brothers at the mission were most hospitable to the officers and their men.

On September 17 the "entire Coeur d'Alene nation" assembled for a council, at which Wright was seated under a leafy bower erected for the purpose. Wright demanded that the Indians surrender the men who had instigated the attack on Steptoe against the orders of their chiefs, turn over all public or private U.S. property in their possession, and allow whites to travel unmolested through their country. They were also to deliver one chief and four men with their families as hostages for the tribe's good behavior, to be taken to Fort Walla Walla.[85] Some of the chiefs made speeches, and then the Indians, after conferring among themselves, agreed to Wright's terms and signed a preliminary treaty. The timely appearance of Donati's comet, which illuminated the September sky, helped convince the Indians that the white man's medicine was strong. Following the council there was considerable fraternizing and trading between the troops and Indians, and Wright was convinced that henceforth the Coeur d'Alenes would be staunch friends. As a gesture of goodwill, Polatkin was released while the whites were at the mission.

It must be remembered that General Clarke was determined to punish the instigators of the attack on Steptoe: "They must suffer for their disobedience, and atone for the guilt into which their bad acts have brought their people."[86] The Indians were adamant against turning over their warriors, knowing all too well the fate that probably awaited them. Father Joset arranged a compromise—that the Steptoe "criminals" would be surrendered as temporary prisoners, with the assurance that their lives would be spared.[87] Time was running out for Wright with cold weather approaching and supplies being depleted. He knew that without Joset's help there would have been no treaty of any kind and possibly would have been more war. Wright decided that, if the Indians agreed to his other terms, acceptance of one deviation from his terms was the only realistic course to follow. This was, after all, a preliminary treaty, presumably to be followed later by a formal treaty for ratification by the government.

The next day the column left the mission with its prisoners, hostages, and some Coeur d'Alene guides and marched thirteen miles down the right bank of the Coeur d'Alene River. Most of September 19 was spent ferrying the command across the river in Indian canoes and the collapsible boats of the quartermaster department. The column passed south of Lake Coeur d'Alene, crossed the Saint Joseph's River on the twentieth and twenty-first, and continued westward. After marching about five miles farther, they encamped. A few chiefs and braves came into the camp. They told Wright that they were Coeur d'Alenes, but they were actually Palouses interested in learning whether they would be granted peace terms similar to those of the Coeur d'Alenes. On September 22 the column moved eighteen miles over rolling, pine-studded country to a campsite on the Ned-whauld River (Latah Creek) just east of the present-day community of Spangle. The Spokanes had been assembled earlier at that location by Father Joset, who remained to serve as interpreter. Kamiakin and Tilcoax had been there also but, becoming fearful, had departed before the arrival of the troops.

Hanging Camp on Latah Creek

The next morning, September 23, a council was held with the Spokanes. Wright made the same demands of them as he had of the Coeur d'Alenes. The chiefs "acknowledged their crimes" in lengthy speeches and agreed to sign the treaty. Garry, Polatkin, and Melkapsi, who had sent the letters to General Clarke, were present. Melkapsi, a Coeur d'Alene, had missed the previous council and now desired to be one of the signers of the treaty. Wright berated him for the tone of his letter but allowed him to affix his mark to the document. Also present were representatives of several smaller tribes whose warriors had fought against

Wright. Wright informed them that henceforth they would be on the same footing as the Spokanes if they conformed faithfully to the terms of the treaty. Enclosed with Wright's subsequent report to Clarke were copies of the two treaties and an expression of thanks to Father Joset "for his zealous and unwearied exertions in bringing all the Indians to an understanding of their true position."[88]

That evening the Yakima chief Owhi, Kamiakin's brother-in-law, came into the camp expecting amnesty. Wright reminded him that he had not returned with his people on the Naches River in 1856 as he had promised and had him placed in irons. Wright ordered Owhi to summon his son Qualchin, who was on the lower Spokane River, and threatened him with death if Qualchin did not appear.

Qualchin had instigated numerous murders, robberies, and attacks on whites both east and west of the Cascade Range during the past three years. In June he had been wounded while leading an attack on a large party of miners on their way to the Fraser River gold strike. A messenger Wright sent for Qualchin did not reach him, but, inexplicably the next morning Qualchin rode into the camp accompanied by his attractive wife, Whiet-alks, and his brother Lo-kout. In his laconic report to headquarters, Wright announced, "Qual-chew came to me at 9 o'clock this morning, and at 9 1/4 a.m. he was hung."[89]

The same morning Brevet Major Grier and three companies were sent to the Steptoe battlefield, twelve miles to the south. Mullan, who accompanied the party, later told of the melancholy experience of finding the bones of their colleagues and the recovery of the two buried howitzers. The men erected a cross at the site, using the shafts of one of the gun limbers. The remains of Gaston, Taylor, and a few others had been buried and so had not been scattered by wolves. Grier's men gathered the bones and took them back to the camp for burial at Fort Walla Walla.[90]

That evening many Palouse Indians began coming into Wright's camp on Latah Creek, now referred to as Hangman's Creek. He had previously warned the Palouses of se-

vere treatment if they were found with the hostiles. He
seized fifteen of the warriors whom he knew had joined in
the war against the U.S. forces. One he mistakenly believed had killed a wounded sergeant of Steptoe's command. Two had stolen cattle in the Walla Walla Valley. Six
"of the most notorious" were summarily hanged; the remainder were placed in irons for the march.[91]

Wright's attitude toward the Palouse Indians was far
harsher than his feelings toward the Coeur d'Alenes or the
Spokanes. The Palouses had fought against the whites in
the Cayuse War of 1848, the Yakima War, and the three
battles of the present conflict, whereas the Coeur d'Alenes
and Spokanes had been friendly in the past. In fact, they
boasted that they had never shed white blood. The Palouses had also been involved in the murder of miners and
numerous thefts of cattle and other property.

Wright left the Latah Creek camp on the morning of the
twenty-sixth. The next day an express from Colville over-
took them, seeking troops for that area. Wright regretfully
informed the messengers, and later Clarke, that he could
not have included Colville in his itinerary without sacrificing more important objectives. Since the only problem in
that region was pilferage, Wright did not feel that it merited his attention.[92]

The march continued for four cold, rainy days, at the
end of which Wright camped beside the Palouse River.
Another large group of Palouse men, women, and children came into his camp. At a council on the thirtieth
Wright castigated the Palouses and told them to bring in
all property in their possession belonging to the government. He then demanded the surrender of the men who
had murdered the two miners on their way to Colville in
April. One was brought forth and hanged immediately.

Wright then had all of his prisoners brought out. Three,
found to be Yakimas or Walla Wallas who had left their
country to wage war against the United States, were hanged
on the spot. None of the men hanged had been included
in the agreement that he had made with Father Joset con-

cerning the Coeur d'Alenes and the Spokanes. Finally he demanded one chief and four men, with their families, as hostages. Wright declined to make a treaty with the Palouses but said that he might consider it the following spring if they obeyed his orders to allow whites to travel through their country and to deliver any of their people involved in murder or robbery. He warned them that if he ever had to return to their country on a hostile expedition he would wipe out the entire tribe.[93]

On the same day he wrote to Clarke, "Sir: The war is closed. Peace is restored with the Spokanes, Coeur d'Alenes and Pelouses [*sic*]. After a vigorous campaign the Indians have been entirely subdued, and were most happy to accept such terms of peace as I might dictate." He summarized his accomplishments: two battles won; 1,000 horses and cattle captured and either killed or used; barns and caches destroyed; Owhi in irons; Qualchin and ten other "murderers and thieves" hanged; treaties made; property restored; agreements reached that whites were to travel unmolested; hostiles not to be harbored; the Steptoe attackers delivered; hostages taken; the two howitzers recovered.[94]

On October 1, Captain Keyes, with the artillery battalion, one troop of dragoons, and the packtrain, crossed the Snake River; the rest of the column followed a day later. When Wright appeared at the river, the little garrison at Fort Taylor fired a welcoming cannon salute. On October 2, Lieutenant Mullan left to report to department headquarters at Fort Vancouver, and Lieutenant Owen left to resume his duties as adjutant at Fort Dalles.

Fort Taylor was abandoned on October 3, and the command set out for Walla Walla. As they were crossing the Tucannon, Owhi, strapped to his saddle and with his feet chained, attempted to escape. He struck Lieutenant Morgan, who was guarding him, in the face with his whip and bolted. Wright had planned to take Owhi, an important prisoner, with him to The Dalles and possibly send him to the presidio in San Francisco. Believing that his career was at stake (he later became a brigadier general), Morgan

dashed off in pursuit. He fired his pistol, wounding Owhi
and his horse. Owhi was then killed by some dragoons who
had been attracted by the commotion.[95]

Return to Fort Walla Walla

Wright and his command marched twenty-six miles in cold
wind and rain on October 4, reaching Fort Walla Walla
about noon on the fifth. There they found the inspector general, Colonel Mansfield. The command proudly
marched onto the parade ground, although they were rag-
ged, disheveled, and begrimed after sixty days in the field.
Mansfield inspected them and found the men in a high
state of discipline and their weapons in perfect order. He
told Wright that he was highly gratified with the result of
his inspection.[96] The next day the officers were invited to
Colonel Steptoe's quarters to meet Colonel Mansfield, and
"a handsome collation was provided." On the seventh the
remains of Taylor, Gaston, and three enlisted men were
buried with full military honors.

The last act of the campaign occurred two days later,
when a council was held with the Walla Walla and Cayuse
Indians. Chiefs Lawyer and Looking Glass and a number
of the friendly Nez Percés were also present. Thirty-five
warriors admitted having fought in the two recent battles.
Among them were three Walla Wallas who had also been
engaged in the murder of whites and Wie-cat, who had
failed to deliver Steptoe's last message, and had attempted
to arouse the valley Indians. They were handed over to the
guard and hanged. Wright reported that he gave the Cayuses "some good advice which I think will benefit them."[97]
These hangings made a total of sixteen Indians executed
by Wright.

After the battles an Oregon paper exulted: "No event has
ever done so much to secure the safety of our settlers as this
victory. The people of this territory owe a debt of gratitude to the officers and soldiers under Colonel Wright."[98]
A more cynical view was expressed by Superintendent
Christopher Mott, an investigator for the Indian Service,

who thought it was the hangings rather than the battles that had resulted in the subjugation of the Indians.[99]

Wright brought with him to Fort Walla Walla thirty-three Indian men, women, and children. Some were warriors who had attacked Steptoe; others were hostages. He left the Indians at the fort and on the ninth wrote Clarke that, "having finished the business the general desired," he would now leave for his old headquarters at Fort Dalles.[100]

Wright submitted an informative report about this time regarding his command's equipment, which General-in-Chief Scott ordered the army's chief of ordinance to read. Wright considered the improved Jaeger rifle carried by the Ninth Infantry the best arm he had ever seen in the hands of a foot soldier, although he recommended strengthening the guide sights and bayonet studs. Wright complained that the new rifle muskets of the Third Artillery, in spite of their long range and accuracy, were too long and possessed an unfortunate tendency to burst. The rubber and gutta-percha canteens were far inferior to those made of tin. Wright's chief complaint concerned the shoes issued to his men: the leather was bad, the threads worse, and some wore out after three days.[101]

Garnett's Raid

Most of the time Wright had been in the field, Major Garnett, commander of Fort Simcoe, had been out as well, having left the fort on August 10, three days after Wright's command moved out. Coordination between the two columns was out of the question, since communication between them was difficult, and neither knew the other's itinerary.

Garnett took with him Company D of the Fourth Infantry and three rifle companies of the Ninth Infantry. His command consisted of eight line officers, a surgeon, and 306 enlisted men. Garnett had no dragoons, so he mounted ten men from each company of the Ninth Infantry and placed them under the command of Lt. Jesse K. Allen. Also in Garnett's column were 225 pack animals and fifty civilian packers and herders. One company was left to garrison Fort Simcoe.

Garnett was eager for a fight but, unlike Wright, did not have the luck to encounter a large band of Indians. The command headed due north to the Kittitas Valley. On August 15, Garnett reported from the upper Yakima River that Lieutenant Allen had been shot and killed during a predawn raid on a small hostile camp. "There is reason, however," Garnett added, "to fear that he was shot accidentally by one of his own men." Allen's detachment captured twenty-one men, fifty women and children, seventy horses, and fifteen head of cattle.

Garnett reported, "Three of the men, having been recognized as participants in the attack on the miners, were shot, in compliance with my general instructions on this subject."[102] A fourth of the miners' attackers was shot attempting to escape, and a fifth found and killed later. Several days after the shootings, Lt. George R. Crook, later a major general and famous Indian fighter, along with Company D of the Fourth Infantry, located another Indian camp on the Wenatchee River. Five "wanted" men were pointed out to him by the chief; Crook seized, bound, lined them up, and shot them. Crook later remarked, "This whole business was exceedingly distasteful to me, and as my 2nd Lieut. Turner rather enjoyed that kind of thing, I detailed him to execute them."[103] Splawn reports that at least one victim of execution, left for dead, survived and recovered from his wounds.[104]

By the end of August most of the Indians in the area had taken refuge in the mountains, and Garnett had trouble finding them. Six of those involved in the attacks on the miners were still at large, but repeated expeditions over difficult mountain trails failed to reveal them. Garnett continued farther north to the vicinity of the Hudson's Bay Company's Fort Okanogan, at the junction of the Okanogan and Columbia rivers.

On September 15 he started for home; supplies were running low and shoes wearing out. He had received news of Wright's victories. He moved down the Columbia and then traveled west from Priest Rapids to Fort Simcoe, reaching there on September 27, after forty-five days in the field and a march of 550 miles. His losses consisted of Lieutenant Allen and one enlisted man.

In his final report Garnett commented that the successes of his expedition "though small have repaid us however for the labor." He felt that his severity had had a salutary effect on the Indians. Owhi, Skloom, and Qualchin had fled with the remaining handful of attackers of the miners and could not be found.[105] Garnett's campaign was later described as brief and ineffectual. Attacks on passing miners continued, and two months later another detachment was required to seek the murderers of more whites.

Garnett's return to Fort Simcoe was marred by personal tragedy. His wife had died of "bilious fever" on September 17, and six days later their seven-month-old son had died. A messenger sent to tell him of the deaths had been unable to find him; not until he was within fifteen miles of home did he learn what had happened. He was granted leave to take the bodies to his wife's home in New York for burial. In 1861 he resigned his commission to join the Confederate forces. As a brigadier general and adjutant to Gen. Robert E. Lee, he was killed in action at Carrick's Ford during the Cheat River Battle.

Clarke Faults Wright's Treaties

The Indian war in Washington, and particularly Steptoe's defeat, caused concern in the nation's capital and led to the realization that strong measures were required. On September 13, 1858, the Department of the Pacific was divided into two parts. General William S. Harney was placed in command of the newly created Department of Oregon, which included Washington, Oregon, what is now Idaho, and parts of Montana and Wyoming, with headquarters at Fort Vancouver. General Clarke was to assume command of the other division, the Department of California, with headquarters in San Francisco.

Gen. Newman S. Clarke, commander of the Department of the Pacific during the Indian War of 1858. Courtesy California State Library.

On October 2, Clarke reported to army headquarters from Fort Vancouver:

> The short, and on our side nearly bloodless, campaign is over. The sudden assembling of the troops took the Indians by surprise; their energy and superior arms threw them into consternation; the expenditure in life and treasure in a long war has been saved, peace is obtained, and a control over the most warlike of the Pacific tribes, which need never be lost. The energy and good leading of Colonel Wright and Major Garnett are seen in the fruits obtained. Their officers and men received their commendations, they have proven good soldiers, patient, enduring, and active. I commend the zeal of all concerned to the General-in-Chief.

The only sour note at this time was Clarke's dissatisfaction with Wright's treaties. On October 10, Clarke reported from Port Townsend on Puget Sound, "There are now no hostile Indians; the work of the troops is finished, and I am able to withdraw to the seaboard the summer reinforcement for operations elsewhere." However, enclosing Wright's preliminary treaties with his report, he commented, "With the form of some of these articles, and the matter of others, I have been obliged to report my disapproval." [106]

Before Wright's campaign Clarke had stipulated that Wright was not to ask for the passage of soldiers and citizens through Indian country as a concession but to demand it as a right. Wright, he said, should have insisted on that condition. Moreover, he said, "The objections to the acceptance of the conditional surrender of prisoners are patent." He conceded that enough had been done to secure the submission of the Indians and give security to the border; although he felt obliged to note these departures from the spirit of his orders, he had no desire to magnify them into grave evils.

What did these preliminary treaties actually say? The treaty with the Coeur d'Alenes stipulated:

1. Hostilities between the United States and the Coeur d'Alene Indians were to cease.

2. The Coeur d'Alene Indians agreed to surrender to the United States all property in their possession belonging either to the government or to individuals.

3. The men who commenced the battle with Lieutenant Colonel Steptoe contrary to the orders of their chiefs were to be surrendered, and one chief and four men, with their families, were to be given to the officer in command of the troops as hostages for their future good conduct.

4. The Coeur d'Alenes promised that all white persons could travel through their country unmolested and that Indians hostile to the United States would be kept out.

5. The officer in command of the U.S. troops promised that if the foregoing conditions were complied with no war would be made upon the Coeur d'Alene nation and that the men who were surrendered, both those who commenced the fight and the hostages, would in no way be injured and within one year would be restored to their nation.

6. When the foregoing articles had been complied with, a permanent treaty of peace and friendship would be made.

7. This treaty was to extend to the Nez Percé Indians.

Eighteen Indians affixed their marks to this treaty, and twelve of Wright's officers signed as witnesses.

The articles of the treaty with the Spokane Nation were essentially the same, except that no mention was made of a future permanent treaty. Clarke's endorsement read:

The fifth article in each of these treaties is disapproved in so far as it accepts the conditional surrender of those Indians guilty of commencing the attack on the troops.

An unconditional surrender was demanded by me before the troops were sent into the field; less should not have been accepted afterwards.

A surrender of the guilty conditioned on their immunity from punishment is futile.

It is now too late to repair the error; the prisoners are but hostages and as such will be kept as long as it may be proper to do so.

The agreement to admit troops and citizens to pass through

the country had better have been a demand than a part of the treaty, but this matters not much, as we have the substance.

Some of this seems like quibbling, especially from a man who was not himself engaged in treaty making. Wright saw that Clarke's insistence on punishment of the attackers, which to the Indians meant hanging, was a stumbling block to any sort of agreement and, in fact, a precipitating factor in the war. Seeing his supplies dwindling and winter coming on, Wright had granted some concessions as a sensible compromise. Perhaps Clarke recognized his own unreasonableness, for on the same day he wrote of his objections, he issued Orders No. 4, which were later printed and widely distributed:

> HEADQUARTERS DEPARTMENT OF THE PACIFIC
> Fort Vancouver, W.T. October 7, 1858
> Brevet Brigadier General Clarke tenders to Colonel Wright and Major Garnett, 9th infantry, his thanks for the zeal, energy, and skill displayed by them in leading the troops against hostile Indians. Also to the troops for their bravery and intrepidity in action against the Indians.
> By command of Brigadier General Clarke.
> W. W. MACKALL,
> Assistant Adjutant General.

By mid-October, Clarke was in San Francisco, now headquarters of the new Department of California. Although he was no longer in command of the northern division, he believed that he should make his views known. He now strongly recommended approval of the Stevens treaties and the opening of the interior to settlers. In view of Wright's subjugation of the Indians and the lure of newly discovered gold lodes, he saw this policy as the best means of maintaining the pacification.

On November 10, General-in-Chief Scott issued General Orders No. 22 from his headquarters in New York. They gave a brief account of Wright's campaign and said:

> Those severe blows resulted in the unqualified submission of the Coeur d'Alenes, the dispersion of the other tribes, and it is not doubted, ere this, in the subjugation of the whole alliance.

Results so important, without the loss of a man or animal, gained over tribes brave, well armed, confident in themselves from a recent accidental success, and aided by the many difficulties presented by the country invaded, reflect high credit on all concerned.

Colonel Wright is much to be commended for the zeal, perseverance, and gallantry he has exhibited.[107]

A brief accolade for General Clarke follows, for planning and organizing Wright's and Garnett's campaigns and for gathering the forces and supplies necessary for success. In Scott's report to the secretary of war he commended the activities of Clarke, Wright, and Garnett and noted that peace had been established by their victories.

Secretary of War John B. Floyd, in his report to the president dated December 6, 1858, gives a brief account of the campaign and adds:

[It] was prosecuted with great activity and vigor by Colonel Wright of the 9th infantry, who gave battle to the Indians on several occasions, always routing them completely. After beating their forces, capturing many prisoners, and destroying large amounts of property, and laying waste their country, the Indians surrendered at discretion, with their wives and children, and sued abjectly for peace. The criminal offenders amongst them, heretofore guilty of murder and rapine, the chief instigators of all dissatisfaction amongst those tribes, and the immediate cause of the recent hostilities, were surrendered, tried, and executed.

A permanent peace has been established by treaties entered into with them, and the army has been already distributed to points where the presence of a force was greatly needed. The officers and men of the command deserve the thanks of the country for the efficient and soldierly manner in which they have borne themselves in the prosecution of the campaign.[108]

Although higher authorities were less disturbed than Clarke about the details of the treaties, the brevet for Wright, for which he and many of his officers were hoping, did not materialize. It is easy to speculate that Wright was held down by the machinations of the southern clique which dominated the army, from the secretary of war down. But Wright occasionally made allusions to other, personal reasons, the exact nature of which remain obscure.

In the fall of 1860, upon the death of General Clarke, a letter to the editor took exception to his obituary notice in the *Weekly Alta California.* In no sense belittling Clarke's actions in connection with the Indian War of 1858, the writer pointed out that it was Wright who had done the fighting, achieved the victories, and subdued the enemy. The letter read, "The judgment, gallantry, professional skill and precise knowledge of the foe—of Colonel Wright, supported by the ability and zeal of his officers and the good conduct of the troops achieved the success of the campaign." This, the letter pointed out, Wright accomplished "in less than one hundred days, so that not the least sign of hostilities has since been noticed."[109]

The Reverend Charles Wadsworth, in his eulogy at Wright's funeral in 1865, referred to Wright's successful termination of the Indian troubles and stated that "none of the tribes, then in the field, have since raised a hostile gun, and the name of General Wright serves to remind them of their humiliation and refresh their wholesome terror of the American Army."[110] Most recent writers have been disparaging of Wright's accomplishments.[111] Some have vilified him, referring to him as a pitiless incarnation of evil, a sadist who enjoyed the "Roman holiday spectacle" of his hangings, calling him the "shifty colonel," and even questioning his sanity and sobriety.[112] Yet, one writer concedes, "considering the provocation of two defeats by the Indians and the Cascades attack, the army was content with a remarkably restrained victory—one not entirely satisfactory to at least a part of [Washington and] Oregon's citizens."[113] However, most citizens of the time felt that a great deal had been accomplished. The need for future warfare with the tribes involved was eliminated, the interior was opened for settlement, and Senate ratification of the Stevens treaties was forthcoming.

To evaluate Wright's conduct by modern standards is unfair and misleading. Twentieth-century Americans have a far greater concern for civil liberties and the rights of minorities than was prevalent in Wright's lifetime—in the era of manifest destiny, when the nation was expanding rapidly. The Indian was regarded as an aboriginal nuisance who stood in the way of the advance of civilization. At the time of Wright's arrival at Fort Vancouver the territorial authorities were offering a bounty of eighty dollars for the heads of hostile warriors.

The government had led the white immigrants to believe that the lands they had struggled so hard to reach were theirs for the claiming. The government wanted the land filled with settlers and the Indians placed on reservations. The civil authorities and the settlers had long been angered by the failure of the army to afford them the protection to which they felt themselves entitled. Many had lost friends and loved ones. Bancroft has estimated that between 1845 and 1856 more than 700 whites were killed by the Indians in the Oregon country, few of these in actual battle.[114] Victor put the figure at 160 per year between 1850 and 1862, over half being "unprovoked murders." Writing in 1894, she referred to the Indian as "a wild man . . . a wild animal on his way to be a man," and said that the ethical and moral parts of him were undeveloped.[115] With the prevalence of attitudes such as these, one can begin to understand some of the pressures Wright experienced.

Besides his browbeating and threatening the Indians, Wright is most often criticized for his hangings and the destruction of the horse herd. However, as one historian has observed, "so crucial were horses to the Plains Indians' way of life that the United States Army made killing them a major objective."[116] The orders that Harney had received for the prosecution of the campaign of 1858 indicated that destruction of the Indian herds was to be part of his task.[117] Certainly Wright could not have kept or used the whole herd, and he did summon a board of officers to help him reach a decision about their disposition. Destruction of an enemy's transport is still an important part of modern warfare.

In regard to the hangings, there is no doubt that Wright administered "summary justice" to the Indians he regarded as war criminals. None received a formal trial, although Wright usually reported that he conducted a careful investigation in such an instance. A "careful investigation" in the field probably meant that he asked them a few questions. Many of these Indians were known to him personally or to his officers. Their misdeeds were widely known and included robbery, murder, and waging war against the United States outside their own territory. Many had already been warned that they would be severely dealt with if they took up arms on the side of the hostiles. Some admitted their guilt; others were indicted by fellow tribesmen during the confrontations.

Although the Spokanes and the Coeur d'Alenes were involved in the attack on Steptoe and in the subsequent battles, none of them were hanged. Presumably the agreement with Father Joset precluded this punishment. Wright's written orders do not say specifically what he was to do with the "criminals" from any of the tribes except that he was to obtain their submission, guard them closely, and await further orders, but he must have had a tacit understanding with General Clarke.

When Garnett reported the execution by shooting of ten Indians involved in the attack on the miners he said that it was done "in compliance with my general instructions on this subject," and again, "in compliance with my orders." Garnett's reports say nothing about a trial or a court of officers. That their orders to "punish" certain miscreants meant "execute" was obviously understood by both commanders. Clarke, in commenting on Garnett's actions, commends him for capturing "and doing justice upon the greater number of those who attacked the miners." Clarke, though quick to criticize Wright's treaties as too lenient, had no complaint regarding the hangings.

After the Steptoe disaster Wright experienced a dramatic change of attitude toward the Indians. Previously he had been sympathetic to them, but now he regarded him-

self as an agent of vengeance. A number of factors contributed to this reversal. First, he believed that the Indians had
not kept the promises they had made to him during the
preceding two years. Second, he was still smarting from
the criticism he had received for his conduct of the Yakima
campaign. Third, along with the change of commanders
of the Pacific Department had come a change in the army's
philosophy regarding the Indians. But above all, Wright
had felt the defeat of his subordinate Steptoe as a personal
blow. To Wright's credit he never made predawn attacks or
raids under a white flag of truce on Indian villages. The
indiscriminate slaughter of men, women, and children,
perpetrated by other commanders on the Sioux at Ash Hollow, the Cheyennes at Sand Creek, and at Black Kettle's
camp on the Washita, or on the Blackfeet on the Marias
River, would have been repugnant to him.

One can only wonder how the campaign against the
Spokanes, Coeur d'Alenes and Palouses would have been
conducted and how the Indians would have been treated
had General Harney arrived a few months earlier and
been in charge.

11.
Under a New Commander

GENERAL WILLIAM S. HARNEY, a native of Tennessee, who was placed in command of the newly created Department of Oregon, was a controversial character. To some he was the army's foremost Indian fighter; others pejoratively referred to him as the "Squaw Killer." Although it was said of him that "Harney uses a rope to good purpose," there is no question that he had served his country long and faithfully, if at times insubordinately. His whole life was marked by contentiousness and a tendency to act independently without the sanction of his superiors.

He arrived at Fort Vancouver on October 24, 1858, with orders from the secretary of war to prosecute with the greatest possible vigor the campaign commenced by General Clarke. The hostile bands were to be thoroughly chastised and subdued. There was to be no cessation of the campaign for the winter, that being

> the most favorable season for striking at the homes and herds of the hostiles. The fall of snow, at no time sufficient to prevent the ready operation of troops in the valleys lying between the Cascade and Rocky Mountains, where the Indians dwell and graze their animals in winter, is nevertheless, so great in the mountain passes as to prevent their passage by the Indians. Their families and herds will thus be readily reached by the troops, and no exertions should be spared to capture the first and destroy the last. No overtures of friendship should be made to any tribes before the chastisement of the hostiles. It would be taken as an evidence of weakness or fear, and exaggerate rather than relieve the evils of war with these people.[1]

Three years earlier Harney had been responsible for the infamous Ash Hollow massacre of the Brulé Sioux.[2] Just before that campaign began, Col., Bvt. Brig. Gen., Ethan Allen Hitchcock, who later served as adviser to President Abraham Lincoln and Secretary of War Edwin M.

Stanton, resigned from the army rather than serve under Harney.

One can imagine Harney's disappointment when, on his arrival at Fort Vancouver, he found the fighting over and the opportunity for glory gone. He talked of renewing the campaign against the Indians and made disparaging remarks about the officers who had engaged in the recent expedition, especially its commander, George Wright. Keyes remarked, "The Harney clique spoke in derision of our battles in which not a man was hit and their prejudices inclined them to withhold *all credit* from Wright and his associates, a majority of whom were Northern men."[3]

Harney brought with him the veteran Jesuit missionary, Father Pierre-Jean De Smet, ostensibly as chaplain to the troops but actually as peace envoy to the Indians. Because of his influence with the Indians and their affection for him, particularly the mountain tribes whom he had visited previously, the sixty-year-old De Smet soon set out on a six-month peace tour of more than 1,600 miles. Part of the time he was snowbound at the Coeur d'Alene mission, but ultimately he got as far east as the Flathead country in western Montana. He found the Indians confused and restless but, as a result of Wright's campaign, no longer interested in war.

At Fort Walla Walla in November, 1858, De Smet was able to obtain the release of the Indian hostages and prisoners held there, since by their exemplary conduct in captivity they had earned the goodwill of the army. Wherever he went he was well received, leading him to say, "The country, I have reason to believe, will remain quiet." This tranquillity was, of course, due in no small measure to his own efforts.[4]

One of De Smet's projects was to bring a delegation of chiefs from the tribes he had visited to meet the new commander at Fort Vancouver. Amazingly, this group included the most sought-after instigator of them all, Kamiakin, and his brother Skloom.[5] Skloom proved to be too ill to travel, and Kamiakin, becoming suspicious of the interference of Indian agent John Owen, slipped away when the party arrived at Walla Walla. Harney was furious at the failure of what he regarded as a great coup, especially since he had already told the War Department that Kamiakin and Skloom were on their way to see him.

The following summer De Smet accompanied the chiefs back to their tribes and then returned overland to Saint Louis. Harney expressed great appreciation to De Smet in personal letters and official dispatches for his help in restoring calm.

Harney's Changes

Meanwhile, Harney, within a few days of his arrival at Fort Vancouver, opened up the interior by inviting settlement near military posts, although the Stevens treaties were not ratified until March 8, 1859. Indian investigator Mott protested this action on "the mere ipse dixit of a military commander." He believed that the infiltration of whites before the time stipulated in the treaties would weaken the Indians' confidence in the promises and good faith of the government.[6]

Reporting to army headquarters, Harney enclosed further copies of Wright's treaties without adverse comment. Referring to these and to a letter from Wright, he says, "It will be seen . . . that a material change has been effected in the minds of these savages, as regards the power as well as the determination of the government to carry out its measures concerning them."[7] On October 28, Wright had written him:

> With regard to the present disposition and feeling of the various Indians with whom I have been brought in contact during the late campaign, I can assure the general that we have nothing to apprehend. The Nez Perces, Spokanes, Coeur d'Alenes, Pelouses, Walla Wallas and other tribes residing on both banks of the Columbia River and its tributaries, are now regarded as entirely friendly.[8]

Harney reported to army headquarters that he found the troops at Fort Vancouver "through culpable neglect" unsupplied with proper clothing because Wright's repeated requisitions to San Francisco had been ignored.[9] Another source of annoyance to Harney was the subsidiary position of his headquarters to Fort Dalles, the regimental headquarters of the Ninth Infantry, of which Wright retained command. Harney set about strengthening Fort Vancouver and stripping The Dalles of its importance. The extravagant construction costs at Fort Dalles had provoked numerous complaints, so downgrading was easy. Fort Simcoe he turned over to the Indian Department.[10]

Harney informed army headquarters that from a strategic standpoint Fort Walla Walla was the most important post, and on June 15, 1859, he placed Wright in command there. Harney also sent expeditions to explore southeastern Oregon, build roads in the area, seek reservation sites, evaluate the disposition of the Snake Indians, and protect emigrants on the Oregon Trail. Meanwhile, the War Department authorized Lieutenant Mullan to complete the military road from Walla Walla to Fort Benton.[11] The road was never heavily traveled, and its usefulness declined after the Northern Pacific Railroad came through in 1883.[12]

Following Harney's order opening the interior to settlement, miners and settlers poured into the area. During 1859, Harney visited the various posts in his command. He deplored the defenseless state of Puget Sound, with its lack of heavy ordinance and war vessels, while Great Britain had warships at Victoria and Esquimalt.

But Harney's most pressing problems at this time were disciplinary.[13] Within a few months of his arrival at Fort Vancouver, his treatment of his junior officers, many of whom had been serving with Wright, produced chaos. For one who was so often insubordinate to his superiors in the army, he was extremely intolerant of any disobedience or disrespect by his subordinates. By the time Harney had been at Fort Vancouver a year and a half, two of his officers had been court-martialed, one had resigned in protest, another had been confined to quarters incommunicado, and a fifth was listed as a deserter when he fled after drawing a pistol on Harney.[14]

General-in-Chief Scott was outraged by the accounts of the capricious arrests and their devastating effect on morale. He ordered certain offenders released and their alleged offenses stricken from their records.

The U.S. Army vs. the Hudson's Bay Company

There were continual squabbles with the Hudson's Bay Company. In 1849, the United States established a military post, Columbia Barracks, on the bluff behind Fort Vancouver. Initially relations between the Hudson's Bay Company and the army were cordial, but as time passed, the army increasingly disregarded the company's property rights. The situation became critical in 1860, when Harney commandeered a tract of company property for a drill ground. Old buildings and fences in the area were removed, and an aged, retired company employee was evicted. Company officials lodged a formal protest, but finally, in view of the declining fur trade, the encroachment of American settlements, and the hostile attitude of the army, they decided to abandon their holdings and move their operations to Victoria.[15]

Later, when Col. George Wright succeeded to the command of the Department of Oregon, he suspended further destruction of the Hudson's Bay Company's buildings and improvements and informed headquarters that the company had left the Oregon country in May. He called attention to the partly demolished buildings and asked for further guidance.[16] The unsightly structures were still standing in September, and he again requested authority to demolish them and erect a new departmental headquarters. Months passed without a response from headquarters, but time, plunder, fire, and decay gradually solved part of the problem.

Among those who appreciated the presence of George Wright at Fort Vancouver were the Sisters of Charity of Providence, who had come from Montreal in response to a request from the bishop of Nisqually, A. M. A. Blanchet. The original group, consisting of Mother Joseph and four

others, had arrived at Fort Vancouver on the *Brother Jonathan* on December 8, 1856. They had started a school, an
orphanage, a home for the aged, and a hospital, the first
of a chain that eventually extended from Alaska to southern California. The sisters came to know Colonel Wright
well and received many kindnesses from him.[17] He made
lumber available to them for some of their buildings and
allowed them to solicit funds from the soldiers on payday.
Benefits, bazaars, and band concerts were held at the post
to help finance their charitable work.[18]

The San Juan Island Controversy

Although Harney's conduct in the matter of the Hudson's
Bay Company's properties led to diplomatic exchanges
with Great Britain, it was his actions in another affair that
led the United States perilously close to a war with that nation and resulted in his removal from command.

When the boundary was established between the United
States and Canada at the 49th parallel, an exception was
made of Vancouver Island, the southern end of which extended a short distance below that line.[19] The Treaty of
Washington, made in 1846, said nothing about the smaller
islands in the area, only that the boundary between Vancouver Island and the mainland was to be established in
the middle of the channel between them. At the time the
treaty was made, the matter was of little consequence, but
as the citizens of each nation became interested in the development of these islands, the question of ownership assumed importance. Actually, there were two main channels, the Strait of Haro, west of San Juan Island, and the
Strait of Rosario, east of Orcas Island. The Americans
held that Haro was the main waterway, while the British
claimed that Rosario was the channel to which the treaty
makers had been referring.[20]

In 1852 the Oregon territorial legislature established
county government for the islands north of Puget Sound;
the following year, when Washington became a separate

territory, Island County was held to be a part of Washington. Later that year the Hudson's Bay Company began grazing sheep on San Juan Island. The company was informed that it would have to pay U.S. customs, a notion at which the British scoffed, saying that the disputed islands were under British jurisdiction.

Governor Stevens sought guidance from Secretary of State William L. Marcy, who told him to avoid conflict without implying concession to British claims and assured him that the matter would be settled between the two governments. Meanwhile, Americans took up claims on San Juan Island and soon outnumbered the British.

One of the American settlers was Lyman Cutler, who had staked a claim near British headquarters on the island, fenced it in, and planted a garden. Hudson's Bay Company pigs knocked down his fence and rooted up his potatoes. On June 15, 1859, the only casualty of what came to be known as the "Pig War" occurred when Cutler shot a pilfering porker. A delegation of company officials called on Cutler, who denied that his act had taken place on British soil. He was threatened with arrest and trial in Victoria. News of these events spread rapidly and were magnified by both the Puget Sound settlers and the army.

Harney immediately decided to occupy the island with U.S. troops. One of Wright's officers, Captain George E. Pickett, and Company D of the Ninth Infantry were sent to build a fort at the southern end of San Juan Island, allegedly to protect the settlers from Indians, but actually to safeguard them from interference by British authorities.[21]

Pickett promptly issued a proclamation that San Juan Island was U.S. territory and that only U.S. laws and courts would be recognized. The British demanded that Pickett leave. By the end of July the British had three well-armed warships anchored in the bay below Pickett's little breastworks. Harney sent him reinforcements, and Pickett declined to depart, saying that he would fight to the last man if British troops landed. Hudson's Bay Company officials could not believe that Pickett's only orders came from Harney at Fort Vancouver. Summer was almost over before anyone in Washington, D. C., or London heard about these events. President James Buchanan was flabbergasted and sent General Scott to Washington Territory to investigate.

Scott reached Fort Vancouver on October 20. He held meetings with Harney and Pickett and then suggested to James Douglas, governor of the new crown colony of British Columbia, that a force of not more than 100 men of each nation be left on the island to protect the rights of their citizens and defend them against hostile Indians. Douglas initially wanted all U.S. troops removed but finally agreed to joint occupancy. Pickett was ordered back to Fort Bellingham, and his troops were dispersed to mainland posts. A force of British marines was installed at the northern end of the island, and a company of infantry was left at the southern end.

Scott departed for the East early in November. Incredibly, the following spring, Harney placed Pickett back in command on San Juan Island. When word of this assignment reached him, an angry Scott wrote to Secretary of War John B. Floyd that Harney considered San Juan Island "as a part of *Washington Territory*. . . . If this does not lead to a collision of arms, it will again be due to the forbearance of the British authorities." Scott said that he had found both Harney and Pickett proud of the "*conquest*" of the island and jealous of interference.[22] When President Buchanan was informed of this latest development, Harney was relieved of his command, and Wright was placed in charge of the Department of Oregon. Harney was ordered to report to Washington, D.C., where he was officially reprimanded by the secretary of war.

Final settlement of the boundary dispute was delayed by the Civil War, Reconstruction, and troubles in Europe; however, cordial relations between the two local commanders and the troops managed to keep the peace.

The boundary question was ultimately referred to Kaiser Wilhelm I of Germany, as a prestigious and impartial arbiter. The Kaiser's decision favoring the Canal de Haro as the boundary was announced on October 21, 1872. The British garrison was withdrawn, and the San Juan Islands became part of the United States.[23]

Wright Relieves Harney in Command, 1860

When Wright assumed command of the Department of Oregon on July 5, 1860, the San Juan Islands were peaceful. He left Pickett in command there, since, freed of Harney's influence, he had done a good job of maintaining order among the often raucous civilians and had kept peace with the British. Pickett resigned from the army in June, 1861, to join the Confederate forces. He attained his greatest fame as the major general who led the heroic but futile charge at Gettysburg.

Wright requested official recognition for the military reserve on San Juan Island and confirmation of a new military reservation known as Fort Colville, eleven miles southeast of the Hudson's Bay Company's Fort Colvile. Because warlike Indians from the British possessions threatened to make trouble on Puget Sound, he ordered the reoccupation of Fort Townsend, which had been abandoned when Harney sent the garrison to San Juan Island. He also sought authority to concentrate the troops in his department for instruction, as the army had once done at Jefferson Barracks. He felt that the men, scattered at multiple small posts, knew little of "big operations" and would profit by attending a "school of practice." The army, however, did not approve the idea.[24]

Because of the unprotected state of the northern part of his department, Wright wanted to establish a military reservation at Point Defiance. The post, he said, would be of strategic importance to Puget Sound. He also wanted to establish a post at the mouth of the Columbia River because of the close presence of a number of British warships. Again his requests were denied. Southern influences in the War Department were opposed to strengthening Pacific Coast defenses.

Wright was distressed to find the quartermaster depart-

ment of the Oregon district $400,000 in debt. He com-
plained to the quartermaster general that the steamboat
company on which the army primarily depended had been
obliged to borrow money at high interest rates because of
unpaid government bills. Because of the company's importance for the movement of troops and supplies he hoped it
would not be forced out of business by financial problems.
Wright told Adj. Gen. Lorenzo Thomas that he needed
money for his headquarters and for the rest of his department, as well as funds for recruiting to replace the men
who had been mustered out and for new uniforms.

When Wright took over the command of the Department of Oregon, he appointed Capt. James A. Hardie of
the Third Artillery as his departmental adjutant. Hardie
was one of his veterans, a man for whom Wright came to
have a high regard. In December he was obliged to report
Steptoe AWOL; nothing had been heard from him since
he departed on leave.[25]

Trouble with the Snake River Indians

Although Wright tended to be a bit euphoric about his
subjugation of the Indians in Washington Territory, he
must have known that all was not peaceful in the southern
part of the department, what is now central and eastern
Oregon and southern Idaho. In January, 1860, the Reverend Edward R. Geary, who had succeeded Nesmith as superintendent of Indian affairs, submitted a report to the
commissioner of Indian affairs in Washington, D.C.; he
enclosed a communication he had received from Capt.
H. D. Wallen, Fourth Infantry, who had commanded a
wagon-road expedition between Fort Dalles and the valley
of the Great Salt Lake the previous summer.

Wallen reported that in August, 1859, the Digger Snake
Indians had staged a destructive raid on the Warm Springs
Reservation in central Oregon, which contained mainly
Wasco, Paiute, and Tyigh Indians. The Digger Snakes
were very poor and subsisted mainly on insects, fish, roots,
and seeds. Although armed only with primitive spears,

bows, and arrows, they were described as expert thieves. Having had little contact with the whites, they had no guns or ammunition. Although the Diggers made occasional predatory raids, their recent attack was thought to be in reprisal for the slaughter of several members of the tribe by the reservation Indians. Wallen regarded them as relatively harmless.

Wallen encountered the Mountain Snakes or Bannocks east of the Blue Mountains at Salmon Falls on the Snake River, where they were fishing. He described these warriors as athletic, well armed, formidable, and not at all impressed with the power of the whites. They roamed in bands of sixty or seventy warriors for several hundred miles along the Snake River from old Fort Boise as far south as the California Road. These bands constituted a considerable annoyance to parties of emigrants heading for California.[26]

Wright certainly was aware that there had been trouble in eastern Oregon the summer he took over the command of the Department. On June 27, 1860, Capt. A. J. Smith reported being attacked by hostile Snakes near Harney Lake in southeastern Oregon and eagerly awaiting the arrival of Maj. Enoch Steen, who was camped on Beaver Creek. When Wright heard of Smith's predicament, he ordered three companies of the Third Artillery under Bvt. Maj. George P. Andrews to march to the scene of activity and a squadron of dragoons under Brevet Major Grier to move from Fort Walla Walla on the Boise Road and report to Steen.

Two days later Steen reported that he had received Smith's message and was moving to join him. He suggested that two companies of dragoons be sent to patrol the headwaters of the John Day River to guard emigrants. He also reported having defeated some Indians and requested more rations. Later in July, Wright reported to the adjutant general that Steen had surprised a small party of Snakes on the headwaters of the Malheur River and captured several of them.

In contrast to his misgivings before the 1858 campaign,

Wright predicted a speedy victory for his troops in the field. On August 13 he reported that Andrews had reached his destination, Grier was on the Snake River, and Steen was moving into the Snow Mountains south of Lake Harney. By September 3, Steen had carried out several "active scouts." The Snakes had been scattered and driven west of the Blue Mountains. Steen had seen signs of large numbers of Indians, but there had been no more battles, although the Wascos who were accompanying him had killed a few hostile Indians.

On September 1, Wright ordered Steen to return with his command to Fort Dalles and the other troops to return to their respective stations, believing that there was nothing more for them to do in the field that season.

On the twentieth, Wright sent what proved to be a fatuous and tragically inaccurate report to army headquarters. He stated that travel east of the Cascade Mountains in Washington Territory was now safe, even for a person traveling alone. Between the Cascades and the Columbia River there had been no trouble with the Indians since Garnett's campaign, and Wright himself had taken care of the area east of the Columbia. He conceded that the Snake Indians had caused difficulties in eastern Oregon (and what was to become Idaho Territory in 1863) but said that military operations had made the emigrant routes "perfectly safe," although a post was still needed near old Fort Boise.[27]

As he wrote this, he was unaware that eleven days earlier one of the worst massacres in the history of the Oregon Trail had taken place.[28] Major Grier and his two companies of dragoons had spent several weeks in the area, protecting the main body of emigrants. Grier had found no evidence of large numbers of Indians anywhere along the trail. Supposing that all travelers had passed the dangerous area, he returned with his command to Fort Walla Walla. He had scarcely left the area when the slaughter began.[29]

Although Grier had been informed that the last of the year's emigrants had passed the last danger point, in fact, a party of forty-four persons remained on the trail—seventeen men, four women, and twenty-three children. With their eight wagons and cattle they had safely completed the long pilgrimage over the plains. The group had been escorted by troops from the Portneuf River near Fort Hall, in what is now southeastern Idaho, to a point about three days' travel above Salmon Falls. Four discharged soldiers had joined the party at the Portneuf.

At the falls, about 140 miles down the Snake River from the mouth of the Portneuf, the travelers found the attitude of the Indians threatening. For the next few days all was quiet as the little caravan moved onward along the southern bank of the Snake River until it reached a point about 50 miles below Salmon Falls. There about noon on September 9, the train was suddenly attacked by a large band of Mountain Snakes.

The emigrant party formed a corral with their wagons about 100 rods from the river and put up a spirited defense, during which four of their men were killed and several others wounded. During the heat of the engagement the four discharged soldiers mounted their horses and fled.

After thirty-four hours of continuous fighting, the emigrants broke the corral and tried to reach the river to get water. A withering fire from the Indians forced them to abandon their wagons and attempt to flee. Two more men, two women, and three children were killed as the corral broke up. The rest of the party escaped as the Indians occupied themselves with plundering the train. The whites made their way to the Owyhee River, where they camped, but soon they saw that the Indians were watching them and had lighted signal fires.

Seven persons who later tried to travel onward on the road were killed by the Indians, as were two of the soldiers who attempted to cross the Blue Mountains. A third soldier named Snyder reached a camp on Willow Creek in central Oregon with the first news of the disaster. He had traveled day and night for a week and was almost starved. Until two brothers named Reith reached the Umatilla Agency October 2, he was thought to be the only survivor.

Upon their arrival the agent in charge immediately sent out two mounted men with a pack animal and a day later a wagonload of supplies. After eight days these men returned, weary and discouraged. They had seen footprints but no survivors.

On October 4, Superintendent Geary sent the Indian commissioner a preliminary report of the massacre, adding that as soon as Major Steen had left the Snake country near Malheur and Harney lakes, aggressions had resumed against the Warm Springs Reservation. Forty horses had been stolen and the residents feared an attack. Geary told the commissioner that he had informed Wright of these "frontier troubles" and added that he had no doubt that Wright's "experience and energy will prompt him, at the earliest moment practicable, to make such a disposition of the forces, as will prevent further disasters and punish these miscreants." [30]

On the same day Wright ordered Capt. F. T. Dent, the brother-in-law of Ulysses S. Grant, to organize an expedition to set out from Fort Walla Walla with four officers, 100 mounted men, and a packtrain. Dent was to proceed to the scene of the massacre, assist any survivors he could find, and, if possible, punish the murderers. [31] G. W. Abbott, the Indian subagent, said, "[Dent] is a prompt, energetic, and efficient officer, and is activated by a proper spirit, as are also the officers and men under him; and if it is in the power of man to accomplish aught for the benefit of any survivors of the party, if any exist, he will do it." When this search party set out, Jacob Reith accompanied it. [32]

On October 31 an express from Captain Dent reached Fort Walla Walla with the news that on October 27 he had recovered twelve of the lost emigrants: three men, three women, and six children. [33] "They were found in a state of perfect nudity, having been stripped by the savages and left to perish. . . . They were in a state of extreme emaciation, their bones almost protruding from their skin." [34] The survivors, "after consultation and prayer," had eaten the bodies of four children who had died, and were devouring the disinterred remains of one of the men when Dent found them.[35] Wagons were sent from Walla Walla with food, clothing, and other articles for the sufferers.[36]

Among those who had been killed were Mr. and Mrs. Alexis Van Orman and their seventeen-year-old son, Marcus. Four other Van Orman children, three girls and a boy, were known to have been taken captive by the Indians. Of the forty-four persons in the party there were fifteen known survivors, the twelve rescued by Dent, the Reith brothers, and Snyder. Dent buried such bodies as he could find.[37] Because of snow in the mountains there could be no thought of a punitive expedition or any attempt to rescue the captives at that time.

Superintendent Geary, in a report to the Indian commissioner in Washington, D.C., expressed his opinion that the only way to protect immigration into the Pacific Northwest was to establish military posts in the heart of the Snake Indian country. Without such protection, he said, immigration by land to the West Coast would virtually cease. Geary added, "These Indians should not be permitted to escape punishment for their past cruelties and must be taught to respect our power which they now hold in contempt."[38]

Wright sent his first report of the disaster* to army headquarters on October 10.[39] After relating such details as were available to him, he observed that the Snake Indians in the southeastern part of his command were not numerous but that they "lurk and steal." He told of the expensive, frustrating, and largely futile scouts by the troops, who pursued an invisible foe without a home. The subjugation of such nomads might take years. He emphasized the need for improved roads and added that large, well-organized emigrant parties who kept in close contact were comparatively safe. He believed that escorts rather than additional small posts were needed. Troop columns operat-

---

*The catastrophe occurred not far from the scene of the better-known massacre of the Alexander Ward party on August 20, 1854.

ing between Utah and the settlements, leaving at known intervals, could protect the emigrant wagon trains but that small, isolated parties would have to travel at their own risk.

Four weeks later, after receiving Dent's report, Wright assured the adjutant general that every effort would be made to rescue the four prisoners when the deep snow blocking the mountain passes had melted. Through the persistent and heroic efforts of an uncle of the Van Orman children and the aid of the army, one of them was rescued two years later.

Later in October, Wright forwarded to headquarters his plan for a vigorous spring campaign against the Snake Indians. If other areas in his command remained quiet, troops could be drawn from most of the posts east of the Cascades and the weakened posts strengthened with new recruits. He would mobilize two columns against the Snakes, one from Fort Dalles moving south and east and one from Fort Walla Walla moving south. They would meet and establish a post near old Fort Boise, scour the Salmon River country east of the Snake River, and move along the emigrant road in the direction of Fort Hall near present-day Pocatello, to protect immigration to the settlements. A garrison would be left at Fort Boise by the returning columns in the fall.[40]

By the time the spring campaign was to take place, the first guns of the Civil War had been fired against Fort Sumter and the first battles fought. The events on the remote Pacific Northwest frontier were of little interest to anyone except the small number of citizens who lived there.

Civil War Days: 1860–1861

IN NOVEMBER, 1860, Abraham Lincoln was elected sixteenth president of the United States, with Sen. Hamilton Hamblin of Maine as vice-president. In December, South Carolina declared its union with the other states dissolved. Other southern states followed in rapid succession, and in February, 1861, seven of them established the Confederate States of America with a new constitution based on states' rights and slavery and Jefferson Davis as president. Before Lincoln was inaugurated in March 1861, all U.S. forts, arsenals, and navy yards in the seceding states had been captured by the Confederates except Fort Sumter, in Charleston Harbor, and Fort Pickens, at Pensacola.[1]

George Wright's brother-in-law, Col. Edwin V. Sumner, was ordered by General Scott to escort the new president from Springfield, Illinois, to Washington, D.C. When he was informed that the Pinkerton Detective Agency planned to smuggle Lincoln into Washington in disguise because of a plot against his life, Sumner, an old dragoon, is said to have called the plan "a damned piece of cowardice. . . . I'll get a squad of cavalry, Sir, and *cut* our way to Washington, Sir!"[2]

On April 12, 1861, the Confederates fired on Fort Sumter, and the Civil War began. Four more states left the Union, and President Lincoln issued his first call for volunteers. The first major battle of the war, at Bull Run, Virginia, on July 20, 1861, resulted in a rout of the Union forces under Gen. Irvin McDowell. Following this disaster thirty-four-year-old Maj. Gen. George B. McClellan was placed in command of the Army of the Potomac.

Department of Pacific Consolidated

The chief problems initially confronting the Army in the Department of the Pacific were the activities of secessionists and of the hostile Indians. In addition, regular army troops were constantly being shifted east for the war effort, necessitating their replacement by volunteers.

In the states and territories of the Pacific Coast began a fierce struggle between southern sympathizers and Unionists for dominance. At first many Californians were undecided about which cause to support. Some people advocated neutrality, believing that California was too remote to have any effect on the national controversy. A substantial number of citizens favored secession, which meant joining the Confederacy, while others wanted to form a Pacific Republic. The vast majority, however, were loyal to the Union, especially after the fighting started.[3]

The army merged the military departments of California and Oregon into the Department of the Pacific and placed Col. Bvt. Brig. Gen. Albert Sidney Johnston in command. This department comprised all the states and territories west of the Rocky Mountains between the Mexican and Canadian borders.

In March, Secretary of State William H. Seward learned from Sen. James W. Nesmith of Oregon that General Johnston's loyalty to the Union was in question. Captain Erasmus D. Keyes, now serving as military secretary to General Scott, was ordered to California to investigate. At his discretion he could send Johnston to Washington, D.C., and if necessary devolve the command upon his old chief, Col. George Wright. The next day, however, Scott changed his mind and ordered Colonel Sumner to proceed to San Francisco to assume command of the Department of the Pacific. Keyes later said that his mission had been canceled because Scott knew of his eagerness to see Wright assume the department command.[4] Relations between Scott and Wright had long been strained, possibly because Scott viewed Wright as a protegé of Worth's. Other reasons remain obscure, but there is no question that at this time in Wright's life Scott consistently opposed him.

Scott admired Sumner, who had fought in the Mexican War and in numerous campaigns against the Indians. He was four times the commanding officer at Fort Leavenworth and had served in New Mexico and Kansas during the turbulence preceding the Civil War. Finally he was given command of the Department of the West with headquarters in Saint Louis. After he escorted Lincoln to Washington, the president had him promoted to brigadier general. Sumner was married to Margaret Wright's sister, Sara Pettit Montgomery Forster, of Erie, Pennsylvania, whom he had met during his first military assignment at Sacket's Harbor.[5]

Brigadier General Sumner assumed his new command in San Francisco on April 25, 1861. Three days later he requested authorization to place Wright in command of the department if Sumner was needed elsewhere.

Johnston had tendered his resignation earlier in the month and left for the East, and a warrant was issued for his arrest. He subsequently became a major general in the Confederate army and lost his life a year later in the Battle of Shiloh.

Captain Pickett, who was still in command of the strategically important and internationally sensitive post on San Juan Island, also tendered his resignation from the army. He was relieved and his company replaced by a company of the Third Artillery. On June 25, Lt. Philip Owen, Wright's son-in-law, was promoted to captain and in September was ordered to relieve Lt. Philip Sheridan of his command at Fort Yamhill when Sheridan was ordered east.[6]

Governor John G. Downey of California, in response to a request from Secretary of War Simon Cameron, began the task of raising volunteer regiments to relieve the regulars for duty in the East. The volunteers were needed to guard the central Overland Mail Route and later to control the activities of secessionists in the San Bernardino area, who had become increasingly bold since the news of Union reverses. After Downey was replaced by Leland Stanford in the election of 1861, Wright thanked the departing governor for his assistance and cooperation.[7]

From 1861 to 1865, 17,500 volunteers were mustered into service. Of these, only 500 were allowed to leave the Coast and fight in the East. These men had volunteered to

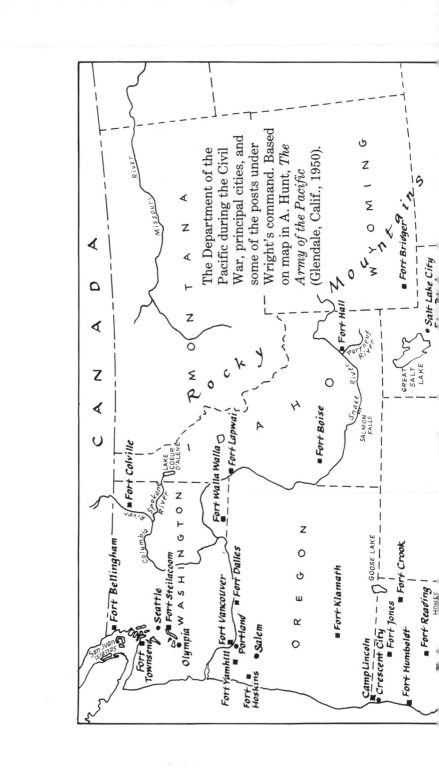

The Department of the Pacific during the Civil War, principal cities, and some of the posts under Wright's command. Based on map in A. Hunt, *The Army of the Pacific* (Glendale, Calif., 1950).

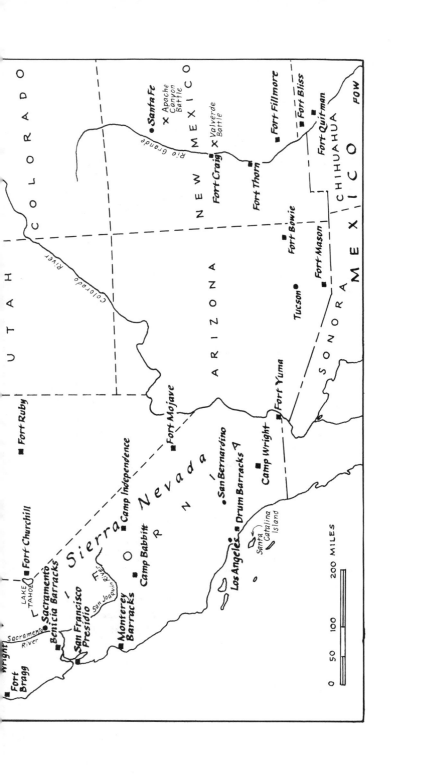

help fill the quota of the state of Massachusetts. The army was reluctant to ship men east because of the expense, and no draft was ever levied west of the Rocky Mountains. More than 16,000 of the volunteers came from California, where eight regiments of infantry and two of cavalry were raised. The state of Oregon and Washington Territory, even less populous, were able to raise their quotas only by enlisting Californians. During the war more than 500 volunteers lost their lives on duty in the West.[8]

Sumner did much to expedite the withdrawal of regular army troops for the East until only the Ninth Infantry, four companies of the Third Artillery, and a detachment of ordinance remained on the Coast. He viewed the threat of Indian disturbances as insignificant compared to saving the Union. To cope with possible threats at sea, he authorized the arming of Pacific mail steamers and later furnished details of soldiers to help protect those ships.[9]

Many officers were withdrawn from federal regiments to command volunteer regiments or transferred to the zones of combat. One by one Wright's officers were taken away from him. One of the first to go was his adjutant, Capt. James A. Hardie. The affection and concern that Wright felt for those serving under him is indicated by a letter that he wrote to Hardie on his departure:

HeadQuarters District of Oregon
Fort Vancouver, W.T. May 3d 1861

My Dear Captain:
I cannot part with you without expressing how highly I appreciate you both personally and officially, and the deep regret I feel at severing a connexion which has afforded me so much pleasure during the last three years.

For your kindness in consenting to perform the duties of Asst. Adjt. General during my command of the Department and District of Oregon, I beg you to accept my warmest thanks-The zeal, ability and intelligence, which have distinguished your performance of the arduous duties imposed upon you, deserve the highest commendation.

I must now bid you adieu, my dear Captain, praying for the

health and happiness of yourself and family, and assuring you of the sincere friendship

> Of your friend & svt.
> G. Wright
> Col. 9-Infy.[10]

Wright's Concern About His Rank

Promotion accompanied many of these transfers, making Wright uncomfortably aware of his own lack of recognition. On May 16 he reviewed his military service in a long letter to Simon Cameron, the secretary of war:

> Headquarters 9 Infy. U.S.A.
> Fort Vancouver, W.T. May 16, 1861

Hon.[bl] Simon Cameron
Secy of War
  Sir,
  In presenting myself before my Government as an applicant for higher rank in the Army, I am fully sensible of the delicate position in which it places me, and it has not been without extreme reluctance that I have decided to address the Hon.[bl] Secretary of War.
  During a long service in the Army, it has been my fortune to receive many honorable notices from my Government- *Three* Brevets in time of War, and lastly *appointed* to the rank I now hold, when the Army was increased in 1855- Under these circumstances, I feel that I can approach the Government without presumption.
  Frankly confessing that I have aspirations for higher rank, yet I would not arrogate to myself any superior merit or claim to advancement.
  I take the liberty of enclosing herewith a memorandum of my military antecedents, and beg leave, most respectfully to request its perusal by the Hon.[bl] Secretary.

> With great respect
> I have the honor to be
> Your Obd. Svt.
> G. Wright
> Col. U.S. Army[11]

Wright pointed out that, with the exception of a few months, he had been on constant duty for thirty-eight years and had always exhibited a patriotic devotion to the Union.

A month later, in another letter to Cameron, he complained that he was assigned to a post remote from the theater of active operations and called attention to the promotion of many of his junior officers to the grade of general by brevet. He hoped that his services in the campaign of 1858 justified his appeal for such a promotion.[12]

The complaint of a disgruntled colonel in the remote Pacific Northwest may not have aroused Cameron's interest. The first great battle of the Civil War had just ended in a rout of the Union forces at Bull Run. A few months later, policy and procedural differences between Cameron and President Lincoln led to his replacement by Edwin M. Stanton. When a scandal in the War Department was revealed, Cameron was censured by Congress.

In June, Wright wrote to Senator Nesmith. This letter reveals the intensity of his patriotism and his belief that he had been discriminated against by superior officers and secretaries of war who entertained southern sympathies.

> Headquarters Dist. of Oregon
> Fort Vancouver, W.T. June 11, 1861
>
> My Dear General:
>
> Before this reaches you, events of the greatest magnitude will doubtless have taken place in the Eastern states, but I trust that our national Capitol will be in repose, and that the Congress of the United States may be undisturbed in their deliberations for the welfare of the Union. I need scarcely say, that I am for the preservation of this glorious Union; it must be preserved intact; not a single star shall fall from that brilliant galaxy- I have prayed that this difficulty might be settled peacefully, but if all the efforts of true patriots North and South fail to accomplish that desirable end, it must be crushed. Let those men, both North and South, who have been instrumental in bringing about this terrible state of affairs, be driven from their country, as unworthy citizens of the Republic.
>
> I have no sectional prejudices; I love the whole country, North, South, East and West, and will fight to preserve this

Union. I have no sympathy with any man, no matter from what section he may come, who is not for the Union, now and forever, one and indivisible.

I have served nearly thirty-nine years in the army, and whether battling with the savage foes in the far West, or deadly hummocks of Florida, or contending with the hosts of Mexico on many a well fought and always victorious field, I have always turned with affection to my native land, and offered up a heartfelt prayer for the Union- God grant that this struggle may soon cease, and that peace may be restored, and our glorious banner, with its thirty-four stars, proudly wave on every housetop from Maine to Texas, and from the Atlantic to our own loved Pacific shore.

The entire people in this country are for the Union. There may be some diversity of opinion as to the *best* mode of settling the difficulty, but all agree that it *must* be preserved.

If we, of the army, remain in this country, it is not probable that we shall be called upon for very active service. But seeing so many of their brother officers who happen to be in the East, promoted to high rank, it begins to arouse the spirit of the young military aspirants for distinction.

I was made a *Colonel* on the bloody field of Molino *Sept.* 8, 1847, but it was only a *Brevet* until March, 1855. But I have not rested very tranquil, under certain *Brevets* of my juniors over me, and I shall not do so. Had I hailed from south of Mason and Dixon's line, I might have obtained a *Brevet* in 1858; but unfortunately I was born in the frozen regions of the North. I cannot, however, now consent to be brought into active service without advancement; not that I could for a moment abandon my flag or country in this, her hour of peril, but I would prefer fighting in the ranks, to occupying a position, without looking forward to preferment.

With great regard,
very truly your friend,
G. Wright[13]

Wright's concern was valid; before the war ended, seventeen of his subalterns had become generals. When the war broke out, the Union army had only 4 general officers; before it ended, there were 583, with an additional 1,367 holding that rank by brevet. In 1860 there were 76 field-grade officers; of 19 colonels, 11 had fought in the War of

1812 as officers. Wright, in his fifty-eighth year, was considered an antique by some of his superiors. The Civil War proved to be a young man's war. Most of the enlisted men were under twenty-one; the average age of brigadier generals was thirty-seven; of major generals, thirty-nine. Of the generals, 217 came from West Point, with Norwich University a close second, but 188 were inexperienced civilians. Many of the reverses suffered by the Union army early in the war were the result of poor leadership. The casual awarding of commissions to untrained civilians was a reflection of the administration's belief that it could not ignore the claims of politicians and remain in power. Paying political debts and reconciling different factions was part of saving the Union.[14]

Indian Affairs

Wright's Oregon district was reasonably calm at the outbreak of the war. Joint occupancy of San Juan Island seemed to be working satisfactorily, at least as a temporary measure.

Concerned about the influx of miners onto the Nez Percé Reservation, Wright sent a company of dragoons there mainly to protect the rights of the Indians, who had always been friendly and loyal. For the first time the Nez Percés were becoming hostile, and Wright feared they might join up with the Snakes. In spite of their growing animosity, Nez Percé scouts were sent to determine the truth of a rumor that the Snake Indians were still holding the Van Orman children captive.[15] In June, 1861, Wright informed headquarters that he had no additional troops to spare. He was authorized to call on the governors of Washington and Oregon for volunteers if he needed them.

Wright was able to prevent a serious uprising at the Cascades by sending troops to the area. The Indians were easily subdued, fearing that Wright might hang them, and they remembered the good advice he had given them in the past.[16]

During the first year of the war the Indians raided several emigrant trains near the Great Salt Lake. In one attack twenty whites were killed, and the survivors were robbed of all they owned. Snake Indians were still being caught and hanged for complicity in the previous year's raid near Salmon Falls.[17]

Assistant Adjutant General Don Carlos Buell, following a tour of inspection of the military posts in northern California, reported that in the recent past more than 200 Indians had been killed by U.S. troops. He recommended stopping the slaughter unless there was confirmation of further Indian depredations. After Sumner was placed in charge of the Pacific Department, he ordered that information-gathering detachments be sent out whenever there was news of uprisings and that punishment be administered only if evidence of guilt was incontrovertible, and then only in proportion of the offense. He was informed that whites were shooting Indian males for trivial misdeeds and raping the women and stealing the children to sell into servitude.[18]

Buell was ordered east in August to assume command of the Kentucky Volunteers. Richard C. Drum became adjutant general of the Pacific Department, in which capacity he served for the rest of the war.

Later in November, Wright reported to the assistant adjutant general in Washington, D.C., that because of the severity of the winter the Indians in many areas were starving. He suggested that an appropriation of $20,000 to feed them would save the government vast sums; it was cheaper, he said, to feed the Indians than to fight them. The Columbia River froze over, and snow was deep in the northern regions and in the mountains. In California roads were blocked and operations delayed by steady rain. Floods caused the deaths of many people and cattle. Sacramento was flooded, and the legislature was forced to adjourn. Many buildings were washed away, and Fort Yuma became an island.[19]

Because of the persistent Indian problems in the area, the seven northern counties of California were designated by the military as the Humboldt District. Colonel Francis J. Lippitt, whose request to raise a regiment and take it east had been rejected by the War Department, was placed in command. Governor Downey had prophetically remarked to Sumner that "an experienced colonel would be especially needed as second in command to Lippitt. You will see [why]!"[20] Lippitt, an austere New Englander, would prove to have difficulties in his new command.

Skirmishes continued as before, with the Indians murdering settlers, plundering and burning their homes, and stealing cattle, and the whites, in turn, abusing the Indians.

Confederate Activities in California and the Southwest

The activities of the secessionists on the Pacific Coast were a source of constant concern. In a few communities they constituted a majority, and a large number lived in southern California. Pockets of disloyal citizens and secret societies were known to exist throughout the western states and territories. It was learned that the Confederates hoped to capture Baja California and the border states of northern Mexico. They also planned to seize the mail steamers conveying treasure to the East and convert them to privateers. As a deterrent, the Pacific Department ordered that any vessel flying the Confederate flag and attempting to enter U.S. waters was to be seized on sight.

Actually, Confederate plans in the West were even more ambitious. Confederate Brig. Gen. Henry H. Sibley was sent to Texas to organize an expedition to conquer New Mexico, Arizona, and possibly part of California. An advance guard of mounted rifles under Col. John R. Baylor began moving up the Rio Grande. Early in July rebel troops occupied Fort Bliss, and a few weeks later seven companies of the Union army's Seventh Infantry surrendered to them near Fort Fillmore. Baylor issued a proclamation taking possession of the Territory of Arizona for the Confederacy, declared himself governor, and settled down to await the arrival of Sibley and another regiment under Col. William Steele. The nearest remaining Union troops were farther up the Rio Grande at Fort Craig under Gen. Edward R. S. Canby. This encroachment by the Confederates necessitated moving the Butterfield stages and the mail from the southern to the central route, by way of Salt Lake.[21]

In August, Scott ordered Sumner to command a major expedition to Texas by way of Mazatlán to recover public property and drive off insurgent troops, with the assistance of Brig. Gen. J. W. Denver. On leaving the Department of the Pacific, Sumner was to turn over his command to Wright. Sumner was pleased at the prospect of seeing action but full of misgivings about the long trek across the desert. Six newly raised companies of volunteers were assembled at San Pedro to prepare for Sumner's expedition.[22]

Reinforcements were sent to Fort Yuma on the Colorado River to guard against an invasion of California and to intercept secessionists heading eastward to join the Confederacy. The two companies of the Sixth Infantry sent for this purpose were under orders never to surrender to the rebels. Sumner informed General Scott that there was considerable evidence of subversive elements on the West Coast, but the disturbances that he had feared might erupt on election day that fall had not materialized.

Wright in Command of Department of Pacific

On September 9, Sumner's orders to prepare the Texas expedition were revoked. The next day orders were issued that the troops gathered for the southern overland route were to march on the twentieth under Col. James H. Carleton. Sumner was to report to army headquarters in the East, and Wright was to proceed to San Francisco to relieve Sumner temporarily. Denver was then to replace Wright, who also was to proceed to army headquarters. Denver received orders in Ohio to go to Washington, D.C., and then go on to California.

On September 13, Col. Benjamin F. Beale, who had briefly commanded the Pacific Department until Johnston's arrival, replaced Wright in command of the recreated Dis-

trict of Oregon. Being in poor health, he was superseded
within a month by Col. Albemarle Cady. Wright reported
to San Francisco and a few weeks later was placed in command of all troops in southern California. The seven counties in this area had been designated a separate military
district on September 25.[23]

Sumner was delighted to be ordered to the principal
scene of war activity and relieved to be freed of the responsibility for what he regarded as an expedition of almost insurmountable difficulty.

He urged Wright to stamp out disloyalty in southern
California, set up a strong supply base for the Southern
Expedition at Warner's Ranch in San Diego County, and
keep Fort Yuma secure. In one of his first reports from
southern California, Wright said that the anti-Union feeling in that section had been greatly exaggerated. Admitting that there were some southern sympathizers, he denied that they were ready to revolt; men who had nothing
to lose were the "reckless" ones. With the troops at his disposal he believed that there was no danger from external
or internal foes.

In his first general order he announced that there would
be no leaves longer than twenty-four hours; that officers in
command of troops were to enforce rigid discipline and attend to the instruction of their officers and men; and that
the object of U.S. troops was to afford peace, protection,
and security to U.S. citizens and to enforce obedience to
the Constitution and laws of the United States and California. Referring to his nine years' service on the Pacific
Coast, he appealed with confidence to California's patriotic
citizens for assistance and cooperation.[24]

Californians vigorously protested the appointment of
Denver. Formerly secretary of state of California, congressman, commissioner of Indian war debt, and governor
of Kansas, Denver had run against Latham for governor
of California. He also had an unsavory reputation for
killing prominent people in duels. Sumner sent word to
Cameron that many officers said they would resign if they
were placed under Denver; it would be a fatal mistake to

put him in command of California volunteers and would even impede recruiting. Moreover, Denver was suspected of entertaining southern sympathies and was regarded as lacking in military skills and totally unfit for command. Ultimately, Denver was ordered to Wheeling, West Virginia.[25]

Wright received a copy of Special Order No. 160, which had been issued at army headquarters in Washington, D.C., on September 30. Brigadier General J. K. F. Mansfield was placed in command of the Department of the Pacific and ordered to San Francisco without delay. Wright was promoted to brigadier general of volunteers and ordered to return to the command of the Columbia River District under Mansfield.[26]

But on October 13, Sumner sent word to Wright: "Come here immediately, by stage if quicker than by boat. Denver is to relieve you and you then go East." Wright transferred the command of the Southern California District to Carleton the next day. On October 20, Sumner relinquished command of the Department of the Pacific, which devolved on Wright, who assumed the position on the same day. This was also the day on which telegraphic communications with the East Coast were established.[27]

Sumner, at age sixty-four, became the oldest corps commander in the Army of the Potomac. As commander of the Second Corps he was promoted to major general and fought in numerous battles of the Peninsular Campaign, in one of which he was wounded. In January, 1863, after the Battle of Fredericksburg, he asked to be relieved of his command and two months later died of pneumonia at the family home in Syracuse, New York.[28]

This was a difficult time for Wright. Before telegraphic communication was established, orders took weeks or even months to arrive, and with the recent and numerous changes he had no idea what he was supposed to do. He was not aware that Mansfield's orders had been changed two days after they were issued and that Mansfield had been ordered to report to Major General Wool at Fort Monroe, Virginia.[29]

Wright, having received Special Order No. 160 by

this time, wrote an agonized letter to his brother-in-law, Sumner:

San Francisco, Cal. Oct. 26, 1861

My dear Friend:

The blow has fallen. I am crushed. Mansfield is assigned to this Command and I am appointed a Brig.-Gen. of Volunteers and ordered to command the Columbia River District, having a few companies of volunteers scattered over an immense region of country. And even this is not an independent command but a dependency of the Department. As the Senior Colonel of Infantry and in fact of the whole Regular Army on duty this appointment gives me hardly any additional rank. Had it been in the Regular Army I should have gained nearly my position at the commencement of the war. I never asked for or sought a commission in the Volunteers. Had it been given me five months since, it would have been better but to make me a brigadier now when more than a hundred have been appointed, young officers of the army and civilians it looks as if I was to be victimized at all hazards. I had the strongest documents and the united influence of several delegations from different states and it was looked upon as a settled matter that I was to be appointed in the Regular Army. I have met with opposition and it must have been from high quarters and powerful. They have succeeded and I am down for the present, but I shall not remain quiet, cost what it will. I am bound to front out this business.

I am peculiarly situated. I cannot decline even this appointment without sacrificing all my future prospects. The night is dark and the winds howl, but with a stout heart and a strong arm I will weather the storm. I love my country. I love the Union. I will sacrifice all, life if necessary to shield our old flag under which you and myself fought and won some little honor on the bloody fields of Mexico.

No fancied personal injustice can lessen my love for my country.

Your
friend,
G. Wright.[30]

In a letter to Asst. Adj. Gen. E. D. Townsend on October 28, Wright requested reconsideration of the order of September 30:

I have served on the Pacific Coast more than nine years; six of them passed in the dark valleys of the Columbia River, or in pursuing the savage foe in the mountain fastnesses on the eastern borders of Oregon and Washington. Under these circumstances I appeal with confidence to the General-in-Chief, and pray that I may be ordered to service in the field.[31]

On November 3, Wright wrote to Adjutant General Lorenzo Thomas that his appointment as brigadier general of volunteers had placed him in an anomalous position: "Officers of my own regiment and gentlemen who won their spurs under my command now rank me." He assured the War Department that wherever he might be assigned he would devote his best energies and lay down his life if necessary for the preservation of the Union and its institutions.[32]

With all the conflicting orders Wright felt confused and frustrated. Being bypassed for promotion had been a source of great humiliation, but not being allowed to play an active part in the defense of the country he loved, in its most critical hour, was the bitterest blow of all. Having devoted his life since the age of fourteen to the development of military skills and experience, he believed that those talents should be utilized. It was unthinkable to him that a loyal and competent officer should be shunted aside while others with less ability and seniority were already seeing action in the momentous battles in the East. The promotion to brigadier general of volunteers was almost an insult to a West Point graduate and career soldier. Members of the regular army constituted the elite in the profession of arms, and only promotion in the regular army officer corps would be meaningful to him and affect his seniority.

Wright's nemesis, the venerable Lt. Gen. Winfield Scott, resigned his position on November 1, and Lt. Gen. George B. McClellan was appointed general-in-chief. Finally, on November 19, McClellan officially assigned Wright to command the Department of the Pacific, a position he was to hold until July, 1864. He was also to retain the command of his old regiment, the Ninth U.S. Infantry.[33]

Feeling that now his prospects for action and advance-

ment might improve, Wright again wrote to his old friend
Hardie, who was now a colonel on McClellan's staff:

San Francisco, November 29, 1861

Dear Sir:

A month since I received my appointment as Brig Genl of
Volunteers. You can imagine my astonishment, that I should
have been appointed at this late date. As the Senior Colonel in
the Army, it gives me but little additional rank. I accepted, I
could not decline without abandoning all hopes for the future. I was at the same time ordered to remain in command of
my old District, Oregon, a dependancy of this Dept, which was
to be commanded by Mansfield. However, after the retirement of Genl Scott, things began to look a little brighter on
my side, and Genl. McClellan has assigned me to the command of the Dept, and ordered me to keep the 9th Infy
here—one company has already gone east. I *know* that Genl
Scott has opposed me throughout, you know the reason. It is
an old affair, and was aggravated by my letter written to Army
Head Quarters when Johnston was placed over me. It has been
intimated to me that Thomas has been opposed to me, I know
not on what account, as I am not aware I ever had any difficulty with him. . . .

I hear, unofficially, that you have accepted a position on
Genl McClellan's staff. I congratulate you, but you should
have been made a General before this and I hope you will
be soon.

We have not much news here; although we have a strong
party of *sympathizers,* all is quiet; yet I am not lulled into a false
security. My troops are on the alert, occupying all the salient
points toward our foes. The overland mail is a failure at this
season of the year, and were it not for the Telegraph we
should be badly off for news. . . .

Please present our kind regards to Mrs. Hardie,

Very truly your friend
G. Wright.[34]

In his letter Wright assumed that Hardie was aware of the
reason for Scott's long-standing antipathy. One can only
surmise that it may have related to something that transpired during the troubled days of the Mexican War, when
his former mentor General Worth was having his bitter

feud with Scott. The letter to headquarters regarding the rebel Johnston, to which Wright refers, has not been found. There is no clue why the adjutant general, Lorenzo Thomas, might have opposed Wright.

Carleton Expedition

It was obvious to its new commander, Col. James H. Carleton, that the estimated time of departure for the Southern Expedition would be far later than September 20. Carleton was a respected dragoon officer who had served in the army for twenty-three years. He had helped control the Canadian border disturbances, had earned a brevet in the Mexican War, and since then had spent much of his duty on the southwestern frontier.[35] He never seemed overwhelmed, as Sumner had been, by the magnitude of the task of directing the Southern Expedition. His attention to the details of planning, training, and logistics associated with the mission of what came to be known as the "California Column" was truly impressive. Carleton's most recent orders simply stated that he was to proceed with his regiment to Warner's Ranch as soon as possible and establish a camp there and that Fort Yuma was to be further reinforced to provide additional service as a jumping-off point for any expedition to Texas.

Lieutenant Colonel Joseph R. West, Carleton's second-in-command, who was sent ahead to Fort Yuma in November with three companies of infantry, was soon able to report that he had taken over control of all the Colorado River ferries. When he learned that Denver was not to assume command of the volunteers, West sent Carleton a letter that typifies the army rivalries of the day: "The news about Denver is glorious. Is not general Wright now in our way? . . . I would be better pleased to hear of his being transferred to a more active field. . . . When you get the department and I get the district there will still be fresh worlds to conquer."[36]

Major Edwin A. Rigg, who with four companies of the

First Infantry California Volunteers had established the camp at Warner's Springs, which was named after Wright, wrote to Carleton that the location in north-central San Diego County was beautiful but the climate objectionable because of frequent storms and constant winds that blew their tents down and kept the air full of sand. He suggested moving to the site of the Butterfield Stage station at Oak Grove, fifteen miles west. Rigg wrote Carleton from Camp Wright that the news of Wright's promotion was received in camp "with every satisfaction." He hoped that the camp could be removed to the new site soon. This location was not only healthier but more strategic for guarding the mountain passes through which rebels might be moving east. The move was authorized a few days later.[37]

Carleton ordered Rigg to hold any suspicious parties passing through the area and to be particularly alert for a party led by former California assemblyman Dan Showalter.[38] Showalter was a southern sympathizer who had killed a fellow legislator in a duel following an argument that took place while the assembly was considering a resolution in support of President Lincoln the preceding spring. Showalter was now on his way to Texas with a band of seventeen armed men to fight against the Union. Major Rigg intercepted some of their letters and learned their location; they were captured on November 24 by a detachment from Camp Wright.[39] They were incarcerated along with other political prisoners at Fort Yuma for five months, and then they were released in response to Lincoln's Amnesty Proclamation. Showalter ultimately became a lieutenant colonel in the Confederate army.

Wright first learned of the capture on December 5 in a dispatch from Rigg. Carleton reported to Asst. Adj. Gen. Richard C. Drum at departmental headquarters that all the prisoners had taken an oath of allegiance but added his opinion that they would take any oath in order to get to Texas.

On December 9, Wright reported to Thomas his plan for recapturing the forts in Arizona and New Mexico and reopening the southern mail route. He said that he had

1,500 men ready to carry out this operation. "Why," he asked, "continue on the defensive when we have the power and will to drive every rebel beyond the Rio Grande?" He added that he was also eager to occupy Guaymas, on the Gulf of California, to keep it out of rebel hands. McClellan approved his overall plan but sad nothing about Guaymas.[40]

Carleton was notified that McClellan had approved Wright's plan and ordered to take the First Regiment of Infantry California Volunteers, a battalion of the First Cavalry California Volunteers, and a battery of four light guns with a detachment from the Third Artillery. Supplies would be sent overland or by sea to the mouth of the Colorado River and then by sailing vessel and river steamer to the supply base at Fort Yuma.

Now that Wright was responsible for the whole Pacific Department, he had many more secessionists to worry about. Small parties continued to organize in southern California to travel east to the aid of the rebels. Wright further reinforced Fort Yuma and ordered all boats and ferries on the Colorado River seized. No one was allowed to pass beyond the river without showing evidence of fidelity to the Union. Wright was determined to crush any attempt at rebellion and suppress any assault on the government or its institutions by word or deed, even if this policy meant infringement of some individual rights.

When Governor J. W. Nye wrote of his concern about the activities of secessionists in the territory of Nevada, Wright replied: "It behooves us to be watchful. . . . I shall not assume a threatening attitude, for the purpose of warning our enemies to refrain from unlawful acts, but pursuing the even tenor of my way, ever observant of impending events, and ready at all times to enforce a due respect and observance of the Constitution and laws of our country."[41]

Wright believed that the only way he could securely hold his political prisoners was by ignoring writs of habeas corpus, though Thomas wired him that he could not lawfully do this. Within a month, Secretary of State Seward wrote Edwin M. Stanton, secretary of war, that in view of secessionist activities in California it might be wise to suspend

the writ of habeas corpus. This letter was forwarded to
Wright, who was directed to "act as the public safety re-
quires." Later Congress authorized the president to suspend the writ when he deemed it necessary, and the California legislature formally approved the action. Wright
soon found it necessary to resort to other extraordinary
measures and further restrict civil liberties to curb secessionist activity.[42] Carleton directed Capt. David Ferguson
in San Bernardino to seize any traitors there if he was sure
of their guilt. He was not to respond to writs of habeas corpus without the commanding general's approval.

On November 13, McClellan ordered Wright to send
one or two regiments to protect the central overland mail
route. Wright was unable to do so because of the late-
ness of the season. He assigned the task to Col. Patrick E.
Connor and his Third Regiment of Infantry, California
Volunteers.[43] Connor had been a soldier since the age of
nineteen and was a Mexican War veteran. After his companies were organized, four were sent to garrison forts
in the Humboldt District and the remainder spent five
months in training at Benicia Barracks. The regiment then
assembled in Stockton to prepare for the long march to
Salt Lake City.[44]

Concerns About Mexico

During his long tour of duty on the West Coast, Wright
had developed a lively interest in Mexico. In the latter part
of 1861 he expressed to Townsend at army headquarters
concern about the unstable government of the Mexican
state of Sonora and the vulnerability of its strategically important seaports. He said that the United States should occupy the state temporarily to facilitate regaining Arizona
and to prevent the Confederates from acquiring a Pacific
port.[45] His fears were valid, for even as he wrote of his apprehension, Confederate Lt. Col. John R. Baylor was informing his superiors how important Guaymas would be
for their plans. Baylor saw it as a place "where we must get
most of our supplies."[46] General Sibley requested from

Don Ignacio Pesqueira, the governor of Sonora, permission for Confederate use of the port of Guaymas. Following his request he sent Col. James Reily to the capitals of Sonora and Chihuahua to enlist Mexican recognition and support.

Reily wrote his superiors a gloating report of his visit with the governor of Chihuahua and announced that the Mexicans would permit no marching of California troops through Mexico. This ban of Union troops represented the first recognition of the Confederate States of America by any foreign power, albeit only a state. Reily described Chihuahua as a fine neighbor but one that would be improved by coming under the Confederate flag. Then he voiced the widely held dream that if Sonora and Chihuahua were acquired southern California would soon follow and that with a railroad from Texas to Guaymas this region would become "a great highway of nations."[47]

Through the efforts of a citizen named F. H. Waterman and a correspondent for the *San Francisco Evening Bulletin,* W. G. Moody, the United States obtained copies of General Sibley's letters to Governor Pesqueira of Sonora. The U.S. consuls at Guaymas and Mazatlán were informed, and the letters were carried by a former consular official to San Francisco, where they reached Wright. It became apparent that under the pretext of chasing hostile Indians Sibley was attempting to gain Confederate access to the border states of Mexico, which, among other things, would cut the U.S. line of communication between the Gulf of Mexico and the Gulf of California.[48]

Although Pesqueira's response was not known, Wright assumed that he had declined. Wright wrote to him, pointing out that, in view of the friendly relations that existed among Sonora, the government of Mexico, and the United States, concessions to the rebels would be a hostile act. He continued:

> I need not point out to Your Excellency the utter ruin and devastation which would inevitably befall the beautiful State of Sonora should the rebel forces obtain a foothold within its

limits, as in that event it would be indispensably necessary that the frontier should be passed by the U.S. forces, and our enemies pursued, possibly to the city of Guaymas. I beg your Excellency to rest assured that under no circumstances will the Government of the United States permit the rebel horde to take refuge in Sonora. I have an army of 10,000 men ready to pass the frontier and protect your government and people.[49]

Should Sibley's forces enter Sonora, Carleton was to pursue without regard for boundary lines. Wright also alerted Commodore Charles E. Bell, commander of the Pacific Fleet, who dispatched the *St. Mary's* to Guaymas.

One of Wright's serious worries was the defenseless state of the Pacific ports. He asked the chief of engineers on the Pacfic Coast, Col. Rene E. DeRussy, to prepare plans for defensive works around San Francisco harbor. Alcatraz and Fort Point were soon strengthened, although they had only about half the guns they needed. Oregon and Washington had no coastal protection at all, but the other harbors were of little importance compared to San Francisco, with the navy yard at Mare Island and the arsenal at Benecia. During the next few months Wright obtained cannons from the navy for harbor defense and held conferences with Governor Stanford and the military committee of the assembly in the hope of obtaining help from the state in arming the land approaches.[50]

Wright's Sons on Active Duty

Although Brig. Gen. George Wright burned with desire to serve in what he regarded as a more important and active capacity, his position as commander of the Department of the Pacific was no sinecure. What happened on the West Coast, particularly in California, was of great importance to the Union. In addition to suppressing secessionist activity and maintaining a steady flow of men and gold to the East, Wright had important responsibilities in relation to the countries bordering the United States. Mexico was in a state of turmoil, and European powers were seizing the opportunity to make threatening gestures, as the Confederacy cast covetous eyes toward the Mexican border states. While primarily responsible for the military security of the vast western domain, Wright was increasingly drawn into the diplomatic and political arena. Although his military career had hardly prepared him for this role, throughout the war he managed to retain good relations with the leaders of the states and territories within his department and those of neighboring Sonora and British Columbia.

During the autumn of 1861, both of Wright's sons entered the army. His younger son, John, who was beginning his third year at the U.S. Military Academy, was placed on active service with most of the members of his class. He was commissioned a captain and assigned assistant adjutant general of the Kentucky Volunteers on the staff of Gen. Don Carlos Buell. Thomas Wright had gone to California from Washington Territory and offered his services. On October 2 he was commissioned first lieutenant and regimental quartermaster of the Second California Volunteer Cavalry.

Wright's wife, Margaret, who had been with him at most of the posts at which he served in Washington Territory went with him to San Francisco, where they lived together throughout most of the Civil War years.

Civil War Days: 1862

THE YEAR 1862 was an eventful one in the East. In February, President Lincoln issued his Amnesty Proclamation, which directed that all political or state prisoners currently held in military custody were to be released upon subscribing parole (that is, pledging to refrain from any disloyal act). Those who kept their parole were granted amnesty for any past offenses of treason or disloyalty.

The navy and army began successful joint operations against the Confederates on the Mississippi and Tennessee rivers. General Ulysses S. Grant won a costly victory against Generals Albert S. Johnston and P. G. T. Beauregard at Shiloh in April. The Peninsular Campaign was initiated, and, because of his procrastination, McClellan was relieved of supreme command by Gen. Henry W. Halleck in July.

The second Battle of Bull Run was fought at the end of August with little more success for the Union forces than in the first. In its aftermath on September 1 former Washington Governor Isaac I. Stevens was killed leading a charge against Thomas J. ("Stonewall") Jackson's corps at Chantilly.

In September, President Lincoln issued the Emancipation Proclamation freeing the slaves—there was little point in trying to save the Union with the chief cause of the rebellion still present. This act turned the Civil War into a crusade for human rights and liberty and lessened the likelihood of any foreign nations aiding the South.

On February 20, 1862, Wright reported to Adjutant General Thomas, "We have peace . . . but not quiet." Wild excitement had prevailed since the telegraph had brought news of Union victories in the East that resulted in the capture of Forts Henry and Donelson.[1]

By this time Wright had settled into his departmental

command. He was working hard to establish good relations with the governors, local officials, and prominent citizens of the Pacific slope. He was totally dedicated to the preservation of the Union and to carrying out the policies of the Lincoln administration.

Carleton Column

While Carleton continued to train his men, accumulate adequate supplies, restore wells, gather forage, and repair storm-damaged roads, events of moment were taking place at his destination. Confederate General Sibley had begun a move up the Rio Grande with a large body of troops. He crossed to the east bank of the river near Fort Craig where General Canby was encamped and on February 20 occupied a position at Valverde, six miles farther north. The next morning Canby attacked him but was defeated, losing sixty-five men to Sibley's thirty-six. A brief truce was declared so that the dead could be buried and the wounded removed. Sibley then moved on to Albuquerque, which had been abandoned by Union troops. Santa Fe then surrendered with little resistance.[2]

By March 10 news of the Confederate gains still had not reached Wright. He wrote Thomas that the strength of Sibley's force was exaggerated and that with Canby at his front and Carleton on his flank there could be no doubt of a Union victory. On February 28, Capt. Sherod Hunter with 100 Confederate soldiers occupied Tucson. The next day Hunter was joined by Colonel Reily, who raised the Confederate flag over the city plaza.[3]

When spies brought Carleton word of the occupation of Tucson, he sent a cavalry detachment under his old friend Capt. William A. McCleave to capture or destroy Hunter and his band. McCleave was warned to use spies and avoid possible traps, but that experienced old soldier walked into one. Scouting the area, McCleave and eight of his men encountered Hunter at the Pima villages on the upper Gila River and were captured. When the news reached Carleton, he was dismayed and incredulous. A flying column that included the remainder of McCleave's eager command was sent to recapture him. The troops arrived too late to rescue McCleave before he had been evacuated, but four months later he was exchanged for two Confederate lieutenants.[4]

On February 14, Lieutenant Colonel Rigg announced that he was desperate for clothing; some of his men were almost naked. He later confirmed rumors that the Confederates in Tucson were confiscating all property belonging to Union supporters. Colonel West reported that one-half of his command at Fort Yuma was in a state of mutiny because Company A, First Infantry California Volunteers, refused to drill while they were wearing their knapsacks. Carleton sent West a letter to be read to his men, giving them one hour in which to reflect on their rebellious conduct. Any men who still refused to obey were to be mustered out without pay. Carleton urged forbearance, since he did not wish to see soldiers of his regiment disgrace themselves. In the end all but thirteen men complied. The thirteen were put in the guardhouse, and Carleton asked Wright to discharge them from service.[5]

In his official report to Wright, Carleton commented that the Confederate successes in Arizona would make his task harder to accomplish. He complained that some of his juniors were now brigadier generals in the Union army but promised to do his best in spite of the odds. It is ironic that he chose Wright to complain to about his lack of promotion.

Carleton informed Wright's assistant adjutant general, Col. Richard C. Drum, that he planned to establish a sub-depot for supplies at the Pima villages, two hundred miles east of Yuma. When his column headed out, he would leave six companies of infantry and three of cavalry at Camp Latham, near Los Angeles, and detachments at other principle southern California cities. Residents of these cities had reported that secessionist activity was increasing as news of the impending troop departures circulated, in spite of efforts to maintain tight security.[6]

As news of the Confederate gains reached California,

Carleton came under criticism for his apparent delay in getting his column under way; some sources went so far as to attack his loyalty. Wright expressed his confidence in Carleton and his officers and observed that his opinion was shared by "all true friends of our country on this coast." Those casting false suspicions on his officers were worse than traitors, he said. Carleton thanked Wright for his backing but said that he could not put his troops in the field until he was sure that his men would have enough to eat. Wishing to strike a good blow for his country, he said, he had no desire to arrive on the Rio Grande in disarray.[7]

On April 19, Wright was finally able to report to Adjutant General Thomas that Carleton's column was beginning to move. Carleton's troops moved eastward in installments, marching at night across the deserts. Scouts and stragglers were often attacked by Apaches. As Carleton's column moved east, Canby found it necessary to appeal to Governor William Gilpin of Colorado for reinforcements. Gilpin sent a regiment of Colorado Volunteer Infantry under Col. John P. Slough, along with two companies of cavalry. On March 25, marching on Santa Fe, 380 of these men under Maj. J. M. Chivington encountered the Confederates at nearby Bernal Springs and soundly defeated them. On the twenty-seventh, Colonel Slough and his main force met the Confederates at Apache Pass and won a resounding victory. Chivington was able to capture and destroy the Confederate supply train after routing its guards.

Following this defeat Sibley retreated to Santa Fe with his remaining troops, and, by abandoning his sick and wounded and what was left of his wagons and artillery, he was able to reach Fort Bliss, Texas. Captain Hunter and his band of cavalry did not leave Tucson until May.[8]

Carleton finally reached Tucson on May 20. Early in June he wrote several letters to General Canby informing him of the California column's presence, congratulating him on his victory over Sibley, and assuring him of Carleton's utmost cooperation. The ill-fated dispatches were carred by three messengers; two were killed by Apaches, and one was captured by the Confederates, but somehow the word reached Canby.[9]

On May 21, West reported the bloodless reoccupation of Tucson, and a few days later Carleton announced that the overland stage from Independence to Los Angeles could resume as soon as the rebels were driven out of Mesilla.

Although he had still not learned the nature of Governor Pesqueira's reply to Sibley, Wright recommended seizing Sonora if the rebels entered that state. Finally, in June, Pesqueira replied to an inquiry of Carleton's, assuring him that Sonora's actions would correspond with Carleton's own friendly ones. Colonel Reily's assertions were exaggerated, he said. No arrangement or agreement had been made between the Confederates and Sonora except to respect the rights of neutrality. Wright received a similar letter from Pesqueira expressing friendship and sympathy for the American Union and none for the Confederates.[10]

On June 8, Arizona was placed under martial law until the arrival of the duly appointed civil authorities. Wright proudly reported to Thomas that Carleton's column from California had achieved perfect success. It had crossed the deserts without significant loss of men or property, had recovered Arizona and established military law, and was now advancing to cooperate with Canby.

Wright apologized for the expense of his two major expeditions but pointed out that the distances traveled and guarded were immense and the actual loss to the government of men and property was small. He also asserted that it would be cheaper to supply Arizona through Guaymas or Lobos and that he had sent a detachment to survey the route.[11]

By August, Wright was able to announce that the Union flag was flying over all of Arizona and that Eyre's command had reached the Rio Grande and raised the flag over Fort Thorn on the Fourth of July. By the end of August all remaining forts in the area extending south to Fort Quitman in Texas were in U.S. hands. Carleton was promoted to brigadier general and replaced Canby in command of the Department of New Mexico, and his troops were now detached from the Department of the Pacific. Arizona was made into a separate district with Col. Joseph R. West in command. Much praise was due Carleton, said Wright; all his aims had been accomplished.[12]

In August, Carleton wrote Canby asking how he might be of service, adding, "The gallantry of the troops under your command has left us nothing to do on the Rio Grande."[13] After all his planning, training, instruction, and indoctrination he found himself with Apaches, but no rebels, to fight. However, he emphasized that the march of almost 1,000 miles across the Great Desert in summer with almost 2,000 men and 2,000 animals was a creditable military achievement. Canby was able to offer him all the supplies he needed and even some subsistence funds. Canby did not think an invasion of Texas from the west was practical but said that he could certainly use reinforcements from California.

Carleton reported to Wright that much of the column's success was due to the labor and zeal of his second-in-command, Colonel West, and recommended that West be promoted. In the report summarizing his expedition, Carleton concluded, "I beg to thank General Wright for the confidence he always reposed in me . . . [he] has kindly overlooked [my] imperfections."[14]

Eyre carried the final dispatches back to the headquarters of the Department of the Pacific and with them the colors of the regiment, which had been hoisted over the reoccupied forts. Rumors of Confederate plans to reinvade the Southwest continued to circulate for a time, but came to nothing, although several attempts were made by the rebels to raise troops for the purpose. On occasion the reports seemed credible enough to warrant requests for reinforcements.

Dealing with the Secessionists

In February, 1862, Wright sent Thomas a copy of a letter he had written to S. A. Parker, postmaster of San Francisco and acting postal agent for the Pacific Coast. Wright told

Parker that he regarded a newspaper published in Jackson-ville, Oregon, the *Southern Oregon Gazette,* as incendiary, abusive of the government, and treasonable and asked Parker to prohibit its transmission through the U.S. mails or its acceptance at post offices for distribution. Parker issued the necessary orders to his postmasters and mail contractors. Wright then wrote to some of his district com-manders, telling them to scrutinize the newspapers in their districts and ban them from the mails if they seemed dis-loyal. Wright's actions inevitably provoked complaints that he was attempting to stifle freedom of speech and restrain the freedom of the press.[15]

In the fall of 1862, Wright again wrote Parker: "Sir, I have to request that you will give instructions excluding the following named newspapers from the United States Mails and Post Offices; also prohibiting their transmission by any Express Agency or Company, viz. *Stockton Argus*—Stockton, *San Jose Tribune*—San Jose, *Tulare Post*—Visalia, *Equal Rights Expositor*—Visalia." The letter was endorsed by Louis McLane, general agent of Wells, Fargo & Co., order-ing the company's agents to comply strictly with Wright's request.[16]

Henry Barrow, the U.S. marshal for southern Califor-nia, sent Wright a letter in April saying that he respected the general but that dissatisfaction was growing in the region because Wright was not aggressive enough in deal-ing with secessionists. Wright's reply to Barrows is worth noting, since it ecxplains his philosophy regarding the matter:

> I shall not hesitate a single moment in using the most strin-gent measures for the suppression of treason or disloyalty to our Government, and the officers in command of United States troops will arrest and hold in confinement all persons against whom such charges can well be established. I fully concur with you as to what should be done, and the only diffi-culty we have to encounter is as to the best manner of accom-plishing the object in view. When I do arrest persons, to hold them safely they must be removed beyond the reach of a civil process, or such writs disregarded. Soon I shall send addi-

tional forces to the southern district and place an experienced officer in command, who will be instructed to confer freely with yourself and other civil officers of the United States in that quarter.[17]

To implement this commitment, he issued orders to all officers commanding districts and posts. He ordered that political prisoners were to be sent to Fort Yuma but two months later Thomas wired that no such action was to be taken in regard to the secessionists arrested. Thomas's rebuffs of Wright were sometimes snidely worded; Thomas apparently also entertained some antipathy toward Wright.[18]

To Thomas, Wright reported that many men in his department were rebels at heart but that, being in the minority, they were harmless as long as they were watched. He wrote, "It has been my aim not to create any unnecessary alarm in the public mind on this coast, but to watch closely the progress of events and be ever ready to crush any attempt to raise the standard of rebellion on the Pacific."[19]

On April 30 Wright issued a proclamation from his headquarters in San Francisco:

Whereas, it having come to the knowledge of the undersigned that there are certain persons, either holding office under the rebel government, or aiding and abetting the enemies of the United States, and that such persons are owners of real estate or personal property within the limits of this military department, it is hereby declared that all such estates and property are subject to confiscation for the use and benefit of the United States.

It is further declared that all sales and transfers of real estate or personal property by any person or persons holding office under the rebel government or who may be aiding or assisting the enemies of the Union, whether made by them personally or by their agents, shall be null and void.[20]

One may well imagine the furor that greeted this edict. The proclamation, while it may appear overzealous, was one of the few means Wright had of aiding the war effort. Since he could not participate in the fighting, he was determined to enforce his authority against secessionists as far as the law allowed. In General Order, No. 34 of September 17, 1862, he called attention to the fact that in July Congress had passed an almost identical act.[21]

Lieutenant Colonel Robert Pollock reported to Drum that he had sent an officer as a civilian spy to ascertain the existence of an armed rebel force in Merced. The operation had revealed that certain elements disliked the Union, but not to the extent of opposing the government or avoiding taxes. Some westerners with nothing to lose had cheered Jefferson Davis and the Confederacy, but most of them had moved on. Union loyalists were alert, and no serious trouble was anticipated, said Pollock, but stringent orders from departmental headquarters backed by a strong military force were the chief means of keeping the disloyal element subdued.[22]

Wright ordered Col. George S. Evans to spend the winter in the vicinity of Visalia, where he had established Camp Babbitt, to keep an eye on secessionist activity. In December, Evans reported that there were more secessionists there than "anyplace this side of Dixie." They were organized and armed and went about shouting disloyalties and insulting the soldiers. The *Equal Rights Expositor*, having been denied use of the mails, bitterly denounced its censors. Numerous fights broke out, and one soldier was mortally wounded. Wright ordered Evans to arrest and confine anyone preaching sedition or harassing the troops and to send the ringleaders to Alcatraz. Captain Moses A. McLaughlin, who was in command of Camp Babbitt, arrested three Visalians who a few days before Christmas had ridden past the troops on dress parade shouting, "Hurrah!" for Jeff Davis and Jackson. He said he needed reinforcements before he could seize the leaders, since the rebels were "gathering like locusts." McLaughlin had ignored a writ of habeas corpus that had been served on him by the secessionists and was expecting a sheriff's posse to attempt to liberate his prisoners.[23]

McLaughlin was reinforced by a company of cavalry, and on January 6, 1863, he arrested L. P. Hall and S. J.

Garrison, the editors of the *Equal Rights Expositor*. But later in the day he received orders to release any political prisoner willing to take a loyalty oath. All but Garrison complied, but even he was soon released, and the newspaper continued its treasonable invective.[24] Violence erupted in March when Hall and Garrison referred to the troops at Camp Babbitt as "cossacks." That night thirty soldiers, acting without orders, broke into the *Equal Rights Expositor* office, destroyed the presses, and pitched type, paper, and ink into the street. They sent up cheers in front of the rival pro-Union paper, the *Visalia Delta*. Major John M. O'Neill, who was in command at that time, furnished the editor of the *Delta* with a guard to prevent any secessionist reprisal. He also had the town patrolled with a strong force and ordered the arrest of three soldiers and one citizen.[25]

Connor Expedition to Utah

Early in the spring Wright was again directed by army headquarters to protect emigrants and the central Overland Mail route. He responded that he had enough men at Fort Churchill in western Nevada to offer protection as far east and north as Salt Lake and Fort Bridger in what became Wyoming Territory until the snow melted in the mountains. Governor Nye and Wells, Fargo's Louis McLane had assured him that troops were not then needed on that route. By July the snow had melted sufficiently that Wright could order Col. Patrick E. Connor to cross the Sierra Nevada and move toward Utah Territory to protect the central Overland Mail Route. Connor took with him seven companies of the Third Regiment of Infantry California Volunteers and five companies of the Second California Volunteer Cavalry. By August 5 he had reached Fort Churchill, where he assumed charge of the Military District of Utah.

In October, after a personal reconnaissance, Connor led his troops to Salt Lake City, on the outskirts of which he established Fort Douglas. He designated that post as his headquarters, because it afforded a good position from which he could observe Mormon activities.[26] Connor was astonished at what he regarded as the iniquity of Mormonism and the disloyalty of its leaders and their adherents. His reports included frequent diatribes against the Mormons, who, for their part, regarded the location of his post as a threat and an insult. Connor, however, believed that the fort's proximity to the center of activity provided the only means of protecting properly the federally appointed officials of the territory.

Three punitive expeditions had been sent from Oregon since the 1860 Snake River Massacre. On at least one of these expeditions a few of the survivors of that massacre accompanied the troops, hoping that they could identify some of the culprits. In August, Col. Justus Steinberger reported he had met with Zachias Van Orman at Fort Walla Walla. He was a resident of Oregon and the brother of Alexis Van Orman, who with his wife had been killed in the Snake Massacre of 1860. Their four captured children had been seen by a friend of Van Orman's in Cache Valley, Utah Territory, but he had been unable to rescue them because of the exorbitant ransom demanded by the Indians. Van Orman originally planned to accompany an expedition led by Col. Rueben F. Maury against the Snakes in the hope of recovering the children, although he personally had found no trace of them on three previous attempts. Instead, Van Orman went on to Salt Lake and accompanied troops from Fort Douglas under Maj. Edward McGarry. Unknown to Van Orman, by this time only the ten-year-old boy remained, his three sisters having died in captivity.[27]

When Connor arrived in the Utah District that summer, he found the Snake Indians on the rampage. Emigrants and settlers were being massacred, mail and telegraph stations attacked, agents killed, and horses stolen. Early in November, Connor sent Major McGarry out from Fort Douglas to punish the marauders. He soon encountered hostile Indians and took a large number prisoner; twenty or more were killed attempting to escape after they had been disarmed. A few Indians were sent out to bring in the murderers; when they failed to return, four hostages were shot.[28]

On November 22, McGarry met Zachias Van Orman in Cache Valley, where the latter had found Chief Bear Hunter, who held Van Orman's young nephew captive. After a skirmish on November 23, Bear Hunter and twenty of his braves surrendered. They were held as hostages until the boy was delivered the next day.[29]

Wright sent his commendation to Connor and McGarry for their successful performance of the delicate task of rescuing the Van Orman boy. Wright believed that the courage, dedication, and persistence of the boy's uncle was beyond praise.

On January 29, 1863, Connor, with 200 soldiers, engaged 300 warriors of the same tribe of Bannock Shoshones on Bear River in what two months later would be Idaho Territory. One of the few pitched battles involving fairly large forces, this engagement was fought in bitter winter weather and in deep snow. A total of 224 Indians were killed, including Bear Hunter and two other prominent chiefs. Connor lost 15 men killed and 53 wounded, of whom an officer and 6 enlisted men later died. Many of the soldiers suffered from frozen feet. For this victory Connor received congratulations from General Halleck and was promoted to brigadier general.[30]

Connor believed that the Mormons often helped the Indians, encouraged their attacks, kept them informed of his movements, and profiteered on supplies sold to the troops. In September, 1862, Connor had written to General Halleck that he now had enough cavalry to protect the Overland Mail Route. Early in the winter Halleck had wired Wright that the Overland Mail Company, the Post Office Department, and the Department of the Interior had urged that Connor be removed to Fort Bridger to check the Indians in that vicinity. Wright replied that a strong force was needed at Salt Lake City. Connor had told Wright of the efforts of the "real governor" of Utah, Brigham Young, and his satellites to get the command "dissevered." Young, he said, had boasted that he would be rid of Connor by spring and would continue to oppose and resist U.S. officials. Young regarded Fort Douglas as contrary to his interests.[31]

In February, 1863, S. S. Harding, the duly appointed governor of Utah Territory, told Wright of his anxiety concerning the possible removal of Connor's troops, which he felt would be a disaster for the federal officers and their supporters. He said that in effect the United States would be abandoning its sovereignty. Wright assured the governor that he was reinforcing, not removing, Connor.

A few days later Connor reported a mass meeting of the Mormons, who had requested the resignation of Governor Harding and two federal judges. Young had assembled 1,500 armed men, raised a flag, and mounted cannons and seemed to be trying to provoke a conflict between the Mormons and the troops. When told of this, General Halleck urged Connor to exercise restraint.[32]

Martial Law in Round Valley

The force at Wright's disposal for use on the coast was comparatively small because he had sent out two major columns. Wright, however, required troops to cope with the persistent Indian problem throughout the Department of the Pacific. The most pressing need was in the Humboldt district, which included present Sonoma, Napa, Mendocino, Trinity, Humboldt, Del Norte, and Klamath counties of California.

Colonel Lippitt submitted an ambitious plan for the removal of the hostile Indians from the Humboldt District. Wright informed him that no troops were available to carry out his grandiose scheme and that the job of setting up reservations and keeping the Indians on them belonged to the Indian Bureau. As an alternative, Lippitt set up three new posts with the available men, whose number had been reduced by desertions and mutiny.[33]

In March, Lippitt made a tour of his district. He described the country as "more Alpine than Switzerland": for hundreds of miles around there was no level spot more than twenty yards wide. Instead, there were high mountain ridges, streams rushing through deep and precipitous canyons, and almost impenetrable forests. He found many buildings that had been burned by the Indians and ranches abandoned by cattlemen. In reprisal the whites had recently massacred 150 peaceable Indians. Lippitt issued orders that one-half of each garrison was to be in the field constantly. The purpose of the command, he informed his men, was not to make war on the Indians but to collect them on reservations, where they could be protected from white outrages. The men were to avoid bloodshed and killing except in self-defense.

When murders of travelers and settlers continued, the troops were instructed that guilty Indians were to be exterminated. Armed white men found to be accompanying Indian bands were to be hanged. The citizens of Humboldt County petitioned Wright to take steps to prevent the Indian war from continuing indefinitely. Lippitt was reinforced by several companies of volunteers and admonished not to spread himself too thin. Unhappy with Lippitt, citizens in a number of communities appealed to Governor Stanford to persuade Wright to give them arms with which to defend themselves.[34]

The citizens in the Humboldt District made constant appeals for protection, but their reports of depredations often proved false. Citizens were eager to make money working for the government or furnishing supplies to military parties. When whites took the law into their own hands, they often overreacted and killed any Indians they found, frequently for trivial offenses.

A frustrated Lippitt wrote to Assistant Adjutant General Drum about citizens' charges regarding his conduct and competence and asserting his ignorance of Indian warfare. He admitted his unfamiliarity with the "difficult and laborious wolf hunting," as he called such activity, and said that he would be more than happy to resign. He also mentioned the high mortality rate from illness among his Indian prisoners, of whom he now had more than 800. He was unable to keep the Indians in his district on reservations if they did not wish to stay. Dispiritedly, he said that the only result of the past summer's campaign had been to convert peaceful Indians into hostile Indians. To shoot men, women, and children was unworthy of the troops of a civilized nation but seemed to be the only way the Indians could be kept under control.[35]

Finally, Lippitt became desperate enough to order his commanders to abandon their pacific policy and show the Indians no quarter, except women and children. However, the men had difficulty finding Indians to kill or capture, since the Indians would attack without warning and then disappear. Surprisingly, Wright cotinued to praise Lippitt's activity and zeal to headquarters, promising that he would bring a speedy termination to the Indian disturbances in northern California. He informed Lippitt that this goal should be attained even if it meant hanging every Indian engaged in hostilities.[36] Wright often spoke glibly of hanging Indians, but so far as is known his only hangings were those after the Cascades Massacre and during the campaign of 1858.

The Indians had little better to expect from the Confederates than from the United States. Colonel Baylor sent this directive from headquarters of the Second Regiment, Texas Mounted Rifles, to Capt. Thomas Helm of the Arizona Guards:

> The Congress of the Confederate States has passed a law declaring extermination to all hostile Indians. You will therefor use all means to persuade the Apaches or any other tribe to come in for the purpose of making peace, and when you get them together, kill all the grown Indians and take the children prisoners and sell them to defray the expense of killing the Indians. Buy whisky and other such goods as may be necessary for the Indians and I will order vouchers given to cover the amount expended. Leave nothing undone to insure success, and have a sufficient number of men around to allow no Indian to escape. Say nothing of your orders until the time arrives.[37]

George M. Hanson, the superintendent of Indian affairs for the Northern District of California, sent Wright several

requests for troops to be sent to Round Valley in Mendocino County to protect the Indians from whites who he
said had threatened to kill all the Indians on the local
reservation and had even made threats to assassinate its
supervisor.[38]

Early in October, Superintendent Hanson again complained to Wright about matters in Round Valley. Whites,
he said, were turning their cattle loose to feed on Indian
crops so that they could sell their own to the government.
The reservation was overrun by whites who were abusing
the Indians and forcing them to starve or steal unless the
government fed them. He asked Wright to declare martial
law and send troops to remove the whites from the reservation. Wright ordered Lippitt to comply with the request.
Lippitt talked with James Short, supervisor of the Round
Valley Reservation, who told him that he had received no
funds from Hanson for salaries for himself, a physician, or
other employees and had been obliged to use several thousand dollars of his own funds. Hanson claimed that he had
not received the necessary funds from Washington, D.C.,
but it was later found that he had obtained $14,000, which
he had spent on the Smith River Reservation.[39]

Hanson, after a visit to Round Valley, told Commissioner of Indian Affairs William P. Dole that the Indians
were leaving the reservation because of the settlers' threats
and plunder of their crops. To Wright he wrote that he
had not exaggerated facts and that the Indians who had
been killed for allegedly stealing cattle had not been guilty.
He thought that the settlers would like to be ousted by the
troops so that the government would have to reimburse
them for their "improvements."[40]

In November, Lippitt sent Capt. Charles D. Douglas
with his company to Round Valley. He was to erect quarters, aid the Indian superintendent when needed, protect
government agents and Indians, and arrest anyone who
tred to drive out the Indians or who advocated treason. He
was to disregard writs of habeas corpus and if any magistrate or civil officer interfered, he was to arrest him.

Douglas named the post he established Fort Wright.

After he declared martial law, the white citizens of Round
Valley held a mass meeting protesting his presence and his
attempts to remove them. Denying culpability, they asked
for a copy of the charges against them and requested an
investigation. Captain Douglas became convinced that
there was no truth to the charges against the settlers; all of
them seemed to be law-abiding and peaceable.

Douglas then blamed Hanson and Short for the reservation's upheavals. He found the reservation neglected, the
Indians totally lacking in care, their crops not even fenced
in. When the whites had slaughtered twenty-three Indians
the previous summer, the supervisor had made no effort
to learn the names of any of the persons involved, nor had
he attempted to prevent the killings. The Indians who had
been killed were said to have been a wild, unruly group
against whom the settlers acted in self-defense. The mis-
management of the reservation, he said, was a disgrace to
the government. The reason the settlers sometimes refused to sell supplies, said Douglas, was that they were
never paid.

At the beginning of 1863, Douglas reported that Indian
bureau officials had done nothing for the support of the
reservation Indians for the coming year. An assistant had
tried to fence the crops but had been stopped by his supervisor. Short, he observed, frustrated all that his assistant
tried to do and should be ousted, especially since he seemed
to have no knowledge of the extent or resources of the reservation. Douglas thought the area well suited for a reservation if it was managed by a competent agent.[41] Douglas
has recently been accused of being naïve and gullible.[42]

At the end of January, Wright sent the Hanson and
Douglas reports to army headquarters and suggested that
the reservation required the attention of the Interior Department. He observed that no improvement seemed likely
under the present system, and a few days later he revoked
martial law.[43]

The whole affair received a good deal of newspaper
coverage. An account in the *Daily Alta California* for Janu-

ary 24, 1863, referred to an editorial in the *Mendocino Herald*. General Wright, the paper said, had urged Douglas to use extreme caution. At the court of inquiry held at Fort Wright on December 18, Short was quoted as saying that he had had no trouble with the settlers. He stated there were 1,500 Indians on the reservation and admitted that it was badly managed. According to the paper, the investigation showed that Hanson was afraid or guilty of some other motive and that the greatest need was for a suitable custodian rather than soldiers.[44]

Indian troubles flared up in other parts of California as well. In mid-March, 1862, Wright had to send troops to Owens Lake. Cattle taken there by whites for sale to the miners had been eating grass that the Indians cultivated for use of the seeds as food. The Indians retaliated by burning all the houses in the Owens River valley, killing a number of whites and stealing or killing their cattle. An armed party of civilians had been beaten back by several hundred Indians but was able to subdue them after the arrival of the soldiers.

In early June, Wright sent Lt. Col. George S. Evans with several companies of the Second California Volunteer Cavalry from Camp Latham near Los Angeles on a four-month expedition to Owens Lake. Before it was over, Evans was to report that many of his men were shoeless and dressed in clothes made from barley and flour sacks. Wright ordered the Quartermaster Department to have the men properly supplied immediately. Throughout the summer and autumn Colonel Evans's expedition in the Owens River valley resulted in a number of skirmishes; a few Indians were killed or captured and a number of their rancherias burned.[45]

On April 25, Wright ordered Capt. George M. Price and Company M, Second California Volunteer Cavalry, to look into reports of Indian problems at Honey Lake and Pyramid Lake on the California-Nevada border. He observed to Price, "I have generally found that by hanging a few of the worst Indians, peace and quiet is soon restored."[46]

In New Mexico, Gen. James H. Carleton, now in command of the department, was attempting to subdue the Apaches, who continued to raid, steal, and murder.

In February, a petition came to Wright from citizens in Oregon and Washington requesting a post on the Payette River on the road to the Salmon River mines for protection against the Snakes. It added that for forty days the temperature had been between five and forty degrees below zero, hardly a propitious time for maneuvering troops.

The following month Wright informed Col. Albemarle Cady at Fort Vancouver that Col. Thomas R. Cornelius was on his way with his newly raised regiment of Oregon Volunteer Cavalry for service in the mining district to protect the emigrants coming from Fort Hall. During the summer they were to establish a new Fort Boise. The Indians who had been involved in the wars of 1855–56 and 1858 were now peaceful, and it was the Snakes who were responsible for most of the troubles. Approximately 10,000 immigrants made their way to Oregon during the summer of 1862.[47]

Wright complained to the commissioner of Indian affairs in Washington, D.C., that much of the conflict with the Indians was due to the encroachment of whites on their lands before the treaties allowing whites such access had been ratified. The system of managing Indian affairs on the coast was a miserable failure, he said, and great sums of money were being expended without benefit to the Indians or the government.[48]

In mid-April, Col. Justus Steinberger, having almost filled out his regiment of Washington Territory Volunteers by recruiting in California, was ordered to move with it to Fort Vancouver and take over command of the District of Oregon from Colonel Cady. Two months later Wright was obliged to write him:

San Francisco June 29th 1862

My Dear Friend:

I have received your note of the 6th inst.-I am very glad to hear that you are getting along so well in Oregon. At no distant day, I have no doubt you will be able to fill up your regiment; soon a reaction among the mining gentlemen will take place & doubtless many good men can be obtained—one full company, (84 men) is now at Alcatraz, & I think we shall get another company soon.

I have received no official advices from Washington in relation to Genl. Alvord. He has received his appointment and orders to report to me for *temporary* duty; but whether it is designed to call him East or not, is not known—He was ordered to report to me by letter from Vancouver. I have telegraphed for instructions but as yet cannot communicate—the wires have been down for nearly 2 weeks, & we are in a terrible state of suspense and anxiety as to how the war is going on—Of course I shall have to assign Genl. Alvord to your district; assuring you at the same time, that all your acts thus far have my cordial approval, & that I have full confidence, that if left in command, you would not disappoint the expectations of the Government.

I hope my friend Cady is getting well. I shall be glad to see him—Present my kind regards to him, as well as to Lugenbeel & the gentlemen near you.

> With great regard,
> Very truly yr friend
> G. Wright.[49]

In the meantime, Steinberger was to move the Oregon Cavalry Regiment east of the Cascades with headquarters at Fort Walla Walla. One company was ordered to the Nez Percé country, and two companies were sent to the Salmon River mining district and later to Fort Hall to protect the emigrants.

Upon relinquishing his command, Steinberger wrote that his policy had been to prevent outbreaks and aggression on either side rather than to subdue hostilities: "In being relieved of [this] command, I have no stronger desires than to have the approval of the officer [Gen. Wright] under whose orders I have had the honor to serve."[50]

Brigadier General Benjamin Alvord assumed command of the Oregon District on July 7, 1862. One of the first letters Alvord received on assuming command was from Charles Hutchins, Washington Territory Indian agent, who

requested troops at Fort Lapwai to protect the Nez Percé's
from the "vicious" whites and liquor sellers. Alvord complied with his request. In the fall Wright ordered the troops
who had been sent there to erect quarters and remain for
the winter.[51]

Governor Pickering complained from Olympia that in
spite of Wright's efforts more emigrants than ever were
being robbed and murdered along the Snake River road.
He demanded that troops be sent at least as far east as Fort
Boise and, further, that two or three posts be established
in the area and occupied the year around. He wanted action *now*, not the usual delayed farce. He asked Wright to
cover the cost of sending a messenger to carry a memorial
from the legislature to Congress recommending these
measures. Wright said he had no authority for such an expenditure. He informed Pickering that a new post was
being planned for the Boise area and suggested that if the
emigrants observed the rules recommended for their protection there should be no difficulty. If the emigrants did
not follow the customary route but separated into small
parties heading to different destinations, it would be impossible to furnish an escort for every party. Wright said
that he thought the number of murders had been exaggerated and that he had ordered Alvord to investigate and
punish murderers.[52] Wright is often criticized for overzealous punishment and warmongering when a police action would have sufficed, but here he was clearly advocat-
ing a police action to Pickering.

In a subsequent letter to the governor, Wright confessed
that he was well aware of the needs of Oregon and Washington: "I shall ever retain a lively interest in the welfare
of the people of Washington Territory and the State of
Oregon. For six long years my home was among these
hardy pioneers, engaged most of the time in battling our
savage foes. I left them at peace, prosperous and happy
and pray they may continue so."[53]

In November, Wright told Thomas that peace in the
Oregon District was due to Alvord's prudence and foresight. However, Wright was still concerned about the situa-

tion on the Nez Percé reservation. He announced that if
these Indians, of whom the veteran army officers thought
so highly, could not receive government protection by
other means he planned to declare martial law in the area.[54]

Mexico and the European Powers

In addition to his concerns about uprisings by secessionists
and Indian warfare, Wright also worried about the possibility of war with a foreign country. Great Britain, France,
and Spain had taken advantage of America's preoccupa-
tion with the Civil War to blockade the east coast of Mexico
in an effort to force the government of President Benito
Juárez to pay its debts. England and Spain withdrew in
April when it became apparent that Emperor Napoleon
III of France planned to use the unpaid loans as an excuse
to invade Mexico. He sent in 30,000 troops, who reached
Mexico City during the summer, and installed his puppet,
Prince Maximilian, as emperor of Mexico.

In May, while Pickering was en route to assume his
duties as newly appointed governor of Washington Territory, he acquired some information at Acapulco that
prompted him to direct a terse note to President Lincoln:
"France will take and keep Acapulco and Western Mexico.
Prevent them."[55]

Another source of anxiety on the coast was the appearance of a British warship at Guaymas. Its purpose was
to apply pressure on the Mexican government to pay its
debts to Great Britain. British warships also remained at
anchor off Vancouver Island. In February, Company D,
Third U.S. Artillery, was taken to San Francisco from San
Juan Island, and Capt. Lyman A. Bissell with Company C
of the Ninth Infantry was sent as a replacement. By now a
sizable unruly element existed on the island, some with
southern sympathies, and Bissell faced a formidable task
in trying to keep order.[56]

In September, Wright sent Seward a copy of a letter
from one A. Ainsa addressed to the Mexican representative in Washington, D.C., requesting that a U.S. post be

established in Sonora to protect the Mexicans from American Indians and seeking right of transit for supplies for Arizona by way of the port of Lobos. Wright suggested that Seward forward these requests to the U.S. legation in Mexico, but Seward declined.[57] Wright also sent Thomas a copy of Major Ferguson's report on the advantages of the overland supply route through Sonora and announced that he was planning to ship the next supplies by that route.[58]

Throughout the year Wright attempted repeatedly to impress Adjutant General Thomas with the importance of sending Union troops to occupy Guaymas, supported by ships of war. Wright believed that the news of Carleton's column being assembled in the southern part of the state of California, preparing to advance against them, would cause the rebels to flee southward toward Guaymas, since it was Sonora they really wanted, not Arizona. He was sure that there would be no objection from Mexico to a temporary occupation by U.S. troops. The war and state departments, however, preferred to walk the tightrope of neutrality.

Strange Doings at Port Townsend

Alvord was particularly concerned about the defenseless condition of the Columbia River and Puget Sound and wanted an ironclad steamer and heavy coastal guns for each area. He called attention to the presence of British warships at Esquimalt, on Vancouver Island, and informed army headquarters that the British were fortifying Esquimalt harbor. He reminded the assistant adjutant general that Congress had appropriated funds for the defense of the Washington and Oregon coasts and expressed the hope that some funds would soon be made available. Engineer DeRussy had already sent plans to Washington, D.C., for defending the mouth of the Columbia River, but no action had been taken.[59]

Wright shared Alvord's concern, but he may have been more amused than alarmed by the ridiculous performance of a few federal officials in the Puget Sound area. On May 26, Wright received a letter from James H. Merryman, the acting collector of the U.S. Revenue Service at Port Townsend, Washington Territory. Wright had authorized the chief collector, Victor Smith, to use some vacated military barracks for a marine hospital and for the reception of sick and wounded soldiers. Smith was a personal friend of Secretary of the Treasury Salmon P. Chase, who had persuaded President Lincoln to appoint Smith. Merryman informed Wright that he had reported Smith to the secretary of the treasury for embezzlement and official misconduct, alleging that Smith was appropriating hospital and other funds for his own use.[60]

In August, Maj. G. W. Patten at Fort Steilacoom reported to Wright that Smith had returned to Port Townsend on the revenue cutter *Shubrick* after a visit to Port Angeles, where he proposed to move the customhouse. When Merryman demanded to see his authority to remove the official papers and books, Smith had the *Shubrick* load its cannons and train them on the town and sent an armed guard to seize the documents. The citizens of Port Townsend had supported Merryman but feared that their town might be destroyed if they continued to do so. Reluctantly they turned the records over to Smith, who took them to Port Angeles. The citizens complained to the governor.

Eleven days later Patten reported that he had accompanied Governor Pickering and his party to Port Townsend by steamer. A hearing was held, and warrants were issued for the arrest of Smith and Lieutenant Wilson, commander of the *Shubrick*. The U.S. marshal boarded the cutter as it came ashore with the mail, but Smith and Wilson refused to accept the warrants. The marshal made a second attempt to board the cutter after it had moved away from the shore, but when he rowed out to serve his warrants, the ship's paddle wheels were set in motion to churn up the water so that he could not approach. Smith then sailed away for San Francisco.

Wright informed Patten that he saw no difficulty for the army in the course pursued by the federal officers, because the solution to this absurd problem was the responsibility of the civil authorities. Peter H. Watson, assistant secretary of war, sent the pertinent correspondence to Secretary of the Treasury Chase.[61]

On September 12, Patten made his final report on the subject. The *Shubrick* had returned to the sound and was now at Olympia. Smith and Wilson had consented to a legal investigation, thus avoiding the possibility of a collision between the territorial authorities protecting the citizens and the officers of the U.S. Revenue Service, whose conduct was bizarre if not criminal. Although charges against Smith were ultimately dismissed by Chase, extreme local pressures finally led the president to replace him. Vocal in his opposition to Smith was Dr. A. G. Henry, Lincoln's former physician, who had been appointed surveyor general of Washington Territory.[62]

Wright's First Year in Command of the Pacific Department

On the anniversary of his assumption of command of the Department of the Pacific, Wright pointed out in a letter to Thomas that he had spent ten years on the coast, one in command of the department. During that time swarms of people from all over the world had rushed in, some with no loyalty to the U.S. government; fortunately that number was small compared to the loyal Americans. He hoped that his efforts had contributed toward preserving the Union, and he expressed his appreciation for the cooperation he had received from the governors and state officers as well as from the citizens.[63]

In many of his reports to headquarters Wright made reference to the harmony that existed between state and federal officials and the military, and asserted that complete reliance could be placed on the civilian authorities for their support in enforcing laws and War Department orders. A recent writer has described Wright's rapport with three California governors, John F. Downey, Leland

Stanford, and Frederick F. Low, as a model of successful civilian-military cooperation.[64]

Wright often conferred with state and territorial governors about the need for more volunteer regiments. When the governors issued calls for volunteers, Wright urged citizens to respond promptly and to rally under the protecting folds of what he often referred to as the "glorious old Star-spangled Banner." Although he was proud of the large number of patriotic citizens who had volunteered, supplying them with weapons was another matter. Halleck periodically protested that no arms or artillery were available, particularly for the militia, which the governors used for local emergencies. Unlike the regular volunteers, these men were not mustered into the army.

Wright was chronically short of funds with which to pay contractors, teamsters, and other employees. Yet he was gratified by the vast sums of money and supplies that the citizens of his department had contributed to the war effort and for the sick and wounded soldiers in the East.

For the first time since his Florida days Wright became ill. In November he requested authority for a temporary removal of his headquarters to Sacramento. He complained that he was suffering from "asthma," the only "affliction" he had ever had, and this only in San Francisco. Sacramento, being the seat of government and the residence of the governor, would be a more convenient site for the transaction of departmental business. He also commented that he had never traveled farther than Sacramento since taking command and requested permission to make a tour of his department.[65]

Wright followed with interest the military careers of his sons. In 1862 John in particular had seen a great deal of action in the East. He had participated in all the engagements fought by the Army of Ohio and on June 30 had been promoted to major for gallantry under fire at Shiloh. In October he had again distinguished himself in the Battle of Perryville. Thomas continued to serve with the Second California Volunteer Cavalry.

Civil War Days: 1863

THE UNION CELEBRATED many victories in the East in 1863, after an initial setback at Chancellorsville. Working with the freshwater navy under Adm. David D. Porter, Gen. Ulysses S. Grant besieged and captured Vicksburg. During the first three days of July, the Confederacy reached its high point at the battle of Gettysburg, but ultimately Gen. George G. Mead forced Gen. Robert E. Lee to retreat.

On July 7 California's gubernatorial candidate, Frederick F. Low, wired Secretary of War Stanton, "Give result in Pennsylvania, citizens anxious." President Lincoln wired back: "General Mead . . . beat Lee at Gettysburg, Pa. at the end of three days battle. . . . Vicksburg surrendered to General Grant on the glorious old Fourth."[1] In September the Confederates were again defeated in the Battle of Chattanooga.

In September, Low, now governor of California, wired Lincoln: "Loyal California sends greetings. The Union, State and Congressional tickets are elected." A message to Stanton said, "California by her votes bids you and the Army Godspeed." Stanton thanked Wright and Low for the good news of the election. "Our military operations on this side," he said, "are progressing favorably in every direction."[2]

The Carleton Column on Occupation Duty

As the new year began, General Wright remained in command of the Pacific Department, responsible for protecting it against enemies within and without. All military operations conducted by his subordinates were subject to his approval and under his direction. It was a monumental task. An example was Carleton's operation. Ironically, after all the careful planning and the epic march, the Carleton column reached its objective too late to participate in the fighting. However, the mere knowledge of the column's imminent arrival helped influence the outcome. The Confederates had been driven out of the Southwest by other units, and the column settled down to occupation duty.

Quiet reigned in Arizona except for occasional murders by Apaches and resulting pursuits by soldiers. Pimas and Maricopas were armed to help fight the Apaches, and those who brought in scalps were rewarded with gifts of guns and ammunition. The Papagos and Navajos also indicated a desire to help the soldiers. The soldiers were encouraged to prospect for minerals in their spare time. Major Theodore A. Coult, who was now in command of western Arizona, reported that, in addition to problems with the Apaches, robberies and murders occurred almost daily at the mines, and skirmishes with bands of California highway robbers and thieving Mexicans were common.

In January the Western District of Arizona was abolished, and Major Coult was transferred to the Department of New Mexico. In severing his connection with the Department of the Pacific, Coult expressed heartfelt regret at leaving and gratitude to General Wright for "the kindness and courtesy with which I have ever been treated by the General commanding and the heads of the several departments in San Francisco."[3]

Secessionists: Seizure of the *J. M. Chapman*

The activities of the secessionists in California were becoming increasingly overt and violent. On March 15, 1863, Drum informed Wright that a privateer had been seized in San Francisco harbor. Drum had learned of a Confederate plot to purchase and arm the schooner *J. M. Chapman* and use her to prey on commerce on the coast. He conferred with the commander of the U.S.S. *Cyane*, the port collector, and the police, and a plan was laid to trap the conspirators and seize the vessel. The chief conspirator, Asbury Harpending, had obtained a letter of marque from Jefferson Davis. Funds for the enterprise were furnished by Ridgley Greathouse, and the vessel was procured by Alfred Rubery.[4]

As Wright reported to Thomas, when the ship set sail, allegedly for Manzanillo, she was seized by a party from the *Cyane* at the request of the port collector. Fifteen heavily armed men were found hidden in the hold and, instead of the machinery listed on the manifest, the cargo consisted of cannons and munitions. The seizure, Wright said, had "a happy effect." The leaders were placed in irons in solitary confinement at Alcatraz. Papers indicating their treasonous intentions were offered as evidence at their trial, and all were found guilty. Each of the chief conspirators was sentenced to ten years in prison and fined $10,000. The other prisoners and the crew were released after taking an oath of allegiance.[5]

Three months later, Wright heard that Rubery might be pardoned, and he wired Stanton reminding him that Rubery had been one of the principals in the "*Chapman* affair." "No reason for him to be object of executive clemency. Feeling here strong against this." Lincoln, however, pardoned him because he was a British subject, and Wright ordered him to leave the country within thirty days.[6]

Within a few days of the *Chapman*'s capture Wright alerted Captain Selfridge at Mare Island that other vessels were known to have sailed to prey on Union shipping and asked him to send the steamer *Saginaw* to the rendezvous point of the rebel vessels. Selfridge agreed but a few days later countermanded the *Saginaw* voyage because of rumors that a military organization in Napa County was about to attack the navy yard. Captain Julian McAllister at Benicia was warned to watch the Pacific mail steamers for possible attempts to seize their cargoes of arms for the newly raised troops.

In April the *Saginaw* left the harbor, and the *Cyane* was needed at the navy yard, leaving only the *Shubrick,* which had been ordered down from Puget Sound, to police the harbor. Wright informed Governor Stanford that Captain Selfridge had withdrawn the *Saginaw* and the *Cyane* and urged him to call out militia in Napa and Solano counties to quell the threatened insurrection, which might jeopardize the security of Mare Island. Wright asked the Corps of Engineers to survey Mare Island for the installation of protective batteries of artillery.[7] On April 7, Wright issued a proclamation to the citizens of the Pacific Coast, setting forth the blessings of peace and the penalty for disloyalty:

> You are far removed from the scenes of war and desolation; a war which has drenched in blood the fairest portion of our beloved country; a war to preserve our Union and our free institutions against the assaults of traitors—traitors to their God and traitors to their country; who, disregarding the precepts of the great Washington, seek to destroy our very existence as a nation. During the war which has been raging for the last two years in the Eastern States you have enjoyed all the blessings of peace and prosperity within your borders. No family hearth has been made desolate. The wailings of the widow and orphan are rarely heard in this favored land. So far you have been exempt from the scourge of war. Are you prepared, then, to sacrifice all these blessings, to prove recreant to yourselves, to the nation, and to the high and holy trust transmitted to you by the founders of our Republic? No. Already I hear the welkin ring with shouts of acclamation: "The Union shall be preserved." Although the great mass of people on the Pacific Coast are eminently patriotic and devoted to the Union, yet, fellow-citizens, we must not disguise the fact that we have traitors in our midst who are doing all in their power to involve this country in the horrors of civil war. To all such persons, I say, pause, and reflect well before plunging into the yawning abyss of treason; an indignant people will rise in their majesty, and swift retributive justice will be your certain doom.

The *Sacramento Daily Union* published this proclamation, adding, "Secession newspapers please copy."[8]

Some people feared that Union reverses in the East might lead to war on the coast. To Wright, the public apprehensions were not entirely groundless, but were exaggerated. He told Thomas that he had tried to rouse the loyal citizens to their sense of duty by holding mass meetings and forming Union Leagues. The governors and high officers stood united in their support of the Union.

In May, Wright was notified by Col. Clarence E. Bennett at Camp Drum that armed parties of Confederate sympathizers were stealing government horses. Wright ordered his son, Maj. Thomas Wright, to proceed with two infantry companies to protect the Union element in that perennial trouble spot San Bernardino and to prevent further thefts. Later he sent Thomas Wright to Solano County to investigate possible disloyalty there.[9]

In August violence flared again in Visalia, where the commander reported that one of his sergeants had been shot and killed by a known rebel. A detachment sent in pursuit of the murderer was frustrated when the man's friends spirited him away. Sometimes problems arose with overeager Union supporters. On one occasion vigilantes in Los Angeles threatened to lynch local prisoners, but Drum was obliged to tell the sheriff that the army could not help him protect his jail from a mob unless help was requested by the governor and ordered by Wright, the commanding general.

Connor and the Mormons

In Salt Lake City, Gen. Patrick Edward Connor was still dismayed by the disloyal conduct and ethics of the Mormons. He suggested either dividing the territory into four parts so that it could be adequately controlled or reinforcing him and allowing him to declare martial law.

Connor called Wright's attention to a report by one of his officers that exemplified the sentiments that he saw daily. A detachment of troops under Col. George S. Evans was involved in a skirmish with some Indians in the center of a Mormon village. The inhabitants simply stood and watched, offering no help. What was worse, they informed the Indians of every move by whites and furnished the soldiers with false reports regarding a relief expedition. Wright forwarded the report to Thomas, saying:

> I beg leave to ask your attention to the statement of Col. George S. Evans, Second Cavalry California Volunteers in rela-

tion to the conduct of the Mormons. It was only a continuation of their perfidious acts which commenced when our troops arrived in Utah. But I trust the day is fast approaching when retributive justice will be meted out to these worse than open traitors to their country.[10]

Connor was sure that the Mormons were inciting the Indians to raids and massacres on the Overland Mail Route. His troops had a few skirmishes with the Indians and recaptured many stolen horses and burned Indian lodges. He requested reinforcements, saying that unless they arrived soon the Overland Mail Route would be broken up and the emigrant route impassable. Wright suggested to acting Gov. Orion Clemens of Nevada Territory that he organize three or four companies of volunteers to move over the Overland Mail Route toward Salt Lake City. Halleck had suggested trying to raise troops in Nevada or Utah or from the emigrant trains since the Sierra Nevada would be impassable until July, and help coming from California would not be able to get through. Wright wondered whether it would be possible to reinforce Connor from the Missouri frontier.[11]

Connor suggested two solutions to the Mormon problem. He felt that the first solution, to increase the use of the military in fighting them, was impractical and preferred encouraging Gentile (that is, non-Mormon) settlement. He encouraged his troops to prospect for minerals, hoping that their discoveries would attract miners and settlers. He was now at peace with the Indians in most of his district, and the emigrant roads were safe. Highway robbers, not Indians, were the main hazard to the Overland stages at this time. Wright commented to Assistant Adjutant General Townsend that he had impressed upon Connor the importance of a conservative policy toward the Mormons when he had assigned him to Utah but added that only through Connor's forbearance and sound judgment had a collision with the sect been avoided.[12]

Wright received a letter from Gov. James D. Doty of Utah commending Connor for improving relations with the citizens and trying to maintain peace. Doty emphasized the importance of keeping troops in Salt Lake City to uphold the U.S. authorities. Wright sent the letter on to army headquarters.[13]

Early in June, 1863, Connor announced that he had made a treaty with a large Snake band and thought that the Indian troubles in his district were almost at an end. A week later, however, he had to admit that the southern Utes had commenced hostilities. He was reinforced by two companies of California Volunteer Infantry and a detachment of cavalry and by October had made treaties with the Utes and the remaining Snakes.[14] After the Indian troubles in this district were settled, Connor believed that he might as well withdraw to California since he did not have enough troops to "coerce" the Mormons, and his presence had become an irritant rather than a source of awe. The stage and telegraph line, he said, could be guarded by four companies of Nevada cavalry.

The Indians on the Coast

The Humboldt District continued to be the site of most Indian-white confrontations. Lippitt said that the only result of a strenuous winter expedition was that three Indians had been killed. Conflicts with the Hoopas and Klamaths persisted. Civilian and government packtrains were ambushed; mules, supplies, personal effects—and occasionally soldiers' lives—were lost. In the West warfare took place on an individual and personal basis, in contrast to the vast armies and mass casualties in the East. Settlers and the army tended to blame the Indian agents, who promised everything but often gave nothing.

Lippitt complained about the whiskey shops near the military posts, which no commander had been able to close. At one post on the average sixteen soldiers were imprisoned in the guardhouse each day for drunkenness, and soldiers' clothing was being stolen and sold to the grogshop operator for liquor.

Several months earlier Lippitt had suggested that volunteer companies made up of experienced hunters and mountaineers could do a better job than regulars in the Humboldt District. On January 21, Wright asked Governor Stanford to raise four companies of this specialized infantry to serve as long as needed in the area, and the next month he requested an additional six companies. Stanford issued the necessary calls. Wright informed the adjutant general that because of continuing problems in the Humboldt District the troops were being replaced by men familiar with the country.[15] Early in June, Lippitt was ordered to take charge of and assign the mountain companies as they were formed. Small detachments were needed to cover vast areas—a reliable force with good officers ready for any service.

By the end of the month Lippitt was complaining of the constant criticism he and his soldiers received from the *Humboldt Times*. He said that he would be happy to be relieved from his odious assignment. Two weeks later his wish was granted when Wright relieved him of his command of the Humboldt District and replaced him with Lt. Col. Stephen J. Whipple, First Battalion Mountaineers, California Volunteers.[16]

When Whipple learned of the proposed withdrawal of Lippitt's command, he immediately requested more troops, since the Indians were well armed and more aggressive than ever. In General Order no. 6 Whipple announced to his men that they were at war only with the hostile Indians and that no one else was to be molested. They were to avoid killing women and children; males who surrendered were to be treated as prisoners of war.

Whipple soon confronted many of the problems that had faced his predecessor. He could capture hundreds of Indians, but making them stay on a reservation was virtually impossible. On September 17 Drum sent Whipple a memorial from Weaverville saying that nine whites had been killed in the preceding two days. Mountain troops were sent to the community's relief. The entire Humboldt District seemed to have flared into active hostilities.

Whipple commented that he often learned of unusual

events in his district through exaggerated rumors appearing in the San Francisco newspapers. However, he acknowledged that the Indian situation was still "threatening." Many of the Indians had left their homes and joined the "bad chiefs" in the mountains. Settlers had abandoned their farms and were congregating for protection. The whites, for their part, were not blameless. Whipple particularly deplored what he considered one of the most heinous offenses of the time, the kidnapping and selling of Indian children by unscrupulous whites.[17]

In August, Indian Superintendent Hanson forwarded to Wright a letter from the supervisor of the Mendocino Indian Reservation. A shanty had been burned; the circumstances were unknown, but Indians were being blamed. Citizens seeking to chastise the perpetrators usually killed any Indians they encountered—most of whom were innocent, since the guilty would be on the alert. Hanson also complained of drunken soldiers prowling in search of Indian women and urged that the indiscriminate slaughter of Indians be stopped.

In September, Hanson complained that Whipple disliked him, abused him verbally, and blamed him for the Indians leaving the Smith River Reservation. Douglas reported from Fort Wright that hundreds of Indians were dying because of gross neglect by the supervisor. A similar tale of sickness and death owing to agent incompetence followed from Camp Bidwell at Chico.[18] Capt. Henry Mellen at Fort Crook, in the Pitt River country, said that the only Indian trouble in the past year had resulted from the lawless acts of white settlers who, in turn, accused Mellen of protecting bad Indians. Wright forwarded the messages to Whipple.

Wright's report to Washington, D.C., for October indicated that the Pacific Department was quiet except for the Indian disturbance in northern California. Peace could not be promised in the Humboldt District unless the Indians were removed to distant reservations, he wrote. He proposed to try an experiment, using some Indians as workers on the Angel Island fortifications.[19]

In southern California, at the end of March, there were said to be 1,100 Indians in the Owens River Valley. Companies were sent from Fort Churchill and Camp Babbitt to prevent uprisings. One of the companies from Camp Babbitt, under Capt. Moses McLaughlin, raided an Indian camp near Keysville. Between 30 and 40 of the warriors, identified as hostile, were shot or sabered to death. The others were released along with the women, children, and aged.[20] Subsequently McLaughlin reported that 1,000 Indians from the Owens River Valley were on their way to the Tejon Reservation. He said that the depredations and fighting could have been avoided by the earlier presence of troops. He received Wright's commendation for his activities.[21]

In reply to a request from Mono County in November for a military post, Wright said, "You must bear in mind, gentlemen, that I have a great many urgent calls for troops to protect our hardy pioneers against Indians . . . and a still more important business on hand to look after traitors within our borders, and to be prepared to meet foes from without." He said that he would do what he could but suggested raising militia in California or Nevada. He believed the government would be willing to arm these volunteers. That very day he received word from Governor Nye that a military company had been raised in Nevada, and, a few days later, another.[22]

Wright had previously told headquarters that he could not send troops everywhere they were needed and asked permission to arm the militia that Governor Stanford had raised. Halleck replied that he had insufficient weapons to arm mustered volunteers and none could be issued to militia. He would, however, help fortify San Francisco.

Early in the spring Alvord sent troops from the District of Oregon to erect the new post that Halleck had finally approved, forty miles east of old Fort Boise. Drum said that Alvord would have to depend on what troops he had and any he could raise in Oregon for garrisoning the new Fort Boise. Alvord reported that he had given arms to the Oregon militia raised by Gov. Addison Gibbs because the secretary of state of Oregon had told him that Wright had given his approval. Wright exploded, "This won't do!" He had received word that the secretary of war had backed Halleck in saying that there were to be no arms for militia.

Governor Gibbs said that he could not raise militia if he could not arm them. As a result, in July, Alvord was forced to dispatch volunteer troops to Canyon City, on the headwaters of the John Day River, where five white men had been killed by the Indians and 1,500 miners needed protection. Superintendent J. W. P. Huntington estimated that at one time there had been 10,000 miners in the Oregon District.[23]

The only good news, from the white point of view, was that a new treaty had been made with Nez Percé Chief Lawyer, which Superintendent Calvin P. Hale regarded as a great success. By its terms the Indians relinquished nine-tenths of their land. According to Hale, there was no further need for troops at Fort Lapwai.[24]

In southeastern Oregon the Snakes were killing and marauding again. Governor Gibbs said that he had 150 men ready to enlist and fight, but Alvord replied that he still had no authority to furnish them with arms. He reminded the governor that if Oregon had been more successful in its efforts to raise six companies of volunteer cavalry there would not have been an Indian problem. Finally, in response to complaints from the governors of Oregon, California, and Nevada, Halleck relented and told Wright to issue arms to state militia on a loan basis.

Wright's Problems with the Army

In May, 1863, recruiting centers for the regular army were closed. With eligible males joining the volunteer regiments, it was impossible to get replacements for the greatly reduced Ninth Infantry and Third Artillery. As time passed, the number of men applying for service with the volunteers and militia began to fall off. Many men were willing to respond, but only for active service in the East. Filling quotas from Oregon and Washington had always been difficult, and Wright reported that Californians resented filling the quotas of other states.

Alvord and other commanders were also confronted with the problem of desertion. The legal tender in which the men were paid was progressively devalued, and they could earn far more in the mines or on road construction. Ironically, settlers who clamored for protection often doubled the cost of transport and supplies when they learned that the troops were coming.

Early in the year Wright had urged that all payments on the coast be made in coin, the currency used in the West. He reported to Thomas that the depreciation of the treasury notes caused much embarrassment and rendered it difficult to make contracts because of a ruinous 30 percent (later 60 percent) discount. Officers and surgeons in Oregon were resigning in protest because of the paper money, and it was interfering with recruiting and purchasing supplies. Later he complained that he scarcely had enough money to pay the board for his wife and himself. Thomas replied, "The General-in-Chief does not perceive the propriety of payment in coin." [25] Two years later, when Gen. Irvin McDowell was department commander, he took up Wright's old complaint, this time addressed to the surgeon general. His medical director, he said, could not live on his pay in legal tender in this "gold country," and contract physicians were becoming unavailable for the same reason.

In the summer of 1863, Wright became involved in an unpleasant controversy when he received a presidential order to take military possession of the New Almaden Mine, a rich producer of mercury-yielding ore in Santa Clara County. Because the events that led to this order had thrown the California mining community into an uproar, on July 9, Wright telegraphed Halleck to request permission to defer acting on Lincoln's order.

Leonard Swett, Lincoln's former law partner, was in San

Francisco as the attorney for the Quicksilver Mining Company of New York, which was suing for possession of the New Almaden Mine. The case went to the U.S. Supreme Court, where, by a four-to-three decision, the present mine operators were held to be in illegal possession. Lincoln signed a writ ordering U.S. Marshal C. W. Rand, to oust the owners and turn the premises and appurtenances over to Swett, who was to act on behalf of the United States.

Numerous officials and prominent citizens wired the president and Halleck urging suspension of Wright's order to take over the mine with a military force. The result, they said, would be "deplorable" and give the secessionists an advantage. Halleck, who as a former president of the Quicksilver Mining Company could hardly be considered a disinterested party, indignantly wired Wright that the secretary of war knew of no order to take over the Almaden Mine. He ordered Wright to desist and obey only orders coming through proper channels and suggested that the order for seizure of the mine had been "surreptitiously obtained." Swett's interest, also, was hardly altruistic. He had gone to California as a representative of the president and of the Quicksilver Mining Company, which was paying him a large fee that would be even larger if he was successful. Moreover, he was a sizable shareholder in the mining company.

On July 15, Wright told Halleck that he had never planned to take military possession but only to furnish the U.S. marshal with a force authorized by an order from the president. Port Collector Low and others had asked him to defer action until further instructions came from Washington, and the marshal had been told to suspend action. Although the government denied having any intention of interfering with any mining interests on the coast except Almaden, antigovernment politicians were creating the impression that all mining interests were at the mercy of the U.S. government.

Lincoln wired Swett that he had received many telegrams begging him to suspend military enforcement of the writ of possession and that Swett was the only one "urging the contrary. . . . I would like to oblige but my duty lies the other way." Not one to give up easily, Swett wired Lincoln that it was now alleged that the mine was on government property.

Finally Lincoln wired Low that there had been a misunderstanding concerning the New Almaden mine. The secretary of the interior, the attorney general, and the president all believed that it was the government's duty to take possession after the Supreme Court declared the Almaden's claim fraudulent. The attorney general had issued a writ, which Lincoln had signed. Nothing surreptitious had transpired, although Halleck was under the impression that military orders had been issued of which he knew nothing.[26]

The members of Lincoln's cabinet were less charitable toward Halleck. Attorney General Edward Bates referred to Halleck's telegram as false, adding that "a liar ought to have a good memory." The president himself called Halleck hasty and indiscreet but, he hoped, "nothing worse." In response to the many presentations from California, Lincoln suspended the writ.

At the end of August, Swett announced that the Almaden matter had been settled in a satisfactory manner by "compromise." In effect this meant that the mine had been acquired by the Quicksilver Mining Company in a forced compromise sale for less than the value of a single year's output.[27] Through no fault of his own, Wright's relations with army headquarters were not improved.

Tiring of the rebuffs from Halleck and Thomas's veiled hostility, in the autumn of 1863, Wright appealed to Assistant Adjutant General Townsend, as one who served long on the Pacific Coast and who would understand the delays and difficulties of complying with War Department regulations. Wright wrote that he had preserved peace over a vast territory and that Arizona and New Mexico had been reconquered. He expressed pride in the performance of the troops sent to Utah as well. In his execution of duties he had frequently been called on to act promptly

and to assume responsibilities that in peace he would have
referred to the general-in-chief and the War Department.
He had never been charged with malfeasance in office or
with disregarding the best interests of the government.
"I have done, and shall do, what seems to be my duty, acknowledging my responsibility to the General-in-Chief,
the Secretary of War and the President of the United
States," he wrote.

He then requested the approval of the secretary of war
for all that he had done in raising, organizing, and ap-
pointing officers for volunteer organizations in the department. "I ask for this because we may experience some
objections by the accounting officers in cases where the
regulations of the Department have not been strictly followed," he said. Wright worried a great deal about the ex-
penses of his two overland columns, and not without justification, considering some of his past experiences. Wright
was working hard and under a good deal of stress. His
appeal to Townsend was simply a search for approbation, sympathy, and reassurance. Among these worried
accounts, one pleasant note appears in Wright's report,
regarding his horseback tour of eastern California and
Nevada and his satisfaction at finding the citizens loyal and
the troops in good fettle.[28]

A Proposal for a Reservation

Almost a year earlier Wright had suggested that the Humboldt Indians should be put on islands off the coast, since it
was impossible to make them stay on the existing reservations. He was convinced that only the removal of the Indians to remote locations could keep them in place and
under control; the alternative was an undesirable but inevitable one—extermination. On November 21, Maj. Henry
Hancock was ordered to evaluate Santa Catalina Island as
a site for a military post, since it might soon become com-
mercially important. Five days later Hancock submitted a
detailed report saying that the island was of great impor-

tance strategically and a good spot for a fort and depot. Accordingly, Col. James F. Curtis at Camp Drum was ordered to send a company of infantry to take possession of Catalina Island. All but a few persons, mainly incorporated miners and owners of livestock, were to be removed, and no new settlers allowed.

On December 21, Wright recommended to the War Department that the twenty-mile-long island be used as an Indian reservation. If this action had taken place two years earlier, he said, he could have placed all the Humboldt Indians there, relieving the troops of arduous service and saving the government a great deal of money. He submitted his plan for colonizing the California Indians and establishing a post at the head of the island's harbor.[29]

On New Year's Day, 1864, Company C, Fourth Infantry California Volunteers, under Capt. B. R. West, left Drum Barracks to take over Catalina Island. About one hundred citizens were evacuated. On February 20, Wright was told that Halleck had asked the Department of Interior to designate the island an Indian reservation. Wright kept Governor Low informed and told him that he thought the site ideal for a reservation. Wright later suggested to Townsend that if the mines were to be worked the whole island should be made a reservation so that unauthorized persons could be removed if necessary. Townsend forwarded the suggestion to the Interior Department.

Specified buildings on the isthmus where the fort was to be built were to be turned over to the troops. A water supply was established, and construction began. The quartermaster was ordered to purchase a schooner for the use and supply of the island. Captain West requested a complete survey of the island.[30] Months passed, and Wright continued to hope that plans for the reservation would receive final approval. He wired Washington asking for a decision from the Interior Department. Finally word was received that Commissioner of Indian Affairs Dole disapproved the project, and in August, Wright ordered Curtis to withdraw all troops and government property from the island. Military personnel and most Californians except the residents of Catalina Island were disappointed at the commissioner's decision.[31]

In November, 1863, another tiresome altercation erupted between the Indian Department and the military, this time in the Klamath Lake region. The site selected by the engineers for a new fort did not suit the interests of the local citizens. The local subagent for Indian affairs was highly critical of Lt. Charles S. Drew, who had been in charge of the project. An investigation absolved Drew of any misfeasance. Wright told the agent that his views had not been requested, whereupon the agent resigned in a huff. Squabbles between army officers and Indian agents regarding authority were frequent and acrimonious. Insignificant Indian alarms often led to urgent requests for troops by the agents, and the army often blamed the agents for causing much of the trouble with the Indians.[32]

In May, Wright sent another letter to his friend Hardie, who had been appointed assistant adjutant general in Washington, D.C.:

San Francisco May 18th 1863
My Friend:

I sincerely congratulate you on your appointment to a position which you are so eminently qualified to adorn, and to which you should have been promoted long since. Far removed as we are from the scenes of war and strife which surround you, yet the people on this coast are in the highest state of excitement; every ticking of the telegraph is listened to with a painful anxiety; the great masses in the country are thoroughly patriotic and devoted to the Union, and determined at whatever cost to maintain it, and preserve this beautiful country for stars to adorn the old flag, that glorious emblem of our nationality. But, we have another class in our midst, doing all in their power to throw this State into the vortex of rebellion; but thank God, their efforts thus far have been a failure. . . .

Your splendid "Army of the Potomac" has again been unfortunate; the magnificent raid of Stoneman shines out brightly in this wilderness of defects—How is it? have we not yet found the right man? We are experimenting at a fearful sacrifice.

General after general ascends the giddy height, and soon falls to raise no more. I pray God, that we may have at the head of each of our armies in the field, men of giant intellect; capable of wielding large armies; men who have the sagacity to call around them the military talent of the country—We cannot afford to jeopardize the safety of our armies and the honor of our flag, by placing them under the guidance of weak and ignorant commanders.

There are always plenty of men ready to claim the prizes and honors of our profession, to accept higher places, no matter how obtained, and "trust to luck" for success; they will not answer our purpose.

I firmly believe that this war will in the end prove highly beneficial to our country; we just now begin to know our power, and peace once restored, we may defy the world in arms. I am afraid that the Army of the Potomac, has been too much afraid of its rear, & that besides making head for Richmond, it had to look to the defense of Washington. Let Washington be more secure and the Army of the Potomac placed under a General with carte blanche; "Objective point" Richmond, and if he don't take it, hang him.

Well, I have faith in ultimate success; this unholy rebellion has nearly reached its culmination; once suppressed, what will become of the arch-traitors, who brought upon our unhappy country this desolating war; already methinks I hear each one inwardly exclaiming,

> "My hour is almost come, when I, to sulphurous and
>   tormenting flames, must render up myself"

If not improper for you to do, I should be glad to get something tangible and reliable from your office, on the occurrence of stirring events.

With great regard,
Very truly your friend
G. Wright[33]

International Affairs

General Carleton was becoming increasingly concerned about France's invasion of Mexico and the approach of her troops to the borders of New Mexico and Arizona. He believed that relations had reached a critical stage, yet the only response he received from headquarters was the admonition to maintain strict neutrality. He was to avoid any military action that might jeopardize friendly relations with France, although officially the United States recognized only President Benito Juárez and the Republic of Mexico, not the government of Maximilian.[34]

On March 9, Wright was presented with a resolution from U.S. citizens on San Juan Island protesting Capt. Lyman A. Bissel's arbitrary conduct. The citizens said that since he was not the governor, they were under no compunction to obey him and were obliged to obey only federal and territorial laws. Wright wrote to Captain Bissel, who was in command at Camp Pickett, that the army was not responsible for U.S. citizens on the island and that law enforcement should be left to civil officers. Since the ownership of the island was still in dispute, Wright said that the agreement which had been made by Lieutenant General Scott and Canadian Gov. James Douglas regarding joint occupany should be adhered to. This was a far different attitude from that of a previous commander of the Oregon Department, General Harney.

Wright informed Alvord of the complaints about Bissell but questioned their validity. He told Alvord to visit the area. Bissell asserted that most of the complaints against him came from liquor dealers, vagabonds, thieves, and those who sought to stir up trouble between Britain and the United States. He pointed out that the British officers had clear authority to deal with troublemakers while he did not.

In May, Alvord told Wright that prominent citizens of Whatcom County approved of Bissell's administration and agreed with his views in regard to the resolution. On May 29, at Alvord's suggestion, Wright authorized Bissell to banish all fomentors of quarrels between the United States and Britain and other offenders of peace and order. Bissell was admonished not to interfere with the civil authorities and to be patient because the ownership of the island would not be determined until the end of the war. By

June, Wright was able to inform Thomas that the Scott-Douglas agreement was being enforced, that cordial relations existed between the British and U.S. commanders, that civil authorities were exercising their proper functions, and that violators would be removed.[35]

On October 1, Wright received an indignant complaint from Rear Adm. John Kingcome, R.N., commander-in-chief of Her Majesty's Naval Forces in the Pacific, that his flagship, the *Sutlej*, had been preparing to drop anchor in San Francisco harbor when it was fired on by the battery at Alcatraz. Wright responded that port regulations adopted by the U.S. government required all vessels entering San Francisco harbor "brought to" and their character ascertained. This was usually accomplished by government steamer under orders of the port collector, in whose absence the duty devolved on the battery commander. All vessels were required to be courteously and promptly checked before they passed the forts.

The commander of Alcatraz, Capt. William A. Winder, gave his side of this comic-opera episode. According to him, the revenue cutter *Shubrick* had left the harbor to assist a wrecked Russian corvette, and Winder had been asked to "bring to" the entering vessels. Both of Winder's small boats were out checking other ships. Suddenly a great warship appeared, being towed in by small boats. Since there was no wind, he was unable to distinguish the nationality of her flag. He fired a blank cartridge from one of his cannons to attract her attention. When this burst was ignored, he plopped an empty shell across her bow.

The *Sutlej* then began firing. Winder thought that it might be a salute to his flag, except that no flags could now be seen anywhere because of the gunsmoke. When he was finally able to see a U.S. flag that had been raised to the masthead of the *Sutlej*, he returned a twenty-one-gun salute. At that point the batteries at Fort Point began firing.

Kingcome huffily informed Wright that he had not complied with the regulations because of the absence of any boats and his lack of awareness of the rules. He regretted

that Wright's report of the affair contained no acknowl-
edgment of the discourtesy to a ship of war of a friendly
nation.

On October 15, Wright sent a mollifying letter to W. L.
Bowker, British consul in San Francisco, since by that time
Kingcome had sailed away. Like a trained diplomat, Wright
expressed distress that Kingcome thought that courtesies
had been disregarded. He pointed out that it was the custom of foreign ships of war to notify the department commander's headquarters to arrange an exchange of salutes.
The government of the United States, he said, enjoins its
officers to treat with respect and courtesy foreign officers
arriving on its shores, and this pleasant exchange of official courtesies between high officers of friendly nations
strengthens the bonds of friendship and maintains understanding between their governments.[36]

When such events occurred, it was fortunate that Wright,
a calm, sensible individual, was in charge of the defense of
the Pacific Coast rather than a rabid Anglophobe seeking
to stir up trouble to advance his own career. Even Wright's
desire to annex the northwest corner of Mexico was based
on sound strategic reasons rather than imperialistic designs. His relationship with the governor of Sonora was
good, and he sympathized with the Mexican people in
their struggle to resist the French. His greatest fear was
that one or more of the European powers would take advantage of those difficult times to extend their hegemony
into North America.

Relations with the Navy

Wright enjoyed good relations with the navy commander
at Mare Island, Capt. Thomas O. Selfridge. Wright lent
him troops to guard the navy yard with its cannons and
ammunition, and Selfridge in return gave him cannons to
fortify San Francisco Harbor. Wright kept the navy informed of the Confederate designs on Mexico, and, now
that Confederate privateers were at sea and France was invading Mexico, he inquired whether any ships suitable for

mounting heavy guns could be made available for the defense of the city.

Selfridge replied that the only suitable ship was being used as barracks for marines and would take a long time to refit; further, his only steamer was presently under repair. The sailing ship *Cyane* was due the following month, and he would order it to lie in the harbor and cooperate with the forts. Selfridge suggested that the city or the state should buy and arm an ironclad steamer.[37]

Wright again told Thomas of his concern regarding the enemy raiders and the need for Union war steamers. Wright also called on Ira Rankin, the U.S. collector for San Francisco, for a vessel to stop all incoming ships before they passed beyond the range of the guns at the harbor entrance. Rankin had none to spare but asked the secretary of the treasury to send a Coast Guard cutter from Puget Sound.

In February the military committee of the California legislature asked what steps the federal government was taking to improve the defense of San Francisco harbor. Both citizens and state officials were concerned. Word was received that the ironclad *Comanche* was on the way to San Francisco, and Stanton told Governor Stanford that batteries for the harbor had also been sent.[38]

In late, July Wright sent the adjutant general DeRussy's reports and drawings for the defense of San Francisco harbor and informed Port Collector Low of their details. The following month Halleck authorized Wright to construct batteries on Point Jose and Angel Island, but on the recommendation of the board of engineers further work at Yerba Buena and Rincon Point was deferred. Wright learned that $100,000 had been assigned for the harbor defenses. Maj. Robert E. Williamson, the engineer assigned to fortify the harbor, had already received $20,000 from public-spirited citizens to begin the project. Wright informed headquarters that the government's prompt action was greatly appreciated by San Franciscans. Low and Mayor H. Coon sent thanks to Lincoln but at the same time requested three ships to help guard the harbor. Wright asked

Captain Selfridge whether the U.S.S. *Independence* could be used for the purpose but added, "But I must recollect I know really nothing at all about ships, and my remarks are only the random thoughts of a soldier."[39]

Confusion arose over who was to do what, and Wright became exasperated at the delay. There was a strong British naval force at Esquimalt. No one knew what the intentions of the French in Mexico might be, and Confederate privateers were abroad. Wright commented to the adjutant general, "If batteries at points designated are to be erected by Engineer Department under special control of that bureau, I presume that no further responsibility will fall on me if they are not ready when wanted." He also told Townsend that he feared the "masterly inactivity system" and worried that the time consumed in planning the best points for batteries might be fatal. "While we are meditating some morning, . . . the enemy's guns will be thundering against the city," he said. Wright reminded the adjutant general that he had a competent engineer and added that if he were disbursing the money granted by the department the batteries would be promptly completed. The next day he ordered Williamson to proceed with the fieldwork on Point San José and Angel Island. He was encouraged by a report that the armament at Fort Point was good, although the garrison was small, and by DeRussy's promise to recommend that all phases of the project start immediately.[40]

In February, Alvord again protested the defenseless state of Oregon and Washington. He enclosed a clipping from the *Victoria Chronicle* describing a plot to seize the Coast Guard cutter *Shubrick*, convert it into a privateer, and use it to seize the mail steamer. The paper also recounted attempts by rebel sympathizers to purchase a steamer in Victoria to prey on federal commerce. Later in the year Alvord wrote Adm. C. H. Bell, commander of the Pacific Squadron at Panama harbor, expressing the hope that a war vessel could be assigned to his district even though construction of batteries at the mouth of the Columbia had been started. He no longer had an effective

revenue cutter, since by that time the *Shubrick* had been
sent to San Francisco harbor. Moreover, no naval vessel
had sailed north of San Francisco in years.[41]

On November 20, Alvord informed Wright that he had
word from U.S. Consul Allen Francis in Victoria about
the designs of rebel sympathizers there to fit out a privateer. Governor Douglas, the consul reported, would use
all means in his power to prevent the outfitting of privateers. Francis thought the U.S. government negligent in
not having a man-of-war in the area and so informed his
superiors.[42]

Wright told Selfridge of this correspondence and asked
that the *Saginaw* be sent north. Selfridge replied that the
Saginaw had been taken over by the Pacific Squadron; however, he reported the matter to Commodore Charles H.
Poor, whose ship, the U.S.S. *Saranac,* was under repair at
the navy yard. Poor responded that he would try to get a
vessel to the area as soon as possible. Later he was forced
to admit that he was unable even to put a man-of-war outside the Golden Gate, since he was having difficulty getting
crews for his vessels because of the low pay. Even the men
on the *Shubrick* were being paid more.[43]

Press Coverage of Wright

At this time Wright began to attract considerable attention
from newspapers and periodicals. Most Union papers were
supportive of his policies. One article, entitled "The Military—General George Wright," referred to him as an up-
right commander and public servant and contrasted his
record of honor and probity in the discharge of great public trusts with the corruption of many government officials.
Possessing more authority than any other official in the
state and bearing great responsibility over an extensive
territory, Wright was accountable for the handling of mil-
lions of dollars of public funds; the procurement of supplies and munitions; the transportation, movement, and
sale of property; and peacekeeping. The article asserted
that no whisper of doubt had ever been heard. About

Wright's faithfulness and integrity conducting these activities had ever been heard.

Owing to Wright's prudent and skillful management of affairs, the coast had been spared the calamity of civil strife. The paper paid tribute to his capacity for restraining the disaffected on the one side and the imprudent zealot on the other. It suggested that these services should commend Wright to the president and the government and that the reward of promotion should follow the "signal good management" of this good soldier.[44]

The *North Pacific Review* published Wright's picture, a long biographical sketch, and a flattering commentary, referring to him as a thoroughgoing and well-tried soldier, an unswerving patriot, and an exemplary citizen who "has won by his conduct both in the field and in the quieter walks of life an enduring claim to the public regard." It attributed the preservation of peace on the Pacific Coast to his prudence and foresight. The article read, "General Wright would probably have preferred a more active field for the display of his military talents, but government could not have afforded a more signal proof of the high estimation in which he is held than by honoring him with the command he now fills."[45]

On the other hand, certain papers, such as the Sonora *American Flag,* believed that Wright was not active enough in suppressing disloyalty and took him to task. The *American Flag* headed its column "Inefficiency of General Wright—He Ought to Be Removed." The paper quoted the *Visalia Delta* as saying that no one in Tulare County believed in the loyalty of General Wright. It claimed that Wright had overruled the attempts of officers at Camp Babbitt to "suppress or modify the black-guardism of the secession newspaper [*Equal Rights Expositor*]." The *Delta* said that it did not dispute his loyalty but believed him inefficient and had no confidence in him: "So far as his presence on this coast was meant to be a restraint on traitors and a protection of loyal citizens, he is of no more account than a wooden man—whether from disloyalty or senility it

Gen. George Wright, commander, Department of the Pacific. The portrait appeared in the *North Pacific Review* in 1863. Courtesy California Historical Society Library, San Francisco.

matters not." The paper suggested that he had been sent to California because he was unfit for duty elsewhere. The state, once betrayed by a predecessor (Gen. Albert Sidney Johnston), was now menaced by the incompetence of a drowsy old man. If he was not in confederation with the secessionists, this "bulky fossil" was a mere tool, sport, and derision for traitors pursuing their work under his venerable nose.[46]

Prosouthern papers were, of course, rabid because of their exclusion from the mails. It would have been impossible to please everyone in the midst of this terrible war. Yet in general Wright, in his acts and proclamations, was beginning to exhibit qualities of statesmanship.

News of Wright's Sons

During the year 1863, Wright received news that his younger son, Maj. John Wright, had been badly wounded at the Battle of Gettysburg and mustered out of service. John had apparently developed an attachment for the state of Kentucky, with whose troops he had served, and after his recovery he settled in Louisville. He was coolly received at first because of its large prosouthern element, but he took up the study of law at the University of Louisville; married Nellie Butler Ewing, the daughter of a prominent local physician; and soon gained widespread acceptance.[47]

Wright's older son, Thomas, resigned from the Second California Volunteer Cavalry but two weeks later was back in service as a major in the Sixth Regiment of Infantry California Volunteers. This move was probably made to expedite his promotion.

15.
Civil War Days: 1864

IN 1864, Gen. William T. Sherman, with 100,000 men of the armies of the Cumberland, Tennessee, and Ohio, began his march on Atlanta and Savannah, cutting a swath of destruction through the southern heartland. On March 9, Ulysses S. Grant was appointed general-in-chief and Halleck remained as chief of staff. Early in the spring Grant began his Virginia campaign. Initially, one reverse followed another, and Grant lost well over 50,000 men. The number of casualties almost destroyed the Union will for victory. Added to the heavy loss of life was the terror inspired by Confederate Gen. Jubal A. Early's raid, which came within sight of the capitol in Washington, D.C. These events resulted in a considerable loss of public confidence in Lincoln and Grant.

On August 29 at their national convention the Democrats passed a resolution demanding immediate efforts to halt the war and nominated Gen. George B. McClellan for president. The same month thirty-three-year-old Gen. Philip Sheridan was placed in command of the Army of Shenandoah. In September he defeated Early and began the devastation of the Shenandoah Valley. On August 5, Adm. David G. Farragut had won a great victory over a Confederate fleet on Mobile Bay, and Union troops captured Fort Morgan a few weeks later, giving the North complete control of the Gulf of Mexico.

During this year the California legislature endorsed administration measures pertaining to abolition of slavery, confiscation, conscription, legal tender, suspension of the writ of habeas corpus, and plans for postwar reconstruction. On November 8, 1864, Abraham Lincoln was overwhelmingly reelected president with Andrew Johnson, former governor of Tennessee, as vice-president.

On March 5 Oregon Gov. Addison C. Gibbs had reported completion of the telegraph to his state and had exhorted, "Let the great Pacific railroad . . . soon follow!" Six months later Gov. William Pickering announced the arrival of the telegraph in Washington Territory and used the occasion to invoke the blessings of God on Lincoln and his officers. Amazingly, in spite of the continuation of the war, work on the construction of the first transcontinental railroad continued from both the east and the west.

Carleton and his men were still in the Southwest, occupying forts along the Rio Grande. In February, Halleck had ordered Carleton to send as many troops as possible down the Rio Grande to cooperate with Maj. Gen. Nathaniel P. Banks's force moving from Brownsville, Texas, to prevent trade between the rebels and Mexico. Banks was also to protect and, if possible, enlist loyal refugees. Admiral Porter's Union gunboats escorted Banks's men up the Red River to Shreveport, whence they were to advance into Texas and join up with Carleton.

In the meantime Gen. Joseph West had been relieved of duty in New Mexico and ordered to report to headquarters of the Department of Arkansas. A month later Carleton informed Halleck that his subordinate West, whom he had praised in previous dispatches, was guilty of "flagrant and criminal neglect of duty" for not obeying orders to have supplies ready for the reinforcements to Banks. As a result, this phase of what was to have been a joint operation was not carried out, and Halleck's order had to be ignored. On April 8, Banks was badly defeated in Louisiana and forced to retire.[1]

In Arizona the Apaches continued to cause considerable trouble, and reinforcements periodically had to be sent to the area. Raids, thefts, and skirmishes occurred with distressing frequency.

Secessionists Still Active

During 1864 numerous Union supporters became convinced that Wright had not been diligent enough in dealing with those who were disloyal. In May, Wright pointed out to the adjutant general that the political status of California had been made clear by the state election the previous September. However, he admitted, the strong opposition party would renew its struggle at the time of the presidential election in November. He claimed that most citizens were satisfied with the policy he had followed and would be supportive but admitted that a radical minority believed that he had been too conservative. Wright intended to use his full power as necessary to preserve peace but refused to be goaded. He complained that whenever he failed to yield to radical demands he was accused of sympathy for the rebellion, in spite of the fact that his men had made many arrests that had led to jail terms. He concluded by remarking that for the past three years he had been laboring for his country, though not on a battlefield, and pointed with pride to the present peaceful condition of the Pacific Coast. If his efforts had contributed to this, he said, he would be happy.[2]

Confederate sympathizers were again reported to be armed and drilling, especially in southern California and Nevada. As the presidential election drew near, the seat of state government in Sacramento and Pacific headquarters in San Francisco were deluged with reports of secessionist activity. The secessionists threatened to use guerrilla warfare if McClellan was defeated in his bid for the presidency. There was also talk of armed resistance to any imposition of conscription. Actually, no draft was ever planned for the coast because of the plentiful number of volunteers and the cost of transporting men to the East.

Troops were sent to as many trouble spots as possible to suppress treasonable activities. Because of Governor Low's concern about a possible raid on the state arsenal and treasury, Wright placed an additional fifty-man provost guard in Sacramento. The military presence in California led many southern sympathizers to move into Nevada, and it became necessary to dispatch a provost guard and additional troops to Virginia City.

In July, Seward informed Stanton that the acting consul

general in Havana, Cuba, claimed to have uncovered a rebel plot to seize southern California and the mail steamers. The information was forwarded to Commodore Poor.[3] Another report came from the consul general in Victoria that rebel sympathizers were again gathering there and planning to seize a vessel. An order had been issued that all passengers were to give up their arms and allow their persons and baggage to be searched when they boarded ships at Pacific Coast ports. All ships entering San Francisco harbor were to be boarded by officials, and no one would be allowed to land or embark without a passport.[4] Undeniably real was the presence on the Pacific Ocean of the Confederate privateer *Shenandoah*, which ultimately destroyed over a million dollars' worth of U.S. shipping.[5]

Connor and the Troops in Utah

On January 4, 1864, J. F. Kinney, former chief justice of Utah and now its congressional delegate, wrote Halleck requesting the removal of Connor and his troops from within the corporate limits of Salt Lake City. They were no longer needed, said Kinney, since the people were loyal. Connor, however, regarded their leader, Brigham Young, as "second only to Jefferson Davis" in disloyalty. Kinney's request drew a blistering response from Halleck. Wright, when he heard of it, wired the adjutant general to reinforce rather than evacuate Fort Douglas.[6] In general, however, affairs in Utah seemed reasonably quiet except for occasional harassment of emigrants on the Oregon Trail by Shoshonis.

Connor was sufficiently concerned about Mormon activity that in July he set up a provost guard in Salt Lake City. However, he was ordered to withdraw it a few days later rather than risk a war with the Mormons, who had responded to his move by putting a thousand men under arms. Wright had his adjutant tell Connor that such a war would be fatal to the U.S. cause in the Department of the Pacific.[7]

On October 16, Halleck ordered Connor to protect the Overland Mail Route as far east as Fort Kearny, Nebraska, since Gen. Samual R. Curtis, who was in charge in that region, was diverted by rebel raids in Arkansas. The troops would remain under Connor's command, although they were out of his district. Connor was thus confronted .with the likelihood of having to wage a winter campaign against the Sioux, Arapahoes, and Cheyennes. Governor Evans of Colorado urged him to bring troops to chastise the Plains Indians soon, for their depredations were reaching new heights.[8]

When Irvin McDowell later assumed command of the Department of the Pacific, he was less sympathetic toward Connor than Wright had been and seemed unaware of the orders that Connor had received from Halleck to patrol eastward. McDowell wrote to the adjutant general that Connor's policy in Utah could have led to war with the Mormons and protested that Connor had no business leaving the department to fight the Indians in General Curtis's department. The situation was resolved when Drum informed Connor that he was no longer needed in Nebraska, since Curtis had held off the enemy.[9]

No Respite from Indian Conflict

On January 26, 1864, Wright reported to Adjutant General Thomas that Lt. Col. Stephen G. Whipple, with his mountaineers and six companies of Infantry California Volunteers, was doing all he could to kill or capture all the hostile Indians in the Humboldt District. On February 6, Wright ordered Col. Henry M. Black to proceed to Fort Humboldt to take command of that district. Wright admonished him to bear in mind the need for decisive measures. He ordered Black to investigate the state of discipline of the mountain troops, the rumor of their opposition to Whipple, and their notion that they were obliged to serve only in the Humboldt District. Wright wrote to State Senator S. P. Wright that he found no fault with Whipple's performance; however, a larger force and a higher-ranking officer were needed in the district because of the continuing plunder and murder of whites by the Indians. Except for these disturbances, which Wright said illustrated the need to evacuate the Indians to Catalina Island, all was quiet in the Pacific Department. Whipple was in agreement; he said that sending some two hundred prisoners whom he had captured to Catalina Island would go a long way toward settling the district's problems.[10]

In reporting the killing in action of thirty or forty Indians, the new commander, Colonel Black, optimistically predicted the war would soon cease in the Humboldt District. Several reports arrived from Maj. Thomas Wright, who had accompanied reinforcements sent to the district. In one report he expressed confidence that strong military pressure was having an impact on the Indians. Black praised young Wright's performance in the campaign.[11]

Activity increased markedly with the arrival of the energetic new commander, Black. Much stolen property was recovered and renegade whites were found among the Indians. Unfortunately for the campaign, in June, Black was ordered back to West Point, his alma mater, as an instructor in military tactics.[12]

In late summer Whipple sent Wright the good news that the Indians in the Humboldt District were tired of fighting and were turning in their arms and moving to the reservations. He believed that the worst of the troubles were over. The district was more peaceful than it had been for five years, said Indian Agent Austin Wiley, although there were occasional reports of shootings and hangings of hostile Indians.[13] In the Trinity River valley, during a drive to herd the Indians onto reservations, white men were found to be keeping forty-five Indian women and helping Indian warriors avoid capture.[14]

In the fall Wright ordered mounted troops to Virginia City and Mariposa County in response to local requests. He was still firmly convinced that moving columns were superior to fixed posts in sparsely populated areas. Troops were required to reoccupy Camp Independence in the

Owens River valley in response to a petition from the settlers. The Indians there complained that they were being hired to work for the whites but were never paid. They threatened to drive the whites away in retaliation. The troops were admonished to prevent abuses by the whites and to protect the Indians.

A hard winter again interfered with some of the troop movements. As usually happened during bad winters, commanders were requesting permission to feed destitute emigrants and starving Indians. The Commissary Department feared that abuses might occur, but the assistant adjutant general in Washington, D.C., granted permission. Each issue or sale was to be decided on its merits and was to be supported by evidence from the commanding officer.[15]

Benjamin Alvord, commander of the Oregon District, replied to one of Governor Pickering's hysterical cries for protection in Washington Territory by reminding him of the measures Alvord had introduced to protect the frontier. During the two years he had commanded the district the first systematc plans for the protection of overland emigration had been laid.[16] Alvord also wrote Oregon Senator Nesmith urging ratification of the Nez Percé Treaty rather than allowing another four-year delay, as had occurred with the previous treaty. Alvord was concerned because of the confusion over whether miners and white settlers could move to the new borders of the Nez Percé Reservation.[17]

In southeastern Oregon horses, mules, cattle, and personal belongings were being stolen by the Snakes, sometimes aided by the Cayuses and others. Expeditions were sent out against them. Near Klamath Lake a wagon train was attacked by members of the Klamath, Goose Lake, and Modoc tribes.

Near Boonville, in Idaho Territory, citizens attacked a band of Indians and turned in their scalps, mostly those of women and children, to the military. The soldiers were shocked to learn that they had killed babies by beating them against rocks. In a fight near Salmon Falls the army killed seventeen Snake Indians.[18]

Withdrawal of troops from the district began in the autumn. In southeastern Oregon the picture brightened with the surrender of the troublesome Snake war chief Po-li-ni and his band at Fort Klamath.[19]

Wright's Loyalty Questioned

In 1863, Wright had received permission to place the recruiting of volunteers under the supervision of military authorities because the governors were unable to conduct it without such aid. Because of the sparse population in much of his department, Wright often found it necessary to send out incomplete units that could be consolidated later. By 1864, however, all mustering of volunteers had been returned to the governors of the various states and territories. Wright was able to report his success in reenlisting most of the regulars on the coast whose terms had expired, but the governors were having less luck with the volunteer organizations. He continued to request arms for militia, but the chief of ordinance accused him of issuing too many guns and obtained a "cease order" from the secretary of war.[20] To Townsend, Wright emphasized the value of the coast to the Union, telling him that immigration was adding almost 100,000 a year to the population.[21]

For Wright, 1864 proved to be a difficult year. With the war dragging on and emotions running high, he was bound to antagonize certain elements. Just as there were men who loathed Abraham Lincoln and all he stood for, there were those who lost no opportunity to vilify Wright. Early in 1864 rumors began circulating that Wright was to be replaced. Southern sympathizers and northern Peace party members objected to his restrictive measures. Fire-eating Union hawks thought him too lax and criticized his failure to respond instantly to the many scattered demands for troops. Yet on January 19 the *Alta California* expressed gratification at being able to announce that the rumor was unfounded and that General Wright would remain at his post as commander of the Department of the Pacific. The article paid tribute to Wright's "considerable administratve abilities" and pointed to his accomplishments while in command, particularly the preservation of peace on the coast: "True to his profession, unswerving in his devotion to the Federal Government, he never failed in the exercise of his duties . . . [or] lost sight of the interests of the people of the Pacific, with whom he has so long been identified and in him they have ever had a willing and urgent advocate." [22] Yet the rumor persisted, and in March Carleton wrote that he was dismayed by the idea of Wright's removal.

In February some newspapers printed vicious attacks on Wright, even going so far as to question the loyalty of the aging patriot. When his loyalty became the subject of a debate in the California legislature, he sent a letter to Joseph Wood, chairman of the military committee. Wood, knowing that the insinuations were unfounded, read the letter in the assembly chamber, and it was published in the *Sacramento Daily Union* on February 15. Three days later it was published in the *Alta California* with a comment from the Sacramento correspondent.

In his letter Wright said that in almost twelve years of service on the Coast, this was the first time his loyalty or devotion to the Union had been questioned. He called attention to the vast size of his department with its sixty military stations and the magnitude of the task of distributing and supplying 5,000 troops to protect citizens from hostile Indians, foes from without, and traitors from within. All his acts had received the approval of his government. While he felt justifiably proud of the state of affairs within the department, he admitted that he had not attempted to please everyone but had followed the course he believed best for the country.

In defending his staff members, particularly his adjutant general, Colonel Drum, he said that their loyalty was "too well established to be injured by fault-finding politicians." As for himself, he would never stoop to defend his loyalty, believing that if he could harbor a thought save for the honor of his country "the very green mountains of my native state would rise in judgement against me."

The Sacramento correspondent added:

What say the croakers to the above? Some men who have been the most active in impugning the patriotism within as well as without the halls of legislation, of the present Commander of the Pacific are by no means invulnerable on the score of loyalty themselves. And not one of these have exhibited in deed, a moiety of that love of country which General Wright has exhibited in the tented field and in the shock of battle. He jests at scars who never felt a wound.[23]

On April 11, 1864, the rumor of Wright's replacement received confirmation when the newspapers reported that Maj. Gen. Irvin McDowell had been appointed to command the Department of the Pacific. The *Alta California* included a biographical sketch of McDowell and an apologia for his military reverses. The editors generally found him acceptable but added, ". . . the necessity for the change which has been made is not very apparent."[24]

Wright's Farewell

On June 21, 1864, from his headquarters in San Francisco, Wright issued a farewell proclamation to the "loyal citizens of the Pacific Coast" on the eve of being relieved of the command of the Department of the Pacific. He reminded them that when he had assumed the command he had been aware of the high trust reposed in him by the government. To illustrate the course he had pursued during his administration, he quoted a letter he had written to the adjutant general of the army at the end of his first year in command in which he had called attention to the value to the Union of "these remote possessions of the United States" and what he had done to preserve their integrity.

After the acquisition of the western lands, and particularly after the discovery of their rich gold deposits, people had poured in from every quarter of the globe. This heterogeneous population, its regional sympathies intensified by the rebellion, had for the most part become loyal citizens. To overcome divisiveness, he had attempted to be watchful and firm and had tried to avoid creating unnecessary alarm by ill-advised acts, regardless of personal consequences. This course, he felt, would be most likely to "secure the respect of political parties of every complexion, ultimately redound to the honor of our Government and country" and, he hoped, contribute to the preservation of the Union. He reminded the citizens of the cordial approval and assistance he had received from the governors and other state officials in his command. In concluding his proclamation, Wright said:

> Acting upon the principles contained in my letter above recited, I now point with pride to the happy and peaceful condition of this country. Entrusted, as I have been, with a high and responsible command, far removed from the seat of the General Government, I have, during the whole period held in my hands the power of peace or war. Had I for a moment yielded to the insane demands of a radical press and its co-laborers, I should have filled my forts with political prisoners to gratify personal hatred—causing such an outburst of indignation at such a course, as to render it almost certain that civil war and blood-shed would have followed.
>
> The Union loving people on this coast are vastly in the ascendant. They have the *power* and the *will* to maintain the integrity of the Union on these distant shores. Let every attempt to raise the standard of rebellion within your borders be crushed.[25]

One of the newspapers called Wright's comments a sweeping denunciation of the loyal press of the state. The paper stated that he had exaggerated the danger of civil war on the coast. However, it referred to him as a veteran soldier

> with a record which entitles him to the respect of all men who value faithful and honorable service. There may be differences of opinion as to his energy, vigilance and peculiar policy, but there is no shadow of excuse for impeaching his patriotism. . . . It is pleasant to turn from what the departing general says to what he has done. Few hands are skilled in use of both sword and pen, and fewer heads can muster at once the art of war and the necessities of politics.

After presenting some biographical data, the paper referred to Wright as a man of experience and fidelity but

suggested that he had been given the coast command because his age precluded active service in the field. It spoke
somewhat disparagingly of his recent military duties but
conceded that "so far as these matters are concerned we
think it may be said that General Wright has done a soldier's duty in a soldier's way." [26]

On June 26 the *Alta California* announced that General
McDowell had sailed from New York on the third of the
month. The *Alta* referred to Wright's farewell order as

> brief and to the point—just the kind of document which a sol-
> dier would pen. . . . To the happy peace we have so long en-
> joyed we are measurably indebted to the wise rule of Brigadier-
> General George Wright. In his hands were the issues of peace
> or war. If he had inclined to the latter, homesteads smoking in
> ruins, devastated farms and ruined cities would everywhere
> meet the eye, while higher military honors might have fallen
> to the share of the General commanding the Department. . . .
> Wherever the lot of General Wright may be cast—whether on
> the battlefield fighting the enemies of his country, or in high
> command, laboring to heal the wounds and scars which the
> war has occasioned, he will carry with him the good wishes of
> all true Californians. He has linked his name indissolubly with
> the history of our young state, and made for himself a fame
> brighter than that which a useless intestine struggle here
> could have conferred. [27]

On June 30 the *San Francisco Bulletin* announced the arrival, amid appropriate cannon salutes, of General McDowell: ". . . known as a notable in the war—mistaken and mis-
understood for awhile but at last appreciated." The paper,
under the impression that Wright was finally going east,
where the action was, congratulated him on the realization
of his long coveted wish:

> General Wright . . . while he has been chafing for more active
> employment has earned—if it is true that "peace has her vic-
> tories no less than war"—the highest title to this country's
> gratitude. By his energy, experience, promptness and pru-
> dence he has contributed largely to maintain peace, harmony
> and quiet on the Pacific Coast while the Atlantic slope is con-
> vulsed with war. He has chosen to attain his object quietly and

without ostentation—he has clearly no taste for fuss and feathers; no relish to display authority where none was required; no disposition to exert extraordinary powers where ordinary ones were quite competent to his purposes. When he leaves us he will take with him the thanks of the people within his Department, and the respect of all who are respectable.[28]

Two days later the *Alta* announced that General McDowell had assumed command of the Department of the Pacific the preceding day and that General Wright had been placed in command of the District of California with headquarters in Sacramento. The article continued, "We presume the Department at Washington, in consideration of General Wright's health, transferred his headquarters from San Francisco to Sacramento."[29] Wright insisted that his health was unimpaired, but a photograph taken in 1863 shows his hair completely white and his features gaunt. He had obviously lost weight and appeared unwell.

Lieutenant Edwin W. Waite was named aide-de-camp to General Wright and acting adjutant general for the District of California. Wright and his wife moved to Sacramento. Colonel Drum was retained as assistant adjutant general for the Department of the Pacific.[30]

Wright may have had some doubt about his authority in his new position, but on September 10, McDowell instructed him to act in all affairs in his district for the best interest of the service.

Bancroft has commented that the "soldierly qualities of General McDowell could not overcome the regret with which Californians suffered the exchange, effected, it was believed, by private enmity. But to escape the condemnation of some in such troublous times was probably impossible."[31] And indeed, not everyone was sorry to see Wright go. On July 19 the *Los Angeles News* reprinted an article from the *Marysville Appeal:*

> The old granny with patriotic buttons on his coat, who has been favored with distinction by the government out of respect for his gray hairs, publishes a farewell address to the people of this state.

We are so well pleased with the announcement of his retirement that our wrath at its unwarranted language is more than appeased. His allusion to the radical press is a direct insult to every Union paper in the state, although only intended for those who have been outspoken in favor of his removal.

There is no distinction in the Union press only as made by the issue whether we should have a live or petrified commander of the department of the Pacific.

But we in common with Union papers feel in too good humor at the retirement of General Wright, old fuss and feathers, to be too severe. We are willing to attach all his faults to the ravages of time and not to any fault of the old man's heart. He departs and as we say goodbye forever, sink all ill will and thoughts of his shortcomings.[32]

A revealing exchange took place between Stanton and Lt. Gen. Ulysses S. Grant the following month. Grant wrote to the secretary of war from City Point, Virginia:

At this particular time it is of great importance that we should have on the Pacific Coast, not only good military commanders, but men who will give satisfaction to the people. From what I learn unofficially, we lack this both in the selection of a commander for the department and for the District of Oregon and Washington. I know Alvord well, I do not think he is fit for command, and he ought to be called East. He is a good man in his intentions and would do well to place on any kind of a board, but I know of no other duty he is eminently suited for. McDowell, if I am not wrongly informed, is likely to do more harm than good where he is. I am in favor of Halleck for that department. He is acquainted with the people and can combine civil with military administration, which is required in that department. McDowell is only a soldier and has never been anything else. It would not be necessary to send anyone to relieve Alvord at present—simply to order him East would be sufficient. If Halleck cannot be spared from where he is, then to restore Wright would do. Have you any information from the Pacific Coast leading you to the same conclusion as to the necessity for a change?[33]

Stanton replied to Grant:

Frequent complaints have reached the Department in respect to General Alvord and I had determined to supersede him as soon as a good officer could be spared. . . . No complaint from any source has been made against General McDowell to the Department and I had not heard that his administration was objectionable to anyone. . . . To make a change so soon ought to require some very good reason for its justification. There had been frequent applications for the removal of General Wright, but as his administration was acceptable to the Department they were for a long time resisted. . . . You know as I do that no man can please all sides in any department, much less in California. But in this as in all other matters relating to military affairs it is the desire of the Department to conform to your judgment.[34]

Grant admitted that he knew nothing official about any dissatisfaction with McDowell's administration; therefore, he was left in command. But this exchange certainly makes it appear that Wright's replacement was a political move, made without consultation with the general-in-chief.

On September 5, headquarters in Washington, D.C., ordered a one-hundred-gun salute from the arsenals at Benicia and Fort Vancouver in celebration of Adm. David G. Farragut's victory at Mobile and Gen. William Tecumseh Sherman's approach to Atlanta. Later in the month more salutes were ordered for Sheridan's victories in the Shenandoah Valley, and in December yet another victory salute celebrated Sherman's occupation of Savannah. Since the war seemed to be nearing a favorable outcome, some regiments were consolidated as enlistments expired. Many soldiers were now being reassigned, with new regiments raised or old ones reorganized.

The Oregon legislature passed a law giving a bounty to volunteers; Washington Territory was without such a law, and soldiers from California who enlisted to serve in that "Godforsaken region" complained vociferously.[35] After all the complaints from headquarters about Wright's liberal policy of furnishing arms to volunteers and militia, he was confronted with a telegram from Stanton to Governor Nye saying that the ordnance officer at Benicia had no right to withhold three howitzers and one thousand Springfield muskets that had been authorized for Nevada troops.[36]

Problems with the Indians had not completely ended with McDowell's assumption of command. In mid-August he complained about the Indian Department's refusal to authorize Wright's plan for the removal of hostile Indians to Catalina Island. He said that many clashes occurred between the military and Indian Department over who was to feed Indian prisoners, their means of subsistence having been destroyed by the constant struggle with the whites. McDowell felt that failure to feed them would result in renewed warfare.

At long last, on December 19, 1864, Col. George Wright, Ninth U.S. Infantry, "for long, faithful and meritorious service" was appointed brigadier general U.S. Army by order of the secretary of war, but even then only by brevet. The order was signed by Col. James A. Hardie, inspector general.[37]

Wright's oath of office as brigadier general by brevet was sworn to and subscribed on May 30, 1865, before notary public Samuel Cross in Sacramento. Cross, a relative by marriage, was also a close friend and legal adviser of the Wrights.[38]

The French Presence in Mexico

One of Wright's greatest concerns in 1864 was the presence of the French in Mexico and French troops and vessels on the Pacific Coast. He complained to a sympathetic Governor Low that the French had begun blockading western Mexican ports and had bombarded Acapulco the previous year. Because the French were sympathetic to the southerners, their presence in western Mexico represented a peril to California, and Wright begged for measures to prevent that "calamity." Arms were again issued to the crews of vessels sailing from San Francisco, and army detachments were often placed on board.[39]

The fact that he had never been authorized to occupy Guaymas was a great source of regret for Wright. His frustration increased after French troops took over most of the state of Sonora during the summer of 1865 and forced

Governor Pesqueira to take refuge at Fort Mason, Arizona.[40] Wright believed that it was essential that the northwestern Mexican states either remain independent or join the United States. Wells, Fargo's Louis McLane urged Wright to apply to the War Department for authority to restore Arizona to the Pacific Department and to keep enough troops available to capture Guaymas when the move seemed advisable. These requests were denied, although Secretary Stanton ultimately did order the reattachment of Arizona to the Pacific Department.

Wright begged the government to keep him informed about its policy in the event of war with France. He told the adjutant general that southern California would be dangerously exposed if French troops occupied Sonora. San Diego, Yuma, and the Arizona forts should be strongly guarded, he said. He enclosed letters from Governor Low and McLane expressing their concern.[41]

At the end of April, Wright again asked for information on government policy, in view of the threatening nature of foreign affairs. To Halleck's inquiry about what emergency required Wright's efforts to raise more troops, Wright replied, "No pressing emergency exists. . . . prudential considerations induced the request." Governor Low rose to Wright's defense, saying that Wright had issued only those arms requested by the governor and that the number was still inadequate. Wright forwarded these letters to the adjutant general and urged him to bring them to the attention of Grant and the secretary of war.[42]

On July 22, Wright notified department headquarters of the arrival in San Francisco of Mexican General Emilio Lanberg to enlist the support of California Mexicans for Maximilian's new imperial government and to ascertain the feelings of people on the coast regarding the presence of the French in Mexico. In fact, the presence of the French at their back door was a source of anxiety and irritation to Californians, and Wright hoped that Mexican guns would prove capable of hurling back the invaders. He suggested that the general be sent on his way.[43]

During the month of August a rather sad tableau began

to unfold. The United States recognized only the Juárez government in Mexico, but with the Civil War in progress the United States wished to avoid any breach of neutrality or embarrassment to a friendly nation, in spite of France's flaunting of the Monroe Doctrine. In November, Mexican General Plácido Vega visited San Francisco, seeking a means of ousting Maximilian. Vega had been assured by local officials that he would have no difficulty transshipping a shipload of arms that he had purchased in Hamburg, Germany, but to his dismay his ship and its arms were seized by the port collector. Vega remonstrated that the French were blockading the ports of Sinaloa and Sonora, yet their vessels were allowed to load supplies in San Francisco.

Meanwhile, Seward, to whom the French ambassador had protested, informed Stanton that vessels were being fitted out in New Orleans and San Francisco to serve as privateers for President Juárez. Stanton ordered McDowell to prevent such "pirates" from preying on French shipping. He cited Lincoln's order of November 21, 1862, which said that no arms or ammunition were to be exported from the United States. Aboard Vega's sloop *Haye* seventy-one cases of war materials and five thousand muskets had been found. Vega claimed that far more had been seized from warehouses on shore.

Vega insisted that the "highest officials" were aware of his acts, but McDowell denied that the army had any such knowledge until the port collector requested help to seize the contraband. McDowell was simply enforcing the presidential order and had nothing to do with the formulation of foreign policy. He was unable to give a date for the return of the seized materials and the vessel but expressed regret at the distress caused to Vega and suggested taking up the matter with the Mexican minister in Washington. The French consul in San Francisco meanwhile demanded to be informed of any vessel being fitted out as a privateer.[44]

McDowell also took custody of the *Colón*, a ship being fitted out for the Peruvian government; his action was approved by the War Department. Negotiations in Washington, D.C., however, led to the release of the vessel the following March.

In April, 1865, McDowell informed Stanton that a storm-battered French fleet was on its way to San Francisco to undergo repairs. Coal had been sent to the damaged vessels on the *Emily Banning*. The port collector said that he had no right to interfere, but this act of aid caused considerable consternation on the Coast. José A. Godoy, the Mexican consul, pleaded with McDowell not to allow the French ships to refit at the Mare Island Navy Yard, adding that Chile had declared even coal war material. Halleck ordered McDowell to accord the French vessels the usual courtesies due to a friendly nation and said that the matter of repairs at the navy yard would be decided when the French minister requested it of the secretary of state.

Officials sympathetic to Mexico kept the wires to Washington humming: the port collector to the Treasury Department, Governor Low to the State Department, and McDowell to army headquarters. But Godoy was finally told that the authorities on the coast could not comply with his request. When the French ships arrived and were under repair, Godoy again protested.[45]

In May, 1865, in McDowell's absence, Drum consulted Wright about the French consul's complaint that Mexico was opening offices in San Francisco to enroll volunteers to help expel the French under the pretext of encouraging colonization.[46] Broadsides had been distributed by the Mexican Constitutional Republican Government of Benito Juárez inviting American emigrants to settle in Mexico. Armed foreigners willing to serve the Juárez government in defending its independence were offered liberal bounties in land, available in $1,000 parcels for privates and $2,000 parcels for officers.[47]

On May 16, 1865, Wright replied to Drum that as long as the United States was at peace with France and Mexico neutrality must be preserved. No recruiting for foreign service was to be allowed nor would bodies of armed men be permitted to sail from any points on the Coast.[48]

In mid-August, McDowell paid a visit to the posts on

Puget Sound. Accompanying Governor Pickering on a visit to San Juan Island, he gave orders that all policing of the American portion of the island was to be conducted by the military. Citizens were permitted to vote and pay taxes, but the civil authorities were to have no further jurisdiction until adjustments were made when the United States was again at peace.[49]

Coast Defense

The various commanders on the seacoast were anxious about their ability to repel foreign or Confederate assaults. Wright asked for some artillery troops to man the coastal defenses, but he was told to train infantry for the purpose. I Company of his old Ninth Regiment of Infantry was sent to man the new batteries at the mouth of the Columbia.

Captain Joseph Stewart at Fort Point reported to Wright that the character of all vessels was being ascertained as they entered the Golden Gate. The *Shubrick* was being used for that purpose and could signal the various harbor batteries to ready their guns if necessary. All incoming ships were to pass south of Alcatraz Island, and harbor defense commanders were ordered to enforce strictly all port regulations. Unauthorized ships were to "bring to" or be fired upon.[50]

On February 17, Wright told headquarters that he had issued 5,000 stand of small arms to militia and had equipped some cavalry and artillery men. He commented that, given sufficient arms, he could equip an army of 75,000 to repel any invasion from the east or in the event of a foreign war. He urged Governor Low to use his influence to keep the U.S.S. *Narragansett* on the coast.[51]

After he assumed command of the department, the defenses of San Francisco harbor became McDowell's worry. Wright accompanied him on a tour of inspection of the fortifications. When McDowell asked for authorization to raise a volunteer regiment of artillery, Halleck again replied that the secretary of war did not approve of raising troops for specific purposes.

Security concerns arose in August when Halleck learned that Captain Winder had permitted photographs to be taken of Alcatraz and, with Colonel DeRussy's consent, arranged for their publication. Wright vouched for the loyalty and efficiency of Winder, about whom doubts had been expressed because his father was a Confederate officer. Regarding the controversial photographs, McDowell wrote Halleck that Winder was simply proud of his installation, not disloyal. The pictures had been taken in compliance with orders from the quartermaster general and were of no strategic value. Their sale would pay for having them made. McDowell suppressed publication of the photographs but said that he had more serious concerns about the security of San Francisco harbor. French and Russian men-of-war were visiting there, their guns covering shipping and the city with no U.S. guns bearing on them.[52]

As the year 1864 drew to a close, Governor Low raised the Eighth Regiment of Volunteer Infantry, which was to receive instruction in defending the seacoast and manning the heavy artillery of the coastal defenses. In the Oregon District Alvord requested appropriations for fortifications and an ironclad steamer on Puget Sound in Washington Territory.

Wright's Address to the Lincoln and Johnson Club

As the crucial presidential election of November, 1864, approached, excitement was becoming intense throughout California. In spite of powerful opposition, Wright told Drum that with "union and harmony in our ranks" he had no fears of the result. Military detachments were sent to many towns to cooperate with the civil authorities in preventing any trouble on election day.[53]

At the beginning of November, Wright, a prominent political as well as military figure, was invited to address the Lincoln and Johnson Club at the state capitol. In his address Wright referred to the current unhappy condition of the country and the ongoing struggle, which would test the permanence of the republican form of government. If our form of government failed, he said, there would be no hope for any nation in the world battling in the cause of free institutions. Union armies were winning glorious victories over some of the traitors attempting to destroy it, and the remainder would be crushed at the polls a few days hence. He urged his audience to be prepared to deal with rebel sympathizers and warned of seditious plans revealed in a letter written by a California delegate to the recent Democratic convention in Chicago.

Among Americans, he said, some men were "enjoying all the benefits of the noblest and best Government the world ever saw" but were working for its destruction. Maintaining the country's institutions and preserving the integrity of the Union was "the imperative duty" of American citizens. Members of the Democratic party were not aware of the depths of treachery into which some of their leaders were attempting to lead them:

> For nearly four years our noble-hearted president has guided the helm of the State with prudence, skill and foresight. With an eye singled for the good of the country he has risen majestically above party consideration, and used the mighty powers entrusted to him for the sole purpose of securing to us and our descendants a country united, free and happy. I say, then, let the humane and noble-hearted man who has consecrated his life to our service, through whose wisdom we have been carried triumphantly this far on the road to victory when the national life was in peril, who is beloved by the army and the people, and whose great soul overflows with patriotic devotion to our cause, receive the sincere, heartfelt thankfulness and gratitude of a free people. Let the wires flash the joyful intelligence across the continent to the Atlantic shores that California, the Queen of the Pacific, has cast her vote for Abraham Lincoln.

Wright urged his listeners to rally to the polls the following Tuesday with the watchword "The Union forever and no compromise with rebels with arms in their hands."

Once peace was accomplished, he continued, it would still not be time to stack arms and disband the army while a sister republic was writhing under the despotic rule of a foreign prince. "We must reach forth a helping hand and gently coerce those foreign freebooters to relinquish their hold on beautiful Mexico and depart from her shore, never to return," he said. Then the world should be told that it is the will of the American people that "the great Monroe Doctrine must and shall be maintained on this continent." Wright concluded his oration with a quotation from George Washington's Farewell Address concerning the duty of all citizens to obey the government that it had been their right to establish.[54]

Wright's talk was no mere political stump speech but a sincere expression of his own beliefs and philosophy. It also illustrated his personal development in the fields of politics and diplomacy. It is said to have been greeted with enthusiastic applause. November 8 passed quietly, and the Union ticket won by an overwhelming majority. After the election Wright sent a letter to Secretary of War Stanton that demonstrates the humiliation he still felt regarding his rank. As in previous letters, he pointed out that he had never received the brevet which it was generally assumed would be bestowed on him for his services in 1858, nor had his request for appointment as a general in the regular army been granted.

After he had been appointed brigadier general of volunteers he had been ordered to Washington, D.C., but the order had subsequently been countermanded. He continued:

> Writhing under the disappointment at not being permitted to take the field, . . . yet I nevertheless yielded without a murmur and for nearly three years I exercised a command over these distant shores, devoting my best energies by day and by night in overcoming the difficulties which surrounded me. . . . Peace and quiet have been maintained and the late elections show that the States of the Pacific are amongst the most loyal of any of the Republic.

Having received no special orders, he had accepted the command of the District of California and now most respectfully asked for an appointment in the regular army.[55]

Activities of John and Thomas Wright

During 1864 Wright's son John resigned his commission, finished his law studies, and started his law practice in Louisville.[56] For part of the year Wright's son Thomas served as a major of volunteers in the Humboldt District. In September he was recalled and ordered to take charge of headquarters and the companies of the Second Regiment of Infantry California Volunteers at the Presidio in San Francisco. On October 3 he was promoted to lieutenant colonel in his new command. By New Year's Eve he was in full command of the Presidio. On January 6, 1865, he was promoted to colonel, and two months later he was breveted brigadier general, U.S. Volunteers, for faithful and meritorious service.[57] Young Wright's good war record must have surprised his father and filled him with pride after some of Thomas's previous performances. It is possible that George Wright even felt a tinge of envy at the speed with which Thomas rose in rank.

16.
Civil War Days: 1865

BY 1865 the Confederacy was sinking fast. In early spring the last battles of the war were fought at Bentonville, North Carolina, and Five Forks, Virginia. On April 3, Union forces entered the Confederate capital, Richmond. McDowell wired Stanton that California was wild with excitement at the news of the fall of Richmond. All the batteries and forts in the department fired salutes.

On April 9, in the McLean home at Appomattox Court House, Lee accepted Grant's terms of surrender. Three days later the ceremony of laying down arms took place. The Confederate raider *Shenandoah*, unaware of the war's end, continued to raid whaling ships in the Pacific until August, when she sailed to England and surrendered.

On April 14, 1865, the nation was stunned by the news of President Lincoln's assassination in Washington, D.C. Wright was concerned about what disloyal elements might do after this tragic event. During the past month he had found it necessary to dispatch troops to several communities in northern and central California to capture conniving southern sympathizers, including some public officials.

Reports were received of rebels running amok in Kernville, California, after they learned of the Confederate army's surrender. Governor Low called on Colonel Curtis to send a military force to protect loyal citizens in San Bernardino, where secessionists were still causing trouble. Horses were stolen, but the presence of the troops forestalled any raids on the community.

On April 16 troops were sent to southern California to suppress the jubilation of the secessionists over the news of Lincoln's death. However, this was hardly the pattern for the rest of the state. A mob in San Francisco, grieved and infuriated, destroyed the plants of four newspapers suspected of disloyal sentiments.[1] Wright requested that civil officers arrest and hand over to the military authorities all persons exulting over the assassination, and he offered the help of troops if needed.

General Order no. 27, Department of the Pacific, issued April 17, called those who rejoiced accessories to the deed and ordered their arrest; newspapers sharing such sentiments were to be suppressed.[2] Hunt writes: "General Wright was master of every situation and refused to be inflamed by local prejudices. . . . To ill-advised persons he abruptly told them to attend to their own business and advised them not to try to supervise military matters."[3] Wright sent four companies of soldiers to reinforce the sheriff of San Francisco because of the excitement there. They were to remain until the conclusion of the funeral services. Col. Thomas Wright was assigned to command the troops participating in local memorial rites for Lincoln.[4]

Apparently the provost guard made many unauthorized seizures, because Wright ordered their commander to stop indiscriminate arrests. Two months later a departmental order announced that thenceforth no civilian was to be arrested by the military authorities.[5]

During the year Wright had another confrontation with the press. When a newspaper printed some of the soldiers' grievances without disclosing their identity, Wright objected that such journalism discouraged enlistment and promoted subversive conduct. He personally investigated some of the complaints and found them groundless. He said that he would stop this attempt to make the soldiers dissatisfied and to cast aspersions on the military administration of the department.[6]

Army Changes

Connor, whose Utah district had been transferred to the Department of Missouri, reported to department headquarters in April that the Indians in his area were "whipped and quiet," the state government was secure, and the mines were being developed.[7] In the Humboldt District quiet reigned, and the members of the Mountain Battalion, who had enlisted for three years, now asked to be released after serving only two years. Their request was approved in May, and the battalion was mustered out July 7 with commendation for its valuable service. The premature disbanding of the battalion almost cost Whipple the promotion to colonel for which he had been recommended.[8]

In March, Alvord was relieved of command of the Oregon District and ordered to report to the adjutant general in Washington, D.C. McDowell expressed surprise and regret, saying that he and all the regional state and territorial governors thought that Alvord had been a competent commander. Colonel Reuben F. Maury, First Oregon Cavalry, took over command of the district.[9]

In January the District of Arizona had been annexed to the Department of the Pacific. This district included Arizona Territory and that portion of California in the Colorado River watershed. B. G. Mason, former provost marshal of San Francisco, was placed in command. A subdistrict under Maj. Charles F. McDermit included all troops in Nevada and the Owens River valley. Wright ordered McDermit's officers to be circumspect in their treatment of friendly Indians and to avoid indiscriminate slaughter.[10]

Indian Hostilities Continue

Although the number and strength of posts were being steadily reduced and recruiting had virtually halted, the end of the Civil War did not bring an end to the Indian fighting. Citizens and governors continued to request troops, especially for the new mining areas in eastern and central California and the Pyramid Lake region of Nevada. As a rule, troops were sent to investigate, and skirmishes with Indians usually ensued.

Not all the commanders' reports were grim. A report from Fort Lincoln, in the Humboldt District, which had been temporarily reoccupied in May, described the nearby Smith River Reservation as beautiful, extensive, well cultivated, and occupied by seven or eight hundred Indians who were thriving under the care of a Mr. Bryson. A few Indians had recently escaped, but they had been promptly recaptured. However, such tranquillity was an exception. Indian attacks on some of the mail stations on the central overland route led to the abandonment of others. Military camps had to be established in the Paradise, Surprise, and Honey lake valleys because of Indian hostilities. From these camps Wright sent out expeditions against the Indians of eastern California and Nevada.[11]

Occasionally Indian uprisings on the Great Plains caused interruptions in telegraphic communications with the East. At one point Connor reported that stage traffic was halted as well. The telegraph company offered fifty dollars in gold, each way, for anyone willing to ride express where the line was out.

An expedition from Fort Churchill to Pyramid and Walker's lakes during March resulted in the capture of some Paiute Indians, who were handed over for trial to civil authorities, since army officers were no longer permitted to execute Indians on their own authority. However, captures were seldom effected without someone being killed.[12]

The Shoshonis had been active in April, firing on citizens, burning their homes, and stealing their livestock. Local whites were ready to start killing Indians since men, women, and children had recently been murdered on the road between Paradise Valley and Surprise Valley. One hundred soldiers were sent to the area.

In May, Major McDermit was ordered to take command of all troops in northern Nevada, after being reinforced by two companies of California Volunteers. Another officer had previously failed to rout 500 hostile Indians, and McDermit was to take over the job. The following December, McDermit engaged in battle a large force of Shoshonis; 120 Indians were killed, and that valuable officer lost his life as well.[13]

On July 21, Wright received a petition from citizens in southern Idaho, forwarded by the newly appointed governor, C. D. Smith, alleging that the road from California had been taken over by Indians and that the stage line had been abandoned, the stations broken up, livestock run off, and four whites killed and their bodies mutilated.[14]

Major John F. Drake wrote that 700 horses had been stolen in one week in the Jordan Valley. Disturbances were also reported at Salmon Falls, at least some of which were caused by discharged employees of the mail contractor, not by Indians. Drake warned that southeastern Oregon, with its Owyhee mines, was more exposed to Indian raids than any other part of the country. He told of extensive depredations and suggested that a military camp near old Fort Hall would be of great value.[15]

The new commander in Arizona, General Mason, said that the Apaches were still attacking small parties and acquiring booty. He believed that they would need "a sound whipping" before there could be peace. At times, he said, the Indians were in virtual possession of the territory. Like his predecessors, he planned to enlist the Pima and Maricopa Indians to help him fight the Apaches. He asked permission to have the Maricopa chief and one or two of his subchiefs visit San Francisco in payment for lending his warriors. Wright told Mason that this could only be done if he mustered the chief into the army, allowing him to resign later if he wished.[16]

In response to requests for protection by Shasta and Tehama counties, Wright suggested reoccupation of his old post, Fort Reading, where he had had very little trouble with the Indians.

Typical of the reports circulating at the time was one that the Indians had burned the Union mills in the Owens River valley, a property worth $30,000, sacked Bend City, and driven out the inhabitants of San Carlos. An investigation revealed that the mill had indeed burned, but the circumstances were unknown. Bend City had not been sacked or San Carlos threatened, and residents had gone to Kearsarge only because business was better and the mines more productive there.

Disharmony persisted between the military and the Interior Department. In May, shortly before his death, Mc-Dermit had forwarded to Wright a telegram that he had received at Fort Churchill. The telegram was from an Indian agent who wanted some cattle to feed his Indians. McDermit suggested that if Indian agents had taken a proper interest in caring for the Indians in the past many of the present troubles could have been avoided. Wright declined the agent's request, saying that if the Indian Department, with its liberal appropriations, could not care for itself the job might better be transferred to the army. He ordered these communications forwarded to the congressional committee investigating Indian affairs on the coast.[17]

On June 27, Wright performed what proved to be one of his last important official acts. He wrote a thought-provoking letter to James R. Doolittle, U.S. senator from Wisconsin and chairman of the joint committee of Congress that was investigating the condition of the Indian tribes. In response to a circular he had received from Senator Nesmith, a member of the committee, Wright confessed that he was happy to write the letter, since he had had considerable experience in the administration of Indian affairs and ample opportunity to observe Indians during his long service in the army. During that time, he wrote,

> I have been in command of many military expeditions against the hostile Indians, especially in Oregon and the territory of Washington, in 1856 and lastly in 1858, when a great combination was formed by many warlike tribes in that country, threatening destruction to all the settlements east of the Cascades. I met the enemy in two hard fought battles, in both of which they were thoroughly defeated and finally sued for peace, and accepting the terms I granted them, they have remained quiet and peaceable ever since.

The number of Indians was decreasing rapidly, Wright said, especially west of the Rocky Mountains, because of wars and the encroachment of whites on their hunting grounds and fisheries and their adoption of vices of the whites. Diseases such as syphilis and pulmonary ailments arose from vicious conduct, intemperance, and exposure. Only among the Indians living in or near white settlements were intoxication, prostitution, and consequent diseases prevalent. Wright was convinced that the only way to prevent extinction of the Indian tribes was to separate them entirely from whites, removing them to new reservations remote from settlements and under military control and jurisdiction. Every Indian family should have land to cultivate, and a portion of the reservation should be set aside for cultivation in common, he said. No "power of alienation" of real estate should be conferred, for the Indians were great gamblers. Schools had a good effect. A Protestant minister should be placed on each reservation; Christian missions had been beneficial and should be maintained.

In this proposed separate Indian territory there was no need for money because whiskey sellers would get it all; the government should furnish whatever goods were necessary. Wright had seen the Indian Bureau operate under the Department of Interior and under the War Department, and he was convinced that management by the latter was more effective. According to Wright, a reservation should be a military colony, governed by law and enforced by arms. Orphans should be placed with the families of Christian whites to be trained and educated.[18]

During his long exposure to the Indians, Wright had come to believe that Indians who were guilty of crimes should receive punishment dependent on the severity of the crime. He did not subscribe to the notion that "the only good Indian is a dead Indian." For a good portion of his life he sincerely believed that the Indian was more often sinned against than sinning.

Wright showed a prejudice typical of many contemporary Americans when he suggested a Protestant minister for each reservation. Yet his bias did not exclude the fine work of the Catholic missionaries when he alluded to the beneficial effects of "Christian missions." During the Indian wars of the Pacific Northwest, Wright often thanked the priests in his official reports.

McDowell Advocates Wright's Mexican Policies

On January 8, 1865, General Grant wrote to General McDowell that William Gwin, former U.S. senator from California, was part of the Maximilian government and was to replace Pesqueira as governor general of Sonora when the French occupied that state. Two years earlier Gwin had defected to the South and had attempted to persuade Emperor Napoleon III to let him set up a colony of Confederate refugees and sympathizers in some of the Mexican border states. Owing to Maximilian's opposition the project was dropped. Grant warned McDowell to be on guard against this "virulent rebel"; in the event of an invasion McDowell was to chase the invading force into Mexico and maintain possession of any land occupied.

McDowell responded he had been interested in the fate of Mexico since the French had taken possession of it. Maximilian had a court, an army, and a government to support, and France expected to be repaid for the cost of her invasion. Much of the revenue for these purposes was expected to come from the northern Mexican states, which Gwin was expected to populate with "Anglo-Saxon and Celtic" settlers.

McDowell had previously told Stanton that it would be incongruous to accept any agent of Gwin's and reminded him that French troops were obtaining subsistence, supplies, and forage from San Francisco. He now stressed to Grant the American strength on land in the West but its weakness at sea; he took up Wright's old refrain that the United States should take over Guaymas and possibly Mazatlán as ports and supply posts if Pesqueira approved.[19]

Halleck, who had been consistently cool to the idea while he was general-in-chief and chief of staff, took up the cry for a Gulf of California post almost as soon as he became commander of the Pacific Division. He wrote to Grant that he hoped that the matter would be kept in view in all future negotiations with Mexico. The boundary line, he said, should be at least as far south as La Libertad. In May, 1865, the executive order banning the export of arms, ammunition, and livestock had been rescinded, and these commodities were now available to Mexico from the United States. No action was ever taken regarding a change in the boundary line, however.[20] Meanwhile, concern and irritation regarding the French presence in Mexico continued to mount on the West Coast.

Wright Prepares to Move North

On June 2, Grant ordered McDowell to relieve and discharge all general and staff officers whom he could dispense with. Stanton informed Halleck that he, Halleck, would soon take over the command of what would now be called the Division of the Pacific and that Gen. Edward O. C. Ord, one of Wright's officers in the 1858 campaign, would command the newly created Department of the Columbia. On June 25, Halleck was ordered to leave for the West; McDowell rather than Ord, was to take over the Department of California.[21]

Then, on June 27, 1865, an order that proved to be fateful for Wright was issued from the adjutant general's office in Washington, D.C. General Order no. 118 divided the United States into five divisions and eighteen departments. The division commanders were to be Maj. Gen. G. G. Meade for the Atlantic Division, Maj. Gen. W. T. Sherman for the Mississippi, Maj. Gen. P. H. Sheridan for the Gulf, Maj. Gen. G. H. Thomas for Tennessee, and Maj. Gen. H. W. Halleck for the Pacific. The Pacific Division was to include departments 17 and 18. Department 17 would be the Department of the Columbia with Brig. Gen. George Wright in command; it was to embrace the state of Oregon and the territories of Washington and Idaho, with headquarters at Fort Vancouver. Department 18, the Department of California, was to be commanded by Maj. Gen. Irvin McDowell. It would embrace the states of California and Nevada and the territories of New Mexico and Arizona; its headquarters would be at San Francisco. The order read: "All officers relieved by this order will, on being relieved by the proper officer, report by letter to the adjutant general for orders. By order of the President of the United States. Signed: E. D. Townsend, Assistant Adjutant General."[22]

On July 28, 1865, the *Alta California* published the following notice:

> Brigadier General Wright, who has been so long identified with the administration of the military affairs of the Department of the Pacific, and recently the General in command of the Department of California, leaves today on the steamer for Oregon, to assume the command of his old District, that of Columbia. During Gen. Wright's lengthy official connection with the people and interests of the Pacific Coast he has won the esteem, confidence and respect of all true American citizens. During the trying times of the early days of the rebellion, General Wright's moderation and clear sightedness carried him and our people peacefully through the surging billows of excitement and fanaticism. His most bitter enemy cannot impugn his honesty or patriotism, although some may differ as to the policy he carried out. A soldier beyond reproach, a courteous and genial gentleman, he leaves hosts of friends behind him to be met by an equal host of friends in Oregon. General Wright is accompanied by his wife and staff, having arrived from Sacramento on Wednesday night. Last evening he was honored with a serenade at the Occidental Hotel.[23]

At this time Col. Thomas Wright was still in command of the presidio at San Francisco. Captain Philip Owen, Wright's daughter Eliza's husband, was in temporary command of Fort Vancouver, which, along with Fort Dalles, Fort Walla Walla, and Fort Boise, had been reduced to depots with caretaker companies. John Wright was practicing law in Louisville.

Evaluation of Wright's Service on Coast

In evaluating Wright's service on the coast, Bancroft wrote the peace in California was due, "if not first, still in great measure to the prudence and firmness of Generals Sumner and Wright, who while the government was withdrawing the regular troops, one regiment after another, raised up others from the people, trained them, and set them to guard half of the public domain, with the inhabitants thereof."[24] James Warner has commented that it was Wright's "sleepless vigilance, unflagging energy and uncompromising patriotism" which served to sustain the authority of the United States government on the Pacific Coast.[25] Most recently John W. Robinson has written:

> Many people in California remembered him as a mild-mannered old gentleman, not in the least impressive but loved and respected by those who served under him. . . . Yet few . . . questioned his leadership ability or his courage. . . . He had a will of iron under his frail hide. He was implacable to political pressure and unafraid to lay his career on the line in defense of what he thought was right.

At the same time he was determined to avoid excessive repression.[26]

With the end of the Civil War, Wright was ready to move back to his old territory, the Pacfic Northwest. His assignments and duties during the war had not been those that, as a trained soldier, he would have preferred. He had desperately wanted to see action and to strike blows for the preservation of the Union, but his age and political enemies had militated against these desires and kept him on the coast. There he had done a creditable job in a difficult situation. Maintaining a balance among the demands of the radical Unionists, the neutralists, and the secessionists had been an arduous and thankless task. Moreover, Wright had had to live with the constant embarrassment of seeing his military and administrative accomplishments go unrewarded by promotion in the regular army. As he had once written to Secretary of War Simon Cameron, "Aspirations for higher rank I *have* always had, and will have, but I have never attempted to depreciate the claims of any officer to advancement."[27] Still, it must have been heartbreaking to see one officer after another, seventeen of whom had served under him in 1858, pass him by.

Despite his disappointments, he was first and foremost a

true soldier. He obeyed orders and carried out assignments, however distasteful, to the best of his ability. He
never seriously considered doing anything less than what
he regarded as his duty. Finally, "notwithstanding the
temptations and responsibilities of his position during
the Civil War, he maintained an unsullied integrity and the
highest purity of personal character."[28]

17.

A Watery Grave

On Friday, July 28, 1865, General Wright set out from San Francisco for Fort Vancouver, Washington Territory, the headquarters of his newly created command, the Department of the Columbia. Accompanying him were his wife, Margaret; his aide-de-camp, Lt. Edward D. Waite, and his orderly, Leach, along with his horse and his Newfoundland dog. The Wrights booked passage on the popular steamship *Brother Jonathan*. Accommodations for the cabin passengers were said to be comfortable and the food and service of high quality. However, the ship's record must have caused misgivings to those who were familiar with it.

The *Brother Jonathan* was a wooden side-wheeler of 1,181 tons, built for shipowner Edward Mills at Williamsburg, New York. It measured 220 feet 11 inches long, 36 feet wide, and 13 feet 10 inches deep, and carried two masts for sails in that day of transition from wind to coal. Its two 33-foot-diameter paddle wheels were driven by a vertical-beam, single-cylinder, 400-horsepower steam engine. Accommodations for 350 cabin and steerage passengers were provided.

In 1851 the *Brother Jonathan* began running between New York and Panama. The next year it was purchased by Cornelius Vanderbilt and transferred to the Pacific, where it ran between Central America and San Francisco. Meanwhile, the forepart of the ship had been rebuilt and a third mast added. By 1853 it was operating under the ownership of the Accessory Transit Company, which was in the business of transporting travelers across Nicaragua and up the coast to San Francisco.[1]

In 1856 the filibustering activities of William Walker caused a halt in the Nicaragua service. Apparently the *Brother Jonathan* operated farther up the Coast during that

S.S. *Brother Jonathan*, ca. 1863. Courtesy National Maritime Museum, San Francisco.

time, for in 1856 she listed among her passengers five Sisters of Charity of Providence traveling from San Francisco to Vancouver (these were the nuns Wright befriended during his tour of duty at Fort Vancouver in 1860).

In 1857 the ship was sold to Capt. John T. Wright (no relation to George Wright), who used it in coastwise service between San Francisco and the northwest ports of Oregon, Washington, and British Columbia under the name *Commodore*. On April 10, 1858, the ship brought confirmation of the gold strike on the Fraser River in British Columbia, and in 1859 it carried the news of statehood to the citizens of Oregon.

In July, 1858, two days out of San Francisco on a run to Victoria with 350 passengers aboard, the ship encountered heavy weather and was forced to turn back. It leaked badly and had enough water in the hold to extinguish the boiler fires. By jettisoning the deck cargo and enlisting the aid of passengers in bailing when the pumps failed, the ship managed to limp back through the Golden Gate. It was sold in December to the California Steam Navigation Company, renamed the *Brother Jonathan,* and placed in drydock for a complete overhaul. It then returned to the northern run. In 1860 it was sold to Maj. Samuel J. Hensley, and soon the *Brother Jonathan* again exhibited signs of structural weakness and once more was placed in drydock in San Francisco, where it was practically rebuilt and returned to service in December, 1861. By this time its structure was of dubious stability. Its history was not unusual for a ship of that era. Overworked and overloaded vessels constituted the main "commercial arteries" for the developing communities on the Pacific Coast before the coming of the railroads and were kept in operation as long as they floated.

Another, less well known incident further marred the seaworthiness of the *Brother Jonathan.* Many years later the widow of her last commander, Capt. Samuel J. DeWolf, wrote:

On the twentieth of July, 1865, the above steamship came into Port at San Francisco, *disabled,* after leaving Portland, Oregon on her way down the Columbia River. She fouled a schooner [the *Jane A. Falkenberg*] carrying away a portion of her forward deck & damaging her hull some eight feet square. The River Pilot, being at the wheel he immediately made for the shore about a mile in the distance on arriving, he boarded his tug, left the Ship. Capt. DeWolf (being in command) after making necessary repairs brought her into Port at San Francisco & at once reported the accident at the Companies office. He also stated, the break being so low it would necessitate their putting her on the drydock as the break could not be reached otherwise.

The owners did not think this major repair necessary and settled for some additional patching. The next eight or ten days were spent piling on freight until the captain protested that he could not take another pound. He was told he could take on more freight or go ashore, so for another twelve hours loading was continued.

Mrs. DeWolf wrote that the night before the ship was to sail the captain and crew held a meeting on board to

decide whether "to leave in a body" or take a chance on
going to the bottom. They knew the risk involved if they
should encounter bad weather, yet they decided to remain
since they would lose any chance of future employment if
they left.[2]

Because of the frequent backlog of freight on the
wharves of San Francisco it was common practice to overload the ships. The *Brother Jonathan*, however, was a damaged vessel that carried only six lifeboats and a supply of
life preservers of questionable efficacy. To overload such a
ship constituted an unconscionable risk. The heavy cargo
on Wright's voyage included machinery for an Oregon
woolen mill, farm equipment, a large quartz crusher, 300
hogsheads of whiskey, and a deck load of railroad rails.
Livestock included Wright's horse and dog and two camels
for the mines. Later rumors circulated that there were vast
treasures of gold aboard, valued at $1 million or more. It is
known that there were $200,000 to pay U.S. troops in the
Pacific Northwest; possibly $400,000 in Wells, Fargo funds;
$76,000 belonging to the Northwest Fur Traders Associa-
tion; $65,000 bound for the Norton Dexter Bank in Seat-
tle; and perhaps a quantity of gold bullion belonging to
the Canadian government. Nevertheless, the cargo was in-
sured for only $48,190.[3]

Captain DeWolf's reputation "as an officer and an experienced seafaring man was unquestioned by the [Califor-
nia Steam Navigation] Company and its patrons."[4] Trust-
worthy and conscientious, he had spent fifteen years sailing
the Pacific Coast and was thoroughly familiar with its features. W. A. H. Allen was first officer; J. D. Campbell, second officer; James Patterson, third officer; John S. Benton,
purser; and Elijah Mott, chief engineer. In addition to the
officers there was a crew of forty-eight men.

The number of passengers has been estimated at between 108 and 300. The discrepancy was due to the fact
that the names of many persons traveling in steerage and
late arrivals did not appear on the list in the company's office. In addition to the Wright party other notables were
on board: Maj. E. W. Eddy, paymaster of the army; Cap-

tain Chaddock of the U.S. Revenue Service, commander of the Revenue cutter *Joe Lane;* Dr. D. R. Ingraham, an army surgeon who had served with the Second U.S. Dragoons in every battle fought by the Army of the Potomac up to Gettysburg; and Anson G. Henry, former U.S. surveyor general, on his way to assume his new position as governor of Washington Territory. Henry was a close friend of the Lincoln family; Abraham Lincoln and Mary Todd had been married in his home. Also aboard was Henry's old nemesis Victor Smith, the former controversial collector of customs at Puget Sound, now a special agent of the Treasury Department; he had survived the wreck of the S.S. *Golden Rule* about a month earlier. James Nisbet, editor and part owner of the *San Francisco Evening Bulletin,* was on his way to Victoria to vacation and to gather evidence in a libel suit against a rival paper. Other passengers were H. Logan, newly appointed superintendent of the The Dalles mint; Joseph A. Lord, a Wells, Fargo messenger; a number of prominent merchants from cities along the coast; and wives, children, personal servants, Indians, and others.[5] One of the passengers was a Mrs. J. C. Keenan, "a business woman engaged in one of the oldest professions in the world. With her were seven girls, seven 'soiled doves' as they were called."[6] She and her string of courtesans were on their way to British Columbia to cash in on the gold strikes. Mrs. Keenan was said to have operated a large beer saloon in Victoria.

The usual description of the sailing of the *Brother Jonathan* depicts a gay scene as she cast off her moorings that noon of July 28, 1865. Champagne corks popped, flags waved, handkerchiefs fluttered, and hands were raised in farewell salutes as the vessel glided out into San Francisco Bay. Mrs. DeWolf tells a different story:

> The anchor raised, steam started, the word given to let go the ropes but not an inch did she move. Upon investigation, it was found she was so deep in the mud she could not move. They waited for the four o'clock tide when, with the help of a tug, she was started on her fatal voyage but so heavy laden, her sides were on a line with the water.[7]

Catastrophic Voyage

Once it was through the Golden Gate, the *Brother Jonathan* encountered a strong headwind and heavy seas. The over-burdened steamer made painfully slow progress up the coast and did not pass Crescent City, near the northern border of California, until Sunday morning, July 30. One well-documented account has the ship tied up and unloading freight Saturday night in Crescent City harbor while Wells, Fargo's Joe Lord spent some time with his wife, who was there visiting her foster parents.[8] In any event, by Sunday morning the ship was again heading north. Many of the passengers were so seasick that they were confined to their berths—if they were fortunate enough to have them.

About four miles northwest of Point Saint George the ship was making so little progress under increasingly violent winds that Captain DeWolf decided that the only hope of saving her was to turn back to Crescent City and anchor there until the storm abated. He could hardly have chosen a worse place for maneuvering a virtually unmanageable vessel: A reef called Dragon Rocks extends six miles out from Point Saint George; some of the fearsome rocks rise 200 feet out of the water, while others are barely discernible at low tide. A commonly used passage existed between the reef and the shore, but DeWolf apparently thought it safer to pass completely around the reef before heading into Crescent City harbor.

What happened next is best told in the words of Jacob Yates, the quartermaster on watch:

> I took the wheel at twelve o'clock [noon], A northwest gale was blowing and we were four miles above Point St. George [two miles north of Crescent City]. The sea was running mountain high, and the ship was not making any headway. The captain thought it best to turn back to Crescent City and wait until the storm had ceased. He ordered the helm hard aport. I obeyed and it steadied her. I kept due east. This was about 12:45. When we made Seal Rock, the captain said, "Southeast by south." It was clear where we were but foggy and smoky in-

shore [numerous forest fires were burning]. We ran till 1:50, when she struck [an uncharted, unnamed rock] with great force, knocking the passengers down and starting the deck planks. The captain stopped and backed her but could not move the vessel an inch. She rolled about five minutes, then gave a tremendous thump, and part of the keel came up alongside. By that time the wind and sea had slewed her around until her head came to the sea and she worked off a little. Then the foremast went through the bottom until the yard rested on the deck. Captain DeWolf ordered everyone to look to his own safety, and said that he would do the best he could for all.[9]

What transpired during the following forty-five minutes has passed into the realm of folklore. Accounts range from scenes of heroic calm to the wildest confusion. There is general agreement on certain facts: mountainous waves continued to crash into the stricken vessel, which was fast breaking to pieces. Two cannon shots were fired as a distress signal, and life preservers were distributed. The first lifeboat, launched under direction of the first mate, was so overloaded that it capsized immediately, and its occupants drowned before the eyes of those on board, although there are accounts of one or two individuals being pulled back aboard the ship. The captain ordered the second mate to lower his boat, which was nearly filled with female cabin passengers. It was promptly swamped by the careening of the steamer.

About this time Patterson, the third mate, who had been asleep in his bunk after being relieved from his watch, made his way to the deck and loaded five women and three children into one of the smaller, newly patented Francis lifeboats. Before he could help any other passengers, ten crew members jumped into the lifeboat and cast off from the ship. As Patterson and his boatload rowed away, Captain DeWolf gave him his last order: "Tell them, that if they had not overloaded us, we would have got through all right and this would never have happened." These nineteen souls somehow made it to Crescent City a few hours later by vigorous rowing and bailing; they were the only survivors of this great maritime tragedy.[10]

George Wright has been described in various accounts as having been in one of the boats, cast into the sea and then pulled back on board, or pleading with his wife to get into a lifeboat. It has been said that Mrs. Wright was in one of the boats that overturned or that she was initially in the little boat that carried the survivors but left it when she found that her husband would not accompany her. The most commonly accepted account is that just before the *Brother Jonathan* gave its last lurch and plunged beneath the waves the general and his wife were seen standing on the deck together, she wrapped in his long military cloak and held in his embrace.

An act of extreme composure is attributed to James Nisbet, who remained with the ship until she sank. He seated himself on a hatch cover, took out his notebook, and, as though he were writing an article for his newspaper, calmly wrote his will, in which he named his brother his executor. He also composed a note to the Caspar Hopkins family, with whom he had been living in San Francisco: "A thousand affectionate adieus. You spoke of my sailing on Friday—hangman's day—and the unlucky *Brother Jonathan*—well, here I am with death before me. My love to you all—to Dita, Belle, Melitie and little Myra; kiss her for me. Never forget Grandpa" [Nisbet, a bachelor, had been called this by the Hopkins children]. The documents were found on Nisbet's body, but the will was refused in probate court because there were no witnesses, and the brother was accused of taking personal advantage of his position as executor.[11]

The *Brother Jonathan* carried three other lifeboats, but most accounts say that they were not launched. In the extremely cold water no one clinging to wreckage or life preservers could have survived for long. Indians standing on the smoke-shrouded bluff of Cape Saint George later claimed to have heard shouted orders and the cries of the drowning.

The reports of the cannon fired at sea were the Crescent

City citizens' first hint of the calamity. A "blue north-wester" was blowing, so they knew that a vessel was in distress. They described the sun as "shining like a red ball" through the smoke of the forest fires and the visibility from the shore as very limited. E. W. McGruder was standing in front of Ben West's saloon after his Sunday dinner and saw a boat come around Lighthouse Point. West came outside, looked through his spyglass, saw the bedraggled survivors in the boat, and said, "There has been a wreck!" He went back into the saloon, where a big poker game was in progress, and told the crowd, all of whom rushed down to the beach. Soon townsfolk and Indians crowded the shore, but the lifeboat did not reach it until almost 5:00 P.M.[12]

The first people the survivors saw were the Indians, and they wondered whether they had been saved from the deep only to meet a worse fate by massacre. The ride from the *Brother Jonathan* had not been easy. Several of the women were in their nightclothes, having just risen from their bunks, where they had been lying ill. The lightly clad women and children sat in the bottom of the boat, shivering and crying, "almost perishing with cold," while the men rowed and bailed. They were taken to a hotel, where they were clothed, warmed, and given assistance by the townsfolk. Although the crew members were later criticized for saving themselves first, one of the survivors, Mrs. Nina Bernhardt, observed, "If there had been more of the passengers and fewer of the crew in that boat it would never have reached land and none would have remained to tell the tale."[13]

Men immediately set out to look for more survivors along the beach. Patterson, to whom Mrs. Bernhardt gave credit for getting the lifeboat to shore, joined the search in spite of his exhaustion. He and some others took boats to the scene of the disaster; the dreadful rock did not appear on the charts of the day, although most of the reef was shown. They found no survivors or bodies, not even any wreckage. Soldiers from Camp Lincoln, six miles north, which had been founded by General Wright in 1862, soon joined in the search and kept bonfires burning on the beach all night.

Emory Wing, of Company C, Sixth Infantry California Volunteers, wrote a letter on August 1, in which he told about General Wright standing on the quarterdeck with the captain as the ship went down. He described the beach patrols and the rescue boats, bonfires burning and cannons firing, but no sign of bodies or wreckage.[14] Reports came in of a crowd of persons huddled near Seal Rock, but a boat sent to investigate found only sea lions. The fruitless search continued for three days. Gradually bits of wreckage began to drift to shore: portions of the steamer's hurricane deck, passengers' beds and trunks, one of the lifeboats, part of a mast, and the ship's wheel.

Aftermath

The day after the tragedy a soldier from Camp Lincoln rode 130 miles in fourteen hours through the redwood forests and the rugged mountains of the Coast Range to Jacksonville, Oregon, where the nearest telegraph was located. He arrived there at 9:30 P.M. on August 1, and soon the wires carried the first news of the "Appalling Calamity," as the next morning's *Daily Oregonian* headlined it. The first news was scant, merely an account of the dispatch that the soldier carried for Col. R. C. Drum, the assistant adjutant general in San Francisco.[15] The dispatch, dated July 31, stated:

> At 2:00 p.m. yesterday, the steamer *Brother Jonathan* struck a sunken rock and sank in less than an hour, with all on board except 16 persons [plus 3 children] who escaped in a small boat, the only survivors of the ill-fated ship. No other trace of the vessel is left. I was out last night on the beach with 14 men; shall keep a party out on the beach. General Wright, family and staff are supposed to be lost. Full particulars by mail.

The dispatch was signed by "Thomas S. Buckley, Captain, 6th Infantry C.V., Commanding."[16]

On August 2 the *Daily Alta California* published a passenger list[17] and the next day reported that the *Sierra Nevada* had passed Crescent City at noon that fateful Sunday heading southward and had not found the weather so "remarkable" as to prevent the safe launching of lifeboats unless the *Brother Jonathan* sank instantly.[18] On board the *Sierra Nevada,* returning from an official visit to Victoria with Schuyler Colfax, Speaker of the House of Representatives, was Samuel Bowles, the distinguished editor of the *Springfield Republican.* When he learned of the fate of the *Brother Jonathan,* Bowles wrote:

> We passed her and her fatal rock only an hour or two before their sad collision; and we readily join, as you can imagine, in the wide tide of feeling that the disaster creates here. The genial old General Wright, long and honorable in service, and beloved throughout the Pacific states, and Mr. Nisbet of the *Bulletin* editorial staff, we knew, and had experienced their hospitality.[19]

Albert Richardson, author of *Beyond the Mississippi,* also described threading the reef and the anxiety he had felt. The ship on which he was traveling from Victoria had hoped to meet the *Brother Jonathan* and obtain recent San Francisco newspapers. The rendezvous did not occur: "two hours after we passed the reef, she reached it, struck a rock and in 45 minutes went to the bottom." He added, "There must be a best way of launching boats under such circumstances, . . . some way for a man with Nisbet's nerve and calmness to save himself if he only knew it."[20]

The news of its worst maritime disaster stunned the people of the West Coast. All flags in coastal cities and on ships in their harbors flew at half-mast. The *Evening Bulletin* for August 2 expressed the hope that in view of the meager details available some of the facts might have been exaggerated and the loss of life not as great as reported.[21] It seemed impossible that so few could have been saved from a wreck in broad daylight so near the shore, and with almost an hour to save passengers.

Later Mrs. DeWolf became convinced that her husband had not run into an uncharted rock but that the heavy quartz crusher had broken loose and plunged through the previously damaged part of the hull. She also believed that there were a good many more passengers on board the steamer than the usual estimates. She believed that the blame for the disaster rested squarely with "the Officers of the Steam Navigation Co. & their adherents."[22] Rumors of mutiny and piracy circulated, and it was even said that the Confederate raider *Shenandoah,* which was still thought to be at large and unaware the war was over, might have been involved.

The *Evening Bulletin* for August 3 confirmed the bad news.[23] The *Alta* contained a dispatch from Patterson: "All boats returned and nothing seen of wreck. We have given up all hopes."[24] On August 5 the Jacksonville *Oregon Reporter* denounced what it called the wanton sacrifice of hundreds of valuable lives to the cold-blooded avarice of the steamship companies. The *Brother Jonathan,* it said, was an old, unsafe hulk, and to send out men, women, and children in worn-out, condemned coffins was nothing short of murder. The editor was not one to mince words. Referring to General Wright, he said:

> It is with severe grief that we announce the tragic death of the newly appointed commandant of the District of Oregon by the wreck of the *Brother Jonathan.* The cause of civil order, public and private right has lost a noble and most gallant friend. At a time when excitement, violence, and a species of maddening fanaticism ruled the hour, General Wright held the supreme military command on this coast. . . . The influence of prominent politicians, the frenzied clamor of a licentious press and prostituted pulpit were powerless however, in swerving him from the path of duty he had chosen. . . . His prudence, foresight, firmness, and wisdom spared the Pacific Coast . . . from civil war. The Department of Oregon to which he has been but recently appointed, particularly has reason to deplore his loss. After such a man as the imbecile Alvord had held command of this state, it needed the military talent, and administrative abilities of such a man as Wright to draw order out of confusion and protect our frontiers from the frequent and daring incursions of hostile savages. Noble deeds and

character enshrined in the hearts of people he served are more enduring than a granite monument.[25]

On August 4 the *Daily Alta California* published a eulogy to Brigader General Wright, which said in part:

When a noble and brave soldier falls in the heat of battle, the sorrow that must be felt is in a measure assuaged by the fact that the perilled life [was lost] in a noble cause—the defense of the land of his birth and the institutions of his Government. We are apt, however, when we learn the sudden taking from our midst of a faithful soldier, to lose sight of the great good he accomplished in his official career. But a few brief days and we chronicled the departure of Brig. Gen. George Wright, to take command of the new Military District of Columbia. We little thought that it should be our duty to pen the notice of his death, for we have no reason to doubt that he, with the illfated passengers of the *Brother Jonathan,* has found a watery grave.

California and the Pacific coast may well put on sables, for one of the truest and best of men has been taken from among us. As a military chieftain, his record stands among the most distinguished of American generals. Not alone was he great, in the field-where masterly ability characterized his every action—but his diplomatic tact, as evinced during the trying period of the past four years, enabled our people to enjoy the blessings of peace.

Gen. Wright was a soldier, and had a record that any great and good man might feel proud of. . . . As an officer, he won the respect and esteem of all; as a man he was kind and genial; as a citizen, he filled all the various positions with credit to himself and the flag he served and so revered. His loss is a public calamity, yet the keen edge of sorrow is tempered when we all know that, covered with years and honors, he surrendered life in the discharge of his duty.[26]

The same day the *Evening Bulletin* announced the dispatch of the steamer *Del Norte* to the scene of the wreck. On board were Col. Thomas Wright, a party from the *Bulletin* office, and others who hoped to recover the bodies of friends and relatives.[27]

The sea was reluctant to give up its victims, but nine or

ten days after the wreck bodies began to drift ashore. Every day three or four would be recovered by boatmen at sea or found on the beach. One account said: "Horrible discoveries were made in caves among the rocks. Dead faces showed white from tangled seaweed, wild eyes stared up from shallow pools left by receding tides."[28] Forty-five corpses were recovered near Crescent City and another thirty scattered between Gold Beach, at the mouth of the Rogue River, and Trinidad and Humboldt Bay. Among the bodies recovered were those of Margaret Wright, Lieutenant Waite, and James Nisbet. C. C. Steward transported many of the bodies in his dray to a large warehouse near Battery Point, which was used as a morgue. He recalled that nearly all the bodies were wearing life preservers but little if any clothing. Scavengers had been at work, and some bodies were found with fingers cut off, presumably for the rings. Rumors of survivors murdered by the Indians proved false.

Many of the bodies, though well preserved and easily recognizable, were never identified since the lack of garments made identification by strangers almost impossible. Some of the bodies and the few survivors were taken back to San Francisco on the *Del Norte*. A special cemetery was established at Crescent City, where many of the victims were interred; some bodies discovered in more remote areas were buried where they were found. Years later, after the Crescent City graveyard and its markers had lapsed into decrepitude, an attractive memorial park with a suitable monument was established on the spot.

After the return on August 10 of the *Del Norte* to San Francisco with the surviving passengers and crewmen, the *Alta* was able to give the public the full particulars of the tragedy. Eventually the *Alta* published lists of the bodies that had been identified and gave detailed descriptions of the unidentified corpses. Although the body of Wright's horse had drifted in near Trinidad, obsequies for Wright were deferred in the hope that his body would be recovered.

On August 17, General McDowell officially announced General Wright's death. The order pointed to his long, prominent connection with the West Coast, where he had established himself in the respect, affections, gratitude, and confidence of the people by the exercise of every high quality that distinguished a soldier and gentleman, his gallant services in the field, and his administration of the Pacific Department. Since there seemed to be little hope of recovering his body, his memory was to be honored at all posts in his late command by display of the national flag at half-staff, the firing of thirteen guns at noon, and the wearing of the "customary badge of mourning" by the officers and colors of the Ninth Infantry for thirty days.[29]

Commenting on the order, the *Alta* referred to Wright as "a soldier and gentleman who will ever be remembered with gratitude by Californians as one who rendered our country and state services in the hour of direst necessity."[30] The following week a similar order was issued from the Department of the Columbia. It included the observation: "It is seldom that we are called upon to mourn the loss of an Officer more universally known and respected alike for his varied and distinguished public service, his sterling integrity, untiring devotion to business, constancy in friendship, loyalty to government and genial social qualities." Regimental orders of the Ninth Infantry announcing his death stated: "Without bloodshed, he accomplished the work of a statesman and soldier, protected the honor of his country's flag and preserved the peace."[31]

A biographical sketch written in later years concluded with this envoy:

> Rest, white haired veteran, 'neath the murmuring waves;
> No more the sounds of war disturb thy sleep;
> Our land, all strewn with patriot-warriors' graves,
> Gives one proud conquest to the mighty deep![32]

The rest of the nation did not learn of the sinking of the *Brother Jonathan* until August 26. The *New York Times* account, headlined "Another Great Disaster," attributed the delay to the interruption of telegraphic communication with the Pacific Coast.[33] On October 13 the *Daily Alta California* announced that Colonel Drum had just learned of the recovery of the remains of the late General Wright at Bay Flat, near Shelter Cove, Mendocino County, 150 miles from the scene of the disaster. The body was badly decomposed but was identified from clothing and otherwise. The body of Mrs. Wright, which had been recovered soon after the wreck, was at a funeral home awaiting the arrival of her husband's body on the *Del Norte*.[34]

Obsequies for Wright

The *Alta* for October 18 announced that the bodies of the general and his "esteemed partner in life and death" would be buried together at Sacramento, where a monument to their memories was proposed.[35] Military authorities had considered sending the bodies east for burial or interring them beside California's other honored dead at Lone Mountain. However, the *Sacramento Bee* reported that Sacramentans who knew the general and his wife and were aware of how much they loved the city had convinced General McDowell that the Wrights looked on Sacramento as their home and that they "should find sepulcher in the beautiful cemetery of the Capital City."

On learning of Wright's death, the editor of the *Bee* had earlier written:

> Of the many who have found a watery grave we may mention the late commander of the Department of California, General George Wright, who with his excellent wife and his manly young adjutant, Edward D. Waite, are among the drowned. We cannot bring the mind to believe it . . . it seems but yesterday that the veteran with fatherly kindness clasped our hand, with the goodness which was the great element of his generous nature, bade us farewell. Prisoner of death with his loving wife who had blessed his life and shared with him the vicissitudes and joys that are intermingled with a soldier's career. . . . He had the pleasant memories of a well spent life and the

consciousness of a career of unbroken honor to soften the asperity of his sad death. Upwards of forty years had he worn the uniform of his country, and sank to rest with name, sword and honor untarnished, . . . his faithful and loving wife beside him.[36]

On Saturday, October 21, 1865, funeral services were held at the Calvary Church in San Francisco with the Reverend Charles Wadsworth, D.D., officiating. The coffins containing the remains of General and Mrs. Wright were placed together in front of the pulpit in the charge of a military guard of honor. Colonel Drum escorted Mrs. Philip (Eliza Wright) Owen, followed by Mrs. Drum and Captain Owen, to a pew in front of the coffins. Colonel Thomas F. Wright was not present, having been transferred to Arizona, where he was in command of the Second Regiment of California Volunteers. Dr. Wadsworth's address made such an impression on his listeners that Generals Halleck and McDowell, Colonels Drum and Babbitt, and others persuaded him to permit its publication. He said in part:

> General George Wright was personally known to most of you. His long residence among you in times that truly and mightily tried men's souls, and the admirable qualities of head and heart that he displayed, amid all those trials, won the respect and affection of all honest men and true patriots; and seldom has a whole community experienced and expressed profounder grief than at the terrible disaster which so suddenly ended his earthly career . . .
>
> During the War of the Rebellion, by his prudence, firmness and conciliation he won universal confidence and respect. . . . Few of you know indeed the depth of your indebtedness to this true patriot soldier, for few understand to what extent the principles inspiring that terrible revolution were widespread, and working in your own golden state. But the pen of history will presently record that it was, under God, the untiring energy, the sleepless vigilance, cool judgment and uncompromising, yet unpretending patriotism of General Wright and his coadjutors which saved this state from becoming a theatre of civil conflict.

Referring to Mrs. Wright, Wadsworth continued:

> Nor are we forgetting that he comes not here alone—side by side as they walked in loving life—husband and wife, partners, helpers, companions, sharers together in all the toils and cares of earth, so in the last and mighty fellowship of death do they journey together to the grave. As the wife of such a man, the sharer of his gentler labors, the solace of his toils, the mother of his honorable children, the light of his dwelling, the dispenser of his noble hospitalities, the one friend loved above all others, nearer than all else . . . on whom he lavished all his deepest love. . . . Her life was rounded in his life—his honor is her honor—his praise her praise; one faith, one love, one hope. Blessed in their united life of love—and, even in that terrible form of death, blessed at least so far, that it did not divide them.[37]

After the services a procession marched to the Sacramento Steamboat Wharf. The route down Montgomery and Jackson streets had been cleared by mounted guards, and the procession moved on to the mournful music of the "Dead March" played by the Second U.S. Artillery and Ninth U.S. Infantry bands. The Ninth U.S. Infantry escort, marching in column of platoons, led the way; the hearses followed, driven abreast; then came the pallbearers, led by Generals Halleck and McDowell, walking on either side. The officers of the various posts in and around San Francisco, regular and volunteer, came next, and the escort of honor, consisting of the regimental staff of the Ninth U.S. Infantry with two sergeants from each company marching behind the hearses followed them. Major General William S. Rosecrans and a number of other distinguished officers marched in the procession, the military portion of which closed with Company A, First Cavalry California Volunteers, and a section of the First California Guard (Artillery) with two guns. The entire military contingent was under the command of Brigadier General French, Second U.S. Artillery.

Citizens in carriages followed the military cortege, and the sidewalks were crowded with people who had been unable to gain admission to the church. At the entrance to the wharf the escort formed double lines and presented arms as the coffins were carried to the boat on which they were taken, under a special guard of honor, to Sacramento. All the flags in the city were at half-mast to honor the memory of a soldier and gentleman and his respected and beloved wife.[38]

One cannot escape the conclusion that the elegance and magnitude of the funeral was in some measure a reflection of the guilty consciences of some of the politicians and military figures who had defamed Wright in life. It is possible they were trying to make restitution to Wright for the neglect and calumny to which he had often been subjected.

Early the next morning the coffins were removed from the steamer in Sacramento and taken to the senate chamber, where they lay in state. While the transfer was taking place, church and fire bells tolled, and all day the flags of the city were displayed at half-mast. About 2:00 P.M. the coffins were removed to the Congregational Church on Sixth Street, where a brief service was held by the Reverends I. E. Dwinell, F. Charlton, and M. C. Briggs.

The coffins were then taken to the City Cemetery in a procession led by General Howell and his aides, followed by the Fourth Regiment of California Militia under Colonel Hamilton. Music was provided by the Ninth U.S. Infantry and Camp Union bands, which were followed by the Sacramento Light Artillery and Company C of the Second Cavalry. Wright's hearse was drawn by six black horses and accompanied by the pallbearers, among whom were Governor Low, Adj. Gen. G. S. Evans, Colonel McGarry, Colonel Bowie, and Chief Justice Sanderson. They were followed by a horse owned by the general, led by a groom.

Then came a hearse drawn by four bays with the body of Mrs. Wright. Among her pallbearers was B. B. Redding, for whom the city of Redding is named. Twenty-three carriages with mourners, including Lizzie Wright Owen and friends of the Wrights, were followed by the Sacramento Hussars, the Pioneer Association, the Sacramento Turn-

The Wrights' grave, City Cemetery, Sacramento, California. Courtesy Eastern Washington State Historical Society.

verein, and several fire-fighting companies. Thirty-five carriages and buggies with citizens brought up the rear. The funeral cortege, more than a mile long, was the largest ever witnessed in the city and required half an hour to pass a given point. Interment took place in the cemetery's state plot. Three volleys were fired over the graves by Colonel Hamilton's battalion.[39]

Shortly after the first news of the sinking of the *Brother Jonathan* arrived, the *San Francisco Call* suggested that it would be proper for the people to take some steps to do honor to the memory of a good citizen and patriotic soldier: "Solemn and imposing obsequies and an appropriate monument would at once symbolize the heartfelt sorrow of the people over their loss, and convey to coming generations the great esteem they feel for the memory of one who had served his country for nearly half a century."[40]

Governor Low, in his eulogy, referred to Wright as the general "to whose loyalty, fidelity and military ability, the people of this state are so much indebted for the peace and good order that prevailed here during the dark days of the Republic." But a recent writer has pointed out that the bitterness of radical Unionists followed the old general to the grave; their opposition blocked efforts by the state to provide a suitable memorial.[41]

At the sixteenth session of the California legislature in 1866, a bill was introduced to authorize an appropriation of $5,000 to erect a monument to General Wright in the state burial ground. The bill failed, and a similar one was presented the following year. This time the Finance Committee failed to recommend its passage.[42] Finally Judge Samuel Cross, counsel for the administrator of the Wright estate, sponsored an act to permit him to erect a monument in the state burial ground, but there is no record of legislative approval.[43] In 1872 the remains of Wright and his wife were removed to the Cross family plot in the old Sacramento City Cemetery. There Cross erected a monument "of lofty and tasty design, which could not have cost less than $2,000."[44] On it appears the inscription:

Gen. George Wright, U.S.A.
and his wife
died
July 30, 1865
Lovely and pleasant in their lives,
and in their death they
were not divided

18.
Epilogue

GENERAL GEORGE WRIGHT was not soon forgotten. Almost a year after his death, in an address delivered before the first annual Celebration of the Society of California Volunteers, held in San Francisco, William Gouverneur Morris, former adjutant Second California Cavalry, captain and assistant quartermaster, U.S. Volunteers (Bvt. Maj.), paid tribute to their "late beloved commander."

Morris reminded his listeners of the respect and affection in which Wright had been held by those who served under him and the pleasure Wright had derived from their attainments. Morris attributed the peace and "unexampled prosperity" that California enjoyed during the war to the "masterly, energetic and *thoughtful* policy" initiated and followed by Wright.

Of particular interest is Morris's statement that Wright had

> the implicit confidence and trust of our late martyred President. The policy pursued here was approved by him and dictated, I might say, by his own hand. I fain would read you an autograph letter from President Lincoln to General Wright, a letter that would forever silence the vile slanderers who traduced him during life, but it is not here; where is it? floating unseen upon the broad expanse of the Pacific, where the eye of the Almighty rests alone upon it.

Morris believed that posterity would do Wright justice and that the monument to his memory that the last legislature had failed to authorize would yet be raised by the grateful state of California. "See that you all enact your part in having this done," he said.

Morris vehemently denounced Wright's enemies, going so far as to say that "to the wicked machination of his traducers, does he owe his death," since they had been responsible for his removal from command and change of station.[1]

By this time, April, 1866, Col. Thomas Forster Wright had been honorably mustered out of service. However, the peaceful life of a civilian did not suit his adventurous spirit, and on July 28 he obtained a commission in the regular army as first lieutenant with the Thirty-second U.S. Infantry. He served as regimental quartermaster from July 15, 1867, until May 12, 1869. On January 31, 1870, he was transferred to the Twelfth U.S. Infantry and was adjutant of that regiment from March 8 to June 8 of that year.

In January, 1873, Company E, with which Lieutenant Wright was then serving, was sent to operate against the Modoc Indians in the Lava Beds of northern California. In February Company G, under Lt. Charles P. Eagan, joined Company E, and both companies were ordered into action after the massacre of Gen. E. R. S. Canby and his peace commissioners on April 11. Severe fighting occurred on April 15 and 17. On the twenty-sixth, Company E, with two batteries of the Fourth Artillery, engaged the Indians and suffered terrible losses. Four officers, including Wright and Gen. Lorenzo Thomas's son, and eighteen enlisted men were killed, and two officers and sixteen enlisted men were wounded. Forty-two-year-old Lieutenant Wright's remains were interred next to his parents in the State Burial Ground in Sacramento City Cemetery.[2]

Eliza Wright's life was not a happy one. Her husband, Capt. Philip A. Owen, resigned from the service on December 31, 1873, because of poor health. On February 11, 1876, Asst. Q.M. Gen. Rufus Ingalls instructed the depot quartermaster in Washington, D.C., to hire Owen as a clerk at $125 a month to assist in the briefing of claims.[3]

The Owens had three children, among them a daughter, Margaret, and two sons, Frank, who later served as second lieutenant in the Eighth Infantry, and Montgomery M., born in Washington Territory. Montgomery died in San Francisco in 1861 at the age of two years, three months, and is buried with General and Mrs. Wright in Sacramento.[4] The first federal census [1860] of Washington Territory lists him as ten years old, but that document differs from the newspaper notices of his death.[5]

Captain Owen died on August 28, 1879, five and a half years after leaving the army.[6] Eliza was left destitute and in failing health. In 1880 she petitioned Congress for a pension of fifty dollars a month, pointing out that no member of her family had ever received a pension. Her first request was submitted to the 46th Congress, second session. Senator J. T. Farley, a member of the Committee on Pensions, reported: "She has no claim under existing laws. The committee did not feel the facts of the case would justify them in granting her a pension." The committee asked that the petition be postponed indefinitely.

The committee's action seems a rather cavalier way of dealing with a woman whose husband, father, and two brothers had served their country long and ably. Similar bills to authorize pensions were introduced before Congress in 1887, 1888, and 1890, but no benefits resulted, though strong supporting letters were written by Gen. Philip Sheridan and other high-ranking officers.[7]

In the meantime, Eliza Owen had returned to Norwich to live with her aunt, Mrs. Olive P. Newton. By the time her last petition was under consideration by Congress in 1890, Lizzie Owen was well past caring whether her pension would be approved. On August 19, at the home of her aunt, she died of heart disease.[8]

The third child of George and Margaret Wright, John Montgomery Wright, enjoyed a long and distinguished career after completing his law studies and earning his LL.B. degree at the University of Louisville in 1866. While he was engaged in the practice of law, he was twice elected to the Kentucky legislature, serving from 1871 to 1875. For the following four years he was adjutant general of Kentucky. During this time he became a highly regarded editorial writer on the Louisville *Courier-Journal*. In 1878 he organized the Louisville Board of Trade and became its first superintendent. In 1880 he was appointed captain of Company F of the Louisville Legion in the state militia. He was general manager of the Southern Exposition, held in

Louisville in 1883, and two years later was its president. He was a founder and the first president of the prestigious Pendennis Club.[9]

In 1888 he was appointed marshal of the U.S. Supreme Court to succeed President Lincoln's former secretary, John G. Nicolay.[10] He filled that position with distinction for almost twenty-seven years and is remembered with warm affection by those who worked with him. A man of diverse interests, he once published a book of poetry. He and his wife, Nelly Ewing Wright, had two daughters: Jean Wright Swope, also a writer of prose and poetry, and Margaret Forster Wright, who married William W. Hawkins,[11] who was then on the staff of the *Courier-Journal* and later became board chairman of the Scripps-Howard newspapers. John Montgomery Wright died on January 2, 1915, and is buried in Arlington National Cemetery.[12]

Timbers reported to have come from the wreck of the *Brother Jonathan* can be seen at the Lighthouse Museum, in Crescent City, California. A bell from the ship that had been on display there has been stolen. Two steering wheels from the vessel were recovered. For many years one of them decorated Soville's Saloon in Crescent City. In the mid-1940s it was acquired by Louis E. Wacksmuth and since then has been displayed in his Dan and Louis's Oyster Bar in Portland, Oregon. The other wheel is in the Oyster Bar of Los Angeles's Jonathan Club (which was not named for the ill-fated ship).

Many efforts have been made to find the remains of the ship and recover its treasure. It is said that in 1914 the Canadian government sent hard-hat divers to search the area for a month or two. In 1922 an amateur diver, Al Thayer, began searching and at one time thought he had located the hull, but found nothing of any value. Nine years later Payton Parks was likewise said to have identified the wreckage. Other divers using scuba gear continued the search.[13] In recent years efforts have been aided by sophisticated modern equipment such as loran, range finders, sidescan sonar, proton magnetometers, and computers but so far without success. Recovery efforts have not been made easier by the fierce currents and frequent storms that prevail along that area of the Coast. A tidal wave struck the region in 1964.[14]

Wright's estate was administrated in Sacramento Probate Court by Samuel Cross in November, 1866. Wright died technically intestate, because his will went to the bottom of the ocean with the *Brother Jonathan*. One of the witnesses was dead, and the other had moved away. Thomas Wright acted as administrator since his brother was in Kentucky and his sister in Washington Territory. The estate was divided equally among the three children, and from her share Eliza repaid $500 Judge Cross had advanced her. George Wright left $1,533 in 175 shares of Fireman's Fund Insurance Company stock; $7,050 worth of real estate in Oakland, San Francisco, and Vermont; and other real and personal property valued at $1,575. Margaret held ninety shares of New York Central Railroad Company stock worth $9,270.[15]

Several forts were named for Wright during his lifetime, and he continued to be so honored after his death. The important military post at Oak Grove, on the route from Los Angeles and San Diego to Fort Yuma, was called Camp Wright. Established in 1861, it was abandoned in 1866. Between 1862 and 1875 Fort, later Camp, Wright was occupied in Round Valley, Mendocino County, California. In 1858 the first steamer on the upper Columbia, running between Celilo Falls and Lewiston, was called the *Colonel Wright*. It was dismantled in 1865, but it is said that a coastal steamer also was named after him. At one time there was a Wright General Hospital at the Presidio in San Francisco and a Wright Camp near the Presidio. While working on his military road between Fort Walla Walla and Fort Benton in 1861, Lt. John Mullan established a winter camp at the junction of the Big Blackfoot and Clark Fork rivers in the Bitterroot Mountains, which he called Cantonment Wright.

In 1897 Fort George Wright was constructed on the outskirts of Spokane, Washington, on one thousand acres donated by the town's citizens. Its first occupants arrived in
1899, a company of black troops from the Twenty-fourth
Infantry Regiment, veterans of the Spanish-American War
and the Indian Wars. Subsequently various companies of
infantry and one troop of cavalry were stationed there.
Three of Wright's former regiments served at the post: the
Eighth Infantry, the Third Infantry, and, from 1922 to
1942, the Fourth Infantry. During the 1930s a Civilian
Conservation Corps camp shared the site. During World
War II the Army Air Corps took over, and later Air Force
officers from nearby fields were housed there. The fort
was declared surplus by the government in 1958. Two
years later the Sisters of the Holy Names of Jesus and
Mary moved Holy Names College, which they had established in Spokane in 1907, to the site and changed the
name to Fort Wright College. In 1925 a public school on
the site of old Fort Dalles was named the George Wright
School.

Historic markers have been placed at the Four Lakes
and Spokane Plains battlegrounds, at Fort George Wright,
at the Horse Slaughter Camp site on the Spokane River
near Liberty Lake, at the "Hanging Camp" at Smyth's Ford
on Latah Creek, and at the site of Camp Wright in Oak
Grove, San Diego County. The Wright monument still
stands in the old City Cemetery in Sacramento.

What, then, is Wright's place in history? The descendant
of a pioneer Vermont family, imbued at a young age with
the Puritan principles of piety, probity, and diligence, he
spent his entire life from the age of fourteen in the army,
most of it on the frontiers of the expanding United States.
As the responsibilities of his profession increased, he displayed qualities of leadership, thoroughness, and good
judgment. As a young company grade officer, he participated in the Seminole and Mexican wars, where he won
the confidence and esteem of his superiors.

His identification with the Pacific Coast, where he spent the latter part of his career, began in 1852, when he assumed command of Fort Reading, California, during the gold rush. His first important responsibilities began when he was appointed commander of the Ninth Infantry and placed in charge of the Columbia River District. During this period Wright's basic differences in philosophy regarding the handling of Indians and the conduct of the Yakima War led to difficulties with the governor of newly organized Washington Territory. The settlers and their officials accused him of being too sympathetic to the Indians and claimed that he preferred palaver to fighting. Wright's attitude underwent a dramatic change after the defeat of Col. Edward Steptoe in 1858. During that year he proved himself a capable field commander. A combination of careful planning, rigorous training, strict discipline, and superior weapons led to two important victories by his troops and effected the subjugation of the Spokane, Coeur d'Alene, and Palouse Indians. These victories also cooled the ardor of other tribes for a war of extermination against the whites. In 1860–61 he reestablished cordial relations with the British in Canada which had been disrupted as a result of the so-called Pig War.

Wright's greatest challenges and service to his country occurred after the outbreak of the Civil War, when he assumed command of the vast Department of the Pacific. It was a period of frustration and disappointment for him; he was far from the major scenes of action of the war and was repeatedly bypassed for promotion. However, Wright's responsibilities were heavy. It fell to him to prevent the Confederate troops from reaching the coast, to control the secessionists, to protect his department from foreign threats, and to maintain a steady flow of gold and supplies moving east. He performed each of these tasks successfully. Far from the bloody battles of the Civil War, he had to assume broad political and diplomatic functions in addition to strictly military ones. Throughout the great struggle he got along well with the governors and other civil authorities in the states and territories within his command and was able to maintain friendly relations with the Canadians on the north and Mexicans on the south. Many citizens believed that the coast enjoyed the blessings of peace and was spared the horrors of war because of Wright's good judgment, imperturbability, sense of justice, and wise management, for which not only the Pacific Coast but the entire nation stood in his debt. In the opinion of many, General Wright did his country a great service in its darkest hour.

As an officer Wright earned the respect of those who served under him; as a gentleman he was refined and genial; as a citizen he filled his various responsibilities with credit to himself and the flag he served. His conduct and policies were said to have earned the written approbation of President Lincoln, though that document and other important papers were lost with the sinking of the *Brother Jonathan.*

During his lifetime Wright made some powerful enemies, civil and military, but he was regarded by most people on the coast with respect, affection, gratitude, and confidence. Without doubt his greatest contribution lay in preserving peace on the coast by accomplishing the work of a statesman and soldier with firmness and moderation and without bloodshed. One can only hope that Wright, toward the end of his long career, recognized the truth of the saying, "Peace has her victories, no less than war."

Abbreviations Used in the Notes

AGO   See under NA.
BL   Bancroft Library, Berkeley, Calif.
CSL   California State Library, Sacramento
LC   Division of Manuscripts, Library of Congress, Washington, D.C.
MHS   Missouri Historical Society, Manuscript Collection, Saint Louis
NA   National Archives, Washington, D.C.

AGO	Adjutant General's Office	
	M	Microcopy
	LR	Letters Received, M 567
	RG	Record Group
	RLR	Register of Letters Received, M 711
	SR	Appointment, Commission and Personal Branch, Service Report
USMA	U.S. Military Academy	
	CAP	Cadet Application Papers, M 688

OHQ   *Oregon Historical Quarterly*
PNWQ   *Pacific Northwest Quarterly*
USMA   Archives, U.S. Military Academy, West Point, N.Y.

CAP	Cadet Application Papers, 1805–66	
	RC	Records of Cadets
	SLB	Superintendent's Letter Book

WHQ   *Washington Historical Quarterly*
WiHS   Collections of State Historical Society of Wisconsin
WiMH   *Wisconsin Magazine of History*
WSHS   Washington State Historical Society, Tacoma, WA
WR   *War of the Rebellion: A Compilation of the Official Records of the Union and Confederate Armies.* Washington, D.C.: U.S. Government Printing Office, 1897

Notes

Chapter 1

1. M. E. Goddard and Henry V. Partridge, *A History of Norwich, Vermont*, p. 3.
2. Ethan Allen Hitchcock, *Fifty Years in Camp and Field: The Diary of Major General Ethan Allen Hitchcock*, ed. W. A. Croffut, p. 9.
3. Goddard and Partridge, *History of Norwich*, pp. 11–14.
4. Ibid., pp. 4–11, 19–32, 231–33, 250–51.
5. Ibid., pp. 33–41.
6. Ibid., pp. 35, 54–55.
7. Norwich Historical Society, Norwich, Vt., letter to author; July 25, 1976.
8. Ibid.
9. Goddard and Partridge, *History of Norwich*, pp. 250–51.
10. Transcribed from monument.
11. L. C. Aldrich and F. R. Holmes, *History of Windsor County, Vermont, with Illustrations and Biographical Sketches of Some of Its Prominent Men and Pioneers*, p. 500.
12. Register of Births and Deaths, Norwich Town Hall, Norwich, Vt.
13. George W. Cullum, *Biographical Register of Officers and Graduates of the U.S. Military Academy, West Point, New York*. 1:288–90.
14. NA, USMA, M 688.
15. Stephen E. Ambrose, *Duty, Honor, Country: A History of West Point*, pp. 1–86.
16. Lester A. Webb, *Captain Alden Partridge and the United States Military Academy, 1806–33*, pp. 33–155.
17. Goddard and Partridge, *History of Norwich*, pp. 232–33.
18. R. Ernest Dupuy, "Mutiny at West Point," *American Heritage* (December 1955): 22–27.
19. G. M. Dodge and W. A. Ellis, *Norwich University, 1819–1911: Her History, Her Graduates, Her Roll of Honor*, 1:1–141.
20. James T. Adams, *Dictionary of American History*, 3:398.

21. Hitchcock, *Fifty Years*, pp. 48–49.
22. Dupuy, "Mutiny at West Point."
23. Edward S. Wallace, *General William Jenkins Worth: Monterey's Forgotten Hero*, pp. 15–30.
24. Hitchcock, *Fifty Years*, pp. 50–51, 71.
25. NA, AGO, LR, M 567, roll 5.

Chapter 2

1. Ronald H. McRae, "The Third Regiment of Infantry," in Thomas F. Rodenbaugh and William L. Haskin, eds., *The Army of the United States: Historical Sketches of Staff and Line with Portraits of Generals-in-Chief*, pp. 432–51.
2. Louise P. Kellogg, "Old Fort Howard," *Wisconsin Magazine of History* 18 (December, 1934): 125–40.
3. Ibid.
4. Deborah B. Martin, *History of Brown County, Wisconsin, Past and Present*, 1:140–42.
5. Albert G. Ellis, "Fifty-four Years' Recollections of Men and Events in Wisconsin" [MS], 1876, WiHS, 7:207–208.
6. *American Military History, 1607–1958: ROTC Manual*, pp. 157–58.
7. Dodge and Ellis, *Norwich University*, 2:259.
8. NA, AGO, RLR, M 711, roll 5.
9. Francis Paul Prucha, *A Guide to the Military Posts of the United States, 1789–1895*, p. 8.
10. Harry E. Mitchell, "History of Jefferson Barracks" [MS], MHS.
11. Hitchcock, *Fifty Years*, pp. 42–47.
12. Mitchell, "History of Jefferson Barracks."
13. Henry W. Webb, "The Story of Jefferson Barracks" [MS], 1944, MHS.
14. *Missouri Republican* (Saint Louis), April 19, 1827.
15. Elvid Hunt, *History of Fort Leavenworth, 1827–1927*, pp. 12–27.
16. Andrew J. Turner, "History of Fort Winnebago" [MS] 1898, WiHS, 14:65–102.
17. William H. Egle, *Pennsylvania Genealogies: Chiefly Scottish-Irish and German*, pp. 246–47.
18. Ibid., pp. 248–50&n.
19. *Nelson's History of Erie County, Pennsylvania, Containing a History of the County, Its Townships, Towns, Villages, Schools, Churches, etc.*, pp. 172–216, 503–55.

20. Egle, *Pennsylvania Genealogies*, pp. 248–49.

21. Nelson, *History of Erie County, Pennsylvania*, pp. 293–311.

22. Letters to author from Historical Society of Pennsylvania, Philadelphia, Pa.; Erie County Historical Society, Erie, Pa.; Dauphin County Historical Society, Harrisburg, Pa.; National Genealogical Society, Washington, D.C.; the Very Reverend A. E. Mintz, Dean, Saint Stephens Episcopal Cathedral, Harrisburg, Pa.; the Very Reverend H. R. Murray, Dean, Cathedral of Saint Paul, Erie, Pa.; E. B. Hawkins [great-grandson of George Wright]; and W. H. Forster [descendant of Mrs. Margaret Wright's family].

Chapter 3

1. U.S. Congress, House, 16th Cong., 2d sess., Ex. Doc. 110 (1820), pp. 167–69.

2. Hiram M. Chittenden, *The American Fur Trade of the Far West*, 1:346–48, 2:950–51.

3. Frederick W. Hodge, ed., *Handbook of American Indians North of Mexico;* Bureau of American Ethnology Bulletin 30, 2:213–16.

4. George E. Hyde, *The Pawnee Indians*, Foreword by Savoie Lottinville, pp. 83–104.

5. Francis B. Heitman, *Historical Register and Dictionary of the United States Army, 1789–1903*, 1:177.

6. NA, AGO, M 567, roll 48 [Wright's journal of the Council Bluffs expedition]. Material in the following paragraphs is taken from this source.

7. Dale L. Morgan, ed., *The West of William H. Ashley, 1822–1838*, pp. 181, 194.

8. Chittenden, *The American Fur Trade*, 1:391–92.

9. Morgan, *The West of William H. Ashley*, pp. 82, 98, 252.

10. Hodge, ed., *Handbook*, 2:215.

11. Hyde, *Pawnee Indians*, pp. 184–87, 359.

12. Hunt, *History of Fort Leavenworth*, 1926, p. 27.

Chapter 4

1. Mitchell, "History of Jefferson Barracks."

2. Dodge and Ellis, *Norwich University*, 2:458–59.

3. NA, AGO, M 711, roll 7.

4. Charles H. Wadsworth, *An Address Delivered in Calvary Church, San Francisco, on the Occasion of the Funeral Services of Gen-*

eral George Wright, pp. 1–12 (hereafter *Wright Funeral Address*), [courtesy Bancroft Library, Berkeley, Calif.].

5. J. Fair Hardin, "Fort Jesup, Fort Selden, Camp Sabine, Camp Salubrity: Four Forgotten Frontier Army Posts of Western Louisiana," *Louisiana Historical Quarterly* 16 (January–October, 1933): 5–16, 279–92, 441–53.

6. Ibid., pp. 5–26.

7. NA, AGO, M 567, roll 102.

8. Hardin, "Fort Jesup," pp. 279–92.

9. NA, AGO, M 567, roll 115.

10. Hardin, "Fort Jesup," pp. 441–53.

11. NA, AGO, M 711, roll 10.

12. Cullum, *Biographical Register*, 1 : 288.

13. NA, AGO, M 711, roll 10.

14. Record of Births and Deaths, Norwich Town Hall.

15. B. Hutchinson, *The Struggle for the Border*, pp. 266–88.

16. NA, AGO, M 567, roll 155.

17. NA, AGO, M 567, roll 178.

18. NA, AGO, M 567, roll 150.

19. Thomas Wilhelm, *History of the Eighth U.S. Infantry from Its Organization in 1838*. 1 : 9–17.

20. Gordon G. Heiner, Jr., *From Saints to Redlegs: Madison Barracks, the History of a Border Post*, pp. 1–35.

21. Wallace, *General William Jenkins Worth*, pp. 44–46.

22. Kentucky Historical Society, Frankfort, letter to author, May 15, 1968.

23. Wilhelm, *History of the Eighth U.S. Infantry*, pp. 19–20.

24. NA, AGO, M 567, roll 220.

25. Heiner, *Saints to Redlegs*, pp. 37–39.

26. Ibid., p. 39.

27. NA, AGO, M 567, roll 221.

28. Wilhelm, *History of the Eighth U.S. Infantry*, pp. 24–28.

29. NA, AGO, G. Wright, SR.

Chapter 5

1. Hodge, ed., *Handbook*, 2 : 500–502.

2. Edwin C. McReynolds, *The Seminoles*, pp. 76–78.

3. J. K. Mahon, *History of the Second Seminole War, 1835–1842*, pp. 42–49.

4. Ibid., pp. 104–106.

5. Ibid., pp. 321–25.

6. William Hartley and Ellen Hartley, *Osceola: the Unconquered Indian*, p. 193.

7. Hitchcock, *Fifty Years*, p. 129.

8. Mahon, *History of the Second Seminole War*, pp. 261–63.

9. Hitchcock, *Fifty Years*, p. 174n.

10. Ibid., p. 120.

11. Wilson, "The Eighth Regiment of Infantry," pp. 511–13.

12. NA, AGO, M 567, roll 202.

13. NA, AGO, M 567, roll 263.

14. NA, AGO, M 711, roll 14.

15. John T. Sprague, *The Origin, Progress and Conclusion of the Florida War: Facsimile Reproduction of 1848 Edition*, pp. 247–83.

16. NA, AGO, M 567, roll 262.

17. NA, AGO, M 567, rolls 243, 244.

18. NA, AGO, M 567, rolls 260, 261.

19. Sprague, *Origin*, pp. 352, 363–64, 375.

20. NA, AGO, M 567, rolls 260, 261.

21. Sprague, *Origin*, p. 376.

22. Ibid., pp. 437–38.

23. Mahon, *History of the Second Seminole War*, p. 318.

24. NA, AGO, M 567, roll 261.

25. Mahon, *History of the Second Seminole War*, pp. 307–15.

26. NA, AGO, M 567, roll 261.

27. Hitchcock, *Fifty Years*, p. 163.

28. Heiner, *Saints to Redlegs*, p. 40.

29. Mahon, *History of the Second Seminole War*, pp. 315–17.

30. Ibid., pp. 321–25.

31. Cullum, *Biographical Register*, 1:289.

32. Sprague, *Origin*, pp. 554–55.

33. NA, AGO, M 711, roll 16.

34. NA, AGO, M 567, roll 243.

35. Dodge and Ellis, *Norwich University*, 2:458.

36. NA, AGO, M 711, rolls 17, 18.

Chapter 6

1. Horatio O. Ladd, *History of the War with Mexico*, p. 322.

2. Wallace, *General William Jenkins Worth*, pp. 67–71.

3. Hitchcock, *Fifty Years*, p. 204.

4. James K. Polk, *Diary of a President, 1845–1849: Covering the Mexican War, Acquisition of Oregon, Conquest of California and the Southwest*, ed. Allan Nevins, p. 67.

5. Wilson, "Eighth Regiment of Infantry," pp. 513–14.
6. Ibid., p. 514.
7. De Voto, Bernard, *The Year of Decision, 1846*, pp. 291–93.
8. Wallace, *General William Jenkins Worth*, pp. 72–139.
9. NA, AGO, M 567, roll 330.
10. Wilhelm, *History of the Eighth U.S. Infantry*, p. 303.
11. George L. Rives, *United States and Mexico*, 2:357–67.
12. Wilhelm, *History of the Eighth U.S. Infantry*, pp. 303, 362.
13. NA, AGO, M 567, roll 360.
14. Wallace, *General William Jenkins Worth*, p. 128.
15. Wilhelm, *History of the Eighth U.S. Infantry*, pp. 361–62.
16. NA, AGO, M 567, roll 360.
17. Wallace, *General William Jenkins Worth*, pp. 138–40.
18. NA, AGO, M 567, roll 359.
19. NA, AGO, M 567, roll 359.
20. Wilson, "Eighth Regiment of Infantry," p. 517.
21. NA, AGO, M 567, roll 359.
22. NA, AGO, G. Wright, SR.
23. J. H. Smith, *The War with Mexico*, 2:118.
24. Hitchcock, *Fifty Years*, p. 298.
25. Samuel E. Chamberlain, *My Confession*, pp. 226–28.
26. NA, AGO, M 567, roll 359.
27. K. D. Richards, *Isaac I. Stevens: Young Man in a Hurry*, p. 293.
28. NA, AGO, M 567, roll 359.
29. Smith, *The War with Mexico*, 2:144–47.
30. Hitchcock, *Fifty Years*, pp. 297–98.
31. Wallace, *General William Jenkins Worth*, pp. 159–62.
32. Smith, *The War with Mexico*, 2:318–19.
33. NA, AGO, G. Wright, SR.
34. Wallace, *General William Jenkins Worth*, pp. 172–85.

Chapter 7

1. NA, AGO, M 711, roll 21.
2. NA, AGO, G. Wright, SR.
3. NA, AGO, M 711, roll 21.
4. Wilson, "Eighth Regiment of Infantry," p. 519.
5. NA, AGO, G. Wright, SR.
6. William H. Powell, *A History of the Organization and Movements of the Fourth Regiment of Infantry, United States Army, from*

May 30, 1796, to December 30, 1870, Together with a Record of the Military Services of All Officers Who at Any Time Belonged to the Regiment, p. 41.

7. NA, AGO, M 711, roll 21.
8. NA, AGO, G. Wright, SR.
9. Hutchinson, *The Struggle for the Border*, pp. 306–16.
10. NA, AGO, M 567, roll 419.
11. NA, AGO, M 567, roll 420.
12. USMA, RC.
13. USMA, SLB, no. 2.
14. NA, AGO, M 567, roll 439.
15. NA, AGO, M 711, roll 23.
16. USMA, SLB, no. 2.
17. NA, AGO, M 567, roll 439.
18. NA, AGO, M 567, roll 455.
19. NA, AGO, M 567, roll 474.
20. NA, AGO, M 567, roll 456.
21. NA, AGO, M 567, roll 474.

Chapter 8

1. Hubert Howe Bancroft, *History of California*, in *Works*, 6:1–42, 251–351.
2. Ibid., 7:474–94.
3. NA, AGO, M 567, roll 475.
4. Bancroft, *History of California*, in *Works*, 7:445–60.
5. Ibid., pp. 460–61.
6. Ibid., p. 477.
7. Robert W. Frazer, *Forts of the West: Military Forts and Presidios and Posts Commonly Called Forts West of the Mississippi River to 1898*, p. 29.
8. Rosena A. Giles, *Shasta County, California: A History*, p. 122.
9. Edward Peterson, "In the Shadow of the Mountain: A Short History of Shasta County, California" [MS], 1965, Shasta County Library, Redding, Calif., p. 162.
10. Gertrude A. Steger, *Place Names of Shasta County*, p. 75.
11. May Hazel Southern, *Our Storied Landmarks, Shasta County, California*, p. 100.
12. V. H. Dunlap, "Fort Reading Ranch and the Hawes Family," in *Covered Wagon* (Shasta County Historical Society, Redding, Calif., 1963), pp. 22–24.

13. Mae H. B. Boggs, *My Playhouse Was a Concord Coach: An Anthology of Newspaper Clippings and Documents Relating to Those Who Made California History During the Years 1822–1888*, p. 763.

14. Dunlap, "Fort Reading Ranch," pp. 22–24.

15. Bancroft, *History of California*, in *Works*, 7 : 489–90.

16. Returns from U.S. Military Posts, 1800–1916, NA, M 617, roll 993 (Camp Reading, Calif.), May, 1852–June, 1867.

17. NA, AGO, M 567, roll 507.

18. Records of Quartermaster General Consolidated, 1794–1890, Transcription of Archives Concerning Fort Reading, 1852–1860, trans. Dorothy Holt, NA, RG 92, Shasta County Museum, Redding, Calif.

19. NA, AGO, M 567, roll 242.

20. NA, AGO, M 567, roll 530.

21. NA, AGO, M 711, roll 25.

22. *Daily Alta California* (San Francisco), March 30, 1853.

23. *Shasta Courier* (Shasta, Calif.), April 2, 1853.

24. Hitchcock, *Fifty Years*, p. 395.

25. NA, AGO, M 567, roll 491.

26. Bancroft, *History of California*, in *Works*, 7 : 462.

27. Returns from U.S. Military Posts, NA, M 617, roll 993.

28. Hitchcock, *Fifty Years*, pp. 400–403.

29. Bancroft, *History of California*, in *Works*, 6 : 583–603.

30. Ibid., 7 : 462.

31. Mansfield Report on Fort Reading, NA, AGO, RG 94, Manuscript File no. 282.

32. NA, AGO, M 567, roll 508.

33. Giles, *Shasta County*, p. 37.

34. Bancroft, *History of California*, 7 : 464.

35. NA, AGO, G. Wright, SR.

36. *Shasta Courier*, April 14, 1855.

37. USMA, Post Order Book no. 4, 1852–56.

38. Dodge and Ellis, *Norwich University*, 2 : 458.

39. Albert Z. Carr, *The World and William Walker*, pp. 1–221.

40. Ibid., pp. 225–74.

41. Dodge and Ellis, *Norwich University*, p. 459.

Chapter 9

1. NA, AGO, M 567, roll 530.

2. E. B. Robertson, "The Ninth Regiment of Infantry," in

T. F. Rodenbaugh and W. L. Haskin, eds., *The Army of the United States*, pp. 526–27.

3. Bancroft, *History of California*, in *Works*, 7:464n.

4. NA, AGO, M 567, roll 530.

5. NA, AGO, M 567, rolls 530, 531, 550.

6. NA, AGO, M 567, roll 530.

7. NA, AGO, M 567, roll 531.

8. Philip H. Sheridan, *Personal Memoirs of Philip H. Sheridan, General*, 1:71.

9. H. Dean Guie, *Bugles in the Valley: Garnett's Fort Simcoe*, pp. 25–27.

10. Hazard Stevens, *The Life of Isaac Ingalls Stevens*, 1:231.

11. Priscilla Knuth, "Picturesque Frontier: The Army's Fort Dalles," *OHQ* 67 (December, 1966): 293–346; ibid., 68 (March, 1967): 5–52.

12. J. Ross Browne, *Letter to Commissioner of Indian Affairs*, 35th Cong., 1st sess., S. Ex. Doc. 40 (1857), pp. 2–13.

13. Edmund S. Meany, *History of the State of Washington*, pp. 177–79.

14. Lucullus V. McWhorter, *Tragedy of the Wahk-Shum*, pp. 1–16.

15. Frances F. Victor, *The Early Indian Wars of Oregon*, pp. 425–27.

16. Meany, *History of the State of Washington*, pp. 180–84.

17. George W. Fuller, *History of the Pacific Northwest*, pp. 225–27.

18. Wilfred P. Schoenberg, *A Chronicle of Catholic History of the Pacific Northwest, 1743–1960*, p. 38.

19. Denys Nelson, ed., "With the Oblates in Old Oregon" [MS], 1926, Gonzaga University Archives, Spokane, Wash.

20. Sheridan, *Personal Memoirs*, 1:70.

21. Rodney Glisan, *Journal of Army Life*, p. 327.

22. Fuller, *History of the Pacific Northwest*, pp. 228–29.

23. R. I. Burns, *The Jesuits and the Indian Wars of the Northwest*, p. 129.

24. Browne, *Letter to Commissioner of Indian Affairs*, p. 2.

25. Thomas Phelps, *Reminiscences of Seattle, Washington Territory, and of the Sloop-of-War* Decatur *During the Indian War of 1855–1856*, pp. 9–38.

26. Isaac I. Stevens, quoted in W. E. Rosebush, *Frontier Steel: The Men and Their Weapons*, p. 196.

27. Stevens, *The Life of Isaac Ingalls Stevens*, 2:191.

28. Ibid., 2:149–75.

29. George Wright and George Curry, Correspondence, in *Journal of the House of Representatives of the Territory of Oregon During the Eighth Regular Session, 1856–1857*, app., pp. 44–48.

30. William N. Bischoff, *We Were Not Summer Soldiers: The Indian War Diary of Plympton J. Kelly, 1855–1856*, p. 47.

31. Kent D. Richards, *Isaac I. Stevens: Young Man in a Hurry*, p. 291.

32. Fuller, *History of the Pacific Northwest*, p. 233.

33. Bischoff, *We Were Not Summer Soldiers*, p. 47.

34. Sheridan, *Personal Memoirs*, 1:72–84.

35. Richards, *Isaac I. Stevens*, p. 292.

36. Ibid., pp. 262–310.

37. William C. Brown, *The Indian Side of the Story*, pp. 6–7.

38. Burns, *The Jesuits*, p. 28.

39. Isaac I. Stevens, *Messages of the Governor of Washington Territory; Also the Correspondence with the Secretary of War, Major General Wool, the Officers of the Regular Army and of the Volunteer Service of Washington Territory*, p. 82.

40. Ibid., p. 170.

41. NA, AGO, M 567, roll 551.

42. Richards, *Isaac I. Stevens*, p. 295.

43. NA, AGO, M 567, roll 545.

44. NA, AGO, M 567, roll 541.

45. NA, AGO, M 567, roll 545.

46. Stevens, *Messages of the Governor*, p. 199.

47. Richards, *Isaac I. Stevens*, p. 310.

48. Della G. Emmons, *Leschi of the Nisquallies*, pp. 345–47, 355–56, 410–11.

49. NA, AGO, M 567, roll 545.

50. Richards, *Isaac I. Stevens*, p. 298.

51. NA, AGO, M 567, roll 545.

52. NA, AGO, M 567, roll 545.

53. NA, AGO, M 567, roll 545.

54. Glisan, *Journal of Army Life*, p. 367.

55. Knuth, "Picturesque Frontier," pp. 8–9.

56. NA, AGO, M 567, roll 545.

57. Richards, *Isaac I. Stevens*, pp. 306–307.

58. Stevens, *Messages of the Governor*, pp. 90–91.

59. NA, AGO, M 567, roll 545.

60. NA, AGO, M 567, roll 545.

61. Victor, *The Early Indian Wars of Oregon*, pp. 423–24.
62. Browne, Letter to Commissioner of Indian Affairs, p. 4.
63. NA, AGO, M 567, roll 545.
64. Guie, *Bugles in the Valley*, p. 53.
65. NA, AGO, M 567, roll 545.
66. Richards, *Isaac I. Stevens*, p. 307.
67. Heitman, *Historical Register*, 1 : 763.
68. Jerome Peltier, *War Bonnets and Epaulets*, pp. 349–60.
69. P. Knuth, letter to author, May 16, 1969.
70. E. J. Harvie, quoted in Fred R. Brown, *History of the Ninth U.S. Infantry, 1779–1909*, p. 73.
71. James J. Archer, quoted by Guie, *Bugles in the Valley*, pp. 51–52.
72. *Statistics of First Federal Census of Washington Territory, 1860*, comp. and indexed by Mrs. John B. Moyer, Eastern Washington State Historical Society, Spokane, Wash., 1931–2.
73. Egle, *Pennsylvania Genealogies*, p. 261.
74. Sheridan, *Personal Memoirs*, 1 : 121.
75. WR, ser. 1, vol. 50, pt. 2, p. 1273.
76. NA, AGO, M 711, roll 28.
77. USMA, CAP, 1859.
78. G. B. Dandy, quoted in Garrett B. Hunt, *Indian Wars of the Inland Empire*, p. 95.
79. I. G. T., "Indian Campaign in the North," *Overland Monthly* 4, (October, 1884): 399.
80. Fuller, *History of the Pacific Northwest*, p. 237.
81. Ibid., p. 242.
82. Knuth, "Picturesque Frontier," pp. 40–41.
83. Guie, *Bugles in the Valley*, pp. 62–63, 72.
84. McWhorter, *Tragedy of the Wahk-Shum*, p. 15.
85. Guie, *Bugles in the Valley*, p. 64.
86. Robertson, "The Ninth Regiment of Infantry," p. 527.

Chapter 10

1. Benjamin F. Manring, *The Conquest of the Coeur d'Alenes, Spokanes, and Palouses: The Expeditions of Colonels E. J. Steptoe and George Wright Against the "Northern Indians" in 1858*, pp. 264–74.
2. *Message from the President of the United States*, vol. 2, 35th Cong., 2d sess. H. Ex. Doc. 2 (1858), pp. 331–36.
3. Louis C. Coleman and Leo Rieman, *Captain John Mullan:*

His Life; Building the Mullan Road; As It Is Today and Interesting Tales of Occurrences Along the Road, pp. 8–45.

4. John Mullan, *Topographical Memoir and Map of Col. George Wright's Late Campaign Against the Hostile Northern Indians in Oregon and Washington Territories,* in Report of the Secretary of War, 35th Cong., 2d sess. S. Ex. Doc. 32 (1859), pp. 3–10.

5. *Message from the President of the United States,* pp. 341–42.

6. Burns, *The Jesuits,* pp. 164–66.

7. Hiram M. Chittenden and Alfred T. Richardson, eds., *Life, Letters, and Travels of Father Pierre-Jean De Smet, S.J., 1801–1873,* 1:67–68.

8. *Message from the President of the United States,* p. 336.

9. Ibid., pp. 337–39.

10. Ibid., pp. 344–45.

11. Ibid., p. 345.

12. NA, AGO, M 711, roll 30.

13. Peltier, *Warbonnets and Epaulets,* pp. 79–118.

14. *Message from the President of the United States,* pp. 344–54.

15. Burns, *The Jesuits,* p. 224.

16. Rosebush, *Frontier Steel,* p. 210.

17. *Message from the President of the United States,* pp. 346–48. Steptoe's comments in the following paragraphs are taken from this source.

18. Richards, *Isaac I. Stevens,* pp. 299–300.

19. Burns, *The Jesuits,* p. 205.

20. Ibid., p. 228.

21. *Message from the President of the United States,* pp. 354–60.

22. Rosebush, *Frontier Steel,* p. 223.

23. David M. Gregg, Letter, quoted in Hunt, *Indian Wars,* pp. 27–30.

24. Brown, *The Indian Side of the Story,* p. 193.

25. Rowland Bond, *Early Birds in the Northwest: One Hundred Years of Western History from Jacques Raphael Finlay to Dutch Jake Goetz,* pp. 78–88.

26. Burns, *The Jesuits,* pp. 223, 230, 234.

27. *Message from the President of the United States,* p. 349.

28. Manring, *The Conquest of the Coeur d'Alenes, Spokanes, and Palouses,* p. 133n.

29. *Message from the President of the United States,* p. 359.

30. Ibid., p. 348.

31. Ibid., p. 350.

32. Burns, *The Jesuits*, p. 239.
33. *Message from the President of the United States*, pp. 350–51.
34. Ibid., p. 352.
35. Ibid., p. 349.
36. Richards, *Isaac I. Stevens*, pp. 331–32.
37. *Message from the President of the United States*, p. 353.
38. L. V. Reavis, *The Life and Military Services of General William Selby Harney*, pp. 19, 275–80 (hereafter *Life of Harney*).
39. *Message from the President of the United States*, pp. 361–63.
40. Ibid., pp. 363–64.
41. Ibid., pp. 364–65.
42. Ibid., pp. 369–71.
43. Guie, *Bugles in the Valley*, p. 126.
44. *Message from the President of the United States*, pp. 366–67.
45. Ibid., pp. 367–68.
46. Ibid., pp. 372–77.
47. Lawrence Kip, *Army Life on the Pacific: A Journal of the Expedition Against the Northern Indians: The Tribes of the Coeur d'Alenes, Spokans, Pelouzes, in the Summer of 1858*, p. 24.
48. Erasmus D. Keyes, *Fifty Years' Observation of Men and Events, Civil and Military*, pp. 266, 285.
49. George B. Dandy, quoted in ibid., pp. 284–85.
50. Kip, *Army Life on the Pacific*, p. 40.
51. *Message from the President of the United States*, p. 381.
52. Kip, *Army Life on the Pacific*, pp. 41–42.
53. *Message from the President of the United States*, p. 384.
54. Ibid., p. 383.
55. Burns, *The Jesuits*, pp. 276–77.
56. Kip, *Army Life on the Pacific*, p. 43.
57. NA, AGO, M 567, roll 586.
58. I. G. T., "Indian Campaign in the North," p. 399.
59. Burns, *The Jesuits*, pp. 273–75.
60. *Message from the President of the United States*, pp. 386–90, 390–93.
61. Kip, *Army Life on the Pacific*, pp. 51–72.
62. Keyes, *Fifty Years' Observation*, pp. 266–85.
63. Dandy, quoted in Hunt, *Indian Wars*, pp. 91–92.
64. Burns, *The Jesuits*, p. 293.
65. Keyes, *Fifty Years' Observation*, p. 275.
66. *Message from the President of the United States*, pp. 386–90.
67. Kip, *Army Life on the Pacific*, pp. 55–56.

68. Brown, *The Indian Side of the Story*, pp. 236–37.
69. Mullan, *Topographical Memoir*, p. 32.
70. *Message from the President of the United States*, pp. 390–93.
71. Dandy, quoted in Hunt, *Indian Wars*, p. 93.
72. *Message from the President of the United States*, pp. 390–93.
73. Ibid., p. 390.
74. Burns, *The Jesuits*, p. 297.
75. P. Joset, letter quoted in Chittenden and Richardson, eds., *Life of Father De Smet*, 2 : 755.
76. Mullan, *Topographical Memoir*, p. 30.
77. Keyes, *Fifty Years' Observation*, pp. 282–83.
78. *Message from the President of the United States*, pp. 393–94.
79. Ibid., p. 394.
80. Ibid., p. 363.
81. Kip, *Army Life on the Pacific*, p. 71.
82. Keyes, *Fifty Years' Observation*, pp. 272–73.
83. *Message from the President of the United States*, p. 395.
84. Ibid., p. 396.
85. Ibid., pp. 397–98.
86. Ibid., p. 362.
87. Burns, *The Jesuits*, p. 301.
88. *Message from the President of the United States*, p. 399.
89. Ibid., p. 400.
90. Mullan, *Topographical Memoir*, pp. 67–68.
91. *Message from the President of the United States*, p. 401.
92. Mullan, *Topographical Memoir*, p. 71.
93. *Message from the President of the United States*, p. 402.
94. Ibid., pp. 403–404.
95. Morgan, quoted in Hunt, *Indian Wars*, p. 101.
96. NA, AGO, M 567, roll 577.
97. NA, AGO, M 567, roll 577.
98. Kip, *Army Life on the Pacific*, p. 128.
99. Christopher Mott, quoted by Burns, *The Jesuits*, p. 326.
100. NA, AGO, M 567, roll 577.
101. NA, AGO, M 567, roll 577.
102. *Message from the President of the United States*, pp. 371–72.
103. George Crook, quoted by Guie, *Bugles in the Valley*, p. 121.
104. A. J. Splawn, *Ka-mi-akin, Last Hero of the Yakimas*, p. 104.
105. R. S. Garnett, quoted by Guie, *Bugles in the Valley*, p. 125.
106. *Message from the President of the United States*, pp. 405–13. Subsequent quotations from Clarke's account are taken from this source.

107. Ibid., pp. 23–25.
108. Ibid., pp. 3–4.
109. *Weekly Alta California* (San Francisco, Calif.), October 20, 1860.
110. Wadsworth, *Wright Funeral Address*, p. 5.
111. Francine Donner, *Spokane Sampler: Historical Poems and Others*, pp. 7–14.
112. Brown, *The Indian Side of the Story*, p. 316.
113. Knuth, "Picturesque Frontier," p. 42.
114. Bancroft, *History of Washington, Idaho and Montana, 1845–1889*, in *Works*, 31:176.
115. Victor, *Early Indian Wars in Oregon*, pp. v, 499.
116. Benjamin Capps, *The Indians*, p. 47.
117. Reavis, *Life of Harney*, p. 280.

1. Reavis, *Life of Harney*, p. 280.
2. J. P. Dunn, Jr., *Massacres of the Mountains: A History of the Indian Wars of the Far West*, pp. 219–44.
3. Keyes, *Fifty Years' Observation*, p. 288.
4. Chittenden and Richardson, eds., *Life of Father De Smet*, 2:731–45.
5. Burns, *The Jesuits*, pp. 340–44.
6. Mott, quoted in ibid., p. 333.
7. *Message from the President of the United States*, pp. 413–14.
8. Ibid., pp. 414–15.
9. Reavis, *Life of Harney*, p. 294.
10. Guie, *Bugles in the Valley*, pp. 137–40.
11. Coleman and Rieman, *Captain John Mullan*, pp. 25–45.
12. Fuller, *History of the Pacific Northwest*, pp. 316–17.
13. Reavis, *Life of Harney*, pp. 292–94, 300–10.
14. Keith A. Murray, *The Pig War*, pp. 18–19.
15. John A. Hussey, *The History of Fort Vancouver and Its Physical Structure*, pp. 91–114.
16. NA, AGO, M 567, roll 629.
17. Mary McCrosson, *The Bell and the River*, pp. 100–36.
18. C. P. Schlicke, "Nun in Statuary Hall," *Pacific Northwesterner* 24 (Summer, 1980): 42.
19. Fuller, *History of the Pacific Northwest*, pp. 176–79.
20. Meany, *History of Washington*, pp. 240–54.
21. Murray, *The Pig War*, pp. 25–66.

22. NA, AGO, M 567, roll 629.
23. David Richardson, *Pig War Islands*, pp. 143–58.
24. NA, AGO, M 567, roll 629.
25. NA, AGO, M 567, roll 636.
26. U.S. Congress, House, 36th Cong., 2d sess., Ex. Doc. 46 (1860), pp. 5–9 (reprint, Fairfield, Wash.: Ye Galleon Press, 1966).
27. NA, AGO, M 567, roll 629.
28. U.S. Congress, House, Ex. Doc. 46, p. 16.
29. NA, AGO, M 567, roll 629.
30. U.S. Congress, House, Ex. Doc. 46, p. 16.
31. U.S. Congress, House, 36th Cong., 2d sess., Ex. Doc. 29 (1860), pp. 86–90.
32. U.S. Congress, House, Ex. Doc. 46, p. 13.
33. U.S. Congress, House, Ex. Doc. 29, p. 81.
34. U.S. Congress, House, Ex. Doc. 46, p. 11.
35. Fuller, *History of the Pacific Northwest*, p. 261.
36. U.S. Congress, *House*, Ex. Doc. 46, p. 14.
37. NA, AGO, M 567, roll 629.
38. U.S. Congress, House, Ex. Doc. 46, p. 11.
39. J. A. Peltier, "The Ward Massacre," *Pacific Northwesterner* 9 (Winter, 1965): 12–16.
40. NA, AGO, M 567, roll 629.

Chapter 12

1. Samuel E. Morison, *The Oxford History of the American People*, pp. 601–704.
2. Carl Sandburg, *Abraham Lincoln: The War Years*, 1:75.
3. Bancroft, *History of California*, in *Works*, 7:275–85.
4. Keyes, *Fifty Years' Observation*, pp. 420–21.
5. Stanley Francis Crocchiola, *E. V. Sumner, Major General, United States Army, 1797–1863*, pp. 21, 34.
6. M. C. George, "Address Delivered at Dedication of Grand Ronde Military Blockhouse at Dayton City Park, Oregon, August 23, 1912," *OHQ* 15 (March, 1914): 64.
7. *WR*, ser. 1, vol. 50, pt. 1, p. 799.
8. Aurora Hunt, *The Army of the Pacific, 1860–1866*, pp. 26–27, 359.
9. *WR*, ser. 1, vol. 50, pt. 1, p. 512.
10. Letter from Wright, May 3, 1861, James A. Hardie Papers, Library of Congress, Manuscript Division.

11. NA, AGO, M 619, roll 68, W 612.
12. NA, AGO, M 619, roll 68, W 612.
13. G. Wright, Letter to Nesmith, *OHQ* 15 (1914): 133, Nesmith Collection, Oregon Historical Society, Portland.
14. Ezra J. Warner, *Generals in Blue: Lives of the Union Commanders,* pp. 574–75.
15. *WR,* ser. 1, vol. 50, pt. 1, p. 430.
16. Ibid., pp. 575–77, 579–93.
17. Ibid., p. 24.
18. Ibid., pp. 527–32.
19. Ibid., pp. 730–31.
20. Ibid., p. 604.
21. Hunt, *The Army of the Pacific,* pp. 52–54.
22. *WR,* ser. 1, vol. 50, pt. 1, p. 572.
23. Ibid., pp. 613, 633.
24. Ibid., pp. 643–48.
25. Ibid., pp. 607–609.
26. Ibid., p. 643.
27. Ibid., pp. 658, 666.
28. Crocchiola, *E. V. Sumner,* pp. 243–90.
29. *WR,* ser. 1, vol. 50, pt. 1, p. 645.
30. G. Wright, letter to Sumner, October 26, 1861, Spokane Public Library, Spokane, Wash.
31. *WR,* ser. 1, vol. 50, pt. 1, p. 685.
32. NA, AGO, G. Wright, SR.
33. *WR,* ser. 1, vol. 50, pt. 1, p. 730.
34. Letter from Wright, November 29, 1861, Hardie Papers, LC.
35. Hunt, *The Army of the Pacific,* pp. 105–108.
36. *WR,* ser. 1, vol. 50, pt. 1, p. 678.
37. Ibid., pp. 679–87.
38. Ibid., pp. 689–717.
39. Hunt, *The Army of the Pacific,* pp. 70–76.
40. *WR,* ser. 1, vol. 50, pt. 1, pp. 750–63.
41. Ibid., p. 735.
42. Ibid., pp. 791, 827, 836.
43. Ibid., p. 720.
44. Hunt, *The Army of the Pacific,* p. 186.
45. *WR,* ser. 1, vol. 50, pt. 1, pp. 690–91.
46. Ibid., pp. 717–18.
47. Ibid., pp. 766–68, 825–26.
48. Ibid., pp. 988–93, 1012–13, 1030–33.

49. Ibid., pp. 1047–48.
50. Ibid., pp. 760–938.

Chapter 13

1. *WR*, ser. 1, vol. 50, pt. 1, p. 982.
2. Hunt, *The Army of the Pacific*, pp. 58–61.
3. *WR*, ser. 1, vol. 50, pt. 1, pp. 917–18, 944–45.
4. Ibid., pp. 89–90, 939, 951, 966.
5. Ibid., pp. 880–94, 920.
6. Ibid., pp. 873–74.
7. Ibid., pp. 974, 1042, 1066.
8. Ibid., p. 88–143.
9. Ibid., vol. 9, pp. 557–95.
10. Ibid., vol. 50, pt. 1, pp. 1117–18.
11. Ibid., vol. 50, pt. 2, p. 14.
12. Ibid., pp. 59, 60, 94, 101.
13. Ibid., pt. 1, p. 94; ibid., vol. 9, p. 537.
14. Ibid., vol. 9, pp. 565–94.
15. Ibid., vol. 50, pt. 1, pp. 895–96.
16. G. Wright, Letter to S. A. Parker, BL, September 15, 1862.
17. *WR*, ser. 1, vol. 50, pt. 1, pp. 996–98, 1015.
18. Ibid., pp. 1021, 1149.
19. Ibid., p. 1041.
20. Ibid., p. 1041.
21. Ibid., pt. 2, pp. 125–26.
22. Ibid., pp. 203–205.
23. Ibid., pp. 135, 136, 236–64.
24. Ibid., p. 217.
25. Hunt, *The Army of the Pacific*, pp. 340–41.
26. *WR*, ser. 1, vol. 50, pt. 2, pp. 5–6, 55, 187, 195.
27. Ibid., pp. 61–62, 228–29.
28. Ibid., pt. 1, pp. 177–79.
29. Ibid., pp. 181–82.
30. Ibid., pp. 185–87.
31. Ibid., pt. 2, pp. 244–57.
32. Ibid., pp. 314–15, 331–44.
33. Ibid., pt. 1, pp. 803–804, 842–58, 889, 958–59.
34. Ibid., pp. 906–13, 1133–62.
35. Ibid., pt. 2, pp. 50–51, 58–59, 221–22.
36. Ibid., pt. 1, pp. 955–56, 992, 1091.
37. Ibid., p. 942.

38. Ibid., pp. 1084, 1093, 1096.
39. Ibid., pt. 2, pp. 161–63, 168–70, 184–85.
40. Ibid., pp. 199, 202, 248.
41. Ibid., pp. 219, 250, 290, 661.
42. Lynwood Carranco and Estle Beard, *Genocide and Vendetta: The Round Valley Wars of Northern California,* pp. 101–57.
43. *WR,* ser. 1, vol. 50, pt. 2, p. 301.
44. *Daily Alta California* (San Francisco), January 24, 1863, p. 2, col. 2 [courtesy BL].
45. *WR,* ser. 1, vol. 50, pt. 1, pp. 46–49, 145–53, 935–36.
46. Ibid., p. 1030.
47. Ibid., pt. 2, pp. 153–57.
48. Ibid., pt. 1, pp. 968–69.
49. G. Wright to Justus Steinberger, CSL, June 20, 1862.
50. *WR,* ser. 1, vol. 50, pt. 2, p. 4.
51. Ibid., pp. 7–9.
52. Ibid., pp. 189–90, 210, 268–69.
53. Ibid., pp. 290–91.
54. Ibid., pp. 226–27, 243.
55. Ibid., pt. 1, p. 1077.
56. Ibid., p. 1168.
57. Ibid., pt. 2, pp. 99–101.
58. Ibid., ser. 3, vol. 3, pp. 24–35.
59. Ibid., ser. 1, vol. 50, pt. 2, pp. 89–96, 112, 134–35.
60. Ibid., pt. 1, p. 1099.
61. Ibid., pt. 2, pp. 51–53, 70–73, 97, 117.
62. Sandburg, *Abraham Lincoln: The War Years,* 2:626–27.
63. *WR,* ser. 1, vol. 50, pt. 2, pp. 196–97.
64. John W. Robinson, "The Ordeal of General Wright: A Study of Secessionist Sentiment in California, 1861–1864," in *Westerners Brand Book,* no. 16, pp. 153–57.
65. *WR,* ser. 1, vol. 50, pt. 2, pp. 210–11.

Chapter 14

1. *WR,* ser. 1, vol. 50, pt. 2, p. 514.
2. Ibid., pp. 602, 605.
3. Ibid., p. 316.
4. Hunt, *The Army of the Pacific,* pp. 305–10.
5. *WR,* ser. 1, vol. 50, pt. 2, pp. 357–66.
6. Ibid., ser. 2, vol. 5, p. 726.
7. Ibid., ser. 1, vol. 50, pt. 2, pp. 366, 378, 385.

8. *Sacramento Daily Union,* April 10, 1863, p. 2.
9. *WR,* ser. 1, vol. 50, pt. 2, pp. 453–71.
10. Ibid., pt. 1, pp. 204–208.
11. Ibid., pt. 2, pp. 379–495.
12. Ibid., pp. 655–57, 669.
13. Ibid., pp. 582–84.
14. Ibid., pp. 479–81, 658–59.
15. Ibid., pp. 291–94, 303–305.
16. Ibid., pp. 222, 502, 510, 522.
17. Ibid., pp. 536–42, 620–43, 707–708.
18. Ibid., pp. 551–52, 610, 629.
19. Ibid., pp. 566, 637.
20. Ibid., pt. 1, p. 304.
21. Ibid., pt. 2, pp. 376, 473, 491–92, 535.
22. Ibid., pp. 662–63.
23. Ibid., pp. 469, 473, 508.
24. Ibid., pp. 477, 482.
25. Ibid., pp. 303–57.
26. Ibid., pp. 515–26, 574, 593–96.
27. Sandburg, *Abraham Lincoln: The War Years,* 2:613–17.
28. *WR,* ser. 1, vol. 50, pt. 2, pp. 630, 673–77.
29. Ibid., pp. 294, 686–706.
30. Ibid., pp. 714–823.
31. Hunt, *The Army of the Pacific,* p. 250.
32. *WR,* ser. 1, vol. 50, pt. 2, pp. 681–82.
33. Letter from Wright, May 18, 1863, Hardie Papers, LC.
34. Hunt, *The Army of the Pacific,* pp. 179–80.
35. *WR,* ser. 1, vol. 50, pt. 2, pp. 343–472.
36. Ibid., pp. 633–50.
37. Ibid., pp. 294, 297.
38. Ibid., pp. 300–60.
39. Ibid., pp. 531–74.
40. Ibid., pp. 599–606.
41. Ibid., pp. 322–24, 604–605.
42. Ibid., pp. 677–80.
43. Ibid., pp. 681–95.
44. NA, AGO, newspaper clipping in G. Wright, SR.
45. "Brigadier General George Wright" [editorial], *North Pacific Review* 5 (February 1863) [Courtesy California Historical Society, San Francisco].
46. *American Flag* (Sonora, Calif.), March 19, 1863, p. 3 [courtesy Sutro Library, San Francisco].

47. *Louisville Courier Journal* (Ky.), November 28, 1948 [courtesy Louisville Courier Journal].

Chapter 15

1. *WR*, ser. 1, vol. 34, pt. 2, pp. 256, 671.
2. Ibid., vol. 50, pt. 2, pp. 846–47.
3. Ibid., pp. 904–908.
4. Ibid., pp. 911–12.
5. Hunt, *The Army of the Pacific*, pp. 319–20.
6. *WR*, ser. 1, vol. 50, pt. 2, pp. 715–17, 748–51, 778.
7. Ibid., pp. 899–900, 904.
8. Ibid., pp. 1013, 1036–37.
9. Ibid., pp. 1100–1101.
10. Ibid., pp. 733–53.
11. Ibid., pt. 1, pp. 247–307.
12. Hunt, *The Army of the Pacific*, p. 248n.
13. *WR*, ser. 1, vol. 50, pt. 2, pp. 956–57, 1005–1006.
14. Ibid., pt. 1, p. 395.
15. Ibid., pt. 2, pp. 838, 1102–1103, 1120.
16. Ibid., pp. 674–75, 1076–78.
17. Ibid., p. 819.
18. Ibid., pt. 1, pp. 384–89.
19. Ibid., pt. 2, p. 1072.
20. Ibid., pp. 782–83.
21. Ibid., pp. 788–89.
22. *Daily Alta California*, January 19, 1864, p. 2, col. 1.
23. Ibid., February 18, 1864, p. 1, col. 4.
24. Ibid., in Bancroft, "Scrapbook," April 11, 1864, 30:213, BL.
25. Ibid., June 21, 1864, p. 1, col. 2.
26. Bancroft, "Scrapbook," 30:289–90.
27. *Daily Alta California*, June 26, 1864, in ibid., pp. 213–14.
28. *San Francisco Bulletin*, June 30, 1864, in ibid., p. 105.
29. *Daily Alta California*, July 2, 1864, p. 1, col. 3.
30. *WR*, ser. 1, vol. 50, pt. 2, pp. 886, 915.
31. Bancroft, *History of California*, in *Works*, 7:471.
32. *Los Angeles News*, July 19, 1864.
33. *WR*, ser. 1, vol. 50, pt. 2, p. 945.
34. Ibid., p. 949.
35. *Daily Alta California*, June 27, 1864, p. 1, col. 3.
36. *WR*, ser. 1, vol. 50, pt. 2, pp. 980–81.

37. NA, AGO, G. Wright, SR.
38. Samuel Cross, in Biographical File, CSL.
39. WR, ser. 1, vol. 50, pt. 2, pp. 788–804.
40. Hunt, The Army of the Pacific, p. 180.
41. WR, ser. 1, vol. 50, pt. 2, pp. 800–801.
42. Ibid., pp. 833–34, 839–40.
43. Ibid., p. 915.
44. Ibid., pp. 947–1161.
45. Ibid., pp. 1181–1203.
46. Ibid., p. 1232.
47. Benito Juarez, Decree [broadside], August 11, 1864, BL.
48. G. Wright, letter to R. C. Drum, BL, May 16, 1865.
49. WR, ser. 1, vol. 50, pt. 2, pp. 946, 972–74.
50. Ibid., pp. 413, 747–48, 775–76, 802.
51. Ibid., p. 756.
52. Ibid., pp. 925–1083.
53. Ibid., p. 978.
54. Sacramento Daily Union, November 2, 1864, p. 3, col. 2.
55. NA, AGO, letter in G. Wright, SR.
56. Louisville Courier Journal, November 28, 1948.
57. WR, ser. 1, vol. 50, pt. 2, p. 1109.

Chapter 16

1. Hunt, The Army of the Pacific, p. 341.
2. WR, ser. 1, vol. 50, pt. 2, pp. 1196–1228.
3. Hunt, The Army of the Pacific, p. 349.
4. WR, ser. 1, vol. 50, pt. 2, p. 1201.
5. Ibid., pp. 1210, 1261.
6. Ibid., pp. 1137–38.
7. Ibid., pp. 1184–86.
8. Ibid., pp. 1138–1277.
9. Ibid., pp. 1146–94.
10. Ibid., pp. 1121, 1157, 1161.
11. WR, ser. 1, vol. 50, pt. 1, pp. 403–14.
12. Ibid., pt. 2, p. 1068.
13. Ibid., pp. 1177–83, 1243–44, 1289–90.
14. Ibid., pp. 1279–80.
15. Ibid., pp. 1253–54, 1276–77.
16. Ibid., pp. 1247–48, 1251, 1261–63.
17. Ibid., pp. 1237–39.
18. Ibid., pp. 1268–70.

19. Ibid., pp. 1118–60.
20. Ibid., pp. 1219, 1293.
21. Ibid., pp. 1254–67.
22. *WR*, ser. 1, vol. 50, pt. 2, p. 1268.
23. *Daily Alta California*, July 28, 1865, p. 1, col. 1.
24. Bancroft, *History of California*, in *Works*, 7:471.
25. Warner, *Generals in Blue*, pp. 574–75.
26. Robinson, "The Ordeal of General Wright," pp. 153–70.
27. NA, AGO, M 619, roll 68.
28. Anonymous friend, quoted by Wadsworth, *Wright Funeral Address*, p. 7.

Chapter 17

1. Alfred L. Lomax, "*Brother Jonathan:* Pioneer Steamship of the Pacific Coast," *OHQ* 60 (September, 1959): 330–42.
2. Marie DeWolf, holograph, undated, Del Norte County Historical Society, Crescent City, Calif.
3. Newspaper Clipping Scrapbook, Del Norte County Historical Society, Crescent City, Calif.
4. Lomax, "*Brother Jonathan*," p. 343.
5. E. W. Wright, ed., *Lewis and Dryden's Marine History of the Pacific Northwest*, pp. 131–34.
6. Doris Chase, *Humboldt Times*, December 13, 1959 [courtesy Del Norte County Historical Society].
7. DeWolf, holograph.
8. Doris Chase, letter to author, November 14, 1981.
9. Wright, ed., *Lewis and Dryden's Marine History*, pp. 131–34.
10. Lomax, "*Brother Jonathan*," pp. 343–47.
11. Newspaper Clipping Scrapbook, Del Norte County Historical Society.
12. Ibid.
13. *Sacramento Daily Union* (Calif.), August 24, 1865, p. 2, col. 4.
14. *Union Record* (Oroville, Calif.), August 12, 1865, p. 3, col. 2.
15. *Daily Oregonian* (Portland, Oreg.), August 2, 1865.
16. *San Francisco Evening Bulletin*, August 2, 1865, p. 3, col. 4.
17. *Daily Alta California*, August 2, 1865, p. 1, col. 3.
18. Ibid., August 3, 1865, p. 1, col. 3.
19. Samuel Bowles, *Across the Continent: A Summer's Journey to the Rocky Mountains, the Mormons, and the Pacific States, with Speaker Colfax*, p. 216.
20. Albert D. Richardson, *Beyond the Mississippi*, pp. 418–19.

21. *San Francisco Evening Bulletin*, August 2, 1865, p. 3, col. 4.
22. DeWolf, holograph.
23. *San Francisco Evening Bulletin*, August 3, 1865, p. 3, col. 3.
24. *Daily Alta California*, August 3, 1865, p. 1, col. 3.
25. *Oregon Reporter* (Jacksonville, Oreg.), August 5, 1865.
26. *Daily Alta California*, August 4, 1865, p. 1, col. 1.
27. *San Francisco Evening Bulletin*, August 4, 1865, p. 3, col. 4.
28. Anthony J. Bledsoe, *History of Del Norte County, California*, pp. 79–83.
29. NA, AGO, G. Wright, SR.
30. *Daily Alta California*, August 17, 1865, p. 1, col. 1.
31. NA, AGO, G. Wright, SR.
32. Cullum, *Biographical Register*, 1:290.
33. *New York Times*, August 26, 1865, p. 1, col. 4.
34. *Daily Alta California*, October 13, 1865, p. 1, col. 2.
35. Ibid., October 18, 1865, p. 1, col. 2.
36. *Sacramento Bee* (Calif.), August 19, 1899, p. 11, cols. 4–6.
37. Wadsworth, *Wright Funeral Address*, pp. 1–12.
38. *Daily Alta California*, October 22, 1865, p. 1, col. 1.
39. *Sacramento Daily Union*, October 23, 1865, p. 3, col. 1.
40. *San Francisco Call*, August 5, 1865.
41. Robinson, "Ordeal of General Wright," pp. 168–69.
42. Hunt, *The Army of the Pacific*, p. 362.
43. Cross, Biographical File, CSL.
44. *Sacramento Daily Union*, June 22, 1872, p. 8, col. 3.

Chapter 18

1. William Gouverneur Morris, *Address Delivered Before the Society of California Volunteers at Its First Annual Celebration, at San Francisco, April 25th, 1866*, pp. 32–33 [courtesy BL].
2. J. P. Dunn, Jr., *Massacres of the Mountains: A History of the Indian Wars of the Far West*, pp. 543–83.
3. NA, RG 92, Consolidated Correspondence File.
4. *San Francisco Evening Bulletin*, December 21, 1861, p. 3, col. 2.
5. Statistics of First Federal Census of Washington Territory, 1860.
6. Heitman, *Historical Register*, 1:763.
7. Information from Library of Congress, Law Division, included in letter to author from Hon. Thomas S. Foley, July 5, 1967. See also Bibliography.

8. *Vermont Journal*, September 6, 1890, p. 5 [courtesy Dartmouth College Library].

9. Richard H. Hill [director, Filson Club, Louisville, Ky.], letter to author, June 29, 1967, et seq.

10. Thomas W. Waggaman [former marshal, U.S. Supreme Court], letter to author, May 25, 1967.

11. *Louisville Courier Journal*, November 28, 1948.

12. Ibid., January 3, 1915, p. 4, col. 3.

13. R. Nash, "Canadian Gold on California Reef," *Old West* 3 (Spring, 1967): 8.

14. Newspaper Clipping Scrapbook, Del Norte County Historical Society.

15. Probate Records, George and Margaret Wright, Office of Secretary of State, State of California, Sacramento.

Bibliography

Manuscript Materials

Bancroft Library. Manuscript Department. Berkeley, Calif.
    Bancroft, Hubert H. "Scrapbook of Educated Men in California." Vol. 30.
    Juarez, Benito. Decree [broadside]. August 11, 1864.
    Wright, George. Letter to S. A. Parker. September 15, 1862.
    ———. Letter to Richard C. Drum. May 16, 1865.
California, state of. Office of Secretary of State. Sacramento, Calif.
    Probate Records, George and Margaret Wright.
California State Library. Manuscript Department. Sacramento, Calif.
    Cross, Samuel. Biographical File.
    Wright, George. Letter to Justus Steinberger. June 20, 1862.
Chase, Doris [newspaper columnist]. Letter to author. November 19, 1981.
Del Norte County Historical Society. Crescent City, Calif.
    DeWolf, Marie. Holograph. N.d.
    Newspaper Clipping Scrapbook.
Eastern Washington State Historical Society, Spokane, Wash.
    "Statistics of First Federal Census of Washington Territory, 1860." Compiled and indexed by Mrs. John B. Moyer. 1931–32.
Erie County Historical Society, Erie, Pa.
    Letters to author. March 12, 1969. February 3, 1970.
Forster, William H. [descendant of Mrs. Margaret Wright].
    Letter to author. April 3, 1969.
Gonzaga University Archives. Spokane, Wash.
    Nelson, Denys, ed. "With the Oblates in Old Oregon." 1926.
Hawkins, Ewing [great-grandson of George Wright].
    Letter to author. February 19, 1968.
Historical Society of Pennsylvania, Philadelphia.
    Letter to author. November 15, 1968.
Historical Society of Dauphin County, Harrisburg, Pa.
    Letter to author. February 21, 1969.

Kentucky Historical Society, Frankfort.
Letter to author re J. M. Wright. May 15, 1968.
Knuth, Priscilla, OHS.
Letter to author. May 16, 1969.
Library of Congress. Washington, D.C.
Law Division.
Information regarding Eliza Wright's pension application.
Manuscript Division.
James A. Hardie Papers. Three letters from Wright.
Mintz, Arnold E., Dean, Saint Stephen's Cathedral, Harrisburg, Pa.
Letter to author. May 14, 1969.
Missouri Historical Society Library. Saint Louis.
Mitchell, Harry E. "History of Jefferson Barracks." 1921.
Webb, Henry W. "The Story of Jefferson Barracks." 1944.
Murray, Frederick, Dean, Cathedral of Saint Paul, Erie, Pa.
Letters to author. April 7, 1969. April 30, 1969.
National Archives. Records of War Department. Adjutant General's Office. Washington, D.C.
Appointment, Commission, and Personal Files.
Service Report of Gen. George Wright.
Consolidated Correspondence File. RG 92.
Letters Received. 1822–60. M 567.
Letters Received, 1861–70. M 619.
Register of Letters Received. M 711.
Records, RG 94, AGO Manuscript File no. 282.
Returns from U.S. Military Posts, 1800–1916. M 617, roll 993.
U.S. Military Academy. Cadet Application Papers. M 688.
National Genealogical Society. Washington, D.C.
Norwich Historical Society. Norwich, Vt.
Letter to author re Wright family. July 25, 1976.
Norwich Town Hall. Norwich, Vt.
Register of Births and Deaths.
Oregon Historical Society. Portland, Oreg.
J. W. Nesmith Correspondence.
Shasta County Library, Redding, Calif.
Peterson, Edward. "In the Shadow of the Mountain: A Short History of Shasta County, California." 1965.
Shasta County Museum. Redding, Calif.
Transcription of Archives Concerning Fort Reading, 1852–1860.
Transcription by Dorothy Holt of National Archives, RG 92,

Records of Quartermaster General Consolidated, 1794–1890.
Spokane Public Library. Spokane, Wash.
Wright, George. Letter to E. V. Sumner. October 26, 1861.
U.S. Military Academy. Archives. West Point, N.Y.
Cadet Application Papers. 1805–66.
Post Order Book no. 4, 1852–56.
Records of Cadets.
Superintendent's Letter Book No. 2, July 2, 1849–February 15, 1853.
Waggaman, Thomas W. [former marshal, U.S. Supreme Court]. Letter to author. May 27, 1967.

Federal Government Documents

American Military History, 1607–1958: ROTC Manual. Washington, D.C.: U.S. Government Printing Office, 1959.
Centennial of the United States Military Academy, 1802–1902: Addresses and Histories. 2 vols. Washington, D.C.: U.S. Government Printing Office, 1904.
Chief of Military History, U.S. Army. *Army Lineage Book.* Washington, D.C., 1969. Vol. 2. *Infantry.*
Hodge, Frederick W., ed. *Handbook of American Indians North of Mexico.* Bureau of American Ethnology Bulletin no. 30. Washington, D.C.: U.S. Government Printing Office, 1912. Vol. 2.
U.S. Congress. House.
Report of Secretary of War [founding of Fort Atkinson]. 16th Cong., 2d sess. Ex. Doc. 110, 1820.
Message from the President of the United States, Vol. 2 [Indian War of 1858]. 35th Cong., 2d sess. Ex. Doc. 2, 1858.
Letter from Secretary of War, ad Interim [Indian depredations in Oregon and Washington]. 36th Cong., 2d sess. Ex. Doc. 29, 1860.
Letter of Acting Secretary of Interior [Snake River Indian massacre]. 36th Cong., 2d sess. Ex. Doc. 46, 1860.
U.S. Congress. Senate.
Report of Secretary of Interior [J. Ross Browne. Letter to Commissioner of Indian Affairs]. 35th Cong., 1st sess. Ex. Doc. 40, 1857.
Report of the Secretary of War [Mullan topographical memoir]. 35th Cong., 2d sess. Ex. Doc. 32, 1859.

Eliza Wright Petitions to Congress. 46th Cong., 2d sess. S. Rept. 592, 1880. 49th Cong., 2d sess. S. 2797, 1887. 50th Cong., 1st sess. S. 42, 1888. 51st Cong., 1st sess. S. 2841, 1890.

War of the Rebellion: A Compilation of the Official Records of the Union and Confederate Armies. Washington, D.C.: U.S. Government Printing Office, 1897. Ser. 1, vol. 50, pts. 1, 2; vol. 9; vol. 34, pt. 2; vol. 46, pt. 3; ser. 2, vol. 5; ser. 3, vol. 3.

State Government Documents

Stevens, Isaac I. *Messages of the Governor of Washington Territory; Also the Correspondence with the Secretary of War, Major General Wool, the Officers of the Regular Army and of the Volunteer Service of Washington Territory.* Olympia, Wash.: Edward Furst, Public Printer, 1857.

Wright, George, and George Curry. Correspondence. In *Journal of the House of Representatives of the Territory of Oregon During the Eighth Regular Session, 1856–1857.* Salem, Oreg.

Books

Adams, James T., ed. *Dictionary of American History.* 8 vols. New York: Scribners, 1940. Vol. 3.

Aldrich, L. C., and F. R. Holmes. *History of Windsor County, Vermont, with Illustrations and Biographical Sketches of Some of Its Prominent Men and Pioneers.* Syracuse, N.Y.: D. Mason, 1891.

Ambrose, Stephen E. *Duty, Honor, Country: A History of West Point.* Baltimore, Md.: Johns Hopkins University Press, 1966.

Bancroft, Hubert H. *History of California.* In *Works,* vols. 6 and 7. San Francisco: History Co., 1888–90.

———. *History of Mexico.* 6 vols. In *Works.* San Francisco: History Co., 1890. Vol. 6.

———. *History of North Mexican States.* 2 vols. San Francisco: History Co., 1890. Vol. 2.

———. *History of Washington, Idaho and Montana, 1845–1889.* In *Works,* vol. 31. San Francisco: History Co., 1890.

Bean, Walton. *California: An Interpretive History.* 3d ed. New York: McGraw-Hill Book Co., 1978.

Beers, Henry P. *The Western Military Frontier, 1815–1846: Dissertation in History, University of Pennsylvania.* Gettysburg, Pa.: Time and News Publishing Co., 1933.

Billington, Ray A. *The Far Western Frontier, 1830–1860.* New York: Harper & Brothers, 1956.

Bischoff, William N. *We Were Not Summer Soldiers: The Indian War Diary of Plimpton J. Kelly, 1855–1856.* Tacoma: Washington State Historical Society, 1976.

Bledsoe, Anthony J. *History of Del Norte County, California.* Eureka, Calif.: Wyman, 1881. Reprint. Crescent City, Calif.: Wendy's Books, 1971.

Boggs, Mae H. *My Playhouse Was a Concord Coach: An Anthology of Newspaper Clippings and Documents Relating to Those Who Made California History During the Years 1822–1888.* Oakland, Calif.: Howell North Press, 1942.

Bond, Rowland. *Early Birds in the Northwest: 100 Years of Western History from Jacques Raphael Finlay to Dutch Jake Goetz.* Nine Mile Falls, Wash.: Spokane House Enterprises, 1973.

Bowles, Samuel. *Across the Continent: A Summer's Journey to the Rocky Mountains, the Mormons, and the Pacific States, with Speaker Colfax.* Springfield, Mass.: Samuel Bowles and Co.; New York: Hurd and Houghton, 1865. Reprint. Great American Series. New Canaan, Conn.: Readex Microprint Corp., 1966.

Brown, William C. *The Indian Side of the Story.* Spokane, Wash.: C. W. Hill Printing Co., 1961.

Burns, Robert I. *The Jesuits and the Indian Wars of the Northwest.* New Haven, Conn.: Yale University Press, 1966.

Capps, Benjamin. *The Indians.* Old West Series. Alexandria, Va.: Time-Life Books, 1973.

Carr, Albert Z. *The World and William Walker.* New York: Harper & Row, 1963.

Carranco, Lynwood, and Estle Beard. *Genocide and Vendetta: The Round Valley Wars of Northern California.* Norman: University of Oklahoma Press, 1981.

Caughey, John W. *California: A Remarkable State's Life History.* 3d ed. Englewood Cliffs, N.J.: Prentice-Hall, 1970.

———. *History of the Pacific Coast.* Lancaster, Pa.: Lancaster Press, 1933.

Chamberlain, Samuel E. *My Confession.* New York: Harper & Brothers, 1956.

Chittenden, Hiram M. *The American Fur Trade of the Far West.* 2 vols. Stanford, Calif.: Academic Reprints, 1954.

———, and Alfred T. Richardson, eds. *Life, Letters, and Travels of Father Pierre-Jean De Smet, S.J., 1801–1873.* 4 vols. New York: F. P. Harper, 1905.

Coleman, Louis C., and Leo Rieman. *Captain John Mullan: His Life; Building the Mullan Road; As It Is Today and Interesting Tales of Occurrences Along the Road.* Montreal: B. C. Payette, 1968.

Crocchiola, Stanley Francis. *E. V. Sumner, Major General, U.S. Army, 1797–1863.* Borger, Tex.: Jim Hess Printers, 1968.

Cullum, George W. *Biographical Register of the Officers and Graduates of the U.S. Military Academy, West Point, N.Y.* 2 vols. New York: D. Van Nostrand, 1868.

De Voto, Bernard. *The Year of Decision, 1846.* Boston: Houghton Mifflin, 1942.

Dodge, G. M., and W. A. Ellis. *Norwich University, 1819–1911: Her History, Her Graduates, Her Roll of Honor.* 2 vols. Montpelier, Vt.: Capital City Press, 1911. Vol. 1.

Donner, Francine. *Spokane Sampler: Historical Poems and Others.* Spokane, Wash.: Whitworth College, 1969.

Dunn, J. P., Jr. *Massacres of the Mountains: A History of the Indian Wars of the Far West.* New York: Harper, 1886.

Egle, William H. *Pennsylvania Genealogies: Chiefly Scottish-Irish and German.* Harrisburg, Pa.: Harrisburg Publishing Co., 1896.

Emmons, Della G. *Leschi of the Nisquallies.* Minneapolis, Minn.: T. S. Denison, 1965.

Esposito, Vincent J. *The West Point Atlas of American Wars.* New York: Frederick Praeger, 1959.

Frazer, Robert W. *Forts of the West: Military Forts and Presidios and Posts Commonly Called Forts West of the Mississippi River to 1898.* Norman: University of Oklahoma Press, 1963.

Fuller, George W. *A History of the Pacific Northwest, with Special Emphasis on the Inland Empire.* New York: Alfred A. Knopf, 1946.

Giles, Rosena A. *Shasta County, California: A History.* Oakland, Calif.: BioBooks, 1949.

Glisan, Rodney. *Journal of Army Life.* San Francisco: A. L. Bancroft, 1874.

Goddard, M. E., and Henry V. Partridge. *A History of Norwich, Vermont (Published by Authority of the Town).* Hanover, N.H.: Dartmouth Press, 1905.

Guie, H. Dean. *Bugles in the Valley: Garnett's Fort Simcoe.* Portland: Oregon Historical Society, 1977.

Hartley, William, and Ellen Hartley. *Osceola: The Unconquered Indian.* New York: Hawthorn Books, 1973.

Harvie, Edwin J. Quoted in Fred B. Brown. *History of the Ninth U.S. Infantry, 1779–1909.* Chicago: Donnelly, 1909.

Heiner, Gordon G., Jr. *From Saints to Red Legs: Madison Barracks, the History of a Border Post.* Watertown, N.Y.: A. W. Munk Press, 1937.

Heitman, Francis B. *Historical Register and Dictionary of the United States Army, 1789–1903.* 2 vols. Washington, D.C., 1903.

Hitchcock, Ethan Allen. *Fifty Years in Camp and Field: The Diary of Major General Ethan Allen Hitchcock.* Ed. W. A. Croffut. New York: G. P. Putnam, 1909.

Hunt, Aurora. *The Army of the Pacific, 1860–1866.* Glendale, Calif.: Arthur H. Clarke, 1951.

Hunt, Elvid. *History of Fort Leavenworth, 1827–1927.* Fort Leavenworth, Kans.: General Service School Press, 1926.

Hunt, Garrett B. *Indian Wars of the Inland Empire.* Spokane, Wash.: Spokane Community College Press [reprint of 1908 manuscript].

Hurd, Walter R. *The Connecticut.* New York: Rinehart & Co., 1947.

Hussey, John A. *The History of Fort Vancouver and Its Physical Structure.* Tacoma: Washington State Historical Society, 1957.

Hutchinson, Bruce. *The Struggle for the Border.* New York: Longmans, Green, 1955.

Hyde, George E. *The Pawnee Indians.* Foreword by Savoie Lottinville. Norman: University of Oklahoma Press, 1974.

Johannsen, Robert W. *Frontier Politics and the Sectional Conflict: The Pacific Northwest on the Eve of the Civil War.* Seattle: University of Washington Press, 1955.

Johansen, Dorothy O., and Charles M. Gates. *Empire of the Columbia: A History of the Pacific Northwest.* New York: Harper & Brothers, 1957.

Johnson, Louise C. *The Congregational Heritage, 1770–1961.* Woodstock, Vt.: Elm Tree Press, 1961.

Ketchum, Richard M., ed. *The American Heritage Book of the Revolution.* New York: American Heritage Publishing Co., 1958.

Keyes, Erasmus D. *Fifty Years' Observation of Men and Events, Civil and Military.* New York: Charles Scribner's Sons, 1884.

Kip, Lawrence. *Army Life on the Pacific: A Journal of the Expedition Against the Northern Indians: The Tribes of the Coeur d'Alenes, Spokans, Pelouzes, in the Summer of 1858.* New York: Redfield, 1859.

Ladd, Horatio O. *History of the War with Mexico.* New York: Dodd, Mead, 1883.

LaFarge, Oliver. *A Pictorial History of the American Indian.* New York: Crown Publishers, 1956.

McCrossen, Sister Mary. *The Bell and The River.* Palo Alto, Calif.: Pacific Books, 1956.

McCurdy, James G. *By Juan deFuca's Strait.* Portland, Oreg.: Binfords and Mort, 1937.

McRae, Ronald H. "The Third Regiment of Infantry," in Thomas F. Rodenbaugh, and William L. Haskin, eds. *The Army of the United States: Historical Sketches of Staff and Line with Portraits of Generals-in-Chief.* New York: Maynard, Merrill, 1896.

McReynolds, Edwin C. *The Seminoles.* Norman: University of Oklahoma Press, 1957.

McWhorter, Lucullus V. *Tragedy of the Wahk-Shum.* Fairfield, Wash.: Ye Galleon Press, 1968.

Mahon, John K. *History of the Second Seminole War, 1835–1842.* Gainesville: University of Florida Press, 1967.

Manring, Benjamin F. *The Conquest of the Coeur d'Alenes, Spokanes, and Palouses: The Expeditions of Colonels E. J. Steptoe and George Wright Against the "Northern Indians" in 1858.* Spokane, Wash.: John W. Graham, 1912.

Martin, Deborah B. *History of Brown County, Wisconsin, Past and Present.* 2 vols. Chicago: S. J. Clarks, 1913.

Meany, Edmund S. *History of the State of Washington.* New York: Macmillan Co., 1946.

Morgan, Dale L., ed. *The West of William H. Ashley, 1822–1838.* Denver, Colo.: Old West Publishing Co., 1964.

Morison, Samuel Eliot. *The Oxford History of the American People.* New York: Oxford University Press, 1965.

Murray, Keith A. *The Pig War.* Tacoma: Washington State Historical Society, 1968.

Nelson's History of Erie County Pennsylvania, Containing a History of the County, 1st Townships, Towns, Villages, Schools, Churches, etc. Chicago: Warner, Beers. 1884.

Nevin, David. *The Mexican War.* Old West Series. Alexandria, Va.: Time-Life Books, 1978.

Peltier, Jerome. *War Bonnets and Epaulets.* Montreal: Payette Radio, 1971.

Phelps, Thomas. *Reminiscences of Seattle, Washington Territory, and of the Sloop-of-War Decatur During the Indian War of 1855–1856.* Fairfield, Wash.: Ye Galleon Press, 1971.

Polk, James K. *The Diary of a President, 1845–1849: Covering the Mexican War, the Acquisition of Oregon, and the Conquest of California and the Southwest.* Edited by Allan Nevins. New York: Longmans, Green. 1929.

Powell, William H. *A History of the Organization and Movements of the Fourth Regiment of Infantry, United States Army from May 30, 1796 to December 31, 1870, Together with a Record of the Military Services of All Officers Who at Any Time Belonged to the Regiment.* Washington, D.C.: McGill and Wetherow, 1871.

Prucha, Francis Paul. *A Guide to the Military Posts of the United States, 1789–1895.* Madison: State Historical Society of Wisconsin, 1964.

Reavis, L. V. *The Life and Military Services of General William Selby Harney.* Saint Louis, Mo.: Bryan, Brand, 1878.

Richards, Kent D. *Isaac I. Stevens: Young Man in a Hurry.* Provo, Utah: Brigham Young University Press, 1979.

Richardson, Albert D. *Beyond the Mississippi.* Hartford, Conn.: Wiley, Waterman and Eaton, 1869.

Richardson, David. *Pig War Islands.* Eastsound, Wash.: Orcas Publishing Co., 1971.

Ridge, Martin, and Ray A. Billington, eds. *America's Frontier Story: A Documentary History of Western Expansion.* Seattle: University of Washington Press, 1955.

Rives, George L. *United States and Mexico, 1821–1848: A History of the Relations Between the Two Countries from the Independence of Mexico to the Close of the War with the United States.* 2 vols. New York: Charles Scribner's Sons, 1913. Vol. 2.

Robertson, E. B. "The Ninth Regiment of Infantry." In Thomas F. Rodenbaugh, and William L. Haskin, eds. *The Army of the United States,* New York: Maynard, Merrill, 1896.

Robinson, John W. "The Ordeal of General Wright: A Study of Secessionist Sentiment in California, 1861–1864." In *Westerners Brand Book,* no. 16. Edited by Raymund F. Wool. Los Angeles: Westerners Los Angeles Corral, 1982.

Rogers, Fred B. *Soldiers of the Overland: Being Some Account of the Services of General Patrick Edward Connor and His Volunteers in the Old West.* San Francisco: Grabhorn Press, 1938.

Rosebush, Waldo E. *Frontier Steel: The Men and Their Weapons.* Appleton, Wis.: C. C. Nelson, 1958.

Ruby, Robert H., and John A. Brown. *Indians of the Pacific Northwest: A History.* Norman: University of Oklahoma Press, 1981.

———, and ———. *The Spokane Indians: Children of the Sun.* Norman: University of Oklahoma Press, 1970.

Sandburg, Carl. *Abraham Lincoln: The War Years.* 4 vols. New York: Harcourt, Brace, 1939.

Schoenberg, Wilfred P. *A Chronicle of Catholic History of the Pacific*

Northwest, 1743–1960. Portland, Oreg.: Catholic Sentinel Printing, 1962.

Sheridan, Philip H. *Personal Memoirs of Philip H. Sheridan, General, United States Army.* 2 vols. New York: Charles L. Webster, 1888. Vol. 1.

Smith, Justin H. *The War with Mexico.* 2 vols. New York: Macmillan, 1919. Vol. 2.

Southern, May Hazel. *Our Storied Landmarks, Shasta County California,* Redding, Calif.: Shasta County Free Library, 1942.

Splawn, A. J. *Ka-Mi-Akin: Last Hero of the Yakimas.* Portland, Oreg.: Binfords and Mort, 1944.

Sprague, John T. *The Origin, Progress and Conclusion of the Florida War. Facsimile Reproduction of 1848 Edition.* Introduction by John K. Mahon. Gainesville: University of Florida Press, 1964.

Steger, Gertrude T. *Place Names of Shasta County.* Redding, Calif.: Redding Printing Co., 1845.

Stevens, Hazard. *The Life of Isaac Ingalls Stevens by His Son, Hazard Stevens.* 2 vols. Boston: Houghton Mifflin, 1905.

Victor, Frances F. *The Early Indian Wars of Oregon.* Salem, Oreg.: Frank Baker, State Printer, 1894.

Wallace, Edward S. *General William Jenkins Worth: Monterey's Forgotten Hero.* Dallas, Tex.: Southern Methodist University Press. 1953.

Warner, Ezra J. *Generals in Blue: Lives of the Union Commanders.* Baton Rouge: Louisiana State University Press, 1964.

Webb, Lester A. *Captain Alden Partridge and the United States Military Academy, 1806–1833.* Northport, Ala.: American Southern, 1965.

Wilhelm, Thomas. *History of the Eighth U.S. Infantry from Its Organization in 1838.* 2 vols. New York. Printed at Headquarters, Eighth Infantry, 1873. Vol. 1.

Wilson, Richard H. "The Eighth Regiment of Infantry," in Thomas F. Rodenbaugh and William L. Haskin, eds. *The Army of the United States: Historical Sketches of Staff and Line with Portraits of Generals-in-Chief.* New York: Maynard, Merrill, 1846.

Wright, E. W., ed. *Lewis and Dryden's Marine History of the Pacific Northwest.* New York: Antiquarian Press, 1961.

Wright, Marcus J. *General Scott: By General Marcus J. Wright.* Great Commanders Series. Edited by J. G. Wilson. New York: D. Appleton, 1893.

Journals, Magazines, and Pamphlets

"Brigadier General George Wright" [editorial]. *North Pacific Review*, no. 5 (February, 1863). [Courtesy California Historical Society, San Francisco.]

Dunlap, V. H. "Fort Reading Ranch and the Hawes Family." In *Covered Wagon* (Shasta County Historical Society, Redding, Calif.), 1963, pp. 22–24.

Dupuy, R. Ernest. "Mutiny at West Point." *American Heritage* 7 (December, 1955): 22–27.

Ellis, Albert G. "Fifty-four Years' Recollections of Men and Events in Wisconsin." In *Collections of State Historical Society of Wisconsin* (Madison) 7 (1876): 207–208.

George, M. C. "Address Delivered at Dedication of Grand Ronde Military Blockhouse at Dayton City Park, Oregon, August 23, 1912," *Oregon Historical Quarterly* 15 (March, 1914): 64.

Grant, Ellsworth S. "The Main Stream of New England." *American Heritage* 18 (April, 1967): 46–49.

Hardin, J. Fair. "Fort Jesup, Ford Selden, Camp Sabine, Camp Salubrity: Four Forgotten Frontier Army Posts of Western Louisiana." *Louisiana Historical Quarterly* 16 (January–October, 1933): 5–26, 279–82, 441–53.

I. G. T. "Indian Campaign in the North," *Overland Monthly* 4 (October, 1884): 399.

Kellogg, Louise P. "Old Fort Howard." *Wisconsin Magazine of History* 18 (December, 1934): 125–40.

Knuth, Priscilla. "Picturesque Frontier: The Army's Fort Dalles." *Oregon Historical Quarterly* 67 (December, 1966): 293–346; 68 (March, 1967): 5–52.

Lomax, Alfred L. "*Brother Jonathan:* Pioneer Steamship of the Pacific Coast." *Oregon Historical Quarterly* 60 (September, 1959): 330–51.

Morris, William Gouverneur. *Address Delivered Before the Society of California Volunteers at Its First Annual Celebration, at San Francisco, April 25th, 1866.* San Francisco: Francis Valentine, 1866. [Courtesy Bancroft Library.]

Nash, Robert. "Canadian Gold on California Reef." *Old West* 3 (Spring, 1967): 8.

Norwich Women's Club. *Know Your Town: 1940 Survey of Norwich, Vermont.* 1942.

Peltier, Jerome A. "The Ward Massacre." *Pacific Northwesterner* 9 (Winter, 1965): 12–16.

Reimers, Henry L. *When Wright Was Might.* Spokane, Wash.:
    Homestead House, 1983.
Schlicke, Carl P. "Nun in Statuary Hall." *Pacific Northwesterner* 24
    (Summer, 1980): 42.
Turner, Andrew J. "History of Fort Winnebago." In *Collections of
    State Historical Society of Wisconsin* (Madison) 14 (1898):
    65–102.
Wadsworth, Charles. *An Address Delivered in Calvary Church, San
    Francisco, on the Occasion of the Funeral Services of General
    George Wright.* San Francisco: H. H. Bancroft & Co., 1865.
    [Courtesy of Bancroft Library, Berkeley, Calif.]

Newspapers

American Flag (Sonora, Calif.)
Daily Alta California (San Francisco)
Daily Oregonian (Portland, Oreg.)
Humboldt Times (Eureka, Calif.)
Los Angeles News (Los Angeles, Calif.)
Louisville Courier Journal (Ky.)
Missouri Republican (Saint Louis)
New York Times (New York City)
Oregon Reporter (Jacksonville, Oreg.)
Sacramento Bee (Calif.)
Sacramento Daily Union (Calif.)
San Francisco Evening Bulletin (Calif.)
San Francisco Call (Calif.)
Shasta Courier (Shasta, Calif.)
Union Record (Oroville, Calif.)
The Vermont Journal (Windsor, Vt.)
Weekly Alta California (San Francisco)

Index

Abbott, G. W. (Indian subagent): 210
Acapulco, Mex.: 74, 259
Accessory Transit Co.: 327
Adams (ship): 57, 58
Ahtanum Creek, Washington Terr.:
    118
Ahtanum Mission: *See* Oblate
Ainsa, A., requests U.S. post in So-
    nora: 259–60
Alamo, Tex.: 40, 67
Alaska: 65
Alcatraz: 210–11
Alden, Capt. B. R.: 96
Allen, Lt. Jesse K., killed in Garnett
    raid: 186
Allen, W. A. H. (first officer, *Brother
    Jonathan*): 330
Alpowa Creek, Wash.: 147
Alvord, Capt. (later Gen.) Benjamin:
    116; commander, Ft. Dalles, 116;
    commander, Oregon Dist., 257; re-
    sponse to Pickering, 297; urges
    ratification of Nez Percé Treaty,
    297; relieved of command, 317
America, North: 45; Oregon claims,
    65–66
American Fur Co.: 25
American government, insult by
    Pawnees: 32
American Northwest Boundary Com-
    mission: 140
American River: 94
American settlers in Oregon: 66
Amnesty Proclamation: 238
Andrews, Maj. George P.: 207
Angel Island: 285
Antoine (Loup chief): 33
Apache Indians: 266; Carleton at-
    tempts to subdue, 256; raids, 292,
    319
Apache Pass, N.Mex., Slough defeats
    Confederates at: 241
Arapahoe Indians: 20, 28

Appomattox Court House, Lee sur-
    renders to Grant at: 315
Archer, Capt. James J. (9th Infantry):
    136
Arizona: becomes separate district,
    West in command, 243; lawlessness
    in mining area, 265; district an-
    nexed to Pacific Department, 317
Arkansas Dept.: 292
"Arkansaw" River: 34
Arlington National Cemetery: 352
Armistead, Gen. Walter K.: 55
Army of Occupation (Mexico): 67
Army of the Potomac: 213
Ash Hollow, Nebr., massacre of Brulé
    Sioux at: 196–97
Aspen Camp: 164
Aspinwall, Panama: 95, 112
Astor, John Jacob: 25
Atkinson, Gen. Henry: 18, 49; estab-
    lishes Headquarters, Western
    Dept., at Jefferson Barracks, 20; es-
    tablishes Ft. Atkinson, 25

Babbitt, Lt. (later Col.) Edwin B.: 28
Babcock, Rep. Leander: 92
Bad Chief (Grand chief): 34
Baja California: 104
Baker, Oreg.: 128
Ball, 1st Sgt. Edward: 161
Bancroft, Hubert H.: 96, 105
Banks, Gen. Nathaniel P., defeated in
    Louisiana: 292
Barrows, Henry (U.S. marshal for
    southern California): 244
Bates, Edward (U.S. attorney gen-
    eral), comment on Halleck: 277
Battle of Bear River, Idaho Terr.: 249
Battle of Bennington: 6
Battle of Bull Run: 213
Battle of Burnt River, Oreg.: 128
Battle of Cerro Gordo, Mex.: 72
Battle of Chippewa: 15

Battle of Churubusco: 74–77, 82
Battle of Contreras, Mex.: 74
Battle of Four Lakes, Washington
  Terr.: 165–69
Battle of Gettysburg, Pa.: 290
Battle of Molino del Rey: 77–79,
  81–84
Battle of Monterrey, Mex.: 68
Battle of Niagara: 15
Battle of Perryville, Ky.: 263
Battle of Quinn River, Nev.: 318
Battle of Shiloh: 263
Battle of Spokane Plains, Washington
  Terr.: 170–72
Battle of Valverde, N.Mex.: 239
Baylor, Col. John, C.S.A.: takes pos-
  session of Arizona, 224; importance
  of Sonora to Confederacy, 234;
  order to Capt. Helm regarding In-
  dians, 252
Beale, Col. Benjamin F.: 225–26
Beale, E. F. (Indian agent): 94, 98
Beall, Thomas J. (packmaster): 146,
  152
Bean, Jonathan F. (Indian subagent):
  29, 32
Bear Hunter (Bannock chief): captor
  of Van Orman boy, 249; killed in
  Battle of Bear River, 249
Bell, Commo. Charles E. (com-
  mander, Pacific fleet): 236, 286
Bell, John (secretary of war): 84
Belknap, Maj. William G.: at Ft. Leav-
  enworth, 20; in Seminole War, 57,
  58
Belle (ship): 123
Benicia, Calif.: 95, 104
Benicia Barracks: 234
Bennett, Col. Clarence: 268
Benton, John S. (purser, Brother
  Jonathan): 330
Bernal Springs, N.Mex.: 241
Bernhardt, Mrs. Nina (Brother Jona-
  than survivor): 335
Biddle's Harbor, Fla.: 58
Big Axe (Loup chief): 33
Big Cypress (Swamp) Expedition,
  Fla.: 56, 58–59
Big Elk (Omaha chief): 30
Big Eyes (Omaha chief): 29
Big Nose (Republican Indian): 29

Billy Bowlegs (Seminole chief): 57, 59
Bissell, Capt. Lyman A.: commands
  on San Juan Island, 259; com-
  plaints about, 282–83
Black, Col. Henry M., commands
  Humboldt District: 295–96
Blackfeet Indians: 116; slaughter on
  Marias River, 196
Black Kettle (Cheyenne chief), attack
  on camp of, on Washita River: 196
Blanchet, A. M. A. (bishop of Nis-
  qually): 201
Blenkinsop, George (trader at Ft. Col-
  vile): 157
Bliss, Capt. John: 11, 12, 28
Bliss, Rev. Samuel: 5
Blockhouses: Puget Sound area, 117,
  120; Cascades, 122–23, 129
"Bloody Island": 120
Blue Mountains, Oreg.: 208–209
Bolon, Andrew J. (Indian agent):
  murdered, 116, 139–40
Bomford, Capt. James S.: 75
Bonneville, Lt. Col. B. L. E., com-
  mands 4th Infantry: 95
Boonville, Idaho, settlers: 297
Bowles, Samuel: 337
Bradford's Store, Cascades, Washing-
  ton Terr.: 122
Brazos Santiago: 69
Brevet (defined): 38n.
Brewerton, Capt. Henry (supt.
  U.S.M.A.): 88–90
British Columbia: 66
British troops: 5, 6
Brockville, Ont., Wright confronts
  mob in: 46
Brother Jonathan (ship): 202; descrip-
  tion, 327; history, 327–29; cargo,
  330; officers, 330; passengers, 330–
  31; voyage north, 331; wreck, 332–
  35, 352–53
Browne, J. Ross (special agent, Trea-
  sury Dept.); investigates causes of
  Indian War: 120, 133–34, 145
Bruce, James (earl of Elgin and Kin-
  ardine, governor of Canada): 86
Bryson (Indian agent): 318
Buchanan, Lt. Col. R. L. (Fort Hum-
  boldt): 96
Buchanan, Pres. James: 8; inaugu-

rated, 138; and news from San
Juan Island, 205; replaces Harney
with Wright in command of Dept.
of Oregon, 205
Buckley, Capt. Thomas S.: 336
Buell, Gen. Don Carlos: 2; assistant
adjutant general, Dept. of Pacific,
223; commands Kentucky volun-
teer regiment in East, 237; J. M.
Wright serves under, 237
Buena Vista, Mex.: 72
Buffalo, N.Y.: 42
Butler, Gen. William O.: 83–84
Butterfield stages: 225

Cabanné, John P.: 25–29, 35; trading
post, 28, 33
Cache Valley, Utah Terr.: 248–49
Caddo Indians: 38
Cadwalader, Gen. George: 77–80
Cady, Col. Albermerle, commands
Oregon Dist.: 226
Calhoun, Sec. War John C. (secretary
of war): 10, 13, 18
California: 92, 94, 96, 100, 107, 111
California legislature: 103; approves
administration policies, 291
California Steam Navigation Co.: 329
California Trail: 105
Calvary Church, San Francisco: 349
Camargo, Mex.: 69
Cameron, Simon (Lincoln's first secre-
tary of war): 215; censured by Con-
gress, 220; replaced by Stanton,
220
Campbell, J. D. (second officer, Broth-
er Jonathan): 330
Campbell, Dr. John (assistant sur-
geon, Ft. Reading), altercation with
Wright: 99
Camp Babbitt, Visalia, Calif.: 246
Camp Bidwell, Calif.: 272
Camp Drum, Calif.: 268, 279
Camp East Toajaka, Fla.: 55
Camp Foster, Fla.: 58–59
Camp Fowle, Fla.: 55
Camp Independence, Calif.: 296
Camp Jefferson Davis, Miss.: 85
Camp Latham, Calif.: 255
Camp Lincoln, Calif.: 317, 335, 336
Camp McKeown, Wis.: 49

Camp Pedrigal, Washington Terr.:
164
Camp Pickett, San Juan Island: 203
Camp Sabine, La.: 40
Camp Worth, San Antonio, Tex.: 85
Camp Wright, Oak Grove, Calif.: 232
Canada: 41–45, 80; boundary dis-
pute with U.S., 202
Canadian government: 42, 43, 45, 46
Canby, Gen. Edward R. S.: at Fort
Craig, N.Mex., 225; appeals to Gov.
Gilpin for help, 241; commands in
Texas, 242–43; murdered by
Modoc Indians, 350
Cantonment (later Ft.) Leavenworth,
Kans.: 20–28, 32–37
Cantonment Miller, St. Louis, Mo.: 19
Cantonment Wright (Mullan's winter
camp in Bitterroot Mts.): 353
Cape Horn: 95
Caribbean: 108
Carleton, Col. James H.: 240; com-
mands Southern Expedition ("Cali-
fornia Column"), 225; commands
Southern California Dist., 227;
criticism of, 240–41; in command,
Dept. of New Mexico, 242; pro-
moted to brig. gen., 242; offers
Canby cooperation, 243; ordered to
cooperate with Banks, 292
Carleton Expedition (California Ex-
pedition, Carleton Column): 231,
241, 264–65
Carlisle, Pa.: 56, 85
Caroline (ship): 42
Cascade Indians: Cascade Massacre,
122–23; Wright's first hangings,
123; troops prevent uprising, 222
Cascade Range: 98, 120, 122
Cascade Rapids, Washington Terr.:
122, 124
Cascades Massacre, Washington
Terr.: 122–24
Casey, Lt. Col. Silas (9th Infantry):
109, 112–13, 120
Cass, Lewis: governor of Michigan
Terr., 14; secretary of war, 40
Castle Rock Battle, California: 106
Catalina Island, Calif., proposed for
Indian reservation: 278–80
Cayuse Indians: 116, 127

Cedar Key (army headquarters in
  Florida): 61–62
Central American Federation: 108
Central Pacific RR: 97
Chaddock, J. (Captain, U.S. Revenue
  cutter *Joe Lane*): 331
Chapultepec Castle: 78, 82
Charles II, King: 4
Charlotte Harbor, Fla.: 60
Chase, Salmon P. (secretary of trea-
  sury): 260
Chattahoochee River: 50
Chesapeake Bay: 109
Cheyenne Indians: 20; Cheyenne
  prisoner sacrificed by Pawnees,
  31 & n., 32; Sand Creek Battle,
  31–32
Chico, Calif.: 272
Chihuahua, Mex.: 235
Childs, Maj. Thomas: 57
Chile: 309
Chivington, Maj. J. M., defeats Con-
  federates at Bernal Springs: 241
Choctaw Indians: 37
Cholera: 85
Churubusco, Mex., Battle of: 74–77
Civilian Conservation Corps: 354
Civil War: begins, 213; ends, 315
Civil War volunteers: 215–16
Clark, William: 19, 30
Clarke, Col. Newman S. (8th Infan-
  try): 55, 74–75, 155; replaces Gen.
  Wool in command of Pacific Dept.,
  138; visits Columbia River Dist.,
  139; critical of Ft. Dallas construc-
  tion, 139; takes over command
  Northern Dist., 141; opposes Ste-
  vens treaties, 144; arrives at Ft.
  Vancouver, 154; terms for peace,
  155, 179; orders to Wright, 155;
  orders to Garnett, 156; faults
  Wright's treaties, 189–91; com-
  mands Dept. of California, 187;
  death, 193
Clemens, Orion (acting governor, Nevada Terr.): 269
Cleveland, Ohio: 45
Coast defense: 200, 205, 236, 285–
  87, 310–11
Coast Range: 100, 103
Coeur d'Alene Indians, sign Treaty of
  Mission: 179–80

Coeur d'Alene Mission: 178
Coeur d'Alene Mountains: 178
Colfax, Schuyler (Speaker, U.S.
  House): 337
Colón (Peruvian ship): 308–309
Colonel Wright (ship): 353
Colorado River: 231
Columbia Barracks, Vancouver,
  Washington Terr., Col. Bonneville
  and 4th Inf. arrive: 95
Columbia River: 119, 122, 123
Columbia River District: 113
Colville, N.E. Washington Terr.: 146
Comanche (ship): 285
Comanche Indians: 20, 35
Commissary Dept., permits feeding
  of Indians: 297
Committee on Pensions, U.S. Con-
  gress: 351
Commodore: 328; *See also Brother
  Jonathan*
Concord, Mass.: 6
Confederate army in Pacific Dept.
  and Southwest: occupation of Fort
  Bliss, 224; capture of 7th Infantry
  troops near Ft. Fillmore, 224; seek
  access to Mexico border states, 234;
  proclaim possession Arizona, 224;
  Sibley defeats Canby at Valverde,
  N.Mex., 239; Albuquerque, Santa
  Fe, and Tucson occupied, 239;
  driven out of Southwest, 242–43
Confederate States of America (Con-
  federacy, C.S.A., South): 107, 213;
  designs on U.S. Southwest and
  Mexico border states, 107, 235; se-
  cession, 213
Congiato, Rev. Nicholas, S.J.: 157–58
Congregational Church ("Old Meet-
  ing House"), Norwich, Vt.: 9
Congregational Church, Sacramento,
  Calif.: 345
Congress, U.S.: *See* U.S. Congress
Congress of Confederate States: 252
Connecticut: 3–5
Connecticut River, Valley: 3–7, 10
Connor (civilian interpreter), killed in
  Steptoe battle: 149
Connor, Col. (later Brig. Gen.) Pat-
  rick E.: 249, 295; Overland Mail
  Route expedition, 234; crosses
  Sierra Nevada, 247; Ft. Churchill,

247; commands Utah Dist., 247; Ft. Douglas, 247; Battle of Bear River, 249; and Mormons, 248–50, 268, 270, 295
Conrad, C. M.: 92
Continental Divide: 114
Contreras, Mex.: 74
Coon, H. (mayor of San Francisco): 285
Cooper, Maj. Samuel: 56, 58
Cordilleras, Mex.: 73
Cornelius, Col. Thomas R.: 256
Corpus Christi, Tex.: 67–68
Cottonwood Creek, Calif.: 102
Coult, Maj. Theodore A.: 266
Council Bluffs, Iowa: 25
Council Bluffs, Missouri Terr., expedition to: 24–28, 30–32, 93
Cow Creek (Sacramento River tributary, site of Ft. Reading): 97
Crawford, George (secretary of war): 89
Creek Indians: 50
Crescent City, Calif.: 102; Cape St. George, 332; Dragon Rocks, 332; wreck of Brother Jonathan, 333–36; cemetery established, 340
Crook, Lt. George R., on Garnett raid: 186
Cross, Judge Samuel: 306
Crow Indians: 28
Crown Point: 3
Cullum, Gen. George W.: 63
Curry, George (governor of Oregon Terr.): 121
Curtis, Col. James F.: 279
Curtis, Gen. Samuel R.: 295
Cutler, Lyman (settler on San Juan Island): 203
Cyanne, U.S.S.: 265

Dade, Maj. Francis L.: 51
Daley, Rev. J. L.: 136
Dalles, The, Oreg.: 95, 121–22
Dandy, Lt. (later Gen.) George F. B.: on Wright, 137, 159; on attack on supply train, 171
Dartmouth College, Hanover, N.H.: 5, 7
Davidson, Lt. Henry B. (dragoon officer with Wright): 176
Davis, Jefferson: U.S. secretary of war, 99, 103–107, 111, 120; president, C.S.A., 213; letter of marque for J. M. Chapman, 265
Decatur (ship): 120
Del Norte (ship): 339–40
Democratic party: 291, 312
DeMoy, Pvt. Victor: 150
Dent, Capt. Frederick T. (9th Infantry): 112, 146; rescues survivors of massacre, 210–11
Denver, Gen. J. W.: 225, 226
Department of California: 323
Department of the Columbia: 323
Department of Oregon: 187
Department of the Pacific: 105; divided, 187; reunited, 214
DeRussy, Col. Rene E. (chief engineer, Pacific Coast): 236, 285, 311
DeSmet, Rev. Pierre-Jean, S.J.: 198–99
Detroit, Mich.: 44, 86
DeWolf, Mrs. Samuel J.: 329–32, 337–38
DeWolf, Samuel J. (captain of Brother Jonathan): 329
Digger Indians (southern California): 94
Digger (Snake) Indians: 206–207
Dole, William P. (commissioner of Indian affairs): 279
Donation Land Law: 114, 134
Doolittle, Sen. James R. (Wis.), chairman, Committee on Indian Affairs: 320–21
Dorion, Francis: 35
Dorion, Martin: 28, 29
Doty, James D. (governor of Utah): 269
Dougherty, Maj. John (Indian agent): 29, 31–33
Douglas, Capt. Charles D.: 253, 254
Douglas, James (Hudson's Bay Co. official, governor of British Columbia): 204
Downey, John G. (governor of California): 215
Dragon Rocks, Calif.: 332
Drake, Maj. John F.: 319
Drew, Lt. Charles S.: 280
Drum, Capt. Simon: 77, 79
Drum, Col. Richard C. (adj. gen. Dept. of Pacific): 223, 299

Dueling: 19–20
Duncan, Col. James: 79–80, 84
Durieu, Father (Oblate missionary): 118
Dutch settlers: 3
Dysentery: 44

Ebey, Col. Isaac (collector of customs, Port Townsend, Washington Terr.): 138
Edgar, Dr. William F. (assistant surgeon, Ft. Reading): 99
Eighth Infantry: 44–49, 73–77; formed, 44; Patriot War, 44–47; Seminole War, 55, 57; Mexican War, 67; Palo Alto, 68; Reseca de Palma, 68; Monterrey, 68; Saltillo, 68; Veracruz, 72; Cerro Gordo, 72; Puebla, 73; Contreras, 74; Churubusco, 74–75; Molino del Rey, 79–81; Chapultepec, 82; Mexico City, 82–83; Fort Lavaca, Tex., 85
Eleventh Infantry: 77
Elk Horn River: 30
Emancipation Proclamation: 238
Emathla, Charlie (Seminole chief), slain by Osceola: 51
Emigrant Trail: Oregon, 211; California, 105
Engineer Corps, U.S.: 80
England: 47
Equal Rights Expositor (Visalia, Calif.): 247
Erie, Pa.: 23
Esquimalt, Vancouver Island (British naval base): 260
Evans, Col. George S.: Camp Babbitt, Calif., 247; Owens Valley, 255; Mormon village, 268
Evans, John (governor of Colorado): 295
Everglades, Fla.: 57–58, 62
Ewing, Nellie Butler (Mrs. John Montgomery Wright): 352
Eyre, Col. Edward E.: reaches Rio Grande, 242, 243

Fairchild Air Force Base, Spokane, Wash.: 172
Farley, Sen. J. T. (chairman, Committee on Pensions): 351

Ferguson, Capt. (later Maj.) David: 234, 260
Fifth Infantry: 74
"Fifty-four Forty or Fight": 65
Fillmore, Pres. Millard: 94, 103
First Brigade: 68
First Dragoons (Cos. A and E, Ft. Reading): 100, 101, 109
First Division (Scott's army): 69, 74, 77
Flathead Indians: 116
Fleming, Lt. H. B.: 163, 167
Florida: 50, 55, 65, 90; becomes state, 62
Florida War: see Seminole War
Floridians: 62, 64
Floyd, John B. (secretary of war): 138
Fontenelle, Lucien: 30–32
Forster, Hannah Wickerskam (Mrs. Edwin Vose Sumner): 23
Forster, John: 22
Forster, Sarah Montgomery (Margaret Wright's mother): 23
Forster, Thomas (Wright's father-in-law): 23
Fort Atkinson, Missouri Terr.: 25; Treaty of, 25, 32
Fort Bellingham, Washington Terr.: 138
Fort Benton, Mont.: 145
Fort Bliss, Tex., occupied by Baylor: 224
Fort Boise (Hudson's Bay Co. post): 212, 274
Fort Boise (U.S. Army, Idaho Terr.): 253, 273
Fort Bridger, Wyo.: 247
Fort Brooke, Fla.: 51, 63–64
Fort Brown, Tex.: 67
Fort Churchill, Nev.: 247
Fort Columbia (Vancouver Barracks, Washington Terr.): 98
Fort Columbus, Governor's Island, N.Y.: 95
Fort Colville (Hudson's Bay Co. post): 116, 146
Fort Colville (U.S. Army, Washington Terr.): 205
Fort Craig, N.Mex.: see Canby, Gen. Edward R. S.
Fort Crawford, Wis.: 49

Fort Crook, Calif.: 272
Fort Dallas, Fla. (site of present
    Miami): 57–58
Fort Dalles, Oreg.: 95, 117–19, 124;
    replaces Ft. Vancouver as head-
    quarters, Columbia River Dist.,
    113; new construction, 130; criti-
    cism, 130
Fort Douglas, Utah: 247 ff.
Fort Fillmore, N.Mex.: 224
Fort Fowle, Fla.: 55
Fort George Wright, Spokane, Wash.:
    354
Fort Gratiot, Mich.: 86
Fort Hall, Idaho Terr. (Hudson's Bay
    Co. post): 256–57, 319
Fort Harrell, Fla.: 57
Fort Howard, Wis.: 14, 18, 49
Fort Humboldt, Calif.: 96
Fort (formerly Cantonment) Jesup,
    La.: 18, 37–38, 41
Fort Jones, Yreka, Calif.: 96,
    100–103
Fort Kearney, Nebr.: 295
Fort King, Fla.: 55, 60
Fort Klamath, Oreg.: 298
Fort Lane, Oreg.: 103, 113
Fort Lapwai, Idaho, troops sent to
    protect Nez Percés: 258
Fort Lavaca, Tex.: 85
Fort Leavenworth, Kans.: see Canton-
    ment Leavenworth
Fort Mackinac, Mich.: 86
Fort Mason, Ariz.: 207
Fort Miller, Calif.: 99
Fort Monroe, Point Comfort, Va.:
    106–109; yellow-fever epidemic
    near, 111
Fort Naches ("Basket Fort"), Wash-
    ington Terr.: 124–26
Fort Niagara, N.Y.: 42, 86–89
Fort Ontario, N.Y.: 86, 87, 91
Fort Orford, Oreg.: 102–103, 113
Fort Pierce, Fla.: 59, 61
Fort Point, Calif.: 310
Fort Quitman, Tex.: 242
Fort Reading, Calif.: 95–102, 104,
    114; description, 97; floods, 97;
    settlers v. Indians, 96–97; deser-
    tions and illness, 97–98; disciplin-
    ary problems, 98–99; regional

depot, 103; visit by inspector gen-
    eral, 104–105; visit by Gen. Wool,
    105
Fort Simcoe, Washington Terr.: estab-
    lished by Garnett, 128–29; turned
    over to Department of Indian Af-
    fairs, 200
Fort Snelling, Minn.: 18
Fort Steilacoom, Washington Terr.:
    95, 113, 120–22
Fort Sumter, S.C.: 213
Fort Taylor, Washington Terr.: 160
Fort Thorn, N.Mex.: 242
Fort Ticonderoga, N.Y.: 3
Fort Townsend, Washington, Terr.:
    138
Fort Towson, Okla.: 38
Fort Vancouver (Hudson's Bay Co.
    post, Washington Terr.): 201
Fort Vancouver, Washington Terr.
    (U.S. Army, originally Columbia
    Barracks): 95, 113, 117, 120–23
Fort Walla Walla, Wash. (Hudson's
    Bay Co. post): 135, 245
Fort Walla Walla (U.S. Army, Wash-
    ington Terr.): 108, erected by Step-
    toe, 134–35; garrison, 135, 141
Fort Winnebago, Wis.: 49
Fort Wright, Round Valley, Calif.:
    253
Fort Wright (formerly Holy Names)
    College, Spokane, Wash.: 359
Fort Yamhill, Oreg.: 215
Fort Yuma, Calif.: 225
Four Lakes Campsite, Washington
    Terr.: 165
Fourteenth Infantry: 77
Fourth Infantry: 85; Seminole War,
    62; Wright assigned, 85; north-
    western frontier, 87; California, 92,
    94–95; Ft. Vancouver, 113; Yakima
    expedition, 124
Fox River, Wis.: 14–15
Fox-Wisconsin Waterway: 14
France: 259; Napoleon's troops ap-
    proach U.S. border, 281; blockades
    and bombardments of western
    Mexican ports, 306; Wright's con-
    cerns, 306–307; storm-battered
    fleet repaired at Mare I, 309; grow-
    ing concern on U.S. West Coast, 323

Francis, Allen (U.S. consul in Victoria, B.C.): 287, 294
Frederick, Md.: 84
French and Indian War: 3, 5
French consul in San Francisco: 309
French settlers: 15
French traders: 28
Fugitive Slave Law: 91

Gaines, Gen. Edmund P. (commander of Western Dept.): 38–40
Gansvoort, Capt. Guert, U.S.N., commander of *Decatur*: 120
Garland, Col. John: 79–80
Garnett, Maj. Robert S. (9th Inf.): 109, 124, 187; establishes Fort Simcoe, 128–29; conducts raid west of Columbia River, 185–87
Garrison, S. J. (copublisher of *Equal Rights Expositor*): 247
Garry (Spokane Indian chief): 158, 180
Gaston, Lt. William: 146, 149
Geary, Rev. Edward R. (superintendent of Indian affairs): receives report of Wallen Expedition, 206–207; and massacre of emigrants by Snake Indians, 210–11
George Wright School, The Dalles, Oreg.: 354
Gibbs, Addison C. (governor of Colorado); 273
Gilpin, William (governor of Colorado): 241
G.I. Weeks (ship): 46
Glisan, Capt. Rodney (medical officer): 129
Godoy, José A. (Mexican consul in San Francisco): 309
Goff, Capt. F. D. M. (Washington volunteers), at Battle of Burnt River: 128
Golden Age (ship): 112–13
Golden Gate (San Francisco harbor): 287
Golden Rule (ship): 331
Gold strikes: California, 94; Colville, 116; Fraser River, 181; eastern Oregon, 319; Idaho, 222
Goliad, Tex.: 40
Goose Lake Indians: 297
Governor's Island, N.Y.: 56

Grahame, James A. (chief trader at Hudson's Bay Co. Ft. Vancouver): 157
Grande Ronde (Oreg.) Battle: 128
Grand Island, N.Y.: 42
Grand Pawnee Indians: 28–30, 33; Wright visits village, 34
Grant, Gen. (later Pres.) Ulysses S.: 291
Great Britain: 6, 7, 41, 66; Oregon claims, 65
Greathouse, Ridgely: 266
Great Lakes: 14
Great Salt Lake, Utah: 206, 223
Great Spokane Plain: 164
Green Bay, Wis.: 14, 49
Green Mountains, Vt.: 3
Gregg, Lt. David M. (1st Dragoons): 146, 163
Grier, Maj. William (1st Dragoons): 146; leads cavalry charge at Four Lakes, 168; leads party to Steptoe battlefield, 181; on Boise Road, 204
Guaymas, Mex.: 233, 236, 260
Gulf of California: 235
Gulf of Mexico: 40, 235
Gwin, U.S. Sen. William (secessionist): 322

Haida Indians: threaten Puget Sound area, 137; removed from Port Gamble, 137; reprisal, 138
Hale, Calvin P. (Indian superintendent): 274
Hall, E. P. (copublisher, *Equal Rights Expositor*): 247
Halleck, Gen. Henry W.: 249; replaces McClellan as general-in-chief, 238; replaced by Grant, 291; chief of staff, 291; advocates Mexican port, 322
Halleck Tustenuggee (Seminole chief): 55, 60
Haller, Maj. Cranville O. (4th Inf.): 116, 124; defeat by Indians, 117, 119; establishes Ft. Townsend, 138
Hammond, James (assistant surgeon): 163
Hancock, Maj. Henry: 278–79
"Hanging Camp": 180
Hanover, N.H.: 9
Hanson, George M. (superintendent

of Indian affairs, Northern Calif.):
252–55; requests troops for Round
Valley, Calif., 253; complains to
Wright, 272
Hardie, Capt. James A.: Indian
battles of 1858, 166, 306; appointed adjutant, Dept. of Oregon,
by Wright, 206; ordered east, 218;
Wright's letters, 218, 230; on Mc-
Clellan's staff, 230
Hardie's tactics (military): 109
Harding, S. S. (governor, Utah Terr.):
250
Harney, Gen. William S.: 200; Semi-
nole War, 54; Mexican War, 77;
ordered to take charge of Indian
War of 1858, 154; and Ash Hollow
massacre of Sioux, 197; and De-
Smet, 198; commands Dept. of
Oregon, 187; orders, 197; opens
interior to settlement, 199; disci-
plinary problems, 200–201; sends
troops to San Juan Island, 203; re-
lieved of command, 204
Harney (ship): 59
Harney Lake: 210
Harpending, Asbury: 265
Harrisburg, Pa.: 41
Harrison, Pres. Wm. H.: 54
Harvie, Col. Edwin J.: 136
Hawkins, Bvt. Maj.: 69
Hawkins, Margaret F. Wright (wife of
William W. Hawkins, daughter of
John M. Wright): 352
Hawkins, William M. (chairman of
board, Scripps-Howard News-
papers): 352
Hebron, Conn.: 5
Helm, Capt. Thomas, C.S.A.: 252
Henry, Dr. Anson G.: 262, 331
Hensley, Samuel J. (owner of Brother
Jonathan): 329
Hillborough County, Fla.: 64
Hitchcock, Gen. Ethan Allen: 12–13,
19, 100–103; on faculty of
U.S.M.A., 11; in Seminole War, 54,
55; opinion of Harney, 54, 61; in
Mexican War, 67, 81–82; com-
mands Division of Pacific, 96, 99;
replaced by Gen. Wool, 104; re-
signs from army, 197–98
Honduras: 108

Honey Lake, Calif.: 255, 318
Hoopa Indians: 270
Horse Slaughter Camp: 177
Houston, Gen. Sam: 40
Howard, Gen. Benjamin: 14
Hudson's Bay Company: 114; rela-
tions with U.S. Army deteriorate,
201; abandons holdings in U.S.,
201
Huger, Capt. Benjamin: 77, 79
Humboldt District: established, 224;
Indians of, quiet, 296
Hunter, Capt. Sherod, C.S.A.: oc-
cupies Tucson, Ariz., 239; captures
Capt. McCleave, 239
Hunter's Lodges ("Patriot" groups): 41
Huntington, J. W. P. (Indian superin-
tendent): 274
Hutchins, Charles (Indian agent): 257

Icarus (British warship): 108
Idaho Territory: 249, 297
Indian conflicts during Civil War:
Cascades, 222; Snakes, 223, 256,
270, 297; in Owens River valley,
255, 273, 317–19; Klamaths, Goose
Lakes, Modocs, 297; Humboldt
Dist., 270–71, 295; Nevada, 317–
18; eastern Calif., 318; Idaho, 319
Indian Department, U.S., argument
over feeding Indians: 306
Indian lands and gold seekers: 94
Indian Removal Act: 18
Indians: 29; Confederate directive,
252; civil trial for, 318
Indian Territory: 62
Infantry School, Jefferson Barracks:
22
Ingraham, Dr. D. R.: 331
Iowa (Ioway) Indians: 28, 37
Island County, Washington Terr.: 203

Jackson, Gen. (later Pres.) Andrew:
18, 40, 50
Jacksonville, Oreg.: 336
Jalapa, Mex.: 73
James River, Va.: 109
Jefferson, Pres. Thomas: 18
Jefferson Barracks, Mo.: 18–21,
35–37, 85
Jenneson, Lewis L.: 28
Jesup, Gen. Thomas S.: 38

J. M. Chapman (privateer), seizure of: 265–66
Joe Lane (revenue cutter): 331
John Day River, Oreg.: 207
Johns, Lt. Thomas: 46
Johnson, Bill, burns Canadian ship: 43
Johnson, Vice-Pres. Andrew: 291
Johnston, Col. Albert S.: commands Dept. of Pacific, 214; joins South, 215
Jonathan Club, Los Angeles: 352
Jones, Maj. Roger (adjutant general): 42, 69, 85, 91–92
Jordan, Capt. Thomas (assistant quartermaster): 130
Jordan Valley, Oreg.: 319
Joset, Rev. Joseph, S.J.: 150–54, 174–75; tries to prevent attack on Steptoe, 148; expedites treaties with Coeur d'Alenes and Spokanes, 177–81
Juárez, Benito (president of Mexico): 282, 309
Judah, Capt. Henry: 89, 106
Jupiter River, Sound, Fla.: 60

Kansas: 215
Kansas River: 25
Kamiakin (Yakima chief): 116, 120, 125–27, 134; injured in Battle of Spokane Plains, 172
Kearny, Maj. Stephen W.: 18, 37
Keenan, Mrs. J. C.: 331
Kelley, Lt. Col. James K. (Oregon volunteers): 119
Kentucky Volunteers: 237
Kern River War: 96
Keyes, Capt. (later Maj. Gen.) Erasmus D. (Third Artillery): seizes Walker's ship, 103–104; Wright's second-in-command, 158; opinion of Wright, 158–59, 166; erects Fort Taylor, 160; aide to Scott at outset of Civil War, 214
Keysville, Calif.: 273
Key West, Fla.: 64
Kickapoo Indians: 34
Kingcome, Rear Adm. John, R.N.: 283–84
Kinney, J. F. (Utah delegate): 294
Kiowa Indians: 20

Kip, Lt. Lawrence (Third Artillery), on Battle of Four Lakes: 168–69
Kirkham, Capt. R. W. (quartermaster); supervises crossing of Snake River: 161–62
Kitsap (Klickitat chief): 128
Kittitas Valley: 127
Klamath Indians: War of 1852, 96; War of 1854, 96; conflict, 275, 297
Klamath Lake, Oreg.: 297
Klickitat Indians: 122–23
Kootenai Indians: 116

Lake Chalco, Mex.: 74
Lake Champlain: 3
Lake Coeur d'Alene, Idaho: 178, 180
Lake Erie: 23, 49
Lake Huron: 49
Lake Michigan: 14, 49
Lake Ontario: 49
La Libertad, Mex.: 322
La Marche (Cabanné's resident trader to Grands): 34
Lanagen, Ed: 90
Lanberg, Gen. Emilio: 307
Lancaster, Pa.: 7, 23
Lane, Gov. Joseph (Oregon delegate to U.S. Congress): 136
Larned, Maj. C. H., at Fort Steilacoom: 196
Latah Creek (Ned-whauld River, Hangman's Creek): 181
Lawson, Capt. Thomas: 57
Lawyer (Nez Percé chief): 151, 274
Leach (Wright's orderly): 327
Leavenworth, Col. Henry: 17, 37, 38; assumes command of 3d Infantry, 17; at Jefferson Barracks, 18
Leavenworth, Kans.: 20
Lebanon, Pa.: 7, 23
LeDoux, Abraham, wounded by Pawnees: 30
Lee, Gen. Robert E. (commander-in-chief, C.S.A.), surrenders to Grant: 315
Leschi (Nisquallie chief): 116, 120, 128; tries to unite tribes for war, 134
Lewis and Clark Expedition: 19
Lexington, Mass.: 4, 6
Liberty Lake, Wash.: 176
Lincoln, Lt. Abram B.: in Seminole

War, 58; on Canadian border, 90
Lincoln, Pres. Abraham: 213; and
Amnesty Proclamation, 238; and
Emancipation Proclamation, 238;
outrages California mining commu-
nity, 275; reelected, 291; assassi-
nated, 315
Lincoln-Johnson Club: 311
Lippitt, Col. Francis J.: commands
Humboldt Dist., 224; and Indian
hostilities, 250–52; and whiskey
shops, 270; relieved of command,
271
Little Platte River: 20
Lobos Island, Mex.: 68–69
Long Island Sound: 3
Longstreet, Lt. James: 75
Lord, Joseph A. (Wells, Fargo mes-
senger): 331–32
Louisiana Purchase: 25
Louisiana (ship): 112
Louisville Courier-Journal: 351
Louisville, Ky.: 290, 351
Loup Fork River, Nebr., Wright at:
33, 34
Loup Pawnee (Skidi) Indians: 25, 28,
29; Morning Star worship, 31 n, 32;
Wright visits, 33; see also Pawnee
Indians
Low, Frederick F. (port collector, San
Francisco, later governor, Califor-
nia): 263, 270, 293, 310–11
Lugenbeel, Maj. Pinkney: 129
Lyon, Lt. H. B. (3d Artillery): 163

McAllister, Capt. Julian: 266
McCleave, Capt. William H., captured
by Confederates: 239
McClellan, Gen. George B.: com-
mander, Army of Potomac, 213;
general-in-chief, 229; relieved of
command, 238; Democratic candi-
date for president, 290
McDermit, Maj. Charles F.: com-
mands subdistrict in California and
Nevada, 317; killed in battle with
Shoshonis, 318
McDonald, Angus (chief trader, Ft.
Colvile): 148
McDowell, Gen. Irvin: and rout of
Union forces at Bull Run, 213;
critical of Connor, 295; commands

Pacific Dept., 300; seizes Colón,
308–309; inspects Puget Sound
posts, 309–10; advocates Wright's
Mexican policies, 322
McGarry, Maj. Edward: 248–49
McGruder, E. W.: 335
McIntosh, Col. James S.: 79–80
MacKall, Gen. W. W. (assistant adju-
tant general): 123
MacKenzie, William Lyon: 41–42
McLane, Louis (Wells, Fargo agent):
244, 247
McLaughlin, Capt. Moses: 246, 247,
273
McLaughlin, Lt. John T., U.S. Navy:
57–58
McLeod's Fork: 105
McNeil, Col. John: 15–17
Macomb, Maj. Gen. Alexander (com-
manding general of army): 36
Madison Barracks, N.Y.: 44–47, 49,
62, 86
Malaria (ague, intermittent fever): 35,
44, 97
Malco River, Fla.: 57, 58
Malheur River, Oreg.: 207
Manifest Destiny: 107
Mansfield, Col. Joseph K. (inspector
general of army): inspects Ft. Read-
ing, 104–105; inspects returning
troops at Ft. Walla Walla, 184;
ordered to California, 227
Mansfield, Conn.: 4
Many, Col. James B.: succeeds Leav-
enworth in command of 3d Infan-
try, 38
Marcy, William L. (secretary of state):
124
Mare Island Navy Yard, Calif.: 236,
266, 284
Marias River, Mont., slaughter of
Blackfeet at: 196
Maricopa Indians: 265
Mariposa County, Calif.: 296
Marshall, James, discovers gold in
California: 94
Mary (ship): 122, 123
Mason, Capt. James L.: 78
Mason, Col. R. B. (superintendent of
Recruiting Service): 69
Mason, Gen. John S., commands Dist.
of Arizona: 317, 319

Massachusetts: 114
Massachusetts (ship): 3, 69; skirmish
    with Haidas, 138
Matamoros, Mex.: 68
Maury, Col. Reuben F., commands
    Oregon Dist.: 317
Maximilian, Prince: 259
Medical Lake, Wash.: 165
Melkapsi (Coeur d'Alene chief): 157,
    180
Mellen, Capt. Henry: 272
Mendocino Herald: 255
Menetrey, Rev. Joseph, S.J.: 179
Menominee Indians: 15
Merrill, Samuel: 9, 10
Merrimack Valley: 3
Merryman, Lt. James H. (acting port
    collector, Port Townsend, Washing-
    ton Terr.): 261
Mesilla, N.Mex.: 242
Mexican army: 68, 82
Mexican border states: 107
Mexican government: 68, 282, 309
Mexico: 25, 38, 67, 72, 74, 94, 107;
    declares war on U.S., 68; Valley of
    invasion, 74; peace treaty signed,
    83
Mexico City, Mex.: 68, 72–75, 78;
    capture of, 80–83
Miners, Colville, murder of: 116
Minnesota River: 18
Mississippi River, Valley: 14, 18–20,
    37, 49, 55
Missouri: 49
Missouri Indians: 25
Missouri River: 20, 25, 29, 32
Modoc War; Lt. Thomas Wright
    killed in: 350
Molino del Rey, Battle of: 77–78, 90
Mono County, Calif.: 273
Monroe, Pres. James S.: 10, 15, 16, 18
Montana: 114
Monterey, Calif.: 94
Monterrey, Mex.: 68
Montgomery, Elizabeth Reed: 23
Montgomery, Rev. Joseph: 23
Montgomery, Sarah Pettit (Thomas
    Forster's wife, Margaret Wright's
    mother): 23
Moody, W. G. (correspondent, San
    Francisco Evening Bulletin), inter-

cepts C.S.A.–Mexican correspon-
    dence: 235
Moore, Lt. J. A. (1st Dragoons): 100,
    101
Morgan, Charles: 107
Morgan, Lt. Michael R.: 283–84
Mormons: 145; see also Connor, Col.
    Patrick E.
Morris, William Gouverneur (capt.,
    adjutant, assistant quartermaster,
    California Volunteer Cavalry, bvt.
    maj.), address to Society of Califor-
    nia Volunteers: 349–50
Mosheel (instigator of Bolon mur-
    der): 139–40
Mott, Christopher (Indian superin-
    tendent and investigator): 184–85,
    199
Mott, Elijah (chief engineer, Brother
    Jonathan): 330
Mountain infantry: organized, 271;
    mustered out, 317
Mullan, Lt. John (2d Artillery): ac-
    companies Gov. Stevens to Wash-
    ington, 145; commands Indian
    scouts, 159, 160; and construction
    of Ft. Benton–Walla Walla road, 200
Mullan Road: 145, 200

Naches River, Washington Terr.: 124
Nacogdoches, Tex.: 40
Napa County, Calif.: 266
Napoleon III, Emperor: 259
Natchitoches, Tex.: 38
National Highway, Mexico: 73
Navajo Indians: 265
Navy Island, N.Y.: 42
Nelson (Duwhamish chief): 128
Nesmith, Col. James W. (later Gen.,
    Oregon Volunteers): 119, superin-
    tendent of Indian affairs for Wash-
    ington and Oregon, 138; U.S.
    senator, 214
Nevada Terr.: 269, 293
New Almaden Mine, Calif.: 275–79
New England: 3, 4, 8
New Hampshire: 3, 4, 6
New Mexico: 215
New Orleans, La.: 19, 64
Newton, Olive P. (Lizzie Wright's
    aunt): 7

New York City: 69, 85, 109, 117
New York State: 4, 41, 86; legislature,
    91
Nez Percé Indians: 116, 141; treaties,
    116, 156; detachment of, serves
    with Wright, 159; and miners on
    reservation, 122; scouts search for
    kidnapped children, 222
Nez Percé Reservation: 272
Niagara River: 42
Nicaragua: 107, 108
Ninth Infantry Regiment: 109; yellow
    fever quarantine, 111; arrives at
    Fort Vancouver, 112–13; Cascades
    Massacre, 122–23; expedition into
    Yakima country, 124; Ft. Simcoe,
    129; Ft. Walla Walla, 135; Steptoe
    disaster, 149; Battle of Four Lakes,
    166; Battle of Spokane Plains, 171;
    return to Ft. Walla Walla, 184; dur-
    ing Civil War, 218
Nisbet, James (editor, San Francisco
    Evening Bulletin): 334
Norfolk, Va.: 109; yellow-fever epi-
    demic, 111
Norfolk and Hampton Steamship
    Co.: 111
Norfolk (Va.) Evening Star: 111–12
Northern Pacific RR: 200
Northfield, Vt.: 11
Northwest frontier: 86, 92
Norwich, Vt.: 4–5, 8–9, 56
Norwich University (Partridge Acad-
    emy): 11, 17
Nye, Gov. J. W. (Nevada Terr.): 233

Oak Grove, Calif.: 232
Oblate: missionaries, 116; Mission
    Ahtanum Creek, Washington Terr.,
    118–19, 128
Octiarche (Seminole chief): 62
Ogdensburg, N.Y.: 43, 46
Okanogan River, Wash.: 186
Oklawaha River, Fla.: 51, 55
Olympic Peninsula, Wash.: 38
Omaha Indians: 28–30
Oneida (ship): 45, 47
O'Neill, Maj. John M.: 247
Ord, Capt. E. O. C.: 163, 167
Oregon: 102–103, 111–14, 121
Oregon (ship): 112–13

Oregon country: 65
Oregon Territory: 94–96
Oregon Trail: 114; massacre of Ward
    party, 211n.; massacre of Van Or-
    man party by Bannocks, 1860,
    208–12
Oregon volunteers: 117–19, 122,
    124; and Cascades Massacre, 123
Osage Indians: 20
Osceola (Seminole war chief): 51
Oswego, N.Y.: 86, 91, 109–11
Oto Indians: 25, 28
Otsego (ship): 58
Overland mail and stage route: 215,
    224, 225, 242
Owen, Frank (Eliza Wright Owen's
    second son): 350
Owen, John (Indian agent): 198
Owen, Lt. Philip A. (adjutant, 9th In-
    fantry): marries Eliza Wright,
    135–36; relieves Sheridan at Fort
    Yamhill, 215
Owen, Margaret F. (Eliza Wright
    Owen's daughter): 350
Owen, Montgomery M. (Eliza Wright
    Owen's first son): 350–51
Owens Lake, Calif.: 255
Owens River Valley, Calif.: 255, 273
Owhi (Yakima chief): 125–27; cap-
    tured, 181, 183
Owyhee mines, Oreg.: 319
Owyhee River, Oreg.: 209

Pacific Coast: 94, 113–14, 214, 267
Pacific Department (Division): 96,
    114; divided into Departments of
    California and Oregon, 187; re-
    united, 214; redivided, 323
Pacific mail steamers: 218
Pacific Northwest: 94, 104, 114
Pacific Ocean: 114
Paiute Indians: 318
Palo Alto, Mex.: 68
Palouse Indians, meetings with
    Wright: 181–83
Palouse River, Wash.: 148, 163
Panama, Isthmus of: 95
Pandosy, Rev. Charles (Oblate mis-
    sionary): 116–18, 127
Papago Indians: 265
Paradise Valley, Nev.: 318

Parker, S. A. (postmaster of San
  Francisco): 243
Partizan: 288 n.
Partridge, Capt. Alden (son of Sam-
  uel Partridge, Jr., first cousin of
  Roswell Wright); superintendent
  of U.S.M.A., 10; controversy and
  court martial, 10–11; resigns from
  army, 11; founds Partridge Mili-
  tary Academy (Norwich Univer-
  sity), 11, 17
Partridge, Elizabeth Wright: 5
Partridge, Ruth Woodward: 5
Partridge, Samuel, Jr.: 5
Partridge, Samuel, Sr.: 5
Partridge Military School (later Nor-
  wich University): 8
Patriots (Canadian insurrectionary
  party): 41, 45
Patriot War: 41–46, 99
Patten, Maj. G. W.: 261–63; estab-
  lishes Ft. Lane in Rogue River val-
  ley, 103
Patterson (captain of Plymouth Rock):
  112
Patterson, Gen. Robert: 69
Patterson, James (3d officer of Brother
  Jonathan): 330, 332–33, 335
Pawnee Confederacy (Grand, Repub-
  lican, Tappage, Loup tribes): 25
Pawnee Indians: 24–25, 28–32;
  Treaty of Fort Atkinson, 25; vil-
  lages, 30; contempt for American
  troops, 30–32; sacrifice of Chey-
  enne Indian woman, 31 & n.
Payette River, Idaho: 256
Pease Creek: 60
Pend d'Orielle Indians, treaty: 116
Pennsylvania: 8
Perote, Mex.: 73
Pesqueira, don Ignacio (governor of
  Sonora): 242, 307
Peupeumoxmox (Walla Walla chief):
  119; killed and mutilated by Ore-
  gon volunteers, 120
Philadelphia, Pa.: 85
Pickering, William (governor, Wash-
  ington Terr.): 258
Pickett, Lt. George E.: at Churu-
  busco, 75; commands Ft. Belling-
  ham, 140; and San Juan Island

controversy, 203–204; joins South,
  202, 215
Pierce, Pres. Franklin: 100–103, 114,
  124
Pillow, Gen. Gideon J. (commander,
  3d Division): 72, 83–84
Pima Indians: 265
Pima villages: 239–40
Pine Creek, Washington Terr.: 147
Pinkerton Detective Agency: 213
Pinkney, Col. Ninian: 15
Pitt River, Calif.: 105
Platte River: 25, 34
Plattsburg Barracks, N.Y.: 86
Plymouth Rock (ship): 111–12
Point Defiance, Wash.: 205
Point Jose, Calif.: 285
Point St. George, Calif.: 332
Polatkin (Spokane war chief): 157,
  176, 179, 180
Po-li-ni (Snake chief): 298
Political factions in California: 214
Polk, Pres. James K.: 65–68, 83–84
Pollock, Lt. Col. Robert: 246
Port Angeles, Wash.: 261
Port Gamble, Wash.: 137–38
Portneuf River, Idaho: 109
Port Townsend, Wash.: 261
Prairie du Chien, Wis.: 49
Preston, Conn.: 5
Price, Capt. George M.: 255
Priest Rapids, Wash.: 187
Privateers: 284–87, 294; Shenandoah,
  294
Prophet (Otulke Thlocco, Seminole):
  57
Prophet's Landing, Fla.: 57
Puebla, Mex.: 73, 84
Puget Sound, Wash.: 94, 113, 116,
  117
Punta Rassa, Fla.: 57–59
Pyramid Lake, Nev.: 317

Qualchin (Yakima, son of Owhi),
  hanged: 181
Quartermaster Department, U.S.: 255
Quebec: 3
Quicksilver Mining Co. of New York,
  claims ownership of New Almaden
  Mine: 276–77
Quiemuth (Nisqually chief): 128

Rains, Maj. Gabriel J.: 116; commands Fort Dalles, 95; relieved by Wright, 113; Yakima expedition, 117–19
Rand, C. W. (U.S. marshal, San Francisco): 276
Randolph, John (assistant surgeon): 146, 163
Randolph County, Mo.: 37
Rankin, Ira (port collector, San Francisco): 285
Ravalli, Rev. Anthony: 148
Reading, Pierson B.: 97
Recruiting: 17; centers for 9th Infantry, 109
Red Bird (Winnebago chief): 22
Red Bluff, Calif.: 97
Redding, B. B.: 97
Redding, Calif.: 97
Red River, Valley, La.: 37–38
Reeve, Lt. N. D.: 46
Rogue River War: 96, 114
Reily, Col. James (C.S.A.): 235, 242
Reith brothers (survivors of Oregon Trail massacre): 209–10
Republic (ship): 113
Republican Pawnee Indians (Republic Indians): 25, 28, 30, 34
Resaca de Palma, Mex.: 68
Revolution, American: 6–7
Richards, Kent D.: 128
Richardson, Albert (author of Beyond the Mississippi): 337
Rigg, Maj. Edwin A.: 232, 240
Rincon Point, Calif.: 285
Rio Grande: 68
Rochester, N.Y.: 42
Rocky Mountains: 25
Rosalia, Wash.: 147
Round Valley, Calif.: 252–55; martial law, 253, 254; court of inquiry, 255
Royalton, Vt.: 6
Rubery, Alfred: 266
Russell, Lt. Edmund (4th Infantry), killed by Indians: 100–102
Russia: possessions of, 65; Russian men-of-war, 311

Sabine Parish, La.: 38
Sabine River, La.: 38
Sacket's Harbor, N.Y.: 45–46, 49

Sacramento River, Valley: 94–96, 103–105
Saginaw, U.S.S.: 266
St. Augustine, Fla.: 62
St. Joseph's River, Idaho: 180
St. Lawrence River: 45
St. Louis, Mo.: 18–19, 117
St. Louis (ship): 112
St. Lucie Sound, Fla.: 59–60
Salmon, Norvel (British naval captain): 108
Salmon Falls, Idaho: 209
Salmon River, Idaho: 256
Saltillo, Mex.: 68–69, 72
Salt Lake City, Utah: 247
Sam Jones (Seminole chief): 79
San Agustín, Mex.: 74
San Antonio, Mex.: 74
San Bernardino, Calif.: 234
Sand Creek Massacre (Colo.): 128
San Francisco, Calif.: 104, 113, 120
San Jacinto, Tex.: 40
San Joaquin River: 99
San Juan Island controversy ("Pig War"): 202–206
San Patricio Brigade (Irish deserters): 77
Santa Anna, Antonio López de (president of Mexico; commander-in-chief of army): 40, 72–73, 81
Santa Fe Trail: 18–20, 25, 35
Sapine (trader with Loup Pawnees): 33
Satan (Oto): 34
Sauk Indians: 32
Scott, Gen. Winfield: 103, 201; Patriot War, 45; Seminole War, 80, 201; replaces Macomb as general-in-chief, 56; Mexican War, 67–69, 72–73, 82, 83; critical of Worth, 73, 81; quarrel with officers in Mexico, 83–84; presidential candidate, 100; investigates San Juan Island controversy, 204; retires, 229
Schoolcraft, H. R.: 14
Scott River Valley, Calif.: 100
Screven, Capt. Richard B.: 57
Seal Rock, Calif.: 336
Seattle, Wash.: 120
Secessionists: 214; in California, 224–26, 233, 246, 267–68, 293, 315–16; in Nevada, 233, 243

Second Brigade: 79–83
Second Dragoons: 56
Second Infantry: 18, 55, 109; Co. E at
    Fort Reading, Calif., 95
Selfridge, Capt. Thomas O., U.S.
    Navy (commander, Mare Island
    Navy Yard): 266, 284–87
Seminole Indians: 50, 59, 77; Treaty
    of Moultrie Creek, 50; Treaty of
    Payne's Landing, 51; bounty for
    capture, 62; never conquered, 63
Seminole War, 50, 56; first, 50; sec-
    ond, 51–52, 62; hostilities end, 63
Seward, William H. (secretary of
    state): 214, 233
Shasta County, Calif.: 97, 105
Shasta Indians: 96
Shaw, Lt. Col. Benjamin F. (Washing-
    ton volunteers): 128; Battle of
    Grande Ronde, 128
Shelter Cove, Calif.: 342
Shenandoah (Confederate raider): 294,
    315
Sheridan, Lt. (later Gen.) Philip H.
    (1st Dragoons): 119; describes ar-
    rival of 9th Infantry, 113; and Cas-
    cades Massacre, 122–23; invades
    Shenandoah Valley, 291
Shields, Gen. James: 72, 75
Short, James (supervisor, Round Val-
    ley Reservation): 253
Showalter, Dan (southern sym-
    pathizer): 232
Shubrick (revenue cutter): 261, 266,
    310
Sibley, Gen. Henry H. C.S.A.: invades
    Southwest, 224; requests rights of
    access to Sonora, 234; defeats
    Canby at Valverde, 234; occupies
    Albuquerque and Santa Fe, 239;
    driven out of Southwest, 241
Sierra Nevada, Calif.: 247
Sierra Nevada (ship): 337
Simcoe Creek, Wash.: 128
Sioux Indians: 20, 28; Ash Hollow
    massacre of Brulé Sioux, 196–97
Sir Robert Peel (ship): 43
Sisters of Charity of Providence:
    201–202
Sisters of Holy Names of Jesus and
    Mary: 354

Sixth Infantry: escort on Santa Fe
    Trail, 36, 74; occupies Cantonment
    Leavenworth, 36
Skloom (brother of Yakima chief Ka-
    miakin): 198
Slaves and slavery: 50; Fugitive Slave
    Law, 91; Emancipation Proclama-
    tion, 238
Sloat, Commo. John D., U.S. Navy: 94
Slough, Col. John P. (Colorado volun-
    teers), defeats Confederates at
    Apache Pass: 241
Smith, Capt. A. J., attacked by Snake
    Indians: 207
Smith, Capt. Kirby: 80
Smith, Capt. Larkin: 75
Smith, C. D. (governor of Idaho): 319
Smith, Gen. Persifor F. (commander,
    Pacific Div.): 95
Smith, Justin (author): 81
Smith, Victor (port collector): 261–
    62; Treasury agent, 331
Smith River Reservation, Calif.: 253,
    317–18
Snake Indians (Shoshoni): Digger
    Snakes, 206–207; Mountain Snakes
    (Bannocks), 207–212, 248; Bear
    River battle, 249; treaty, 270; raids,
    battles, 318
Snake River: 147, 151, 162, 209
Snelling, Lt. James G.: 75
Snow Mountains, Oreg.: 208
Snyder (survivor of Oregon Trail
    massacre): 209
Society of California Volunteers: 349
Sonora, Mex.: 103
South Carolina: 213
Spain: 18, 38; cedes Florida to U.S.,
    50
Spalding Mission, Lapwai, Idaho: 150
Spangle, Wash.: 180
Spencer, John C. (secretary of war):
    60
Spokane Indians: 127, 180
Spokane River, Wash.: 148
Sprague, Lt. John T.: 59
Stafford, Vt.: 6
Stanford, Leland, Jr. (governor of
    California): 215
Stanton, Edwin M. (secretary of war):
    233, 264

Stark, Dr. (civilian physician, Ft. Reading): 99
State militias: 42, 50, 243, 305
Steele, Col. William, C.S.A.: 224
Steen, Maj. Enoch: 207–208
Steinberger, Col. Justus: 248, 256–57
Steptoe, Maj. (Bvt. Col.) Edward J. (9th Infantry): 109, 124, 144; erects and occupies Ft. Walla Walla, 134–35; background, 144; reconnaissance mission, 145–147; personnel, 146; armament, 146–47; encounter with hostiles, 147; disastrous battle, 149–50; casualties, 149; escape, 150–51; aftermath, 151–53
Steptoe Butte (Pyramid Peak): 147, 151
Stevens, Hazard (Isaac I. Stevens's son): 121
Stevens, Lt. (later Gen.) Isaac I: 116–17, 119–21, 123–25, 127, 135, 153; at Molino del Rey, 80; governor of Washington Terr., 103, 114; superintendent of Indian affairs, 114; railroad survey, 114; Indian treaties, 114; Indian councils, 116, 131–32; pack train captured, 132; censured for declaring martial law, 138; delegate to Congress, 138; complaints re Wright, 138; wants Indian "murderers" turned over for trial, 138; serves in Civil War, killed at Chantilly, 238
Stevens treaties: 114–16, 125
Sumner, Gen. Edwin Vose (Wright's brother-in-law): 214–15, 227; marriage, 23; Mexican War, 77; escorts Lincoln to Washington, D.C., 213; Commander, Dept. of Pacific, 214; arms soldiers for Pacific steamers, 218; tries to slow slaughter of Indians, 223; prepares for march to Texas, 225
Sun Chief (Grand chief): 34
Surprise Valley, Calif.: 318
Sutlej (British ship): 283
Sutter, John: 94, 97
Swanton, Vt.: 45
Swartwout, Samuel (capt. of U.S.S. Massachusetts): 138

Swett, Leonard (former law partner of Lincoln), and New Almaden Mine imbroglio: 275–77
Swope, Jean Wright (daughter of J. M. Wright): 352
Syracuse, N.Y.: 91

Tacubaya, Mex.: 77
Tampa Bay, Fla.: 51
Tappage (Pawnee tribe): 25, 32–34
Taylor, Capt. Oliver H. P., killed in Steptoe battle: 150
Taylor, Gen. (later Pres.) Zachary, in Mexican War: 67–68, 72
Tehama, Calif.: 100
Tehama County, Calif.: 100
Teias (Yakima chief): 125, 127
Tejon Reservation, Calif.: 273
Telegraph: California, 227; Oregon, 292; Washington, 292
Telegraph (ship): 45
Tampico, Mex.: 68
Tenth Regiment (Infantry): 106
Texas: 38–40, 67
Thayer, Maj. Sylvanus: 9–12
Third Artillery Regiment: 109; Co. D, Ft. Reading, 98, 104; serves as infantry in eastern Washington on Wright's campaign, 158, 162; all but four companies sent east during Civil War, 218
Third Infantry Regiment: 14–18; at Fort Howard, 14–18; at Cantonment Miller, 19; at Jefferson Barracks, 19; at Fort Leavenworth, 20; at Ft. Jesup, 37–38; in Seminole War, 62
Thomas, Col. Lorenzo (adj. gen., U.S. Army): 206, 229ff.
Thomes Creek, Calif.: 100, 102
Thompson, Gen. Wiley (Indian agent): 51
Thousand Islands (St. Lawrence River): 85
Thurman, John (mayor of Oswego): 92
Tiger Tail (Seminole chief): 62
Tilcoax (Palouse chief): 176
Timothy (Nez Percé chief): 147, 150
Toppenish Creek, Wash.: 128–29
Totten, Gen. Joseph C.: 90, 92

Townsend, Col. E. D. (assistant adjutant general, U.S. Army): 228 ff.
Treaties, Indian: see *under names of tribes*
Treaty of 1827 (Joint occupancy of Oregon): 65–66
Treaty of Guadalupe Hidalgo: 82, 94
Treaty of Washington, 1846 (Canada): 66, 202
Treaty of Washington (Spain cedes Florida to U.S.): 38
Trinity County, Calif.: 250
Trinity Valley, Calif.: 296
Troy, N.Y.: 44
Truxillo, Honduras: 108
Turner, Lt. (4th Infantry): 186
Twiggs, Col. David E.: dispute with Worth over seniority, 67–68; commands 2d Division, 69, 72, 74
Tyler, Pres. John: 55, 61–63, 67
Tucannon River, Wash.: 180

Umatilla Indians: 116; agency, 209
Union leagues: 343
United States: 14, 25–28, 38, 41, 44–45, 66, 86, 94, 107, 108; war with Mexico, 68; boundary dispute with Canada, 202; recognizes Benito Juárez government, 282, 308
United States (ship): 45
U.S. Army: 9, 40, 77, 125; discord at end of Mexican War, 83; Pacific Dept. divided, 187; relations with Hudson's Bay Co., 201; Civil War victories in East, 238; capture of Richmond, Va., 315; arrest of civilians by military terminated, 316; execution of Indians without civil trial proscribed, 318; reorganization of army departments, 323
U.S. Congress: 7, 14, 18, 44, 66, 106, 114, 120; authorizes Mullan Road, 145
U.S. Department of Interior, squabbles with army: 272, 280, 319, 320
U.S. Military Academy, West Point, N.Y.: 7–13, 44, 88–89, 92, 114, 119
U.S. Navy: 63
U.S. Revenue Service: 262
U.S. Senate: 67–68

U.S. Supreme Court, decision re New Almaden Mine: 276
U.S. volunteer troops: 128, 217–18
U.S. War Department: 20, 69, 83, 92, 111, 127
University of Louisville: 351
Utah Military District: 247
Utah Territory: 249
Ute Indians, treaty: 270

Van Buren, Pres. Martin: 42, 47, 54
Vancouver Island, B.C.: 259
Vanderbilt, Cornelius: 107
Van Dieman's Land: 45
Van Orman, Alexis, Snake River massacre: 211, 248
Van Orman, Reuben: 211, 248–49
Van Orman, Zachias: 248–49
Vega, Gen. Plácido: 308
Veracruz, Mex.: 90; siege of, 72
Vermont: 3
Victoria, B.C.: 201
Vincent (Coeur d'Alene chief): 175
Virginia: 118
Virginia City, Nev.: 296
Visalia, Calif., violence in: 246–47, 268
Visalia Delta: 247

Wadsworth, Rev. Charles: 343–44
Waite, Lt. Edwin W. (aide-de-camp to Wright): 303, 340
Waite, Maj. Carlos D.: 75, 82, 88
Walker, William: 103–104; expedition to Baja California, 103; expedition to Nicaragua, 107–108; expedition to Honduras, 108; execution, 108
Walker's Lake, Calif.: 318
Walla Walla Council: First, 216; Second, 131–32
Walla Walla country: 119
Walla Walla Indians: 141; treaty, 114; battle with Oregon volunteers, 119–20
Walla Walla River, Valley: 116
Wallen, Capt. N. D. (4th Infantry), survey of eastern Oregon: 206
Ward emigrant party: 211
Warm Springs Reservation, Oreg.: 206

Warner's Ranch, San Diego County, Calif.: 226
War of 1812: 8, 19, 50
Warships: American, 108; British, 108, 200, 203
Wasco (ship): 122–23
Washington, D.C.: 40, 68, 85
Washington, Pres. George: 14
Washington Territorial Legislature, protests army's closure of interior: 145
Washington Territory: 114, 121
Washington volunteers: 117, 124, 128
Washita, Battle of (Indian Terr.— Oklahoma): 128
Waterman, F. H., intercepts C.S.A.– Mexican letters: 235
Watson, Peter H. (assistant secetary of war): 262
Wells, Fargo Express Co.: 244, 331
Wenatchee River and Valley, Wash.: 127
West, Capt. B. R.: 279
West, Lt. Col. Joseph R. (Carleton's second-in-command): commands Ft. Yuma, 231; gains control of Colorado River ferries, 231; reports troop mutiny, 240; reoccupies Tucson, 242; commands Arizona Dist., 243; transferred to Dept. of Arkansas, 292; castigated by Carleton, 292
West Coast: 95, 103, 225
Western Department: 18, 38
West Point, N.Y.: see U.S. Military Academy
Whipple, Lt. Col. Stephen J.: 295; commander of 1st Battalion Mountaineers, 271; replaces Lippitt, 271; in Humboldt district, 296
Whiskey: 38, 270
White, Lt. James L. (3d Artillery), in charge of howitzers on Wright campaign: 163, 166
White Mountains, N.H.: 3
White River valley expedition: 120
Whitman Mission, Waiilatpu, Washington Terr.: 119
Wie-cat (Indian messenger): 148, 184
Wild Horse (Tappage chief): 32–33
Wiley, Austin (Indian agent): 296

Williams, 1st Sgt. William C.: 150
Williamson, Maj. Robert S.: 285
Willow Creek, Oreg.: 209
Wilson, Lt. John E. (commander of *Shubrick*): 261–62
Winder, Capt. Charles S. (9th Infantry): 123
Winder, Capt. William A., photos of Alcatraz: 283, 311
Windmill Point, Prescott, Ont.: 45
Wing, Emory (soldier), on sinking of *Brother Jonathan:* 336
Winnebago Indians: 15, 22, 49
Withlacoochee Cove, Fla.: 56
Wood, Joseph (chairman, Military Committee, California legislature), defends Wright's loyalty: 299
Woodruff, Capt. Dickinson: 140
Woodward, Rev. James W.: 9
Wool, Gen. John E.: 17, 105, 113, 117, 120, 122; Mexican War, 72; commander, Dept. of Pacific, 99, 104; on Indians, 120–22, 129–32; on civilian officials and volunteers, 119, 121; closes interior to settlers, 129; orders Wright to meet with Indians in Walla Walla region, 131; relieved of command, 138; replaced by Clarke, 138
Worth, Lt. (later Bvt. Brig. Gen) William Jenkins: 46–47, 61, 64–65, 68, 73, 99; West Point, 12; commands 8th Infantry, 44; Patriot War, 44–47; Seminole War, 55–56, 59–61; regiments in Florida, 56; praises Wright, 63; Mexican War, 67; dispute with Twiggs, 67; Battle of Monterrey, 68; commands 1st Division, 69; siege of Veracruz, 72; Cerro Gordo, 73; Perote, 73; Puebla, 73; criticized by Scott, 73; court of inquiry, 73; Churubusco, 75; Molino del Rey, 77, 81; controversy with Scott, 83–84; death, 85
Wright, Aaron: 5
Wright, Anna: 7
Wright, Betsy: 7
Wright, Ebenezer: 23
Wright, Eliza (George Wright's daughter): 41, 135, 351
Wright, Elizabeth Bliss: 5

Wright, Gen. George: birth and boyhood, 8–9, U.S.M.A., 9–13; 2d Lt.,
3d Infantry, 13–14; Ft. Howard,
14, 17; Partridge Academy, 17; recruiting duty, 17, 41; Jefferson Barracks, 19, 37; regimental adjutant,
3d Infantry, 21, 37; Ft. Leavenworth, 21; 1st Lt., 22; marriage, 22;
expedition to Council Bluffs, 24,
28–32; to Pawnee Tappage village,
32; to Loup village, 33; to Grand
village, 34; to Republican village,
35; birth of older son, 37; confrontations with other officers, 39,
69, 99–100, 125; Ft. Jesup, 37–40;
capt., 41; northern frontier, 41;
birth of daughter, 41; Patriot War,
41–47; Ft. Niagara, 42; 8th Infantry, 44; Madison Barracks, 44; birth
of younger son, 46; confrontations
with civilians, 47–48, 64, 91–92,
111–12; faces mob in Brockville,
46; disciplines company, 46; Camp
McKeown, 49; Ft. Winnebago, 49;
adjutant, 8th Infantry, 55; Big Cypress expedition, 56; Big Cypress
and Everglades expeditions, 57–
58; commands Ft. Pierce, 59–61;
Bvt. Maj., 63; Ft. Brooke, 64; legal
problem, 64; Key West, 64; recruiting, 65; rejoins regiment, 69; siege
of Veracruz, 72; Perote, 73; Battle
of Churubusco, 74–75; Bvt. Lt.
Col, 75; leads assault party, Battle
of Molino del Rey, 79–80; wounded, 79; Bvt. Col, 82; sick leave, 83;
Maj. 4th Infantry, 85; mustering
out troops, 85; joins regiment, 86;
Ft. Ontario, 86, 89–91; complains
about quality of recruits, 86; concern for men serving under him,
90–91; commands Ft. Reading and
Northern California Dist., 95–98,
100–103; Lt. Col., 4th Infantry,
106; Col., 9th Infantry, 106; quar-
antines Ft. Monroe, 111; ordered
to Pacific Coast, 112; commands
Columbia River Dist., 113; to Ft.
Dalles, 113; views on Indians, 121,
127; Cascades Massacre, 122–23;
Yakima expedition, 124, 129; seeks
pardon for Leschi, 128; opposes
ratification treates, 133; meets with
local chiefs, 135; command reduced to Ft. Dalles, 141; prepares
for campaign against Spokanes,
Coeur d'Alenes, and Palouses, 158–
59; battle of Four Lakes, 165–69;
battle of Spokane Plain, 170–72,
170–72; evaluation of victories,
174–75; slaughter of horse herd,
177; Indian caches destroyed, 177–
78; Coeur d'Alene Treaty, 178–79;
Spokane Treaty, 180; "Hanging
Camp" on Latah Creek, 180–82;
visit to Steptoe battlefield, 181;
letter to Clarke, 183; report to Scott
re. equipment, 185; return to Ft.
Walla Walla, 185; Clarke faults
treaties, 189–91; official comments,
191–92; War Dept. views of campaign, 192; evaluation by others,
193–95; Harney commands Oregon Dept., 197; Wright commands
Ft. Walla Walla, 200; Wright replaces Harney, 204; request for
new posts denied, 204; troop and
Indian activity, southern Idaho and
northeastern Oregon, 205–206;
troops withdrawn from Oregon
Trail, 208; massacre of emigrants,
208–12; letters to Hardie, 218,
230, 280–81; concern about rank,
219–22, 230; requests funds for
food for starving Indians, 223; confusion over assignment, 225–29; in
charge of troops in southern California, 226; Brig. Gen. of volunteers, 227; commands Dept. of
Pacific, 227, 229; concern about
Mexico, 232–36, 242, 260; warning
to Pesqueira, 235–36, 242; defenses of San Francisco, 236; responsibilities, 236–37; relations
with public officials, 239, 262–63;
on subversive newspapers, 243;
criticism from U.S. marshal, 244;
orders political prisoners to Ft.
Yuma, 245; confiscates subversives'
property, 245; Conner's troops
march, 247; Wright complains to
commissioner of Indian affairs,

256; and activities of European
powers, 259; and events at Port
Townsend, 261–63; relations with
navy, 266, 284–85; proclamation to
citizens of coast, 267; response to
troop request from Mono County,
273; and devaluation of legal tender, 275; and New Almaden Mine
imbroglio, 275–77; appeal to
Townsend, 277–78; and Catalina
Island as Indian reservation, 278–
80, 295; and France in Mexico,
281–82; welcomes Adm. Kingcome, R.N., 283–84; and harbor
and coastal defenses, 285–87; press
coverage of, 287–90; charged with
laxness in dealing with secessionists,
292–93; loyalty questioned, 299–
300; relieved of Pacific command,
300–301; farewell proclamation,
300–301; press reaction, 301–304;
in charge of California Dist., 303;
Grant-Stanton comments, 304–
305; Bvt. Brig. Gen., 306; address
to Lincoln-Johnson Club, 311–13;
letter to Stanton, 313; response to
Sen. Doolittle's Indian question-
naire, 320–21; assigned command
of re-created Dept. of Columbia,
323–24; evaluation of service on
coast, 324–25; embarks on *Brother
Jonathan*, 327; shipwreck, 333–34;
press comments and eulogies,
338–43; bodies recovered, 340,
342; funeral services and burial,
343–48; place in history, 354–56
Wright, Jemina Rose (wife of Roswell
Wright, mother of George Wright): 8
Wright, John: 5–7
Wright, John, Jr.: 7–10
Wright, John Montgomery (George
Wright's younger son): birth, 46;
applications to U.S.M.A., 136;
leaves West Point, Capt., Kentucky
Volunteers, 237; battles of Perryville and Shiloh, 263; wounded at
Gettysburg, 290; mustered out of
service, 290; studies law, 290; as
editorial writer, 351; as legislator,
351; marshal, U.S. Supreme Court,
352; death, 351

Wright, Margaret Wallace Forster
(wife of George Wright): 23, 65,
139, 237
Wright, Mercy R. (sister of George
Wright): 7–8
Wright, Olive: 7
Wright, Olive Partridge: 5
Wright, Olive Partridge II (sister of
George Wright): 8
Wright, Polly: 7, 23
Wright, Roswell: father of George
Wright, 7–9
Wright, Ruby: 7
Wright, Samuel: 5
Wright, S. P. (California state sena-
tor): 295
Wright, Thomas Forster (George
Wright's older son): birth, 37; Par-
tridge Military Academy, 64;
U.S.M.A., 88–90, 107; accom-
panies Walker to Nicaragua, 107–
108; to Honduras, 108; quartermaster Dept., Ft. Walla Walla, 108;
2d California Volunteer Cavalry,
237; 6th Regiment Infantry, California Volunteers, 290; in Humboldt Dist., 296; commands San
Francisco Presidio, 314; Brig. Gen.
314; joins regular army, 350; killed
in Modoc War, 350
Wright campaign of 1858: advance
party moves out, 159; Ft. Taylor,
160; misgivings, 161–62; Indians'
opinion of soldiers, 162; crossing of
Snake River, 162; personnel, 162–
63; evaluations, 163, 174–75; armament, 164; march north, 163–65;
encampment at Four Lakes, 165;
Battle of Four Lakes, 165–69;
battle of Spokane Plain, 170–73;
march to Coeur d'Alene Mission,
176–78; "Horse Slaughter Camp,"
176–77; council and treaty with
Coeur d'Alenes, 179–80; "Hanging
Camp," 180–82; hostages and prisoners, 180; council and treaty with
Spokanes, 180; visit to Steptoe
battlefield, 181–82; return to Ft.
Taylor, 183; return to Ft. Walla
Walla, 185; inspection by Mansfield, 185; hangings, 186

Wright General Hospital (San
    Francisco): 353
Wyse, Capt. Francis O.: 98–99, 106,
    160

Yakima, Wash.: 122
Yakima Indians: 116, 127; Cascades
    Massacre, 122–23
Yakima River, Wash.: 119, 124, 126

Yakima War: 117, 125–26
Yates, Jacob (quartermaster on *Brother
    Jonathan*): 332–33
Yellow fever: 109, 111
Yerba Buena, Calif.: 285
York, Pa.: 23
Young, Brigham: 249–50, 294
Yreka, Calif.: 100